THE CHURCHES AND POLITICS IN GERMANY

The Churches and Politics in Germany

in Germany

By FREDERIC SPOTTS

Wesleyan University Press

MIDDLETOWN, CONNECTICUT

Library of Congress Cataloging in Publication Data

Spotts, Frederic.
  The churches and politics in Germany.

  Bibliography: p.
  1. Church and state in Germany (Federal Republic,
1949-   ) I. Title.
BR856.3.S6   261.7'0943   72-11050
ISBN 0-8195-4059-5

Manufactured in the United States of America
First edition

To M and J

Contents

Preface   ix

BACKGROUND

    1 German Protestantism – Character and Organization   3
    2 German Catholicism – Character and Organization   22

THE AFTERMATH OF THE WAR AND THE PROBLEMS OF THE
OCCUPATION

    3 The Occupation Era   47
    4 Collective Guilt and Denazification   89

THE CHURCHES' POLITICAL AIMS AND TACTICS

    5 The Political Ethic of German Protestantism   119
    6 The Political Ethic of German Catholicism   149

THE CHURCH-STATE RELATIONSHIP

    7 The Legal Relationship between Church and State   183
    8 The Schools and Other Problems of the Reichskonkordat   208

KEY ISSUES OF CHURCH INTEREST

    9 Reunification, Rearmament, Conscription and Nuclear Arms   237
    10 Social Policy   269

THE CHURCHES AND PARTY POLITICS

    11 The Churches and Christian Democracy   291
    12 The Churches and Social Democracy   324

    Conclusion   351
Appendix   364

Sources   367

Index   400

Maps

The Provincial Churches of the Evangelical Church in Germany   14

The Dioceses of the Catholic Church in Germany   39

Distribution of Confessions in Germany, 1939, 1946   49

INITIATING the first Social Democratic government in nearly forty years Chancellor Brandt told the Bundestag in his formal policy statement on October 28, 1969 that his government wanted to maintain a partnership with the churches and hoped to cooperate with them in their social programs in Germany and the Third World. A month later, Herbert Wehner, the Social Democratic floor leader in the Bundestag, and Georg Leber, minister of transport and sole Catholic SPD member of the cabinet, hurried off to Rome to assure the Pope of the new government's desire for friendly relations with the Catholic church and to encourage the Vatican to accept the Oder-Neisse border. In July 1970 Brandt himself went to Rome to discuss his Ostpolitik and the Oder-Neisse issue with the Pope. The Bundestag statement and the visits represent merely random examples of the interaction of church and politics that characterizes the domestic and foreign affairs of any German government, even a government of the left, even at the present time. That a head of government should find it prudent or necessary to assure the churches of his good intentions, that government leaders should find it advisable or useful to seek Vatican support for an intended major foreign policy initiative—these are probably without parallel.

Throughout modern history the church in Germany has been a key factor in any political equation. "In school and literature, ecclesiastical and political history may be separated from one another; in real life they are always united and interwoven with one another," von Ranke wrote. The interplay of religion and politics is by no means unique to Germany. The whole body of Western political thought and institutions was molded in the most fundamental and decisive way by the tensions in western Europe between sacerdotium and imperium, between Pope and Emperor, between church and state. But Germany is exceptional in two respects. Here the intermingling of religion and politics was closer, the bonds between church and state tighter than elsewhere. Moreover, these ties remained intact far longer than in other countries. The legal and psychological separation of church and state, which largely took place by the end of the eighteenth century in Britain, France, and the United States, is only now occurring in full measure in Germany. Despite the radical political changes Germany has undergone since the Reformation, German society has in many respects been highly stable, and this has especially been the case in the church-state sphere.

In short, through historical circumstances the churches enjoyed a position in German society which was more prestigious and more secure than that of any other institution. This situation was never more clear than during the Third Reich, when only the churches proved themselves able to preserve their independence from the National Socialist system. The churches alone survived the collapse of three Reichs, several catastrophic wars, an accident-prone republic, foreign occupation, and the dismemberment of the country. The circumstances which took the Social Democratic leaders to Rome bind them in a "political succession" going back to Bismarck, Charles V, Henry IV, and every other German ruler who sought, in one form or another, either to maintain or to change the balance between political interests and ecclesiastical claims.

This alliance—or tension—between church and state is largely foreign to the Anglo-Saxon political tradition since the early nineteenth century. Neither the role the churches play in German social and political life nor the decisive influence they exert on the intellect and psychology of the German nation is widely appreciated outside Germany. Germans, on the other hand, take the situation for granted, and apart from producing a substantial body of literature on "Staatskirchenrecht," scholars have never treated the subject comprehensively. Furthermore, the caution of German scholars toward "contemporary history" has diverted serious research away from so current a topic. As a result, there is a sizable void in popular appreciation of an important aspect of postwar German politics. The purpose of this study is to assay the ground and start to bridge the gap. The quarter-century since the war offers a remarkably well-rounded period for study. The immediate postwar years saw the German churches at their most influential since the Reformation. By 1970 German society had undergone such unprecedented secularization that the Jesuit theologian Karl Rahner characterized Germany as a "pagan land with a Christian past and vestiges of Christianity."

The angle of approach here is political and not theological; moreover, the churches are examined primarily as social institutions and not as religious bodies. While this approach admittedly leaves aside their major purpose, in the German context such an analysis runs less of a risk of distortion than would elsewhere be the case, given the important role the churches have played in the country's political and social life. The study confines itself to the Federal Republic, except insofar as the churches as all-German bodies require mention of their circumstances in East Germany. To keep the focus on the underlying structure of events, I have stripped the subject down to its essentials. My primary aim is to describe a situation rather than to prove a thesis, draw a moral, or point out a lesson. But considering the tragedy of German history to lie principally in the failure of liberal democracy to take firm root, I found it impossible while writing to suppress the question of how far the churches since 1945 have contributed to liberal politics and a free society. To the extent that this inquiry amounts to applying a subjective judgment, it may be unfair. In any event, it is a bias to be acknowledged.

The best is the enemy of the good. For an outsider to attempt to cover a broad field of recent events is risky in itself. But to try to describe and illustrate the tangled interaction of religion and politics with information fragmentary, access to documents aleatory, and ecclesiastical and political leaders occasionally determined to conceal the facts presents an even more formidable obstacle. Since it is difficult under such circumstances to feel confident of fully knowing the "inside story" (assuming there is one) in any particular case, one is tempted to abandon the effort of writing anything. But in a democracy most of any "story" has ultimately to be played out in public, and much of the remainder can be uncovered through unpublished sources. In writing this study I was given access to many useful documents and was able to interview—in some cases at considerable length and several times—persons directly involved in the events or the situation described. Together these documents and interviews provided indispensable information, and without them this study would not have been possible in anything like its present form. Normally, however, I have used these sources for my own background information and have usually cited them only in the relatively rare cases where I have quoted or referred to them explicitly in the text. All but a few are therefore identified only at the end of this book in a discussion of sources.

While this text is for the most part current through 1972, substantial passages were written several years ago, and may in minor respects be slightly dated. The two church maps have been drawn to show the ecclesiastical borders during most of the period covered by this study, and therefore do not take into account the division of the Evangelical church in 1969 or the reorganization of the Catholic eastern dioceses in 1972. This is also the case with the outline of the churches' structure in the appendix. After the manuscript was already in galley-proof, the papers of Cardinal Alois Muench, Apostolic Visitator and later Papal Nuncio to Germany, were deposited with the Catholic University of America and made available for research. Some of this material has been cited in the text, though the source references have had to be given in the discussion of unpublished sources at the end of the book rather than in footnotes.

The late Professor Ernst Deuerlein, Professor Ulrich Scheuner, Alexander Kohn-Brandenburg, Professor Günther Koch, and Pastor Wilhelm Niemöller read sections of the manuscript; while the late Pastor Gunter Heidtmann, Professor Baron von Aretin, and Professor Clemens Bauer reviewed the entire text. I am indebted to them all for their comments and criticism. A special word of thanks is due my Foreign Service colleague Philip Wolfson, who read the initial draft of the manuscript and gave much helpful advice.

1 | German Protestantism — Character and Organization

"THE fundamental fact of German history is Martin Luther." Nietzsche's words contain immense historical truth. In no other nation touched by the Reformation did any religious leader have the profound impact on his people that Luther had on the Germans. As the reformer molded and established the very language of his nation, so his reform, directly and indirectly, determined the whole subsequent course of German civilization. Luther launched his reform at a time when medieval institutions were on the point of collapse, and the immediate impact of his ideas was as much to weaken the fabric of feudal society as to loosen the religious hold of Rome. Consequently the Reformation was from the start caught in the political and social turmoil of the period, even though Luther initially rejected the notion that his religious ideas could be construed to have political application. Despite the frequent tension between church and state authorities in the Middle Ages, there was between the Holy Roman Emperor and the Pope an essential identity of outlook and interests. A challenge to one was therefore a challenge to the other, and in defying the Church of Rome, Luther at the same time ignited the latent mass of national feeling. Emperor Charles V had no choice but to try to maintain the religious and political unity of his *monarchia,* and in this way the Reformation became entangled in the political evolution of the German nation.

The Emperor's intervention in turn transformed the religious leader from the reluctant master into the sorry victim of the political upheaval which his reform had touched off. That Luther was forced to place himself under the physical protection of the Saxon Elector both before and after the Diet of Worms (which had put him officially under the ban of the Empire) was more than symbolic. The reformer soon realized that his religion could survive only with the support of friendly princes—as subsequent developments in Austria and Bavaria proved. Once the authority of Rome was broken, it fell upon these princes, as the sole remaining authorities, to maintain

3

the faith. This evolution of events reached its culmination in the famous provision of the Treaty of Augsburg in 1555, which gave each imperial prince the right to choose whether he and his subjects would thereafter be Lutheran or Catholic.

The consequence was one of the central facts of German history: alone of the nations of Europe, the German nation was almost evenly divided between Catholics and Protestants. Not only was the tension between the two more intense than elsewhere; German Christianity also became ecclesiastically regionalized, and Protestantism emerged not as a national church—as in England and the Scandinavian countries—but in the form of independent provincial churches. Protestant princes became, in Luther's own apt phrase, "bishops by necessity," and the churches became virtual organs of the state. This composite of theology and politics, the product of a particular historical situation, became the foundation upon which the Protestant ecclesiastical order was established. The model church ordinance made the civil ruler the *summus episcopus* with complete authority over church property, with total ecclesiastical jurisdiction, and even with the decisive word in dogma. The general administration of the church was placed in the hands of theologians and lawyers—the consistory—who occupied their positions as state officials. In this way the subordination of the church to the state was, within eight years of Luther's challenge to all human authority at Wittenberg, literal and complete.

Although Lutheranism was always the dominant strain in German Protestantism, Calvinism was far from insignificant. Its very different social ethic and church order stemmed from a difference in both theological and historical experience. Calvin's *Institutes of Christian Religion* declared that the church should be paramount in all spheres of life and that secular authority should merely implement the moral order taught by the church. Where the law of God was the law of the state—that is, where Calvinism was supreme, as in Geneva and the Massachusetts Bay Colony—Calvinists practiced outright theocracy. Where, however, the state was ignorant of God's will—that is, where Calvinists were a minority in opposition to the state, as in France and Scotland—Calvinism taught that civil resistance was a duty. In Germany, Calvinists faced a political and religious situation that was mixed and ambiguous. Though specifically exempted from the Treaty of Augsburg, Calvinism became the religion of several of the provincial rulers and, as Lutheranism lost some of its fervor in the late sixteenth century, it spread in certain areas of the north and west. What eventually emerged was a church order that gave the laity a wide authority in an elected synod and a theological attitude distant and critical toward the state.

The course of the Reformation and the political developments of the age, acting and reacting upon one another, were consequently responsible for some of the central features of modern German history: the deep religious division of the nation, the confessional-geographic pattern of society, and the intermingling of religion and politics. German Protestantism itself emerged from the Reformation era territorially fragmented, confessionally divided, organizationally bound to the state, and psychologically tied to the status quo. It has never succeeded in fully liberating itself of these characteristics.

Allowing for the fact that ecclesiastical unity is not a paramount Protestant ideal, the divisions within German Protestantism over the centuries have nonetheless been striking. A *corpus Reformatorium,* a sort of lowest common denominator of Reformation teachings, was adopted by the Imperial Reichstag in 1653, but even the loose cohesion this embodied was dissolved, along with the Holy Roman Empire, in 1806. Following Napoleon's consolidation of the 300 German principalities into thirty states, an equal number of coterminous and autonomous provincial churches (Landeskirchen) were established; this has been the fixed form of Protestant ecclesiastical life ever since.[1] Even subsequent periods of intense nationalism saw slight advance toward closer organizational ties; only in 1852 did provincial church representatives agree to meet on a regular basis, and not until 1922 was a loose federal organization established. This gradual centripetal tendency, temporarily reversed during the Third Reich as a defensive reaction in certain provincial churches to central government interference in ecclesiastical affairs, has progressed little further up to the present time.

Napoleon's action also had the effect of merging Lutheran and Calvinist areas. This process reinforced the impatience of laymen for doctrinal unity but, significantly, it was the state rather than the church that moved in this direction. The resolution of theological differences was long the desire of many Protestant rulers—the Hohenzollerns, for instance, who upon their conversion to Protestantism in 1613 became Calvinists and were monarchs in an

---

1. From that time until 1918 the head of each church was the local monarch, whether Lutheran, Calvinist, or Catholic, who increasingly delegated his authority in part to the religious officials he appointed and in part to his ministry of education and religion. Self-government within the churches was gradually introduced and, particularly in Calvinist areas, the provincial synod became the effective governing body. Even though the fall of the monarchies in 1918 demolished this entire legal structure, the Länder of the Weimar Republic continued to exercise certain supervisory rights over the churches. Only since 1945 have provincial churches been independent of state control, and even this independence has been somewhat compromised by church treaties modeled on Catholic concordats.

overwhelmingly Lutheran area. Frederick William III, who took his position as *summus episcopus* very earnestly, used the three-hundredth anniversary of the Reformation in 1817 as an occasion for decreeing a union of the two confessions in his realm. This "Church of the Prussian Union" was little more than an organizational union, however, since each parish held to its old doctrine and liturgical practices. A number of other unions were subsequently attempted, but only in Baden and the Palatinate were they genuine doctrinal ones. The paradox is that the sum effect of these efforts was, rather than to erase differences, to establish three confessions and to endow some provincial churches with Lutheran and Reformed, as well as United, congregations.

The political consequences of the Reformation also influenced the social character of German Protestantism since the close church-state relationship reinforced the inherent conservatism and patriarchalism of Lutheranism. Troeltsch has described this as "one of the most important events in social history." Protestantism became completely tied to the status quo and taught as a virtual religious code an Erastian and ultraconservative social ethic, while the church "in turn was supported by the social and political forces of reaction, by all the means of power at their disposal."[2] Despite the liberal spiritual climate which grew out of Lutheran individualism and which was the basis of German cultural and intellectual achievements after the sixteenth century, the relationship between throne and altar caused Protestantism as a religious force to fall increasingly out of step with the social trends of modern industrial life. A Christian socialist movement in the late nineteenth century flickered and quickly died and with it the last contact the church had with socialist, liberal, and democratic forces. The workers and urban masses simply ceased religious practice, while the middle and upper classes had little contact with the church apart from ceremonial events. At the height of the Wilhelmine period, according to one church historian's estimate, only about 3 percent of the Protestant population was attending religious services.[3]

Since the Empire, Protestant and Prussian, was broadly considered as the secular culmination of Luther's Reformation, its collapse in 1918 was a staggering psychological blow to church leaders.[4] Although the church-state pro-

---

2. Troeltsch, *The Social Teachings of the Christian Churches*, Volume II, p. 575.

3. Kupisch, *Zwischen Idealismus und Massendemokratie,* p. 133.

4. As one church official declared at a church conference in 1919, "The glory of the German Empire, the dream of our fathers, the pride of every German is gone. The Evangelical Church of the German Reformation is closely associated with this collapse. . . . In the depth of sadness we can do no other than solemnly acknowledge how

visions of the Weimar constitution endowed the churches with many privileges, the Protestant clergy was hostile to the Weimar Republic, generally sided with its archconservative enemies, and longed for a restoration of the Hohenzollerns. Bismarck's picture in the rectories and the "Dolchstosslegende" preached in sermons were the outward signs of an inward nationalistic ardor. The abrupt end of almost four centuries of alliance between throne and altar had constituted a revolution for Protestantism from which it had still not recovered when the National Socialists came to power and appeared to offer a degree of the general restoration which the church desired.

Consequently Protestant officials and clergymen initially welcomed the advent of the Third Reich and in statement after statement enthusiastically described Hitler's rise to power as a divine miracle.[5] Some of them—who liked everything about National Socialism, from its racism to its totalitarianism, had already organized themselves into a "German Christian Faith movement". More respectably conservative churchmen were pleased at the prospect of the replacement of the "political chaos" and "free thinking" of the Weimar era by older political and religious virtues. Apart from a cautious warning against dictatorship uttered by Otto Dibelius in Hitler's presence, no important church figure in the early years of the Third Reich publicly criticized Nazism on moral or political grounds, and few subsequently followed Dietrich Bonhoeffer in condemning it root and branch on moral *and* political grounds. In the general enthusiasm that attended Hitler's rise to power the number of "German Christians" soared, and by July 1933 they were able, with Hitler's assistance, to establish a Nazified "German Evangelical Church" with a National Socialist, Ludwig Müller,[6] as Reich bishop. They soon went

---

much gratitude the Church of our Fatherland owes to its princely protectors and how this deeply felt gratitude will, unforgotten, remain in the hearts of Protestants" (quoted in Fischer, "Der deutsche Protestantismus und die Politik im 19. Jahrhundrert," p. 502). That this feeling is still cherished by some Protestants was evident in 1966 when, upon the enthronement of the new bishop of Schaumburg-Lippe, the superintendent of the church remarked, "We are grateful that the Princely House continues to show us benevolence and we hope that this will remain so in the future" (*Frankfurter Allgemeine Zeitung*, November 8, 1966).

5. The classic collection of quotations is Schmidt, *Die Bekenntnisse und grundsätzlichen Äusserungen zur Kirchenfrage*, vol. 1.

6. Otto Dibelius (1880–1967), as head of the Berlin church, preached before Hitler at the Reichstag meeting in the Potsdam Garrison Church in March 1933. He was imprisoned three times in the Third Reich for anti-Nazi activities; from 1945 until 1966

on to seize power in all but three provincial churches. At flood tide, however, the "German Christians" never quite amounted to a third of the pastorate; somewhat less than 10 percent of the clergy joined the NSDAP.

In their zeal, the government and the "German Christians" overreached themselves; their crude tactics and their threat to provincial church autonomy quickly aroused resistance. There was already some theological queasiness about Nazism. The annual report on Protestant activities, the *Kirchliches Jahrbuch,* in 1932 rejected the party's church program as too outrageous for discussion. In March 1933 the Berlin church sent its pastors a confidential letter taking issue with Nazi racism, while in September the Marburg University theological faculty rejected the Aryan paragraphs of a new church law. Three influential bishops—Theophil Wurm, Hans Meiser, and August Marahrens—while initially well-disposed to the Third Reich, successfully fought to keep their churches out of the hands of the "German Christians." In September 1933 Pastor Martin Niemöller[7] founded the Pastors' Emergency League to unite clergymen who stated in writing they would be bound only by scripture and Reformation teachings and who opposed state interference in ecclesiastical affairs.

---

a key figure in the Evangelical church, he was elected a president of the World Council of Churches in 1954. Dietrich Bonhoeffer (1906–1945), a theologian and leading member of the German resistance whose fragmentary writings, much influenced by Bultmann, have become the foundation of "religionless Christianity" (a term coined by Bonhoeffer). Bonhoeffer and his theology have been more popular outside Germany than within. Symptomatically, when a memorial was dedicated in 1954 at Flossenbürg in commemoration of his execution there, Bishop Meiser of Bavaria refused to attend the ceremony because he considered Bonhoeffer a political casualty rather than a Christian martyr. Ludwig Müller (1883–1945), an army chaplain at Königsberg until selected by Hitler to lead the "German Christians." Like all "Quislings," he was discredited from the start; he committed suicide in Berlin in April 1945.

7. Theophil Wurm (1868–1953) was head of the Württemberg church from 1929 to 1949; thanks to his genius for standing respectably in the middle on every issue, he helped hold German Protestantism together in the Third Reich, established unified church organs in 1945, and as such is the most important Protestant figure in the postwar period. Hans Meiser (1881–1956) was bishop of Bavaria from 1933 to 1955; his tactic was to fight fire with fire, and in 1934, for instance, he appointed an active Nazi and long-time anti-Semite, Heinrich Riedel, to be Bavarian youth pastor. August Marahrens (1875–1950) was bishop of Hanover from 1925 to 1947; his compromises with the Third Reich left him discredited by 1945, though he refused to resign from the bishopric until 1947. In 1933 Martin Niemöller (1892–   ) was pastor in Berlin; from 1937 to 1945 he was an inmate of Sachsenhausen and Dachau concentration camps; from 1947 to 1964 president of the Church of Hesse-Nassau; from 1945 to 1956 head of the EKD's foreign bureau and from 1961 to 1968 a president of the World Council of Churches. In 1967 he received the Lenin peace prize and in 1971 the (rarely awarded) grand cross of the order of merit of the Federal Republic of Germany.

"German Christian" support plunged rapidly after 1933, and by May 1934 anti-Nazi resistance had sufficiently crystallized for a Reich Synod of the opponents to be held in the Rhineland town of Barmen. Here, largely under the influence of Karl Barth,[8] a "Confessing church" (Bekennende Kirche) was organized, based upon a confession of faith in the supremacy of Scripture which might not be changed to suit prevailing ideological or political convictions. Under the circumstances this meeting inevitably led to a radical reexamination of the concept of the Church and its place in society. In theologically demolishing traditional Lutheran subservience to the state, the Barmen meeting brought an end to four centuries of Erastianism.

The "Confessing church" enjoyed such wide support in its claim to being the true Protestant church that the authority of the "German Evangelical Church" was shattered; in the majority of provincial churches "German Christian" bishops were gradually replaced after 1935. The clergy tended to fall into three loose groups: the "German Christians" and other pro-Nazis, the adherents of the "Confessing church," and finally those who sought to find a position between the two. Each of these, however, was further split within itself. Confessing churchmen ran the gamut from those, such as Bonhoeffer, who opposed Nazism on every ground to those, such as Meiser, who only or primarily opposed Nazi interference in church matters—though this attitude, like the Gelasian controversies of the Middle Ages, amounted to a political thrust at the absolute claims of the state. Even the most solid group of opponents, those who declared their adherence to the Barmen principles in writing—amounting to at least 20 percent of the clergy by 1938—was weakened psychologically by disagreements over the best response to the Nazi challenge and physically by the arrest of its most active members by 1941. Altogether during the Third Reich 3,000 pastors were arrested, at least 125 were sent to concentration camps, and 22 are known to have been executed for their beliefs.[9]

The consequences of National Socialism and World War II were disastrous for German Protestantism. Eastern and central Germany, its heartland, were now lost or under Soviet occupation, and Protestant leaders at the end of the war even doubted that the church in those areas would be able to retain its ties with the church in the Western zones. Despite the disappearance

---

8. Karl Barth (1886–1968), one of the great creative theologians of modern times, was the theological heart and soul of German resistance to Nazism. Communism, on the other hand, he regarded as simply a non-Christian and constructive means of coping with the social problem.

9. Figures provided by Pastor Wilhelm Niemöller and Professor Karl Kupisch.

of "German Christians" from the scene, acid resentments among Church leaders remained. The lack of central ecclesiastical leadership, the cleavages among provincial churches, and the political divisions among the clergy threatened ecclesiastical disintegration on a nationwide basis. It was in the face of this challenge, made no easier by the sheer physical chaos in Germany at the time, that the seventy-eight-year old Bishop Wurm cajoled the American Army into giving him a car and permission to tour the Western zones in June 1945 to begin the reconstruction of the church. Encouraged by these soundings, he summoned a general conference in August at Treysa where, despite the presence of such opponents as Barth and Niemöller on the one hand and Marahrens and Meiser on the other, the desire for unity triumphed and a provisional all-German church government, headed by a council, was established. [10] This was the first, but by no means the last, occasion when Wurm and his equally able successors guided the church through troubled times. Their skill, combined with the underlying sense of confraternity revealed at Treysa, has maintained ecclesiastical bonds, no matter how sharp the personal and political tensions among Protestant leaders.

Legally the EKD (Evangelische Kirche in Deutschland) was a new construction. The "German Evangelical Church" was clearly a grave embarrassment to Protestants and too tainted a foundation upon which to rebuild an ecclesiastical structure. Church leaders had consequently decided to treat the 1933 body as nonexistent because of its illegal origin. (At Wurm's request, in December 1945 the Allied Control Council formally annulled the July 1933 law establishing the "German Evangelical Church" though the Allied authorities cautioned Wurm that the status of the provincial churches should not be altered without Allied approval.) As a result of the Treysa decision, the provincial churches, which had been forced to reassert their independence in the years of the Third Reich as a means of defense against Nazi pressure, were now fully sovereign. This circumstance, combined with the strong feeling on the part of Lutheran leaders at the war's end that real ecclesiastical integration could be attained only on a strict confessional basis, meant that any new ecclesiastical organization would be at the mercy of confessional narrowness on the one hand and provincial church autonomy on the other. Under such

---

10. Wurm was elected chairman of the council, Niemöller head of the church's foreign bureau, and Hans Asmussen head of the church chancellery; thus a majority of the council had been members of the Confessing church. The victory for Confessing churchmen was too clearly marked, for it was not long before Meiser was writing to Wurm to threaten to withdraw himself (and presumably the Bavarian church) from the all-church organization.

circumstances the much discussed desire of many confessing church leaders for a united Volkskirche, constructed from the parish upward, never had a serious chance of realization. In the chaotic conditions of 1945 a loose confederation, preserving a basic minimum of organizational continuity and unity, was the best that could be achieved.

When determining at the end of the war the kind of church they wanted in the future, Protestant leaders had to ask what kind they had comprised in the past. This consideration led directly to an acknowledgment of the church's inadequate understanding of its place in society and its specific failure to the German nation in the years of the Third Reich. "Long before churches sank in ruins, pulpits were profaned and prayers silenced. . . . Long before the specious order of the Reich collapsed, law had been falsified," the Treysa conference stated in a message to all Protestant congregations. "Moral standards do not suffice," it added in a message to the clergy, "to measure the depth of the guilt which our nation has brought upon itself. . . . We acknowledge our guilt and are bowed by the weight of its consequences." This examination of conscience and acknowledgment of guilt was made even more explicit at a meeting of the church council in Stuttgart in October, when—in the presence of leaders of the ecumenical council and of Protestant churches in France, Britain, Holland, and the United States—it was declared on behalf of the entire church:

> We know ourselves to be with our nation not only in a great community of suffering but also in a solidarity of guilt. With great pain we say: because of us, infinite suffering has been brought to many peoples and countries. . . . We condemn ourselves because we did not believe more courageously, did not pray more devotedly, did not believe more joyously, and did not love more deeply.
> Now a fresh start is to be made in our churches. [11]

Although the church's statement was deeply resented by much of the German public and by many Protestant clergymen, ecclesiastical leaders, with the exception of Meiser, never wavered in holding to the declaration. The Evangelical church thereby became the only group to associate itself with the German people in a sense of collective responsibility for the Third Reich and its acts. More importantly, in risking odium for the sake of honesty, the church was able to begin to put into practice what had been set in train at

---

11. The text of the statements to the congregations and the clergy are in Merzyn (ed.), *Kundgebungen,* pp. 6–11, 14.

Barmen—a radical new concept of the church's role in society. The core of this idea was that the church's moral responsibility to the nation entailed a political responsibility and—implicit but most important of all—that this political responsibility lies not in passive obedience, but in independent judgment of the acts of the state. Though imperfectly realized, this ideal transformed German Protestantism into a generally progressive institution of postwar German public life and one through which, despite internal restorative tendencies, political dissent could be expressed.

On the purely ecclesiastical side, however, it was not the "Confessing" churchmen who called the tune at the war's end but the arch-Lutherans, who had not opposed Nazism, who explained the national disaster in terms of God's inscrutable will, who saw no need to break with the past, and who were determined to maintain old interpretations of Lutheran creeds. While Wurm and most of the other leaders believed that a full confessional union among Lutheran, Reformed, and United provincial churches was theologically possible, the Bavarians and Hanoverians refused to go beyond a federation of provincial churches, and even this had to follow the establishment of a German Lutheran church. Numerically the strongest group, these ultraconservatives had their way, to Wurm's bitter disappointment, and only after a "United Evangelical Lutheran Church of Germany" (VELKD) was formed in 1948 was a broader Protestant grouping possible.

This wider organization calls itself the "Evangelical Church in Germany" (EKD). Founded in Eisenach in July 1948, the EKD is not a church in a doctrinal or legal sense, but merely a federation of autonomous provincial churches. Its members, in other words, are not individuals but rather the twenty-seven independent provincial churches. [12] The EKD has no creed of its own, and there is no intercommunion among the three confessions or among the provincial churches. The authority of the central organs of the EKD over member churches is limited; theological or liturgical questions are generally not discussed by these bodies. As a consequence, the religious life of the individual Protestant is as much centered on the provincial church as it was centuries ago. In fact, even the old Augsburg principle of *cuius regio, eius religio* remains curiously intact, so that when a Munich Protestant, for instance, moves to Düsseldorf, he automatically becomes United after having been Lutheran—a religious phenomenon known in church circles as a "moving-van conversion."

---

12. See Appendix for a list of provincial churches, their numerical strength, and their leaders.

From the Reformation to the present day, consequently, German Protestantism has been frozen in a state of territorial particularism and confessional division. No ecclesiastical Bismarck has ever emerged to forge a union over these twin obstacles, and as a result there has never been a fully united Protestant church in Germany. In fact, because of continuing Lutheran intransigence over theology, doctrinal differences have been accentuated to the point where, in the opinion of one authority, "the confessional division is greater today than before 1817."[13] At the same time provincial churches have clung so tenaciously to the territorial arrangements set down at the Congress of Vienna that a contemporary map of German provincial churches is, with minor exceptions, identical with a political map of Germany in 1815. (See Map 1) In the postwar German federal system, however, only the borders of the Bavarian and Bremen churches coincide with Land borders. There are also such anomalies as that in Hamburg, where a Protestant may be a member of the church of Hanover, Schleswig-Holstein, or Hamburg, depending upon his address in the city. Despite this archaic and impractical situation, the provincial churches have up to now refused to compromise their autonomy, and they even insist on being individually represented—along with the EKD itself—in the World Council of Churches.

So outmoded are these territorial and confessional divisions that the EKD has necessarily assumed more and more the characteristics of a unified body. Today it unquestionably manifests an unprecedented degree of unity. By handling all social and political matters for West Germany as a whole, and by representing Protestant interests before the federal government and Bundestag, the central church agencies are in a unique position to speak for German Protestants. This situation was first symbolized in 1957, when the chairman of the church council signed an agreement on military chaplains with the federal government, marking the first time in history that "the Evangelical church" had negotiated and entered into an agreement with a national government. The feeling has grown in recent years, however, that this trend has not gone nearly far enough and that it has become unimportant in an ecumenical era whether a Lutheran crucifix, a United cross, or—as the Reformed prefer—nothing is on the altar. Unfortunately, leaders—such as Bishop Lilje, who worked hard prior to his retirement in 1972 for intercommunion and a consolidation of provinical churches in northern Germany—have made little headway against the ingrained conservatism of much of the laity and clergy. The election in 1967 of Bishop Hermann Dietzfel-

---

13. Brunotte, *Die Evangelische Kirche in Deutschland*, p. 33.

The Provincial Churches of the Evangelical Church in Germany

binger, head of the ultraconservative Bavarian church, to the center of authority in the Evangelical church is not a good omen for strengthening the church's central organizations.

The church constitution establishes three such central bodies: a council, a church conference, and a synod. The council is the executive and provides permanent ecclesiastical administration. Its fifteen (before 1966, twelve) members, selected with due regard for confessional and geographic considerations, are elected by the synod and the church conference for a term of six years. As a general rule six members are Lutheran, six United, and three Reformed. Until recently two-thirds of the members were from the Federal Republic and the others from East Germany. Eleven members are clergymen, four laymen. In this way the council is representative of the interests and views of German Protestantism and as a result has had the strength and self-confidence to exercise very real leadership over the years. Following Wurm, council chairman from 1948 until 1961 was Bishop Dibelius, whose stewardship at a difficult time undoubtedly contributed to the steady increase of the body's strength, prestige, and influence. His successor was Dr. Kurt Scharf, Provost and later Bishop of Berlin and Brandenburg. Forbidden by East German authorities from entering East Berlin (despite the fact that he had long resided there and holds an East German passport) and overshadowed by the reputations of his predecessor and his own deputy, Bishop Lilje of Hanover, Scharf did not have an easy time of his term of office, though he was a strong progressive force in the church. He was succeeded in 1967 by Dr. Dietzfelbinger, Bishop of Bavaria, elected over Bishop Lilje, who was considered too committed to the foreign and defense policies of the Federal Republic for the good of the all-German organization.

The synod is empowered to discuss and decide any ecclesiastical matter and to establish the broad policies of the church in both the religious and public spheres. Decisions on doctrinal matters are subject to the concurrence of the confession concerned. Its meetings, usually held once a year, are of great importance in the life of the church and are the occasion of a free exchange of views between the clergy and laity. This has been particularly the case with political matters which have often dominated the synodal meetings. The synod has 120 members, both clergy and laity in equal proportions; 100 of them are delegated by the provincial churches, the remaining 20 being selected by the council. The president of the synod, who is an ex-officio member of the council, is a layman elected by the synod for a term of six years. [14] The church conference, with an appointed member from each provincial church, has come to be little more than an advisory body to the council. Meeting two or three times a year under the chairmanship of the council chairman, it in effect makes sure that the views of the provincial churches are given due weight in EKD activities.

Within the Evangelical Church in Germany there exist three confessional groups or "churches" in the strict sense of the term: the United Evangelical Lutheran Church in Germany (Vereinigte Evangelisch-Lutherische Kirche Deutschlands: VELKD), the Evangelical Church of the Union (Evangelische Kirche der Union: EKU), and the Reformed Federation of Germany (Bund evangelisch-reformierter Kirchen: BRK). These church groups unite certain of the provincial churches doctrinally while, like the EKD, leaving their autonomy intact. The United Evangelical Lutheran Church, to which ten of the thirteen Lutheran provincial churches belong, draws together eighteen million or 41 percent of German Protestants. The Evangelical Church of the Union joins seven of the thirteen United provincial churches and, with fourteen million members, represents 34 percent of German Protestants. Lutheran congregations tend to predominate in eastern and United and Reformed in Western areas and the large cities; confessional distinctions, however, are not made in the EKU. The Reformed Federation joins the two small Reformed churches of northwestern Germany, with a combined membership of 500,000.

This complex structure of federal, doctrinal, and provincial bodies is further complicated by the fact that the primary ecclesiastical unit, the parish, enjoys a high degree of independence. It is the parish itself which holds the legal and practical control of day-to-day church life. The parish not only owns the church structure, the rectory, and the other property, it also has much influence on the appointment of pastors and other officials. Each parish has, independently of the provincial church, full authority in the spiritual and ecclesiastical affairs of the congregation. In view of this complicated and overlapping system of ecclesiastical bodies, it can easily be appreciated that a great practical problem facing the church today is how religious life can be most efficiently organized.

But the church's primary problem—the situation which has molded its outlook and guided its actions in the postwar period more than any other

---

14. Presidents of the synod have been Gustav Heinemann (1949–1955), Constantin von Dietze (1955–1961), Hans Puttfarken (1961–1970), and Ludwig Raiser (since 1970).

consideration—has been the deepening division of the country. [15] East Germany being 85 percent Protestant, the East-West German border divides German Protestants fairly evenly, with 60 percent in the West and 40 percent in the East. Not surprisingly, the Evangelical church has seen its paramount secular responsibility as holding the two parts of the nation together. Being, by the same token, the one really significant institution that linked the two parts of the country, the church's unity was a function of the state of East-West relations. During the first ten postwar years ecclesiastical ties were maintained without difficulty. The Russians, far from hindering Church unity, were helpful and friendly to ecclesiastical officials at the founding ceremony of the EKD in their zone in 1948. When the East German regime was established in 1949, it, too, did not challenge the integrity of the Evangelical church as an all-German institution. In fact, it welcomed the accreditation of an official EKD representative, Heinrich Grüber, [16] as the counterpart of the church's representative in Bonn. Once East Germany was declared sovereign in 1955, however, Pankow inaugurated its strategy of separation of the two parts of Germany, and the Evangelical church was at once drawn into the tragic course of events. Like the National Socialists, the East German authorities ultimately looked forward to a state without a church, but until then they were determined to have a national East German church which supported its political objectives. The provincial churches in East Germany consequently faced a choice of either bowing to Communist demands for a separate church organization or of protecting their political independence, in both cases risking their ties with the West.

The first Communist step in the campaign to split the church was taken in 1955, when Bishop Dibelius—though permitted until 1961 to preach in East Berlin—was forbidden to travel in East Germany. The EKD council was not permitted to meet in East Germany after September 1955, and plans for sessions there of the synod and the church assembly had also to be canceled. However, during the 1950s East German members of these bodies were still allowed to attend sessions in West Germany, and despite sinister warnings at

---

15. The views within the church over the political aspects of this situation, as distinguished from the purely ecclesiastical situation outlined here, are discussed in Chapter 9.

16. Heinrich Grüber as a pastor in 1937 founded an agency in Berlin to help Jews; he was imprisoned at Sachsenhausen and Dachau from 1940 to 1943; he was appointed by the Russians to the Berlin civil government in May 1945 and became dean of Berlin in 1945. In 1962 he became the first Christian to receive an honorary doctorate from Hebrew Union College in Cincinnati.

home, they fully participated in all the work at hand, voting along with their West German colleagues even when the issue concerned the domestic and defense affairs of the Federal Republic. After the spring of 1958, however, the East German government refused to receive Grüber (who was forbidden entry into East Germany after 1960), and it has since then declined to accept a successor. With the erection of the Berlin wall in 1961, virtually all contact between the government and church officials was severed. It was at this point that Bishop Scharf was expelled from East Berlin in spite of his plea to remain. Although East German churchmen are occasionally allowed to attend religious meetings in western European countries, Bishops Friedrich-Wilhelm Krummacher of Pomerania and Gottfried Noth of Saxony were refused permission to attend the 1968 session of the General Assembly of the World Council of Churches at Uppsala because they declined to give up their membership in the EKD council. Most notoriously of all, on the occasion of the celebration in Wittenberg in 1967 of the 450th anniversary of the Reformation, East German authorities forbade the attendance of all but one of the West German Protestant leaders and many foreign visitors as well as two East German bishops.

In such ways the East German regime gradually succeeded in isolating the East German provincial churches. The council and the synod had to hold separate regional sessions and to make ever more extraordinary and secret arrangements to give these divided meetings an all-German character. Until 1968 synod meetings were held simultaneously in East and West Germany, and for several years tenuous contact was maintained by telephone and tele-type and subsequently by couriers. The 1967 synodal session, for instance, managed to hold coordinated voting on the membership of the new council as well as on the new council chairman and synod president. It had become increasingly evident however, that the problems of the church on each side of the border were either too different or too politically charged for the Eastern members to risk involvement. A new church law was therefore approved in 1967, giving each group independently the right to handle matters of unique interest to itself. In 1968 for the first time the Eastern and Western members of the synod met at different times. With that, the curtain had risen on the last act of the struggle for church unity.

In retrospect, the tenacity with which East German church leaders had over the years resisted the pressures on them is somewhat surprising. Their determination had been inspired to some extent by a consciousness of the church's role as a link between the two parts of the country and to some extent by a sense of moral compulsion growing out of the lesson of the Third Reich—that a sacrifice of the integrity of church organization in response to totalitarian pressure could jeopardize the church's spiritual mission. After the German Christians, a "national Christianity" was not a model that any German churchman wanted to follow (with the possible exception of the Bishop of Thuringia, Moritz Mitzenheim, who had been pliant under the Third Reich as well). It was therefore a cardinal principle that the legal framework of the EKD should remain intact, and with considerable courage the Eastern "regional" synod as late as 1967 issued a unanimous statement emphatically rejecting the government's demand for a separate church. The very success of the church in withstanding communist authorities for nearly two decades proved to church leaders and to the world that they could maintain their integrity. It was perhaps this fact that eventually gave them the self-confidence to decide that, given the durability of the East German regime, their ties with the West actually deflected them from meeting the church's responsibilities to East German Protestants. Tied to an all-German organization, they had no body that could effectively coordinate church affairs in the East. Each provincial church was on its own and could to some extent be played off by the government against the others.

The Eastern church leaders finally concluded that their ties with the West weakened rather than strengthened them. In September 1969 the eight provincial churches formally seceded by unilateral act from the EKD and constituted themselves an independent church federation. The East German members of the council and synod declared themselves no longer to be members of the EKD, and the East Berlin branch of the church chancellery was closed. Since the church constitution makes no provision for withdrawal, the step was legally a revolutionary act, even though it was taken after consultation with church officials in the West. Although the Eastern leaders had deliberately refrained from asking for EKD approval, the council (with its eleven Western members) declared a short time later that it "respected" the decision and would consider its functions to extend only to the Federal Republic and West Berlin. In May 1970 the seventy-eight Western members of the synod issued a similar statement. With this—despite official assurances by East German church leaders (to their government's displeasure) and by the Western synod that a "special relationship" would be maintained between the two churches—the Evangelical Church in Germany ceased to exist as an all-German body. Indeed, legal purists maintain that the EKD ceased to exist entirely, since it no longer met the church constitutional definition of being the "communion of German Protestant Christianity." But this unpleasant consideration was put aside for fear that, if any part of the existing structure were unraveled, the entire fabric might come apart. As a consequence of the same political intimidation, the VELKD had split into an East and a West

German branch in December 1968 and the Berlin-Brandenburg church was formally divided in November 1972. With this the only remaining all-German Protestant body is the Church of the Union.

Ecclesiastically, as well as politically, the handwriting had been on the wall ever since it went up in Berlin in 1961, and the church's accommodation to the division of Germany paralleled that of the federal government. Painful though the situation was for the older generation of churchmen, younger church officials in the Federal Republic are generally convinced that the split will have great practical advantages for the church. Because the maintenance of church unity had enjoyed absolute priority over all other considerations, the EKD had been hindered not only from undertaking long-overdue liturgical, administrative, and organizational reforms, but also from giving adequate attention to the crisis that confronts the church throughout Western society. For twenty-five years the whole focus of the EKD was on East-West issues. When it came to practical social problems, the Evangelical church tended to tag along behind the Catholic church and, later on, to abdicate in favor of its own "revolutionaries." Consideration of internal church reform was automatically vetoed because of the risk to the ties across the border.

The division of the church has therefore opened the way for the EKD to reexamine problems that have never been adequately solved since the Reformation. Fresh breezes have already begun to move the church in the direction of liturgical unity among Lutheran, United, and Reformed churches, a consolidation of provincial churches, a diminution of provincial church autonomy, and the establishment of a central organization with broader responsibilities. Apart from the Bavarians, the Lutherans are for the first time spearheading a move for reform, and it is widely anticipated that a Protestant Bundeskirche, or one united church, in the Federal Republic is not far off.

Lay groups—the final aspect of the structure of German Protestantism—have traditionally had as little appeal to German as to other Protestants, though in the postwar period, largely for political reasons discussed below, they enjoyed a substantial importance for a time as forums for discussion and "political education." The two outstanding examples are the Kirchentag, the large biennial lay assemblies and the Evangelical academies, which organize meetings on topical matters (not usually religious) to which experts on the subject, whatever their beliefs, are invited. In addition, two charitable organizations, the Innere Mission and the Hilfswerk, played a notable role in the early postwar years as lay groups for men, women, youth, students, and workers. These groups, relatively small and organized on a provincial church basis, are neither a sociological nor political factor of significance in themselves nor an instrument of indirect ecclesiastical influence. Consequently, when the Evangelical church wishes to achieve some particular objective in the public sphere, it must attempt to do so itself and cannot use lay groups as intermediaries. For this reason it has been correctly observed that the Evangelical church often becomes an open interest group, and ecclesiastical leaders have to stand in the political limelight more than they would like. [17]

The Protestant press is also independent and uncommitted. In quality and circulation (with a total of about four and a half million readers) it is superior to anything of its kind elsewhere in the Protestant world. The outstanding publications, and those with a broad national readership, are weekly newspapers devoted in large part to interpretative articles on current political and social issues. An extensive range of political viewpoints is reflected in them, from pro-Christian Democratic newspapers, such as Dr. Eugen Gerstenmaier's *Christ und Welt* (one of Germany's two best weeklies) and independent but generally pro-CDU ones, such as Bishop Lilje's *Sonntagsblatt,* through uncommitted papers, such as the Evangelical Church of the Union's *Kirche in der Welt,* and finally, to such pro-Social Democratic papers as *Junge Gemeinde* and *Stimme der Gemeinde.*

-----

17. See Breitling, *Die Verbände in der Bundesrepublik,* p. 53.

2 | German Catholicism — Character and Organization

THE political consequences of the Reformation influenced the fortunes and character of German Catholicism as decisively as they did those of German Protestantism. With the treaties of Augsburg and Westphalia, the unity of both the medieval church and the Holy Roman Empire crumbled. Catholics became a sizable but permanent minority in the area of modern Germany. The Catholic church almost vanished from northern, central, and much of eastern Germany. Despite the counter-Reformation, the south and west retained a large Protestant population. Even the Catholic ecclesiastical order was deeply marked by the legal settlements of 1555 and 1648. Catholic princes accepted Rome's dogmatic supremacy, but recognizing the papacy's dependence on their favor and encouraged by the example of Protestant princes, they in practice exercised a control over the church in their area that differed little from that of their Protestant counterparts. Relics of this order can still be found in contemporary church-state arrangements, such as the appointment of bishops and priests. On the other hand, many bishops were simultaneously temporal princes. Three ecclesiastics were prince-electors, and no fewer than twenty-three were prince-bishops. Collectively they comprised the richest and most aristocratic episcopate in the Catholic world—as the sublime palaces, churches, and abbeys of southern Germany remain to show. Individually they personified a relationship between altar and throne that was the reverse of, but no less intimate than, that in Lutheran provinces. As a consequence, while Lutheranism fell prey to state dominance, Catholicism had an equally strong and lasting tendency toward clericalism. Napoleon destroyed this baroque version of the medieval order when he abolished ecclesiastical states, confiscated church property, and drastically reduced the number of principalities. The effect, ratified by the Congress of Vienna, was to impoverish the church and incorporate large numbers of Catholics into Protestant states, complicating the political-ecclesiastical relationship still further.

22

The sum effect of the Reformation and subsequent political developments was to leave Catholics as a body disadvantaged, leaderless, and inse-
cure—a situation that was intensified throughout the nineteenth century.
Most Catholics were small farmers and, after the industrial revolution, workers. Their only chance at a higher education was to take holy orders (even
today a majority of bishops are from a humble, rural background), but those
who did so remained in a closed Catholic milieu. Members of the Catholic
middle class were discriminated against in Protestant areas, and relatively few
succeeded in breaking into the civil service, the army, or the professions.
They generally stood outside the dynamic political and economic forces of
Prussia and the north. In cultural and intellectual life they had a relatively
modest and generally declining impact. After 1815 only Bavaria and Saxony
had Catholic rulers, and with the exception of Ludwig I of Bavaria, they
tended to be indifferent to the interests of their Catholic population. As a
consequence, Catholics increasingly withdrew into themselves and—in a reversal of ultramontanism—turned to Rome for protection and guidance.

At the same time the church's own security was threatened by the
secularist influence of the French Revolution and the consolidation of state
power in the nineteenth century. In defending its traditional prerogatives, the
church became embroiled in disputes with the Josephist governments of the
Catholic south no less than with the authoritarian government of Prussia,
aligning itself with reaction in the former and liberalism in the latter. Even
Ludwig I, whose reign in the first half of the nineteenth century was marked
by a strong Catholic restoration, maintained a ban on Jesuits, and in 1830 he
opposed the church on the religious education of children of mixed marriages. Bavaria was also the first German state to introduce nonconfessional
schools. Its attempt in 1867 to make them the norm set off the first Kulturkampf in Germany. This quarrel became so bitter that by 1870, upon the
proclamation of papal infallibility, the Bavarian government lent support to
the schismatic "Old Catholics," who rejected the dogma, and forbade discussion of the topic from Catholic pulpits. Although the government always
backed down in the end (confessional schools, for instance, were reinstituted
in 1877), the liberal and secularist tone of government prevailed to the end of
the century. In reaction, in 1869 Catholics founded the Bavarian Patriots'
party, a clericalist, reactionary, and Bavarian separatist political movement.
This became the mold for Catholic political activity in Bavaria for almost a
century.

It was in Prussia, however, that the future of German Catholicism—as of
modern Germany—was decided. Here not only had the church to defend its
claims, but Catholics had to fight for equal opportunities in public life. As a

result, Catholicism in northern and western Germany became closely associated with constitutionalism, the demand for civil liberties, and the desire to limit state power. Catholics also favored a strongly federalist system as a device both to circumscribe the authority of the central government and to maximize the influence of Catholics in areas where they predominated. But in Prussia as in Bavaria, what drew Catholics onto the political battlefield was the secularist challenge to church authority in such spheres as civil marriage, schools, and the religious upbringing of children of mixed marriages. This gradually made Catholics a politically conscious group and gave Catholicism an automatic political connotation. In 1848 Catholic deputies at the Frankfurt Assembly formed a "Catholic club" and with that took the first step toward a Catholic political party. Four years later, following a number of anti-Catholic actions by the government, sixty-four Catholics were elected to the Prussian parliament, where they established a parliamentary group. Significantly, as pressure was taken off the church in the relatively liberal era introduced by the Prince Regent in 1858 (who for a time even entrusted the government to a relative from the Catholic branch of the Hohenzollern dynasty), the Catholic group, which had taken the name Zentrum or Center, virtually disappeared.

With the Austro-Prussian war of 1866 and the Austrian defeat at Königgrätz, German Catholicism suffered its worst blow since the Reformation. The dream of Catholic-Protestant parity in a Greater Germany dissolved overnight. The small-German solution meant that German Catholics north of the Alps would be a permanent minority. The church now faced the prospect of incorporation in a state which, whether liberal and secularist or conservative and absolutist, would be inhospitable. In no time Catholic church and political leaders called upon the faithful to close ranks. In December 1870, on the eve of the founding of the Reich itself, the Center party was established with the announced aim of protecting the church's interests.

The anticipated challenge was not long in coming. In 1872 a clash over state supervision of education ultimately developed into a battle over the independence of the church and its teachings—hence, Kulturkampf. Although the practical issues were eventually compromised, the outcome was a serious defeat for Bismarck, since it united Catholics as never before. The Center party emerged from the Kulturkampf as a mass party with enough deputies in the Reichstag to threaten Bismarck's parliamentary balance. Throughout the Wilhelmian era it could count on the election of roughly a hundred parliamentary representatives, and until 1933 most governments were dependent upon its support. Within a relatively short time, and for defensive purposes, Catholicism had become one of the decisive forces of German politics.

The impact of the small-German solution and the Kulturkampf was no less drastic outside the political sphere. Existing social and psychological trends became permanent traits of German Catholicism. The insecurity and inferiority complex of Catholics developed into a "ghetto mentality" that lasted for almost a century. "Catholics lived their own lives cut off from the culture of the nation," an eminent Catholic churchman has written. "They lived in Germany in a world that was intellectually foreign to them. In the universities outside the theological faculties they were scarcely to be found. . . . Even the great writers (such as Stefan George and Rainer Maria Rilke) who were born in the Catholic world broke away from the church which was their mother." [1] This self-imposed isolation, along with fear of ultramontanism, built up the popular impression—far stronger than in England or the United States—that Catholics were somewhat "foreign" and less than completely loyal to the Reich. The psychological scar left upon Catholics went deep; to prove their Germanness, they became obsessively nationalistic—a characteristic the Nazis later took advantage of.

With the state and its twin supports, the bureaucracy and the army, in the hands of Protestants, and with the majority of Catholics among the poor of the nation, German Catholicism found social issues a natural focus of its attention. In fact, it led the Catholic world in this field during the nineteenth century. Taking form as the industrial revolution was getting under way, German "social Catholicism" developed largely as a reaction to the inhumane and materialistic aspects of urban life. Originally the church's underlying approach was paternalistic and retrospective, envisaging a modernized version of the medieval social and economic order based on a corporative system. However, in the hands of Bishop Ketteler of Mainz, these romantic reveries were molded into a program of pragmatic if moderate social reform. Ketteler's ideas tracked the course for Catholicism between liberal and Marxist economics and laid the foundations for Leo XIII's social encyclical *De rerum novarum*. This, too, had a profound and enduring impact on German social and political life. The Protestant worker, faced with a choice between his church and social democracy, left the church and joined the Social Democrats. The Catholic worker did not experience this conflict. Precisely because of the inherent conservatism of German Catholicism, the Catholic church was able to offer him an alternative to both laissez-faire economics and socialist revolution. As a result Catholics maintained their political solidarity. The Center party—and, later, Christian Democracy—became an essentially classless

---

1. Monsignor Robert Grosche, "Der geschichtliche Weg des deutschen Katholizismus aus dem Ghetto," in Grosche and others, *Der Weg aus dem Ghetto,* pp. 15–16.

party, thereby depriving the Social Democrats of a large block of the working-class vote.

Because of its social concern, its clashes with the state, and its exclusion from the Prussian establishment, German Catholicism stood well outside the Wilhelmian order. Consequently, though the collapse of the ancien regime in 1918 completely disoriented the Evangelical church, it left the Catholic church untouched, even if uneasy about the revolution as such, particularly in Bavaria, where the Catholic monarchy had toppled. But now the church saw danger from the other direction—from the liberal secularists who wanted to separate church and state. At the Weimar constitutional assembly the Center party, supported by some Protestant conservatives, turned the laicists' flank and won not only recognition of confessional schools but also church-state articles giving the churches a privileged legal and financial position. Yet typical of the institutions in the republic without republicans, the Catholic church was conservative, monarchist, and antiliberal. "In the Weimar period," one Catholic historian has pointed out, "Catholics—including those at the core of the Zentrum—only partially approved the new state, as something provisional and the lesser of the evils, and left the way fully open for a retreat either into a monarchist past or into the 'more beautiful future' of a Christian corporative state or Christian socialism." [2] In the prevailing Catholic view, the Weimar Republic was at best a liberal and humanistic outgrowth of Protestant ideology. At worst, as in its cultural and intellectual forms, it was generally considered atheistic, materialist, and decadent. With the army, the civil service, and diplomacy still in the hands of Protestants, Catholics found themselves out in the cold almost as much as ever.

German Catholicism between the wars was as much a prisoner of the past as German Protestantism. But while Protestants looked back to the second Reich, many Catholics tended to yearn for a revival of the first. With signs of the Weimar Republic's breakup, this "Reichsschwärmerei" had increasing appeal among the Catholic conservatives. To them—Catholic counterparts, in a way, of the "German Christians"—the ideal of an integrated, predemocratic, preliberal and paternalistic society was not only a solution to the problems of the German republic, but nothing less than the earthly equivalent of the Kingdom of God. This Reich ideal weakened Catholic resistance to the epidemic of nationalism following the Nazi seizure of power. Archbishop Gröber of Freiburg, for instance, in October 1933 declared himself "fully in

---

2. Maier, "Der politische Weg der deutschen Katholiken nach 1945," in Maier (editor), *Deutscher Katholizismus nach 1945,* p. 197.

favor of the Reich government and the new Reich" on the ground that Hitler wanted "a German Reich built on a Christian basis and supported by ethical and moral force." [3]

The position of the Catholic church in the Third Reich was at once simpler and more complex than that of the Evangelical church. Being a tightly disciplined hierarchy, the Catholic church presented a united front to the National Socialist regime and kept its own ranks almost completely free from direct Nazi infiltration. Though the hierarchy was divided in its attitude toward the Third Reich, the Catholic church never had to suffer the humiliation of a "German Christian" take-over of some of its dioceses or of a "Reich bishop" Müller. Churchmen such as Gröber, Berning, and Bertram, who tried to come to terms with National Socialism, remained in the same fold with those like von Preysing, von Galen, and von Faulhaber,[4] who openly opposed it. It was this organizational unity which enabled the Catholic church to prevent "coordination" into the Nazi state. The church's preservation of its autonomy raised a continuous challenge to the Nazi system. It was this probably more than the bishops' condemnation of euthanasia, sterilization laws, and Nazi attempts to interfere with religious life—the effect of which was

---

3. Gurian, *Der Kampf um die Kirche im Dritten Reich,* p. 98.

4. Konrad Gröber (1872–1948) was bishop of Meissen from 1931 to 1932 and archbishop of Freiburg from 1932 to 1948. An enthusiastic supporter of the Third Reich in its early years, he was known as the "brown bishop." In 1933 he became a "sponsoring member" of the SS; though expelled by the organization in 1938, he curiously retained his membership card. After the war he claimed his enmity to the Nazis had eventually been so extreme that they planned to crucify him on the door of Freiburg cathedral. Wilhelm Berning (1877–1955) was bishop of Osnabrück from 1914 to 1955. Probably the most politically naive of the bishops, he saw fit to sit with "Reich bishop" Müller in the Prussian State Council from 1933 to 1945. Adolf Bertram (1859–1945) was bishop of Hildesheim from 1906 to 1914, prince-bishop of Breslau from 1914 to 1919, bishop of Breslau from 1919 to 1930, archbishop of Breslau from 1930 to 1945, and chairman of the Fulda Bishops' Conference from 1919 to 1945. He was created cardinal in 1919 (in petto, 1916). Konrad Count von Preysing-Lichtenegg-Moos (1880–1950) was bishop of Eichstätt from 1932 to 1935 and bishop of Berlin from 1935 to 1950. He was created cardinal in 1946. Associated with the Kreisau circle, he was probably the most thoroughgoing opponent of the Third Reich among the bishops. Clemens August Count von Galen (1878–1946) was bishop of Münster from 1933 to 1946 and created cardinal in 1946. The most open critic of Nazism among the bishops, he gave a famous series of sermons in the summer of 1941 condemning euthanasia, treatment of the Jews, Gestapo terror, and concentration camps. Michael von Faulhaber (1869–1952) was bishop of Speyer from 1911 to 1917 and archbishop of Munich from 1917 to 1952. He was created cardinal in 1921. His public condemnation as early as 1933 of Nazi racialism and hostility to the church was echoed in Pius XI's 1937 encyclical, *Mit brennender Sorge,* of which Faulhaber was the principal author.

offset by their calls for support of the Third Reich—that gave the Catholic church an anti-Nazi reputation.

But institutional factors also drew the Catholic church into a complicated relationship to the Third Reich. Because of its ties to the Center party and its obsession with its own legal position in the state, the church became directly entangled in the crucial events of 1933. Historically, emotionally, and philosophically bound to the Center, the church was also organizationally linked to the party through the many clerical officials who were also Center officials, the most notable of whom was the party chairman after 1928, Monsignor Ludwig Kaas. Neither church nor party could act without implicating the other. On March 24, 1933, the Center party unanimously voted for the Enabling Act which gave Hitler dictatorial powers. At this point the church—reversing its tactic against Bismarck—abandoned the Center. On March 28 the Fulda Bishops' Conference lifted the ban on Catholic membership in the NSDAP. On April 7, 1933, Kaas went to Rome, never to return. On July 5 the Center party voluntarily dissolved itself. On July 20 the Vatican and the German government signed a concordat on behalf of the entire Reich, the first in German history and one of the most important ever entered into by the Holy See. How far the church failed to recognize the Nazi menace, how far it was beguiled by the Nazis' antibolshevism, and how far it was motivated by an attitude of *sauve qui peut*—these are not clear. But amid all the persisting rumors and unanswered questions, it is evident that the church provided some of the tools the Nazis used to destroy the Weimar Republic. The Reichskonkordat, which the Vatican intended as a means of protecting German Catholicism, was under the circumstances a step forward in the National Socialist consolidation of power. Far from strengthening the Catholics' will to resist, the treaty appeared to many of the faithful to signify the acceptability of the regime and the church's desire for a modus vivendi with it. In the succeeding years the church's determination to do nothing that would interfere with its obvious overriding concern, the administration of the sacraments, further limited clerical opposition to National Socialism.

The end of the war found the Catholic church shaken but fundamentally intact. The heartland of German Catholicism lay in the west and the south. Almost four-fifths of German Catholics lived in this area before 1939. Only 6 percent of the population of central Germany, from the Elbe to the Oder, and 30 percent of eastern Germany were Catholic. On the other hand, the vast prewar lay movement was in ruins and the once powerful Catholic press had long ceased publication except for a few official diocesan journals. The hierarchy itself was in a weakened state. Most of the bishops were quite old—the average age was probably about seventy—and they were wearied both by the struggle against the Nazis and by tensions among themselves. Yet despite everything the morale of the German Catholic world was high, a mood engendered by the feeling: we have defeated National Socialism.

What strengthened and encouraged the German bishops more than anything else was the attitude of the Pope. Pius XII, Nuncio to Bavaria from 1917 to 1925 and to Germany from 1920 to 1929, was so Germanophile that he had long been known in Vatican circles as *il papa tedesco*—the German Pope. His admiration of the Germans survived the Third Reich unaltered. The first church figure from Rome able to travel to Germany after the war was the Jesuit Regent of the German College in Rome, Ivo Zeiger, and he reported to Archbishop Frings (as the latter subsequently wrote):

> The Holy Father especially wanted German Catholics and their bishops to be assured of his undiminished love and respect. With tears in his eyes he shook Father Zeiger's hand in saying farewell and asked that his greetings be conveyed con tutto affetto, con tutto amore. . . .
> . . . Despite the wave of hatred which is being directed at the German people from all sides at the present time, the Holy Father wants to help the German people without respect to their confession.[5]

Indeed, the Pope's first postwar public statement was devoted entirely to the relationship of Catholicism to the Third Reich. In this address, entitled "The Church and National Socialism," Pius XII recalled the Nazis' oppression of the church as well as the suffering of the Catholic clergy and faithful. He defended the Holy See for having concluded the Reichskonkordat, maintaining that the church's ability to defend itself had as a result been strengthened. He praised the millions of Catholics "who had never ceased, even in the last years of the war, to raise their voices" and who had maintained a "Catholic way of life and of education." The Holy See had done its best to help them. Its protests, such as the encyclical *Mit brennender Sorge* had brought "light, leadership, comfort and strength to all who took the Christian religion seriously." Even in the ranks of the faithful, admittedly some had been blinded by prejudice or misguided by hope of political advantage. This was not the fault of the church, since "no one could accuse the church of failing clearly to point out the true character of the National Socialist movement and the danger it represented to Christian culture." Then, as if anticipating the postwar controversy that would most dramatically explode upon the world in

---

5. Zeiger's message is conveyed in a letter of September 11, 1945, from Frings to Archbishop Lorenz Jäger of Paderborn. File *CR 25/18*, Diocesan Archives, Cologne. Explicit papal guidance also transmitted by Zeiger is discussed below (Chapter 3, pp. 56–57).

1963 with Rolf Hochhuth's play, *Der Stellvertreter (The Deputy)*, Pius added that he and his predecessor had countered Nazi brutality in "the most suitable and . . . indeed the only effective way." [6]

Not a trace of regret. The church had not erred; it had invariably been percipient, wise, and steadfast. As Father Zeiger, a confidant of Pacelli since the latter's days as Nuncio in Berlin, once commented to a later Nuncio, Alois Muench: Pius XII was "impervious to criticism;" his attitude toward the past was "let critics rave, we did what was right." While the German hierarchy was at least sufficiently embarrassed by the Reichskonkordat to hope that it would rapidly be forgotten, the bishops otherwise needed little prompting from Rome to take a similar stance toward the past. Consequently the Pope's view characterized the attitude of German Catholicism just as emphatically and as enduringly as the lacerating self-criticism of Protestant leaders at Treysa and Stuttgart did that of German Protestantism. Although the bishops realized that the church had exposed itself politically in 1933, they appear neither personally nor as churchmen to have felt a debt of repentance. At his first postwar meeting with the people of Cologne, in the auditorium of Cologne University, Archbishop Frings shocked many of his listeners by speaking, not of the need for spiritual and political atonement, but of the barbarity of the Russians for having summarily executed his brother, a judge in East Germany. This episode typified the general attitude of the hierarchy.

The Third Reich, which radically changed the outlook of the Evangelical church, had, in short, little evident impact on the Catholic church. Having made no mistakes, the hierarchy saw no need of altering course. Living in the past, the heads of the Catholic church grew more and more isolated from the faithful, more and more unaware of social trends. Their point of reference was the security and interests of the church rather than the security of German democracy and the interests of society at large. As their flock had in the past to be guided through the Red Sea of a Protestant Reich, now it had to be protected from the threat of Marxism and atheism. They consequently did everything in their power to revive the old siege mentality. It was not difficult. Catholics were automatically inclined in times of stress to close ranks. But the extent to which in 1945 they still lived in a world of their own was probably without parallel anywhere else. For instance, even those Catholics who were left-wing intellectuals and socialist trade union leaders could not bring themselves to join the Social Democratic party, but, without any

---

6. "The Church and National Socialism," an address to the College of Cardinals on June 2, 1945, in Hermann Schäufele (editor), *Zur Neuordnung in Staats- und Völkerleben.*

clerical prompting, confined themselves instead to clear Catholic forms of political activity—the CDU or, if that were unacceptably conservative, the revived Center party.

But after the initial postwar shock had worn off, after Germany had been ruled by one Catholic-led government after another and after the Vatican Council had adopted a tolerant attitude toward non-Catholics, the "threat" was no longer credible. Some Catholic observers also attribute the crisis of authority in the church to *The Deputy*. Hochhuth's iconoclastic treatment of Pius XII stirred German Catholics to the depths, not alone because Pacelli was sacrosanct to them but because it implied that the Catholic church may have survived Nazism but had certainly not defeated it. With the institution's integrity thus called into question, the church after Hochhuth began to look different to many of the faithful in spite of their outrage at the play.[7] By the mid-1960s Catholic unity and isolation were collapsing. Significantly the new mood was introduced by the laity over the resistance of a largely recalcitrant hierarchy. Once the most obedient flock in the world, German Catholics suddenly became, after the Dutch, the most unruly. Nothing better demonstrated this than the 1968 Catholic assembly in Essen, which was so restive as a result of the encyclical on birth control that a tape recording of a papal message to the session could not be played for fear of provoking an uproar. Cardinal Döpfner bravely read the text—after both the bishop of Essen and the Papal Nuncio declined to do so for fear of being shouted down—but even then took the precaution of deleting several passages.

A year later another incident occurred that reinforced the impact of *The Deputy*. In the summer of 1969 Catholics were mortified by the news that an auxiliary bishop of Munich, Matthias Defregger, while a captain in the German army in 1943, had enforced an order for the execution of seventeen Italian civilian hostages. After the war Defregger, appalled by his involvement in the affair, had devoted himself to a religious life. He had never concealed the facts from his ecclesiastical superiors, but they kept them from the public. When *Der Spiegel* broke the story, it aroused a minor public scandal which contributed to the rethinking current among Catholics regarding the

---

7. In predominantly Catholic cities throughout the Federal Republic, Catholic pressure on local authorities has prevented *The Deputy* from being performed in any theater that is publicly subsidized (as a high proportion are). More than that, as Hochhuth stated in a letter in late 1970, the play "has up to now not been performed on any German stage south of the Main or on the Rhine with the exception of Düsseldorf."

nature of the church and its place in society. A clear expression of this was the comment of a Catholic theologian who remarked:

> Above all I see a chance in the current discussion about Defregger of correcting the distorted picture of a triumphant church of "saints on earth" and of letting it appear more like a society for redemption. Authority in the church, especially the office of a priest or a bishop, is to be understood as service to the community and to society.[8]

Nearly a quarter of a century had had to pass before the serene surface of German Catholicism was broken by such humility.

By this time the German church was deep in a crisis that is still far from resolution. Indeed, the general challenge to authority in the Roman church as a whole reached its theological peak—as theological crises since 1517 usually have done—in Germany, symbolically culminating in Professor Hans Küng's questioning of papal authority in his 1970 book *Unfehlbar?*. There are nonetheless unique aspects of the dissension in Germany. Here Catholics have specific accounts to settle with their bishops. Consequently, the debate over democracy in the church has largely taken the form of a thrust against the hierarchy by a small but articulate group of laymen, priests, and theologians. The hierarchy has been forced to the defensive and, in contrast to its self-confidence and assertiveness during much of the postwar period, is now so uncertain and cautious as to be unable to give a firm lead, either forward or backward.

The reexamination of the concept of the church, which German Protestants had to face in 1945, has been clearly more difficult for Catholics because of the strength of tradition and canon law. The gradual change of mood in German Catholicism after the war has consequently had no impact on Catholic ecclesiastical organization. Each bishop remains supreme in his diocese and is responsible only to the pope. He is assisted by auxiliary bishops, vicars general, and a cathedral chapter, a college of eight canons who act as his advisers in selecting candidates for a successor. Neither at this level nor in the parish does the laity have any function or voice, and in recent years laymen have cast envious glances at Protestant synods with their lay membership, democratic elections, and free discussions of religious and political issues. The clergy as well are becoming restive under the weight of ecclesiastical autocracy. In 1968 priests in the diocese of Cologne, for instance, demanded that all of the diocesan clergy should be consulted before nominations of a

---

8. Johannes Gründel, professor of moral theology, University of Munich, in *Süddeutsche Zeitung*, August 9, 1969.

successor to Cardinal Frings were submitted to Rome. The chapter ignored their appeal but took some cognizance of the progressive mood in the diocese, only to find that the Pope in anger (and in keeping with the Nuncio's advice) availed himself of his right unilaterally to appoint a bishop coadjutor with the right of succession. In this way the Pope deprived the chapter of its normal right to choose among three nominees (a right guaranteed by the Prussian concordat) and installed a man to his own conservative clerical taste: Joseph Höffner, then bishop of Münster, who had not been among the chapter's candidates. The incident illustrated how even modest efforts toward a sharing of ecclesiastical responsibility have so far been unsuccessful. Power is as much as ever centered at the top—sometimes at the very top. The bishops have, however, been forced to make at least a tactical concession to the laity's growing insistence on some voice in church councils and ultimately some role in the church's direction. With their reluctant consent, synods with lay participants were convened in 1971, 1972, and 1973, and while these have lacked concrete results, the sessions have gone some way to appease lay desires for a degree of democracy in the church.

In his Nuncio in Germany the Pope has both a representative to the hierarchy and an ambassador to the German government. In his ecclesiastical capacity the Nuncio is primarily responsible for observing the church's activities and reporting upon them to the Vatican. He also provides the Pope with an evaluation of a chapter's recommendations for bishop and can in this way strongly influence the choice of church leaders. Since some tension between himself and the hierarchy is inevitable, the Nuncio's ecclesiastical role is not an easy one. In Germany it has become increasingly ceremonial. By contrast, an exceptionally important role falls to the Nuncio in his diplomatic capacity. It is he rather than the hierarchy who is responsible for seeing that the terms of the various concordats are carried out and for negotiating any change in their provisions.

The Nunciatur was established in Germany in 1920 and, curiously enough, has continued its activities, despite war and occupation, without a hiatus. Its chancery in Berlin having been destroyed, the Nunciatur moved at the end of the war to the baroque town of Eichstätt in Bavaria where, however ambiguous its legal status after the German surrender, it continued operations. The Nuncio, Archbishop Cesare Orsenigo, although politically somewhat compromised, was instructed by the Pope—contrary to the wishes of the German hierarchy—to remain in Germany. After his death in April 1946, he was succeeded by Monsignor Carlo Colli, who in turn died the following February. Conduct of the Vatican's affairs in Germany was assumed in July 1946 by an Apostolic Visitator, Alois Muench, bishop of

Fargo, North Dakota. Following the establishment of the Federal Republic in 1949, Muench became Regent of the Apostolic Nunciatur and in 1951, when an occupation statute gave Germany the right to conduct foreign relations, he was appointed Papal Nuncio. Muench evidently believed that he was out of his depth both in diplomacy and in German politics, and he allowed the work of the mission to be handled in the early period by Ivo Zeiger, who dealt directly with Father Robert Leiber, Pius' closest associate, and Sister Pasqualina Lehnert, head of the papal household. It appears clear from Muench's papers that these three together handled German affairs to the exclusion of the secretariat of state and largely controlled what information on Germany reached the Pope. After Zeiger's retirement in 1951, the Nuncio's responsibilities were largely taken over by the German hierarchy, an unusual arrangement that eventually caused friction with the Vatican and that necessarily collapsed with the death of Pius in 1958. The following year Muench was made cardinal and removed to Rome. He was succeeded by Archbishop Corrado Bafile who, by general judgment, has not been outstanding in either his diplomatic or his ecclesiastical capacity. It is said that he is inclined to regard German churchmen as Lutherans at heart, while they reportedly consider him a typical Italian conservative whose function as an overseer of their affairs is, in their view, outmoded.

The relationship among the German bishops themselves is marked by complete administrative autonomy on the one hand and strong hierarchical discipline on the other. There is no primate among the bishops, and although most Catholic organizations have traditionally had their headquarters in Cologne, there is no real center of the church. With each bishop jealous of his independence, there is less cooperation among the dioceses than among Protestant provincial churches. Catholics do not, for instance, even have an equivalent of the Evangelical church chancellery. There has, however, been some fairly strong regional collaboration—the Bavarian bishops under the leadership of the archbishop of Munich, the northwestern bishops under the archbishop of Cologne, and the East German church leaders under the bishop of Berlin. While these groupings were especially important during the occupation because of zonal divisions, only the Bavarian and East German churchmen have maintained their links—the East Germans out of continued political necessity and the Bavarians out of antique provincialism.

A broad measure of unity and an outward appearance of unanimity has been preserved by the bishops' strong self-discipline. Sooner a mistake together than the scandal of division—such has been their governing precept. One bishop, moreover, has usually towered over the others in terms of influence. In addition there is a national episcopal conference, where church leaders regularly hammer out a common position on the moral, social, and political issues of the day. Since decisions must have unanimous approval, the pronouncements represent the lowest common denominator but by that very fact the general viewpoint of the entire hierarchy. Although the conference has been recognized in canon law only since 1966, it has always enjoyed immense authority among German Catholics, and its pronouncements have in practice been regarded by the laity as the "official" church position. From 1867, when the first meeting was held, until 1966 the meeting was known as the Fulda Bishops' Conference. It met once a year and was attended only by ordinaries. In response to the Vatican Council's decision to strengthen the collective work of national hierarchies, the Fulda Bishops' Conference was in 1966 given a new statute and renamed the German Bishops' Conference. Now held several times a year, it is attended not only by the ordinaries, but also by the auxiliary bishops as well as the Exarch of Ukranian Orthodox Germans in the Federal Republic and the Berlin vicar general, representing the East German bishops who, since 1961, have not been permitted to attend the sessions. A permanent conference secretariat was also established in 1966; its secretary, Monsignor Karl Forster, is one of the rare observers at the conference. The chairman of the conference no longer serves until retirement but is elected for six years. Though he may be reelected, this rule deliberately diminishes the possibility of a bishop's becoming a de facto primate.[9]

The two postwar chairmen of the bishops' conference, Frings and Döpfner, have undoubtedly been the most powerful influences in German Catholicism since the war. Each typified the mood of the church at the moment while simultaneously contributing to it. Joseph Frings, born to an upper middle class Cologne family in 1887, became Archbishop of Cologne in 1942, chairman of the Fulda Bishops' Conference in 1945 and Cardinal in 1946. The chairmanship and the cardinal's hat, along with his influence gener-

---

9. The Fulda Bishops' Conference was so called because the sessions were held in the Hessian town of Fulda, the site of the tomb of St. Boniface, the missionary who converted much of Germany to Christianity and who in 742 convened in Fulda the first synod of German bishops. Since 1867 the conference has been held with only one break—in 1944 as a result of the disruption of transportation.

An ordinary is the possessor of an ecclesiastical jurisdiction. In the postwar period these have been: twenty-two bishops, three vicars capitular, and two canonical visitors. It was only in 1968 that the hierarchy constituted itself a juridical person, when the bishops established the "Association of Dioceses of Germany." In this capacity the bishops may for the first time own and dispose of property and institute civil action in the courts. The association's members are the bishops or their representatives; its chairman is ex officio the chairman of the bishops' conference. The body normally meets the day before the bishops' conference, and its attention so far has focused on financial issues.

ally, were not so much rewards for outstanding ability as a result of his heading the largest diocese in Germany (the second-largest in the Catholic world). Like many a prince-elector of Cologne, Frings was more attracted to public than to pastoral matters and made his name in this way—though as an outspoken opponent, not of the Nazis, but of the British occupiers. Otherwise Frings was outstanding for almost never standing out. Though politically conservative, he supported left-wing Christian Democrats. He was always concerned about social problems, while strongly opposing social reform. He was against cooperation between the churches but was not anti-Protestant. Old-fashioned and autocratic, he was never beguiled by the pomp of his office and often walked through the streets of Cologne dressed simply as a priest.

His triumph came at the Vatican Council in 1962. With considerable courage and in fluent Latin he assailed curial conservatism and supported liberal forces on the key topics of "sources of revelation" and "the church." News of this stand exploded like a bombshell in Germany, leaving laity and churchmen stunned. Although there is still general mystification as to how it all happened, the commonly accepted explanation is that Frings had rather suddenly become much impressed with a number of progressive theologians and followed their lead. Once back in Cologne, however, his eyesight gradually failed to the point of blindness, and he fell more and more under the influence of archconservative advisers with whom he had always surrounded himself. In 1968 the hero of Vatican I forbade a Catholic memorial service for Martin Luther King because a participant was to be the Social Democratic Minister-President of North-Rhine Westphalia, Heinz Kühn, a lapsed Catholic.

Far different were the background and career of Julius Döpfner. Like the gifted child of many a poor Catholic rural family, Döpfner chose the priesthood as a way to a university education. It was soon clear that there was neither moderation nor modesty in his character. In Döpfner's case theological studies were the introduction to a career of almost unexampled brilliance. In 1948 he became bishop of Würzburg, and at the age of thirty-five he was the youngest Catholic bishop in Europe. His enormous ability and ambition were at first nourished by the counter-Reformation tradition of his diocese. Notorious for his militant intolerance of Protestants and Social Democrats, in 1956 he was nevertheless made bishop of Berlin—a city overwhelmingly Protestant and Social Democratic. Although his distaste for non-Catholics went so far that he was on the point of asking the Pope's permission to refuse the appointment, once in Berlin he experienced a personal revolution. In 1958 he became a cardinal, the youngest in the entire church. By 1961, when he left Berlin to become archbishop of Munich, most persons regarded him as the most tolerant, progressive, and flexible bishop in Germany. Cynics maintained that he had seen the way the wind was blowing and trimmed his sails accordingly. In any event, he emerged from Vatican I as a churchman who wanted to slow down the progressives and drive along the conservatives—an approach he was later to follow at home in both ecclesiastical and political affairs. Pope Paul has such high confidence in Döpfner that he appointed him one of the four moderators of Vatican II. Typically Döpfner took as advisers to Rome Michael Schmaus, one of the most conservative, and Karl Rahner, one of the most progressive theologians in Germany.

Tactically adept at the council sessions, he returned to Germany with his prestige higher than ever. In 1965 he became chairman of the Fulda Bishops' Conference, breaking the century-long tradition of alternating the position between Cologne and Breslau. At this point Döpfner, who had successfully been riding two horses at once, apparently confused the signs in Rome and made a miscalculation from which he has never recovered. He committed himself unmistakably to a progressive course when the Vatican was turning in a sharply conservative direction. As chairman of the advisory group on birth control, Döpfner recommended that the birth-control pill be theologically sanctioned. The Pope felt betrayed, and when *Humanae vitae* was issued, Döpfner in turn felt cheated. Papal displeasure was increased when Döpfner persuaded the Bavarian bishops to give up confessional schools. By this time Döpfner was no longer being received by the Pope and was at one point so discouraged that he gave serious thought to resigning his cardinalate and his archdiocese. No sooner had he regained some of his self-confidence and influence than the Defregger case broke, revealing not only that Döpfner had badly misjudged German public opinion but that he had also failed to inform the Vatican of the auxiliary bishop's background. "In Rome many may have to fight the temptation," the *Frankfurter Allgemeine* wrote on July 25, 1969, "to use the issue for church politics and make of the Defregger affair a Döpfner affair." By 1969 Döpfner had lost much of his influence over the hierachy as a whole and even among the Bavarian bishops. Somewhat surprisingly, however, he was reelected chairman of the Bishops' Conference in 1971.

If the ecclesiastical organization has remained essentially unaltered since 1945, the diocesan structure has by contrast been subjected to intense political stress.[10] The oldest German diocese, Trier, was established about 150 A.D.; the newest, Essen, in 1957. During the intervening eighteen centuries dioceses have been founded, dissolved, reestablished, and territorially altered.

---

10. See appendix for a list of dioceses, their numerical strength, and their leaders.

The most recent major reorganization followed the signature of the Prussian concordat of 1929, when a diocesan structure that had largely disappeared with the Reformation was restored in central and eastern Germany. The only subsequent formal change was the creation of the Essen diocese (out of parts of the dioceses of Cologne, Paderborn, and Münster) for the purpose of intensifying church activity in the Ruhr. Drastic de facto changes, however, have occurred since 1945 both in East Germany and in the German territory east of the Oder-Neisse line which the three wartime allies placed under Polish administration. (See Map 2)

Virtually all the German population either fled or was expelled from the Oder-Neisse area after the war, and the temporary border was soon regarded as final by communist countries and later by world opinion. Until June 1972, however, the Vatican refused to alter the existing German diocesan structure in the area. The result was one of the greatest anomalies conceivable. Four Polish churchmen administered religious affairs in the territory, but they had neither formal ecclesiastical possession of the area nor any connection with the Polish hierarchy. The three German episcopal Sees were situated outside the territory: those of Ermland and Schneidemühl (entirely in Polish territory) in West Germany—Ermland in Münster and Schneidemühl in Augsburg. That of Breslau, which was truncated by the Oder-Neisse line, moved to the East German town of Görlitz in the western portion of the diocese. Each See had a diocesan administration, complete with cathedral chapter, and was headed by a vicar capitular (a titular bishop in charge of a diocese until a bishop is appointed). Moreover, two tiny areas adjacent to the diocese of Breslau—within post-1919 German borders but administered by the Czech dioceses of Olmütz and Prague—were also given representation in the German hierarchy in the form of canonical visitators. These two officials along with the three vicars capitular were, as already noted, full voting members of the German Bishops' Conference. Following the ratification of the German-Polish treaty in June 1972, the Vatican reorganized these dioceses but left the German ecclesiastical positions essentially intact. The vicar capitular of Breslau became the apostolic administrator of Görlitz, and the other vicars capitular were made apostolic visitators resident in West Germany, where they continue to minister to refugees from their respective areas. They remain members of the German hierarchy and, as such, will still have their salaries paid by the government.

Only about half the territory of East Germany is covered by the three dioceses—Berlin, Meissen and Görlitz-Breslau—with seats in East Germany. The remainder is part of various West German Sees—Osnabrück, Paderborn, Hildesheim, Fulda and Würzburg—which were split at the end of the war by

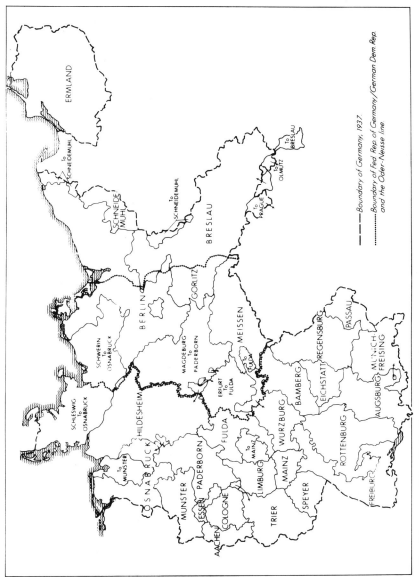

The Dioceses of the Catholic Church in Germany

the Soviet Zone border. To assure effective ecclesiastical administration in this area, special commissariats were established in the East German part of each of these dioceses—in Schwerin for Osnabrück, in Magdeburg for Paderborn and the small eastern portion of Hildesheim, in Erfurt for Fulda, and in Meiningen for Würzburg. As contact across the border became increasingly difficult, the status of these commissariats rose. Each diocesan commissioner (except that of Meiningen) has since the early 1950s had the rank of auxiliary bishop and of "vicar general for the eastern part of the diocese." Meiningen, having a Catholic population of only 30,000, is headed by a vicar general. In the course of time all four church leaders have become virtual bishops in their area.

The Catholic church has been just as much victim as the Evangelical church of the East German government's determination to cut all ties between the two parts of the country. In the Catholic case, however, the communist authorities have moved much more cautiously. The Catholic church is relatively small and weak; its fewer than two million communicants are scattered in enclaves throughout the area. Communist authorities consequently view it with less concern and accordingly subject it to less pressure. On the other hand, the Catholic church enjoys, as it did in the Third Reich, protection in its strict and canonically defined organization. Church authorities can legitimately maintain that they do not have the authority to introduce formal changes of the sort made by the East German Protestants. The church's international structure is an additional shield. The East German government cannot maneuver the Catholic bishops into total isolation and forbid the bishops' periodic *ad limina* visits to Rome except at the cost of a head-on clash with the Vatican, and this it has always sought to avoid.

But in practice the East German churchmen constitute a separate hierarchy. Since 1961 communist authorities have not permitted church leaders in the two parts of the country to have any contact with one another. Cardinal Alfred Bengsch, [11] who was appointed bishop of Berlin three days after the wall went up, resides in East Berlin and is allowed to visit West Berlin only four days a month. To regulate their affairs, the East German bishops and commissioners meet regularly in the "Berlin Ordinaries Conference," and inasmuch as this may not automatically adopt the decisions of the German Bishops' Conference, it amounts to an independent East German bishops' conference. East German authorities have brought increasing pres-

---

11. Bengsch, auxiliary bishop of Berlin from 1959 to 1961, was given the personal title of archbishop in 1962 and made cardinal in 1967. The cardinalate that previously fell to Breslau now appears to be reserved for Berlin.

sure upon Cardinal Bengsch to go the final step and break ties with the church in West Germany. While some churchmen have reconciled themselves to this, the majority of eccleslastical officials in East Germany and the Vatican appear determined at least to put this off to the last possible moment. To alter the present arrangement, anomalous as it is, would leave the church in East Germany weaker still by removing it from the protection of the Reichskonkordat and the West German hierarchy's substantial financial support.

An entirely different sort of structural problem that faced the Catholic church after the war was the reorganization of the lay movement. One of the distinctive marks of German Catholicism and a reflection of Catholics' social isolation was the growth in the late nineteenth century of a lay movement on a scale beyond anything ever established elsewhere in the world. These lay groups were the pride of the church and, along with the Center party, made German Catholicism the most powerful force in German society after Social Democracy. At the peak was the Volksverein für das katholische Deutschland (National Association for Catholic Germany), a combination lay group, adult-education institution, and ideological movement dedicated "to supporting [Catholic] social policy and to immunizing Catholics against revolutionary, proletarian socialism". Founded in 1890, it had 805,000 members by 1914; though membership fell off to 380,000 by 1933, the organization remained a highly influential force in German political life. [12]

The Volksverein, like all other Catholic lay organizations, was dissolved during the Third Reich. After the war some Catholic politicians, such as Adenauer, wanted to revive it and thereby assure the CDU the same army of supporters that the Volksverein had provided the Zentrum. Fearing that the organization might become a political force too independent of the church, the bishops decided against refounding it. The same issue—whether lay groups should be controlled by the clergy or the laity—was long debated as it concerned other lay groups as well. In the end a middle way was found. Lay groups have been endowed with a fair amount of autonomy, and most of them have laymen as top officials. But in virtually all of them priests, as religious advisers, hold important positions, and most of the statutes, which were initially approved by a bishop, may be changed only with his agreement. Moreover, the hierarchy maintains coordinating committees for all the various men's, women's, and youth groups, and these are in the hands of church officials. Lay group leaders are in reality coopted rather than freely elected,

---

12. Höfer and Rahner (editors), *Lexikon für Theologie und Kirche*, vol. 10. pp. 683, 861.

and in practice only an "establishment" Catholic has over the years had any chance of holding high office. As a consequence, the leadership of the lay movement and the bishops have seen eye to eye on important topical issues; the church has been able to maintain a distance from active politics while its views are directly carried over into the political sphere. With lay officials serving at the same time as Christian Democratic officials, the relationship between Catholic groups and the CDU was less one of alliance than of symbiosis. The sum result has been to reduce the lay movement to a mere instrument of the bishops and the party and to destroy its influence in other circles.

A lay group exists for every age, background, interest, and vocation; Catholics are strongly encouraged to participate in at least one of them. It is difficult to establish their precise number, since the purpose of some organizations is far more religious than secular. Although the total number of such organizations and institutes is more than three hundred, probably no more than half of these are lay groups with secular missions. The number of members is even harder to estimate, but during most of the postwar period the eighteen largest groups had about three million members. After seven years of disagreement over the sort of body that should be established to coordinate the work of Catholic lay groups, the central committee of German Catholics was established in 1952. Its statute and membership assure the hierarchy a decisive voice in its activities, and important questions are always discussed with the committee's religious advisor, Bishop Franz Hengsbach of Essen. Occupying the middle ground between the hierarchy and the laity, the central committee can keep both sides continuously informed of the thinking and plans of the other.

There are some 547 Catholic publications in Germany. Circulation has risen steadily since the war and is probably now in excess of twenty-two million. [13] These publications run from periodicals on biblical research and missionary affairs through children's magazines to daily newspapers. Some are official church publications, others are completely independent journals published by laymen. There are four principal categories. The most important ecclesiastical publications are the official diocesan journals and diocesan weekly newspapers, the latter alone with a circulation of two and a half million. There are also seven church dailies, with a circulation of over 500,000—though this is a mere shadow of the church's prewar newspaper empire of 448 dailies in 1932, with a circulation of about three million. In

---

13. Franz Groner (editor), *Kirchliches Handbuch*, vol. 26, pp. 182, 577.

the nebulous area between official and unofficial publications are the periodicals and newspapers of the religious orders and the lay groups. These include such intellectually outstanding publications as the Jesuits' *Stimmen der Zeit* and the Dominicans' *Die neue Ordnung* and extend to large-circulation publications of the Catholic Workers Movement, the Catholic Youth Movement, and so on. There are, to mention the leading types, nine publications for women, eleven for workers, twelve for families, and thirty-two for youth, as well as twelve journals devoted to political, economic, and social questions. The final category is composed of publications by independent Catholic groups and individuals; these include the monthlies, *Herder Korrespondenz, Hochland,* and *Frankfurter Hefte,* as well as the two leading weeklies, *Rheinischer Merkur* and (until 1971) *Publik.* There is, moreover, a Catholic news agency (Katholische Nachrichten-Agentur: KNA), which was established in 1953. Associated with other Catholic news agencies around the world, it reports "Catholic news" as well as general news events of significance to the church.

THE AFTERMATH OF THE WAR AND THE
PROBLEMS OF THE OCCUPATION

3 | *The Occupation Era*

EVEN had there been no Third Reich, the effect of World War II would have been an unprecedented physical calamity for Germany. If there had been no war, the effect of twelve years of National Socialism would have been unparalleled moral disaster. Both together produced an immeasurable catastrophe. The churches alone survived. Organizationally intact and generally prestigious as the only institutions not to have been "coordinated" into the Nazi state, they stood as something solid and reputable amid the boundless moral and material rubble of Germany in 1945. As the principal element of stability in the postwar chaos and as the main source of values for a spiritually starved people, the churches found themselves at the war's end in a position of unique authority.

Their most urgent task was a pastoral one; this was of staggering dimensions, and their ability to cope with it was greatly limited because most church structures were in ruins and a fifth of the clergy had been killed or disabled. The situation was made still more desperate by the influx into Western Germany of almost six million refugees and expellees from the Sudetenland and the territories east of the Oder-Neisse—persons particularly in need of spiritual and material assistance. Hundreds of thousands of refugees suddenly found themselves in towns where there were not even churches or clergy of their confession. As the Apostolic Visitator, Bishop Muench, reported in 1947 to the American Catholic hierarchy:

> Areas that were once predominantly Protestant today have a very substantial Catholic population. For instance, the Diocese of Hildesheim in northern Germany formerly had about 300,000 Catholics; today it has more than a million. Expellee Catholics have added 1,200,000 new members to the Church in the Diocese of Osnabrück. Thuringia, which formerly had about 40,000 Catholics today has 700,000. The Diocese of Berlin previously had about 650,000 Catholics, and now has an addition of 400,000 more. The Diocese of Meissen in the Russian Zone formerly had about 220,000 Catholics, and now had an addition of 480,000 Catholics. . . .

The need of priests, sisters and catechists, not to say anything of churches, schools and rectories is great beyond all powers of description. If 6 million to 7 million Catholics were all of a sudden dumped into an area of the United States not much larger than the two Dakotas, and smaller than Montana, Texas or California, one can get a picture of what the situation is.[1]

This postwar migration, unprecedented in Europe since the sixth century, had profound sociological consequences as well. It shattered the confessional-geographic pattern of society that had evolved out of the settlements of 1555 and 1648 and which had remained intact, except for urban and highly industrialized areas, up to 1945. Prior to the war, in fact, a religious map of Germany looked almost identical to a political map after the Thirty Years War. For four centuries each principality was almost entirely Catholic or Protestant. In those principalities within the present borders of East and West Germany 60 percent of rural counties had a population which was 90 percent of one confession (177 Protestant and 130 Catholic). By October 1946, this was true of merely 82 counties (31 Protestant and 51 Catholic). Only 8 of the 19 urban counties remained in this category. On the local level the change was even more dramatic. One study of the subject shows that in the former Prussian areas of the Federal Republic, for instance, there had been before the war 2,163 boroughs in which quite literally not a single Catholic was resident and a further 2,583 where only one to five Catholics lived.[2] Another 1,098 of the boroughs had not a single Protestant, and 1,153 had only one to five Protestants. This meant that of a total of 11,879 boroughs in this area, almost 60 percent were completely homogeneous in religion. Of the 7,266 Bavarian boroughs, 1,424 contained only Catholics and 140 only Protestants. The situation was roughly similar in other areas. After the arrival of the expellees, in Bavaria there was not a single totally Protestant borough left, and only 9 remained completely Catholic. Of the 95 boroughs

---

1. Bishop of Fargo and Apostolic Visitator in Germany (Alois Muench), "A Brief Survey–The Church in Germany" (undated but evidently written in late 1947), copy in *Catholic Church–Germany,* Modern Military Records.

2. Statistisches Reichsamt, *Statistik des Deutschen Reichs, Band 522, 3, Volks-, Berufs- und Betriebszählung vom 17. Mai 1939* (1941); Ausschuss der deutschen Statistiker, *Volkszählung, Tabellenteil, Volks- und Berufszählung vom 19.Oktober 1946 in den vier Besatzungszonen und Gross-Berlin* (1949); Walter Menges, "Wandel und Auflösung der Konfessionszonen" in Lemberg and Edding, editors, *Die Vertriebenen in Westdeutschland,* vol. 3, passim. The population statistics in the remainder of this as well as the following paragraph are from Menges.

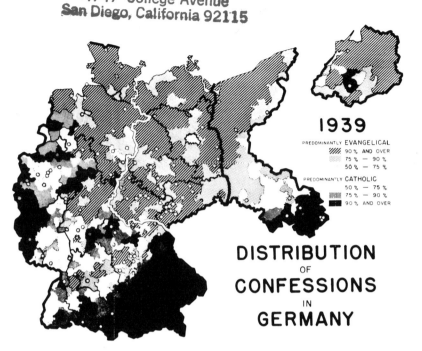

1939

PREDOMINANTLY EVANGELICAL
- 90 % AND OVER
- 75 % — 90 %
- 50 % — 75 %

PREDOMINANTLY CATHOLIC
- 50 % — 75 %
- 75 % — 90 %
- 90 % AND OVER

DISTRIBUTION
OF
CONFESSIONS
IN
GERMANY

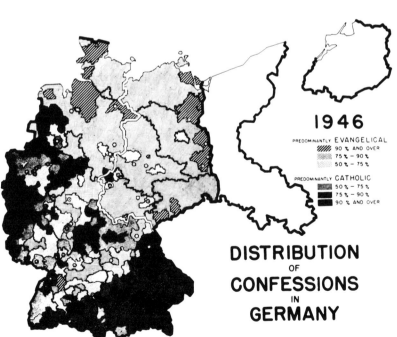

1946

PREDOMINANTLY EVANGELICAL
- 90 % AND OVER
- 75 % — 90 %
- 50 % — 75 %

PREDOMINANTLY CATHOLIC
- 50 % — 75 %
- 75 % — 90 %
- 90 % AND OVER

DISTRIBUTION
OF
CONFESSIONS
IN
GERMANY

in Württemberg which in 1939 were exclusively Catholic or Protestant, only 2 remained so in 1946. Hesse and Schleswig-Holstein lost all such boroughs. Some towns that had formerly been predominantly Protestant became predominantly Catholic. By the same token, since the French Military Government would not permit expellees to enter its zone, Rhineland-Palatinate still had in 1950 as many as 182 wholly Catholic boroughs, more than all the others in the Federal Republic.

Strictly speaking, this radical change did not result from the influx of expellees as such (expellees as a group were almost of the same religious proportions as the prewar population of western Germany) but from the way they distributed themselves. Even though 80 percent of the refugees went to areas predominantly of their own religion, the number of those who did not was so great as to sweep away the old framework. This was a problem for the natives as much as for the expellees, since 80 percent of the expellees had come from communities that had been overwhelmingly and sometimes totally Catholic or Protestant. Most newcomers found themselves in confessionally mixed areas and thus faced a totally new social-confessional situation. Expellees were anxious to adapt themselves to their new surroundings in all but religion, and confessional tension resulted. Many of them consequently resettled in areas predominantly of their own confession; studies have shown that religious considerations were the reason for their moving. In Schleswig-Holstein, for instance, the number of Catholics in almost all counties decreased after 1946. In 15 percent of the boroughs of Schleswig-Holstein every single Catholic left between 1950 and 1953. The same was the case with Protestants in heavily Catholic areas of Bavaria, so that the number of wholly Catholic boroughs increased from 9 in 1946 to 27 in 1950.

The consequence on the community level was to destroy forever the traditional closed Catholic or Protestant society. The psychological hold of the churches was loosened, and community life began to be secularized. Many of the radical changes in German society since 1945—such as the collapse of the confessional school system—can ultimately be traced to the sociological consequences of this drastic alteration of the local confessional structure. A great paradox of the whole situation, however, is that the religious character of broad regions remained as it had been for 400 years—Bavaria, Baden, the Rhineland, the Saar, and the Münster area are still predominantly Catholic, while Schleswig-Holstein, the Hanseatic cities, Lower Saxony, Hesse, and Württemberg continue to be heavily Protestant. Western Germany as a whole, which had been 49 percent Protestant and 46 percent Catholic in 1939, became 51 percent Protestant and 46 percent Catholic by 1950 as a result of the influx of expellees and refugees from eastern and central Germany.

If the postwar situation in this way confronted the churches with some of the most challenging problems in their history, it at the same time conferred upon them de facto leadership of the nation. The only institutions at the end of the war, the churches found themselves inevitably filling the void left by the disappearance of German governmental authority. In the absence of organized political parties, the churches were simply the only bodies in a position to address a communication to an Allied authority and to maintain contacts outside Germany. In towns and villages the pastor, priest, or both became the social focal point, the person to whom most people turned for advice, assistance, and leadership. In the chaos following the collapse, churchmen became civil authorities of great popular influence. Both on a national and a local level an immense responsibility fell to religious leaders, and they generally took it up eagerly. "The German Church," Niemöller is reported to have told the press in *Neue Zürcher Zeitung* for September 3, 1945, "must act as custodian of German national policy so that the human rights of the population might be continually protected." Even after political parties had been revived and Land parliaments established, church leaders were far more free than politicians to speak out in the national interest and to criticize occupation policies. Until a German government was reestablished in 1949, the churches constituted the most powerful and articulate voice of the German people.

In addition to their unique status in Germany, the churches alone had powerful contacts outside Germany through the churches in Britain, France, and the United States. The Catholic church enjoyed the additional advantage of having a Nuncio in Paris and apostolic delegates in London and Washington who were able officially to intervene at high government levels on behalf of German Catholic interests. In Washington, for instance, Archbishop Amleto Cicognani was in frequent touch with the secretary of state over German affairs even before the end of the war. His demarches included appeals that Sudetenlanders (predominantly Catholic) should be settled in western Germany rather than in the Soviet Occupation Zone, demands for the recognition of the continuing validity of Länder concordats, and complaints regarding specific military government practices. At the same time American Catholic and—to a lesser extent—Protestant officials were in frequent touch with the State Department, the War Department and the White House about German church problems and especially about ecclesiastical welfare programs in Germany. While it is difficult to measure the precise impact of these interventions on policy, there can be no doubt that they made government officials keenly aware that difficulties for the churches in Germany would mean immediate difficulties for themselves from the churches at home.

For their part the British, American, and Soviet governments regarded the churches as institutions of great potential value to themselves. In fact, prior to the war's end, at the Yalta conference, representatives of the three powers discussed at length a rather cynical plan to break German morale through spreading the word by way of the Vatican that the churches would be given a major role in German reconstruction after the fall of the Third Reich. In implementing this scheme, the British Minister to the Holy See, Sir Francis d'Arcy Osborne, informed Vatican officials early in February 1945 that the churches "will have a large part to play in saving Germany from chaos after defeat and in educating youth". The Vatican, accepting the proposal at face value, reacted with enthusiasm. As Myron Taylor, President Roosevelt's representative to Pius XII, cabled Washington: "Osborne said matter first conveyed to Montini but Vatican considered of such importance that Tardini called Osborne and spoke at length in optimistic terms as to what the churches including the Protestant could accomplish in post-war Germany. It was obvious to Osborne that the Pope had been apprised of the matter and that he welcomed the Foreign Office suggestion as confirmation of his own desires and hopes." Taylor concluded his report, "Osborne said Vatican reaction more than Foreign Office had expected as point was that suggestion would reach Germany and somehow weaken German resistance". For the first but not for the last time church officials soon would learn that Allied intentions regarding the German churches' role would fail to match their words.[3]

As the invading armies entered Germany, they were, or quickly became, aware of the churches' institutional importance. Military authorities had some knowledge of the churches' record in the Third Reich and a vague recognition of their social strength. Even the Russians went so far as to appoint two clergymen, Provost Grüber and Father Peter Buchholz, to the Berlin City Council in May 1945, and the man they chose as deputy mayor, Andreas Hermes, was known to them not only as a resistance figure but also as a

---

3. The quotation by Osborne is from the Foreign Office instruction to Osborne, a copy of which was given to the State Department with a request for parallel American action (862.404/2-1445 in Box C-729, General Records of the Department of State, National Archives, Washington). Taylor's statement was made in Telegram 39 of February 12, 1945 (740.00119 E W 2-1245, ibid.) Giovanni Montini (later Pope Paul VI) was Substitute Secretary for Ordinary Affairs; Domenico Tardini was Secretary for Extraordinary Affairs.

prominent Catholic politician in the Weimar Republic.[4] Western military officers went much further and very often looked initially to clergymen and church leaders for political advice. The SHAEF Handbook for Germany, which set down Allied military policy during the period of hostilities on German soil (September 1944 to May 1945), in fact directed military personnel to treat church leaders with "deference and respect," to give them special privileges and to consult them on "appropriate community problems."[5] This express direction apart, it was a widely accepted view among Allied officers that as a practical matter churchmen were the least likely persons in a community to have been Nazis and that at the same time they were persons whose advice, if taken, would reduce the risk of trouble with higher headquarters if something later went wrong. In the American Army, Catholic military officers were more apt to approach Catholic church officials than Protestants were to make overtures to the Evangelical church. This circumstance was due not only to greater Catholic group-consciousness (Protestants often looking to trade union officials and Social Democrats), but also to the recognition that a higher proportion of the Protestant clergy had been politically compromised.

As a result, churchmen generally exerted an important influence on the make-up of the initial administrative superstructure at all levels throughout the western zones. The appointment of mayors in Aachen and Mainz was at the recommendation of the Catholic bishops of the two cities; the selection of the mayor of Freiburg and a host of other officials throughout southern Baden was at the suggestion of Monsignor Ernst Föhr; the naming of the mayor of Munich as well as the regional civil governors in Bavaria, the Rhine Province, and Westphalia followed consultation with, respectively, the Archbishop of Munich, the Bishop of Trier, and the Bishop of Münster. Bishop von Galen of Münster himself was asked by British military authorities to form a provisional civil government in Westphalia, and the Americans asked

---

4. While it would be going too far to say that the Russians were friendly to the churches, they were at the very least correct, collecting church taxes and paying the traditional state subsidies. Despite the politically tense situation at the time of the Berlin blockade, they facilitated the entry into their zone of Protestant officials on their way to the founding ceremony of the EKD in 1948. Oppression of the churches started only as Ulbricht secured a freer hand in the mid-1950s.

5. Supreme Headquarters Allied Expeditionary Force, *Handbook for Military Government in Germany Prior to Defeat or Surrender* (1944), Section 849.

Bishop Wurm to head a provisional government in Württemberg-Baden. Both bishops, however, declined, von Galen because it was inconsistent with the Reichskonkordat and Wurm so that he could devote all his efforts to reorganizing the Evangelical church. In the British Zone the first provincial cabinets were appointed after consultation with church leaders, and university professors were chosen on the basis of ecclesiastical recommendation.

The close cooperation during and immediately after the combat phase of operations, when the churches and the military were thrown together by necessity, was followed by a troubled relationship during the four years of military government. Allied occupation policy in the ecclesiastical sphere was drawn up almost as an afterthought in 1944, largely as a result of the difficulties that had arisen between military and clerical officials in Italy; it received little interest at high government levels. The directives were drafted by a joint British-American group, the members of which were far from expert in this field. Armed with a jumble of generalized impressions drawn from a few scraps of out-of-date information regarding the ecclesiastical situation in the Third Reich, the planners produced a policy that was fundamentally contradictory. The churches were to be rewarded for the anti-Nazi aspect of their record by being given complete immunity from interference in their internal affairs. At the same time, because their record had been imperfect and some clergy had been pro-Nazi, they were to be carefully watched as a potential underground movement. The Americans in particular, bemused with the wartime resistance of the churches in German-occupied countries, feared that the German churches might act similarly against the Allies. They cautioned their forces to bear in mind that "the concession of freedom of assembly for religious purposes" might "afford a convenient cloak for a future German underground movement."[6]

Consequently military government policy in the ecclesiastical sphere, to which the French later generally adhered, was one of noninterference combined with a threat of action to prevent possible neo-Nazi activities. The key article stated:

> It is the policy of Military Government to provide protection and fair treatment for all religious elements and to foster freedom of religion and

---

6. Marshall Knappen, *And Call It Peace,* p. 49. Apparently envisaging a virtual civil war, Knappen added, "The safety of our own forces was felt to be the paramount consideration. Under no circumstances must apparent softness encourage underground activity." Knappen was the leading American officer for religious affairs in the SHAEF planning unit and became head of the Education and Religious Affairs Branch of American Military Government.

the maintenance of respect for all churches and other religious institutions in Germany. Subject to military necessity, all places of worship will be permitted to remain open and no restriction will be placed on normal religious activities. Religious Affairs Officers will ensure that religious activities, including sermons, are not used as a cloak for the spreading of political ideas or of propaganda contrary to Military Government directives.[7]

Other articles in the regulations filled in the details. These dealt with such provisions as the return of church property confiscated by the Nazis, the collection of church taxes, and the payment of subsidies to the churches. While subject to the general ban on political activities, clergymen violating occupation rules or found "unsatisfactory" because of their political past were not to be punished or dismissed by military officials but should be reported to their ecclesiastical superiors for appropriate action. The most important point was that the churches were tacitly recognized as the sole institutions above direct military control, as national bodies not generally subject to varying zonal regulations and as exempt from "reorientation" into directions determined in Washington, London, or Paris.

On the whole the forces followed the regulations carefully. Church property was in most cases immediately placed off limits to military personnel. Despite the restrictions upon travel in the early postwar period, clergymen were permitted to go wherever they wished in the Western zones and were frequently given the vehicles and fuel to do so. Contrary to strict regulations against civilian entry into Germany, foreign churchmen were permitted and in some cases encouraged to visit Germany. Regardless of the ban on meetings of more than five persons, which was rigorously enforced in the American Zone until the end of 1945, large meetings of ecclesiastical officials—such as the Protestant meetings in Treysa and Stuttgart—were sanctioned. Religious Affairs officers met regularly with designated church officials to iron out day-to-day problems. The two highest Allied civil officials in Germany—Robert Murphy, political adviser to American Military Government, and Ivone Kirkpatrick, political adviser to the British Forces, both practicing Catholics—had a responsive ear for the churches' problems and interests. It was, for instance, largely in response to an appeal by Bishop Wurm to Murphy that a number of theological faculties were opened in the American Zone by the end of the year and that clergymen and theological students held pri-

---

7. Headquarters, United States Forces European Theater, Office of Military Government (U.S. Zone) *Military Government Regulations, Title 8, Education and Religion* (1945 ff.), paragraph 8–111, Control of Religious Affairs.

soners of war were discharged. In the French Zone the theological schools at the universities of Freiburg and Tübingen were permitted to reopen a few months after the war; they were the first university faculties to be reopened in the French Zone.

The situation was not perfect, however, and there were areas of friction. In the British Zone, for instance, church property seized in the Third Reich was taken over by the military government and returned only after long delay, and Catholics were not immediately allowed to have religious processions. In the French Zone some Protestant church halls and parish houses were seized and in a few cases military personnel were billeted in pastors' residences. In the American Zone the Fulda Bishops' Conference occasioned a series of disagreements between the Catholic bishops and the American authorities. Although this meeting, like that of the Protestants at Treysa, had the express approval of Murphy and Kirkpatrick, a non-Catholic official of the Fulda Military Government detachment banned the meeting as being inconsistent with military security. Once news of this action reached Washington, the War Department promptly countermanded the order. However, as the bishops assembled, a Religious Affairs officer arrived from Berlin and pressed Archbishop Frings to permit him to join the meetings. Pointing out that at the height of the Kulturkampf and even during the Third Reich the sessions had been private and secret, Frings declined to convene the working sessions in the presence of an outsider. The officer wisely decided to withdraw, and the meeting took place without him. In another mishap, the bishops' traditional pastoral letter issued at the conclusion of their conference was censored by American authorities, who deleted three passages, including a reference to confessional schools. Cardinal Faulhaber refused to release the altered text, and it was not until after the apostolic delegate in Washington wrote to Dean Acheson, the acting secretary of state, informing him of the Pope's annoyance at the censorship that the military government finally agreed to permit the message to be circulated in its original form on the following Christmas.

The churches' traditional legal position in the state was not on the whole seriously disputed. The Catholic stand on these issues had been adumbrated by the Pope himself and conveyed to the German hierarchy shortly after the war by Father Ivo Zeiger, who reported to Frings:

> The Holy Father considers the Reichskonkordat of 1933 as well as the individual provincial concordats as continuing to be legal. . . . The three western Allies have let the Holy See know through their Ambassadors they would not question the Concordat.

The maintenance of confessional schools is worth a fight.

If the State should stop payments to the Church, this should not be taken as cause on our part to disregard the obligations of the Concordat vis-à-vis the State; instead the non-payment should be regarded as a delay, not as final renunciation of State obligations. . . .

The censorship of pastoral letters and ecclesiastical regulations should not, in accordance with law, be permitted. This is a matter of a fundamental right of the Church and her freedom. The appearance of Sunday papers for the people is urgently desired even at the price of censorship.[8]

This message inaugurated a period of direct and explicit papal guidance over the German hierarchy (ending only with the death of Pius XII) and helps explain the bishops' unbending obstinacy in holding to the Reichskonkordat and the demand for confessional schools. The Protestants, by contrast, could scarcely have been less dogmatic on these points. At their Treysa meeting they coupled their preference for nonconfessional schools with a willingness to accept confessional schools wherever this move appeared advisable. They would rather have done without church taxes and subsidies, but in 1945 they saw no practical alternative to their continuance.

Although some American officials, particularly in the civil affairs branch, would have liked to have introduced a fairly strict separation of church and state, all four military governments decided to leave existing legal arrangements intact as much as possible, to be eventually dealt with by a German government. (Allied Control Council Law 49 of March 20, 1947, codified this approach as quadripartite policy.) Difficulties arose, however, over confessional schools and the Reichskonkordat. None of the occupation powers at first wanted to permit confessional schools. The Russians flatly disallowed them, although they permitted religious instruction to remain part of the curriculum. The Americans and British originally planned to open only nonconfessional schools but retreated in the face of the Catholic bishops' wrath and—following referenda on the issue—established confessional schools in predominantly Catholic areas of their zones. The French initially decreed that only those confessional schools that had existed in 1933 would be re-opened. Early in 1946 they explicitly recognized the obligation of the Reichs-

---

8. Zeiger's message is contained in a letter of September 11, 1945, from Frings to Archbishop Jäger. File *CR 25/18,* Diocesan Archives, Cologne.

konkordat for confessional schools where these were desired by the population, but they did not carry out this policy uniformly.[9]

Over the status of the Reichskonkordat itself, there was complete divergence. American military regulations stated: "The terms of the Concordat of 1933 remain technically binding and will be respected." The original British directive said nothing on the point, but Educational Directive No. 1 of January 14, 1946, for the British Zone declared that the concordat, while probably still valid, was "temporarily out of force." The French recognized the treaty's school provision, as already indicated, but went no further, perhaps because the Reichskonkordat applied to the Saar, whose legal connection to Germany the French wanted to sever. [10] The Russians would apparently have liked to have had it formally abrogated, along with the nullification of the 1933 law establishing the German Evangelical church, but could not secure Allied Control Council agreement. Whatever the legal differences and ambiguities, none of the military governments in practice ever felt strictly bound by the treaty and went right ahead controlling the travel of bishops, intercepting ecclesiastical mail, and engaging in other practices prohibited by the agreement.

---

9. On December 5, 1945, the Allied Control Council (ACC), in its only policy directive on the topic, recommended the following policy to the four Military Governments: "In matters concerning denominational schools drawing on public funds, religious instruction in German schools, and schools which are maintained and directed by various religious organizations, the appropriate allied authority should establish in each zone a provisional regulation adapted to the local traditions, taking into account the wishes of the German population in so far as these wishes can be determined, and conforming to the general directives governing the control of education. In any case, no school drawing on public funds should refuse to children the possibility of receiving religious instruction, and no school drawing on public funds should make it compulsory for a child to attend classes for religious instruction." *(CORC/P(45)162(Final),* Department of State Archives, Washington) The issue had been referred to the ACC because of church pressure and the negotiating history of the directive suggests that the policy was intended to maintain a semblance of quadripartite unity while permitting American and British military governments to meet the desire in Catholic areas for confessional schools.

10. Headquarters, US Forces, European Theater, Office of Military Government (US Zone, *Military Government Regulations, Title 8, Education and Religion,* Section E: "Church Constitution and Legal Status," Paragraph 8–986; Paragraph 8–987 made a similar provision for the concordats with Bavaria (1924), Prussia (1929), and Baden (1932); but perhaps ignorant of their existence, it made no mention of Protestant church treaties with certain Länder. Control Commission for Germany (BE), *Directive on Education, Youth Activities and German Church Affairs* (November 22, 1945). Repertoire Permanent de Legislation, GMZFO, *Circulaire, Objet: Procédure d'ouverture et de reouverture des écoles confessionnelles* (February 6, 1946).

In short, there was at first a good deal of confusion, caution, and reserving of positions. One principle at least prevailed in the Allied capitals: to interfere as little as possible with the formal church-state relationship. This approach was once summed up by Dean Acheson, acting secretary of state, in a letter to the apostolic delegate. "It is not our policy," he stated, "to approve any change in existing concordatory arrangements unless a Bavarian Government, elected by and representative of the Bavarian people, should request such a change in accordance with popular demand." Regarding education, he wrote: "It is not the policy of this government to oppose the reopening of confessional schools in Germany." And he added, "The entire matter of religious instruction and confessional schools is not, of course, of long-term interest to the Military Government. It is interested to leave ultimate decisions in this matter to the will of the German people as democratically expressed." [11] While it was one thing for Acheson in Washington to sketch out the grand policy line and another for local military officials to know about it and follow it, a modus vivendi on all essentials was reached fairly soon. In practice, therefore, the two sides avoided any serious jurisdictional clash.

The serious quarrels arose in the political sphere, and in spite of their variation in intensity and substance from zone to zone, they had a common denominator. Most basic perhaps was the refusal of the three military governments, in varying degree, to recognize the role which fell to the churches following the collapse of the Third Reich. Even though Allied occupation aims touched the roots of German society, thus raising issues so fundamental that the churches were bound to feel directly involved, there was no inclination by military authorities to consult them, to enlist their cooperation on policy matters, or even to keep them informed of occupation objectives. Moral rehabilitation would be the churches' business while economic, political, and social reconstruction was the concern of the occupation authorities. The fact that the two cannot be out of step was largely ignored by the military in the rush to get Germany on her feet materially.

At the same time church leaders were anything but overjoyed that their country was occupied, divided, and governed by four foreign states. A number of Catholic bishops regarded the Allies in the early postwar period as "the enemy"; in fact, Archbishop Gröber continued to refer to them as such in his pastoral letters throughout the summer of 1945. From the outset of the

---

11. Letter of December 29, 1945 (762.66A/12–445), General Records of the Department of State, National Archives, Washington.

occupation the church authorities anticipated another form of the same sort of struggle they had waged with the Nazis. "As bishop," von Galen's chaplain has written of the Münster prelate on the eve of the Allied victory, "he had shown the rulers of the Third Reich the God-established limits; he would not fear unhesitatingly to do the same now with respect to the new rulers." [12] Under the best of circumstances bishops and generals do not have much in common; the occupation period was scarcely a good time for Allied generals and German bishops to find common ground.

If confrontation was for these reasons likely, it became inevitable as a consequence of the deep gulf dividing the political outlook of ecclesiastical and military leaders. At the Potsdam Conference it was agreed that Germany should be democratized, denazified, and demilitarized; no ecclesiastical leader found it difficult to accept these goals. But the Allies had little notion of what these aims meant in terms either of philosophical premises or of pragmatic policies. In significant ways the military governments soon appeared to believe that German society was so flawed that it would have to be demolished and rebuilt and that the German character was so marred that it would have to be "reoriented" and "reeducated." These notions the churches resented and rejected. In the view of most Catholic and Protestant churchmen, National Socialism had been imposed upon the German people by a group of thugs and accepted by most of the population at first for innocent reasons and later because there was no choice. The thugs—"the couple of Nazis," as Bishop von Galen often put it [13] —had to be removed and the moral damage repaired, but this would be a relatively simple task and one that must not entail political or social disturbance.

This attitude was reinforced by the conviction of most religious leaders at the war's end that Germany was on the threshold of an economic and social misery so profound that a complete proletarianization of society was threatened. It would be difficult to exaggerate the concern of the Catholic bishops in particular that, with widespread destitution in the western zones and the Russians at the Elbe, all of Germany might easily be engulfed by communism. They had no deeper fear and repeated no theme more frequently in their public and private appeals to the three military governments than that the German people could easily sink into a mire of utter despair. In their view, Allied treatment of the Germans merely aggravated the situation and, as Frings warned a representative of Field Marshal Montgomery, this "was push-

---

12. Portmann, *Kardinal von Galen*, p. 232.
13. Ibid., p. 231.

ing the people into the arms of communism." Faced with an occupation policy that a high American Military Government official once described as "exclusively punitive", church leaders quickly came to doubt the motives no less than the wisdom of the Allies. When asked by Montgomery's emissary about the prevailing mood of the German people, Frings responded, "Above all a feeling of great disappointment. After the Third Reich we had expected improvement. Instead everything has become worse." In other words, the basis of the churches' involvement in the problems of the occupation era was not so much a bleeding-heart appeal for Christian charity—though it included that—as a plea for political reason as they saw it. [14]

In a confidential letter to General Eisenhower drafted at their August conference, the Catholic bishops summarized well the specific concerns of leaders of both churches in the months following the war. After emphasizing their desire to cooperate with the Allies in reestablishing civil order, the bishops appealed for urgent action to head off widespread famine; they asked that Germans wanting to stay in the areas east of the Oder-Neisse and the Sudetenland be permitted to remain, and they called for stronger disciplinary measures toward the displaced persons who, they said, were responsible for widespread murder, rape, and robbery. They asked for an end to the internment and dismissal of nominal members of the Nazi party which, in their view, hindered reconstruction by removing experts from vital positions. Finally they called for the release of the millions of German prisoners-of-war and an improvement in their living conditions until that time. [15] Similar petitions were made by Protestant leaders, not only to Allied military authorities, but also to Allied governments, to church groups in Britain, France, and the United States, as well as to the United Nations. It appears doubtful that these appeals were generally taken very seriously by high military government officials.

In any event most practical matters were handled at the local and zonal levels, and here relations varied a good deal. In the early postwar period priests, pastors, and bishops were flooded with letters and oral appeals concerning individual and community problems, with urgent demands to "do something" to put things right. Each Catholic diocese and Protestant provin-

---

14. Frings' remarks from a memorandum of a conversation between Frings and an unidentified British officer on July 19, 1945; File CR 25/18, Diocesan Archives, Cologne. For military government official, see Dorn, "Debate over American Occupation Policy."

15. Letter dated August 23, 1945 in *Fulda Conference—Treysa Conference,* Modern Military Records.

cial church handled such matters individually, a designated liaison official or the bishop himself intervening with the local military commander. Frequently the dioceses and provincial churches in a particular zone acted together. The effectiveness of these contacts depended largely upon the personal relationship between the church official and the military officer; some churchmen enjoyed a considerable influence. For their part the three military governments held different attitudes and followed different policies in their pragmatic dealings with churches.

The basis of British policy was simple: complete noninterference in ecclesiastical affairs. The British, with their Anglican tradition of an established church and bishops sitting in the House of Lords and having to that extent a place in the political system, could grasp what the traditionally close church-state relationship in Germany meant in practice and could recognize that the churches would have strong views on public affairs which they would legitimately wish to express. The British tactic was therefore to give church leaders full liberty to speak out as they pleased and to shun an outright clash with them at almost any cost. Alone among the occupation powers British Military Government did not insist that the churches restrict their criticism of policy matters to private communications submitted through military channels. The British were the only occupiers never to ban or censor pastoral letters and never to intervene in the churches' own denazification. They alone stopped censoring the bishops' mail and their communications with the Vatican.

From the start to the end of the occupation this forbearing approach was stringently tested. The British not only had the most difficult of the four zones, they also faced the most vigorous and closely coordinated group of Catholic bishops in Germany. The northern half of their zone was flooded with Catholic refugees; the diocese of Hildesheim made itself their champion, appealing to the British to take immediate steps to provide housing, schools, food, jobs, and so on. To the British authorities, however, the refugees were only one among a number of overwhelming problems, and pleas for special treatment were considered more annoying than helpful. In some cases the diocese offered direct assistance—for instance, to pay for the cost of housing if construction materials were made available. The British, who did not want the entire body of refugees to remain put, resented the church's interference in a matter of great complexity for which they were responsible. The church was concerned about an immediate human problem and thought that the

British were dawdling; the military government was interested in a long-term solution and considered the church to be impatient. The church feared that, unless effective steps were taken to give refugees work and a reasonable community life, they might turn to communism in desperation. Military government believed that in ecclesiastical circles the refugees' cause was being "used to indulge in covert anti-communist propaganda and to attempt to set the western powers against Russia." [16] Misunderstanding blossomed freely in such ground.

In Westphalia the "lion of Münster," Bishop von Galen, was distressed at the very sight of foreign troops on German soil, describing the onset of the occupation as "the terrible doom now breaking over Germany." Deeply conscious of his role as protector of this overwhelmingly Catholic diocese, he reacted aggressively to the situation. *The New York Times* caught his mood in an interview on April 7, 1945, reporting that he had "made it clear the Germans would have to consider the Allies enemies." In June he turned down a British invitation to head the Westphalian civil government and began instead a campaign of written and oral, private and public criticism of British Military Government. His initial interventions with British officials, during which he engaged in a good deal of fist banging and used language his interpreters hesitated to translate, concentrated on the unsettled social conditions, especially the plundering, murder and rape committed by displaced persons in the area. He accused the British of failing to take the necessary steps to restore order and warned that the result could be the "domination of communism and anarchy." Dissatisfied with the British reaction to his various appeals, von Galen complained in a dramatic sermon in July about events that "can only be explained on the grounds of the hate and thirst for revenge of our former enemies of war." According to him, it was because of British inaction that the German people were on the verge of starvation. The sermon created a sensation and, as with the bishop's wartime attacks on the Nazis, parishoners passed copies of the text from hand to hand. British officials, infuriated by both the matter and manner of von Galen's sermon, demanded a public retraction of his charges. Von Galen refused to withdraw a word, but finally agreed to have published in the official diocesan journal a brief statement, the relevant portion of which simply stated, "The English Military Government has told me that in its measures it is far from being guided by

---

16. "The Clergy's Attitude to German Problems", *British Zone Review,* June 8, 1946. The *British Zone Review* was a semi-official publication. See note 30.

hate or thirst for revenge and that it would neither tolerate the excesses and outrages that I mentioned nor would passively permit an avoidable famine." [17]

Not that he believed his own words. In fact, he was just getting into his stride; in an interview on October 26, 1945, with Fritz René Allemann of the Zurich newspaper *Die Tat*, von Galen took advantage of British permission to speak freely to condemn the military government with wild extravagance. According to him, the liberties taken away by the Nazis had not been restored by the occupation powers; the British Military Government was in many respects an imitation of National Socialism; many of the complaints were the same under the two regimes; political suspects were being put in "concentration camps" and denied permission, which even the Nazis had granted, to receive mail and packages; and in contrast to the Nazis, who pensioned off their opponents in the civil service, the British summarily fired persons they considered undesirable. All this, von Galen concluded, was leading to a political radicalization which ran the risk of producing what he said he feared above all, "nihilism and bolshevism."

The sermon and the interview demolished von Galen's relationship with the British, and though he was always received courteously by local military officials, his interventions were ignored and he was denied access to higher headquarters. In his last Lenten pastoral letter before his death, published in the diocesan journal on February 1, 1946, he confessed sadly, "You may believe me; it pains me bitterly, yes it often makes me deeply sorrowful that I can help you so little, almost not at all, that I must again and again say and write: I have no power, I have no influence on the rulers; yes, it is not even possible for me to bring our distress and your requests to the attention of those offices where decisions are made." By regarding the British as "the enemy" and little better than the Nazis, von Galen destroyed his ability to influence occupation policy. His own chaplain's comment, "He was far more a fighter than a negotiator," [18] sums up his unfortunate relationship with the military government.

But it was in the Rhineland, in the person of Archbishop Frings, that the British faced their real nemesis. As chairman of the Fulda Bishops' Conference and through his vigor and self-confidence, Frings was the most powerful

---

17. Von Galen's statements appear in Portmann, p. 232; Bierbaum, *Nicht Lob, Nicht Furcht,* p. 265; his sermon is in file *CR 25/18,* Diocesan Archives, Cologne.
18. Portmann, p. 243.

Catholic leader in Germany after the war. Throughout the course of the occupation he was so distraught by the suffering of the people that nothing the British did in their zone—from the ban on growing flowers to the dismantling of the Krupp works—escaped his notice or comment. In his view, the situation and how to cope with it were clear. Since Germany had been deprived of her agricultural lands in the East and had to accommodate millions of refugees, large imports of food would have to be arranged. Since housing had been destroyed by bombs, massive reconstruction would have to be undertaken. Since there was an acute fuel shortage, mines would have to be worked at full capacity and coal would have to be imported. Since men, and especially the young men, needed work for psychological no less than material reasons, industry would have to be quickly revived. Since the population was weighed down by a sense of hopelessness, it needed encouragement and friendship.

When, however, the British did not supply food in large quantities; when they confiscated housing for their forces; when they removed some of the coal mined in the Ruhr; when they dismantled factories; and when they introduced a policy of broad denazification and nonfraternization—Frings was first exasperated and then infuriated. During the occupation years he missed no occasion to badger, cajole, criticize, or condemn the British, with the intent of securing policy changes. That the Germans must both hunger *and* freeze, he told Lord Beveridge, "is an act against humanity." [19] To move Germany families out of their homes to make way for British families, he wrote to the Cologne Commandant, "seems to me to contradict all rules of humanity." If the order were not countermanded, he went on, "I request that you not overlook the house . . . where I live. . . . I will then attempt to settle myself in the ruins of the archbishop's palace." [20] Dismantling the Krupp works, he warned General Bishop, Governor of North Rhine-Westphalia, would mean "the ruin of the city of Essen." It would also place "family life, which has already been badly disrupted by war experiences and the postwar years, in the greatest danger because of the dismissal or transfer of workers." [21] Denazification, he stated to the visiting bishop of Chichester and the Catholic bishop of Nottingham, was being carried out so mechanically

---

19. Report on visit to Frings by Lord Beveridge on January 16, 1947, in File *CR 25/18,* Diocesan Archives, Cologne.

20. Letter of July 12, 1946, from Frings to Colonel White, *op. cit.*

21. Report on visit to Frings of General Bishop on March 18, 1948, *op. cit.*

that "the result is the paralysis of Germany." [22] These were all points that Frings drove home at every encounter with a British official (and he appears to have had more frequent contact with them than all the other bishops together) until the policy was altered, the situation improved or the British left.

Frings' concern was not just for the people's suffering but, as he once wrote to Cardinal Griffin, archbishop of Westminster, also for the danger "that many men, also in this country, are driven to despair and then run into unbelief and communism," [23] a theme he repeated in his meetings with military officials. When, following one of the archbishop's lectures on all the errors in the British Zone, the Regional Commissioner for North Rhine-Westphalia, William Asbury, remarked that not every difficulty was the fault of British Military Government, Frings agreed but insisted that much more could be done. So convinced was he of British negligence that in the course of his New Year's Eve sermon in 1946 he claimed that an individual was justified in stealing from common stocks whatever was necessary for his life or health if he could not secure these necessities through his work or from the British. The Cardinal's motivation was that of helping his "Rhineland children" and the verb "fringsen" (meaning to steal what one needs) became part of the German vocabulary. But in the British view, this went beyond criticism of occupation policy; it was an outrageous flouting of the military government's authority and an invitation to grave social disorder. Frings later joked that the British had wanted to arrest him as a result of his sermon, and while it can be taken for granted that such was not the case, Asbury did implore Frings to withdraw the statement, since the theft of coal had increased to a dangerous level and appeared to have episcopal sanction. Frings would not, however, go beyond informing the press that organized forays against coal trains were a menace and that he condemned them. When, toward the end of the occupation, Lord Pakenham remarked that the problems of the British Zone had been more intractable than those of the other zones, Frings responded simply that the British had chosen that area and that they should not have done so if they were not equal to the task.

---

22. Report on meeting between Frings, Chichester, and Nottingham on November 19, 1946, *op. cit.*

23. Letter (original in English) of January 8, 1946, *op. cit.*

But it was not simply that Frings felt that the British had bungled the material situation in their zone; in his view they made a bad situation worse by following a quite iniquitous economic and political line that hàd nothing to do with the occupation as such. The British policy of nationalizing Ruhr industries, for example, would "not serve the worker since the State can be a much more ruthless exploiter of people than the individual capitalist." [24] The British veto of the establishment of a Catholic trade union in favor of a single trade union movement greatly vexed the Cardinal by running counter to his policy of keeping Catholics organizationally separate from non-Catholics. At the outset of the occupation military officials had appointed the Communist party chairman, Max Reimann, as Mayor of Essen and a number of lesser communists as mayors of other towns. This was not a single gaffe, and during the summer of 1946 Frings pointed out to General Balfour, Deputy Military Governor, that the communists were getting far too much and the Christian Democrats far too little newsprint in proportion to their political strength. After having investigated the matter, Balfour admitted the truth of this allegation and promised to take corrective action. Still more blatant, in the Cardinal's opinion, was the partiality shown to Social Democrats over the Christian Democrats. "In the political sphere," he once complained to Asbury, "it seems to me the SPD is, perhaps because of its relationship to the Labor Party, being favored. Even prior to the coming elections, the top positions are being given to SPD people. I believe that such favoritism toward the SPD is not in keeping with the will of the people." [25] Repeating his criticism over a year later to Lord Pakenham, Frings charged "Though the top-level of the civil administration is now consonant with the election results—that is, in the Rhineland largely held by members of the Christian parties—the influence of the SPD in middle-level positions is unjustifiably great." [26]

Worse still than the putative chicaneries and ineptitude of the British, what lay at the heart of Frings' criticism was the Cardinal's conviction that the British were being willfully vindictive—toward the German people general-

---

24. Report of meeting of Frings, Pakenham, and Asbury on September 25, 1947, *op. cit.*

25. Memorandum on meeting of Frings and Asbury on July 5, 1946, *op. cit.*

26. Memorandum on meeting of Frings, Pakenham, and Asbury on September 25, 1947, *op. cit.*

ly and toward the Catholic church specifically. A common refrain in his interventions during roughly the first two years of the occupation was that the British were deliberately not doing all they could to provide food, coal and housing materials "in order, I am convinced," he charged on one occasion, "to punish the people." [27] Increasingly he came to believe that the British aimed at the economic emasculation of Germany. The German people, he argued, did not want to be dependent upon others; but because of British delays in providing fertilizer, for instance, he was driven to the conclusion that "Germany is deliberately being kept completely dependent upon others for food." [28] He could never escape the feeling that the British, in the field and in London, tended to be anti-Catholic. "In the Foreign Office, especially, there must be forces at work which do not have much use for the Catholic Church," he flatly charged. Because military authorities long refused to return a seminary near Cologne which had been seized by the Nazis, he actually went so far as to say, "The behavior of the occupation authority toward the Church resembles too closely that of the past Nazi regime." [29]

For these reasons Frings' mistrust of the British turned into fury, and his fury developed into a hatred that lasts to this day. For their part the British felt that the Catholic bishops simply had no grasp of the problems facing the military government, made no allowance for the limitations upon an exhausted Britain to reconstruct Germany, ignored the worldwide food and coal shortage which meant hunger and cold for everyone in Europe, and overlooked the fact that denazification and dismantling were agreed Four Power policies. They felt victimized by a persistent and unfair campaign that tended to erode their authority and to contribute to the very confusion and despair the bishops complained about. As early as the spring of 1946 a survey of Catholic and Protestant churches in Rhineland and Westphalia described the Catholic clergy as "intolerant and prejudiced" and the church itself as generally hypercritical of British policies, uncomprehending of British aims and,

---

27. Memorandum on meeting of Frings and Colonel Parker, Commandant of Cologne, on January 12, 1947, *op. cit.*

28. Letter of July 21, 1946, from Frings to Military Headquarters of North Rhine Province, *op. cit.*

29. Memorandum on meeting of Frings and Gwynne, Head of Religious Affairs Branch, and Monsignor Smith, Head of Roman Catholic Section of Religious Affairs Branch, on December 10, 1946, *op. cit.*

though influential, altogether a "nationalist rather than a democratic influence in German life." [30]

There can be no final balancing of this account. British officials would have found it much more comfortable to administer their zone without any ecclesiastical interference. Cardinal Frings' innumerable interventions, which he never publicized to gain personal popularity, forced the British to hear—and, at times, to heed—popular dissatisfaction. His points of criticism ran the gamut from fair to preposterous. Dismantling policy, for instance, which he bitterly fought, was probably the most universally unpopular act of the occupation period. It was opposed personally by both Lord Pakenham and General Robertson and probably marked the only issue on which Frings and SPD chairman Kurt Schumacher were in full agreement. Frings, along with Protestant churchmen and political leaders, saved many a factory from demolition. The charge of favoritism toward the SPD was in certain respects valid; as Frings was able to demonstrate, the Social Democrats were preferred at some times, in some places, and at some levels of civil administration. Lord Pakenham's appointment as resident minister, no doubt partly in order to improve British relations with Christian Democratic and Catholic church leaders, was at once confirmation of the fact and evidence that it was not a concerted, consistent policy. In any case, Frings was again able to effect changes where the CDU could not. The archbishop's strictures on living conditions were probably least just and least effective. He showed absolutely no understanding of the plight of Britain herself or of Europe as a whole. The British use of their 1946 dollar loan to supply their zone is perhaps the best gauge of British intentions. Indeed, in the early occupation period, as one German scholar has observed, "the British zone, despite all the structural difficulties, was considered the most humanely administered." [31]

Where Frings really went wrong was in imputing deliberate maliciousness to the British. The charge that the foreign office was anti-Catholic was true only insofar as Frings saw everything in terms of "he who is not for me is against me." The notion that the British deliberately let the German people suffer and starve—which, it is understood, he still believes—was especially unworthy, since the British government was less motivated by thoughts of

---

30. The report, originally secret, was later published in the official *British Zone Review* on June 8, 1946. Curiously enough, a hand-written copy of the secret report itself was in Frings' possession and is today in the diocesan files of Cologne.

31. Schwarz, *Vom Reich zur Bundesrepublik*, p. 734.

punishment than any of the occupation powers. "Though their people," Harold Zink, the American historian and expert on the occupation, has written, "had suffered far more grievously than Americans as a result of the bombing of their cities, the submarine warfare and so forth, there was never in Britain the wildfire of revenge which was kindled in the United States." [32]

Fighting the British tooth and nail was one way of dealing with the occupiers. A different approach was followed by the Protestant church leaders in the British Zone. Throughout the occupation their relationship with military officials was good and often quite cordial. Even when Protestant churchmen strongly disagreed with British policies, they never impugned British motives. The several communist mayors, who were such an anathema to the Catholic bishops, were put out of office in the first round of elections in 1946, and with that, as far as the Protestants were concerned, the matter was closed and forgotten. There was no Protestant apprehension of the Labour government or of cooperation between British officials and German Social Democrats. The Religious Affairs Branch of British Military Government, which Frings considered without influence and better dissolved, operated in the Protestant case as a useful means of contact among the provincial churches, British church circles, and the military government. Religious Affairs officers and British military chaplains, moreover, were anxious to help rebuild the German church. Understanding and confidence, the two most scarce and vital commodities at the end of the war, developed to such an extent that the military government had no problem with the Evangelical church.

A key element in this relationship was the close links which were soon established between the provincial churches and the Church of England, the Church of Scotland, and the Free Churches. This was above all due to the bishop of Chichester. Apart from Pope Pius XII, the German people had no greater champion than Bishop Bell. [33] He realized that German churchmen badly needed encouragement and that the German people would need someone abroad to speak out on their behalf. He enlisted the support of Geoffrey

---

32. *The United States in Germany, 1944–1955,* p. 167.

33. George Bell (1883–1958) was chaplain to Archbishop Davidson from 1914 to 1924; dean of Canterbury from 1924 to 1929; and bishop of Chichester from 1929 to 1958. A pioneer in ecumenical work, Bell was passionately concerned over the plight of the Evangelical church in the Third Reich; he became a friend of Bonhoeffer and in 1942 conveyed the views of German resistance circles to the British government. His denunciation of the indiscriminate bombing of German cities and of the nuclear raids on Japan apparently cost him not only the See of Canterbury but also that of York.

Fisher, Archbishop of Canterbury, and (thanks to the latter's intervention with the government) was by October off on a tour of the three western zones and Berlin. The Primate himself was more reserved toward Germany but began corresponding with Wurm as soon as possible after the war. "I will not," Fisher wrote on October 15, 1945, "in this letter enter upon all of the deep spiritual questions which must arise for discussion, searching the conscience of all Christian people. The great thing is that once more we can be in touch with each other." Expressing his distress at the "terrible physical conditions" in Germany, he assured Wurm that Anglican churchmen were "pressing in every possible way for active steps to be taken to relieve the situation so far as it can be relieved." In November Fisher led a Protestant delegation to the British Zone, and in the fall of 1946 Bell organized the Catholic-Anglican mission which held talks with Cardinal Frings and Protestant church heads. In this way British churchmen not only came to know German church leaders personally and secured firsthand impressions of German conditions, but also took home information which they could use in appealing to the government and to British public opinion. "I realize something of the distress from which you are suffering in Germany now," Bell confided to Wurm on December 14, 1945. "I saw with my own eyes the misery of the deported people. The Archbishop of Canterbury has already called attention to the acute distress in Central Europe in the House of Lords, and I myself described something of what I had seen in the same debate." [34]

These visits and letters not only built up confidence in British church leaders within the Evangelical church but also contributed to a balanced appreciation of British programs in Germany. At the very time Frings was accusing the British of starving the German people, Wurm was writing to Chichester:

> It is with great gratitude that the German people have heard that the United Nations have taken effective steps to meet the coming famine and that especially the English are making sacrifices to help us over the crisis. We shall never forget that. [35]

To this Bell replied:

> What you say about strengthening the spirit of Christian fellowship through personal relations and the hope that such personal relations may

---

34. Fisher's letter, *File 230: Ökumene. Ausland, 1945–1946* (April); Bell's Letter, *File 235: Korrespondenz mit Bischof von Chichester, 1945–1951;* both in Wurm Papers, Württemberg Provincial Church Archives, Stuttgart.

35. Letter (English in the original) of May 31, 1946, *ibid.*

have an effect in the political and economic spheres—and yet the difficulties of that—is only too true. I am in close touch with the Control
Commission and with Mr. Hynd, who is in charge on the British side. I
think churchmen can do something but it is only too easy to exaggerate
their possibilities. . . .

Yesterday an announcement has been made in the House of Commons that bread is to be rationed in this country. And I know from
firsthand contact with the British authorities in Berlin how seriously
they are regarding their responsibilities with regard to the food situation. [36]

In response to Wurm's appeals, Bell and Fisher intervened both privately
with the government and publicly in the House of Lords on two issues of
greatest importance to the Germans: the return of prisoners of war and
denazification. "I wish with all my heart," Bell wrote to Wurm, "that the
prisoners could be returned at once to their own homes, and as you know I
have done what I could, publicly in the House of Lords and elsewhere, to give
expression to the urgency of the need for their release. I will not cease my
efforts." [37] Although the rate of repatriation had already been stepped up as
a result of his previous interventions, the bishop reopened the question in the
House of Lords in February 1947, a debate which Lord Pakenham has
characterized in a personal interview as the most difficult of his parliamentary
career to respond to. Although no immediate result was apparent, Fisher
assured Wurm that the "matter of the repatriation of prisoners-of-war is
constantly in my mind." [38] Not long afterwards the British government
decided to return all prisoners as rapidly as possible.

The British churches were the only organized force in Britain working
for the softening of British occupation policy. The tangible results of their
interventions were relatively limited. But the relationship which Bell and
Fisher developed with the Evangelical church did more than anything else to
maintain a basic confidence in British intentions. Bishop Bell was posthu-
mously awarded the Order of Merit by the German government for his work
on behalf of Anglo-German relations. No tribute, however, could have been
more moving than a line from one of Wurm's letters: "I am constantly grateful to know that I have in you not only a personal friend, but also a Christian
brother who sympathizes with the material and spiritual distress of my people
and my church." [39]

The French attitude toward the churches—like postwar French political

---

36. Letter of June 28, 1946, *ibid.*
37. Letter of March 21, 1947, *ibid.*
38. Letter of April 2, 1947, *ibid.*
39. Letter of November 21, 1947, *ibid.*

policy toward Germany—was characterized by a desire for cooperation but strictly on France's terms. When French conditions were met, the military government's cooperation with ecclesiastical officials was closer than anywhere else in Germany. When, however, a church leader refused to fall in with the French aims, a near Kulturkampf was the result. In practice this situation applied—for good or ill—primarily to the Catholic church. The French Zone was almost two-thirds Catholic and had six resident Catholic bishops. The only resident Protestant leader was Hans Stempel, the President of the Palatine Provincial Church. He played an important role in negotiating with French officials over the return of German prisoners of war in France, but otherwise he had relatively few dealings with the military government.

In the southern part of their zone the French could not at first deal with either of the two Catholic leaders. Archbishop Gröber of Freiburg was badly compromised, while Bishop Sproll of Rottenburg returned physically broken from his banishment by the Nazis. However, in Monsignor Föhr of Freiburg, an eminent anti-Nazi, and Vicar General Kottmann of Rottenburg, the French found two locally powerful figures. A large number of administrative and judicial officials were appointed at their suggestion. Diocesan offices became channels through which much public dissatisfaction was brought to the attention of the French and through which French views were often disseminated. A Catholic official was often able to "fix things" in a way that no church leader elsewhere could. Relations were so close in the early period that Protestants, including Württemberg provincial church officials, were angered by what they considered the excessively pro-Catholic slant of the French. Later, as civilians came to play a greater role in the military government, the relationship lost a good deal of its original warmth.

In the northern half of the zone relations were from the start a good deal less cordial. On the personal level there was intense suspicion between French authorities and the leading Catholic prelate of the area, Bishop Franz Bornewasser of Trier. In the French view, Bornewasser was a reactionary nationalist who had worked incessantly during the 1920s and 1930s for the return of the Saar to Germany and who had played a significant role in the outcome of the 1935 Saar plebescite. As Bornewasser saw it, French Military Government was controlled by Freemasons and communists who sought to undermine the church. To Bornewasser it was outrageous that the French should refuse to carry out the promised school referenda but should instead reopen schools on a nonconfessional basis. Relations became steadily worse, and French authorities were increasingly annoyed by his pastoral letters, which they regarded as politically objectionable, repeatedly warning Bornewasser's clergy against reading them. Matters came to a head in the spring of

1947 over the bishop's pastoral message in celebration of his twenty-fifth anniversary as bishop. This message contained passages—commenting on such events as the French occupation of Trier after World War I and the Saar plebiscite of 1935—which were considered by General Pierre Koenig, the Military Governor, to be an intolerable provocation. Bornewasser was instructed to revoke the message or at a minimum delete certain portions of it. When the Bishop refused, French authorities directly instructed each priest in the diocese not to read designated passages. The unfortunate octogenarian was himself given a severe dressing down by a senior military official and told that French Foreign Minister Bidault as well as the Holy See had been informed of the matter. Deeply wounded, Bornewasser replied to General Koenig that his conscience had not permitted him to withdraw yet another pastoral letter. "French Military Government," he added, "has not exactly handled itself well in making trouble over a pastoral letter for the doyen of the German hierarchy, known even in wide circles abroad for this fight against National Socialism, at the precise movement of his episcopal jubilee." [40]

The core of the difficulty between French and Catholic church leaders lay in the issue of German territorial integrity. The Catholic bishops were among the most zealous opponents of Danish, Dutch, and Belgian territorial claims against Germany as well as of the (minor) separatist groups in the Rhineland and the Palatinate. By taking a lead in these matters, Catholic churchmen reinforced the already lively French impression that they were archnationalists. In the Palatinate, for instance, it was Deacon Johannes Fink, one of the most politically influential persons in the province, who organized opposition to various schemes—in which the French may or may not have been involved—for an autonomous Palatine Republic. "Do not," he once pointedly warned the French provincial governor, "make politics with Quislings." [41] It was Bornewasser, however, who was again caught in the main crossfire of Franco-German dissension over the greatest prize of all, the Saar. Since the Trier diocese encompassed most of the area, Saar separatists sought his open support for its integration with France. Nothing could have been further from Bornewasser's intentions, and the bishop in fact did all he could to oppose the French policy of separating the Saar from Germany. In re-

40. Letter of July 4, 1947, from Bornewasser to Koenig, File *CR 25/18,* Diocesan Archives, Cologne.

41. Quoted in Helmut Kohl, *Die politische Entwicklung in der Pfalz und das Wiedererstehen der Parteien nach 1945* (Heidelberg University doctoral thesis, 1958), p. 152.

sponse, the French deliberately sought to disgrace him—circulating old photographs of Bornewasser giving the Hitler salute and distributing copies of sermons susceptible of a pro-Nazi interpretation. They also sought to defame his vicar general, whom they forbade to enter the Saar. Both sides appealed to the Vatican—the French, as after World War I, for the creation of a separate Saar diocese, and Bornewasser for the ecclesiastical status quo. As in 1934, Rome's Solomonic decision was to leave the area under German ecclesiastical jurisdiction while placating the French with appearances through the appointment of an apostolic visitator to the Saar from June 1948 until 1956 after a popular referendum had again joined the area to Germany.

According to local political leaders, it was in revenge for the role Bornewasser played—for a second time—in the Saar question that the French demanded in 1947 that the Rhineland-Palatinate constitutional assembly delete articles from the proposed Land constitution recognizing the Reichskonkordat and providing for confessional schools. When the members of the drafting committee adamantly insisted on some formula which would permit confessional schools, pointing out that French authorities in southern Württemberg had authorized them in that area, the French finally relented, but only to the point of authorizing a referendum on the question.

French demands for compliance or silence from the churches sums up the American attitude as well. But what was with the French a cynical and pragmatic approach was apotheosized by the Americans as inspired and benign policy. In a preface to a monograph on American policy in the religious field in the postwar period, Harold Zink referred to the fact that "at the conclusion of World War II, the German church was considered by the Occupying Powers as one of the most important instruments for the reorientation of German society." [42] In other words, American Military Government envisaged the Cardinal Archbishop of Munich and the Protestant Bishop of Bavaria, for example, falling in step with the majors and colonels of the American Army to do their bit in remodeling German society along lines determined in Washington. While exaggerating the cognizance taken of the churches by the Americans, Zink's statement accurately reflects the state of mind of the military government at the commencement of its operations in the summer of 1945. Caesar was interested in the Church of Jesus Christ so far as it could further the aims of American policy. The head of the military government,

---

42. McClaskey, *The History of U.S. Policy and Program in the Field of Religious Affairs under the Office of the U.S. High Commissioner for Germany*, p. i.

General Lucius Clay, was still of this opinion when he came to publish his memoirs, *Decision in Germany*, in 1950.

Because of the thoroughly secularized American political tradition, most military government officials appear to have had little or no concept when they arrived in Germany of the strength of the churches in German society; they had the greatest difficulty in grasping—or accepting—the situation after being confronted with it in practice. The army's consultation with church leaders regarding appointments to civil government during and immediately after hostilities was a one-time effort; when military government officials took over, they rarely sought the churches' advice. Thanks to his previous diplomatic experience in Bavaria, France and Italy, Ambassador Murphy well appreciated the importance of the churches. He made a point of seeing the senior leaders of the two churches shortly after his arrival in Germany and continued to follow ecclesiastical affairs closely. But a political adviser to an American military commander is in no position to differ frequently or fundamentally with military policy. There was practically nothing Murphy could do in the early postwar years to alter the military government's general attitude, and this was neither understanding nor even well-intentioned toward the churches. "It was found to be one of the important tasks of this office to overcome a widespread hostile attitude toward the church in Military Government circles—an attitude more often born of ignorance and prejudice than of knowledge and contemplation," one Religious Affairs officer reported upon taking up his duties in 1945. An American churchman, sent by the World Council of Churches to survey the situation in Germany at the war's end, concluded bitterly after his tour, "The Nazi Party could not have been more disinterested in the fate of the Church than the American Military Government, whose policy adhered rigidly to the strict American tradition of complete separation of Church and State." [43]

The military government's attitude not only made relations with the churches difficult, it put policy askew from the start. Instead of seeking ways in which the two sides could cooperate toward commonly agreed objectives, the military government took the position that what it did in the American Zone was strictly its business and that church leaders must either support American programs or remain silent. Public criticism in any form was therefore prohibited, as Ambassador Murphy privately made clear to both Cardinal Faulhaber and Bishop Wurm shortly after the end of the war. Armed, more-

---

43. *History of Military Government for Land Württemberg-Baden to June 1946; Part I: General History* (undated typescript), Modern Military Records, p. 33; Herman, *Rebirth of the German Church*, p. 108.

over, with a full-scale "reeducation" program and all the pent-up political missionary zeal that had, for lack of colonies, no previous outlet, the Americans planned a psychological and political transformation of their part of Germany. While German church leaders respected American political ideas and practices, they did not feel that these could be grafted onto a nation with a wholly different political background, and they tended to resent a foreign army's tampering with the very foundations of their nation's way of life.

With the lines so starkly drawn, it would be more accurate to speak of an impasse than of relations between the two in the early postwar period. The August 1945 letter to Eisenhower by the Fulda Bishops' Conference was considered by American officials to be so presumptuous in making suggestions about how Germany should be governed that the letter was neither forwarded nor even acknowledged. In July of the following year the four archbishops and Cardinal Preysing of Berlin submitted to General Clay a petition addressed to President Truman urging that greater material assistance be given to German expellees from Czechoslovakia and Poland. General Clay refused to forward the petition and in a curtly phrased reply informed churchmen that the expellees had brought their plight on themselves and that the military government was doing its best to cope with the group's problems. The bishops were angered by the military reaction to these and other appeals. At the 1946 session of the Fulda Bishops' Conference, Cardinal Frings took an American liaison officer aside and expressed their dissatisfaction. Concerning the letter about refugees, for instance, the officer reported, "He said that he feared the purpose and objective of the appeal was misunderstood, namely that the successor agency of UNRRA should make some provision for the needs of the German people, a subject matter beyond the jurisdiction of General Clay." [44]

The military government was just as strict regarding critical pastoral letters. The Catholic bishops in the northern half of Germany, for example, issued a pastoral letter for Easter 1946 criticizing denazification procedures, the treatment of German prisoners of war, the conditions in which Germans were being evacuated from Czechoslovakia and Poland, and expropriation of farms under the guise of land reform in the East. The British raised no objection to the letter because, as a British officer was reported in *The New York Times* for April 17, 1946, to have remarked, "it is impossible to interfere with the liberty of the church." American military authorities, however,

---

44. Report (undated and unsigned), in *Fulda Bishops' Conference—August 1946,* Modern Military Records.

asked the bishops to instruct their clergy in that part of their dioceses falling in the American Zone not to read the letter. "Mr. Murphy stated," one official recorded, "that he had lived through the German occupation of France and that our position would gradually become more and more difficult. . . . Military Government would not possibly tolerate public criticism by high church officials but . . . they should direct their grievances and criticism to us through proper channels."[45] The bishops agreed to withdraw the letter in the American Zone, but the story reached the American press, provoking sharp criticism. The Catholic *Commonweal* remarked on May 10, 1946, that it had not "cried down American occupation the way most of its contemporaries have done, because we have tried to appreciate the enormity of the job and the failure of directions from home, and the work, in spite of all, accomplished. Now we are an enemy of Military Government. . . . Not being confirmed in enmity, we look with an angry impatience first for an honest description of what has taken place, and then, no doubt, for a revision of policy which will at least recognize that colonels cannot run the Church and that the heyday of the god-monarch passed with the empire of Alexander the Great."

Treatment of the Protestant bishops was similar, with similar refusals to transmit petitions to American government officials and similar cracks across the knuckles for critical public remarks. One of Bishop Wurm's letters to the archbishop of Canterbury, which had been transmitted by the British Army to London, earned the bishop a visit by Ambassador Murphy, who coldly reminded Wurm that the United States "would not brook public criticism of Allied policies and action in Germany by individual German citizens no matter what their status." American authorities would, Wurm was told, be willing to receive private communications, providing these did not challenge basic policy but looked "to the achievement of our announced purposes in Germany."[46]

Although Wurm and the Catholic bishops in principle accepted the American prohibition on public criticism of Allied policies, the ban obviously contradicted the guarantee of full religious freedom and made some military officials uneasy. Occasionally the flat rule laid down by Clay and Murphy was ignored in the field. At other times ludicrous compromises were solemnly

---

45. "Report concerning Pastoral Letter" dated 15 June 1946 by Theobald J. Dengler, in *Catholic Church Germany,* Modern Military Records.

46. Memorandum of April 19, 1946, by Murphy, in *Bishop Wurm,* Modern Military Records.

propounded, such as that permitting criticism by the churches of "communism but not of Russian communism or of Russia."[47]

These policy weaknesses were greatly magnified by a fundamental difference of political outlook which went far deeper in the case of the Americans than of the other Western occupiers. Not only did American military authorities plan more sweeping changes of German society; they were, in the words of George Kennan, "still deeply affected by . . . the disgraceful anti-British and pro-Soviet prejudices that certain of our military leaders had entertained during the war."[48] It was, however, the menace of communism backed by the presence of the Red Army, as already noted, that was uppermost in the minds of all the Catholic and many of the Protestant bishops. As Marshall Knappen, the head of Religious Affairs in the American Zone, reported of his first meeting with Bishop Wurm: "Over and over again he emphasized the necessity of building up the church as a bulwark against leftist interests. . . . Over and over again I explained to him that Soviet Russia was our associate in the occupation and must not be attacked." Knappen later added with alarming candor, "Our encounters with Bishop Wurm and others of his type had left us almost belligerently determined to find a basis of cooperation with the Russians and so make a success of quadripartite occupation."[49]

The bishops were horrified by the American attitude. A few years later the American government came to share the churches' evaluation of the European situation; but in the early occupation period military officials concluded that the churches were nationalistic, ultraconservative, probably reactionary, and potentially subversive. Allowing for the strong conservatism of some Catholic and Protestant bishops, this judgment was highly subjective. To begin with, military government officials were taught in their training

---

47. Report on Religious Affairs Staff Meeting, June 10–12, 1946, in *Conferences,* Modern Military Records. *The Bavarian,* the Military Government journal for Bavaria, announced this as Military Government policy on June 28, 1946.

48. George F. Kennan, *Memoirs, 1925–1950* (1967), p. 257.

49. Knappen, pp. 100, 145. From the start Knappen grossly misjudged the attitude of the Protestant leadership. In the official report of his meeting with Wurm on June 22, 1945, he warned: "A combined Niemöller-Wurm appeal to Protestant and anti-Russian elements in the United States against American occupation policy appears imminent." Referring to Knappen's report, Ambassador Murphy commented dryly to Washington that in his conversations with the two church leaders "no such intimation" of an appeal was given. In fact, of course, no appeal was ever made. (The two reports are contained in Murphy's Despatch No. 521 of 25 June 1945; 740.00119 Control (Germany) 6–2545, General Records of The Department of State, National Archives, Washington.)

schools that the Protestant church was nationalistic and reactionary. Once in Germany, they tended to see only what fitted their preconceptions. The attitude toward the Catholic church was much less uniform; some circles were quite cordial, while others were inclined to regard the church as a feudalistic institution largely responsible for the state of mind that led to National Socialism.

In addition, clergymen were forbidden to serve in the Religious Affairs branch, and most Religious Affairs officers were both uninformed and unsympathetic toward the churches. The misjudgments that resulted were occasionally breathtaking. At the Treysa conference in 1945, to cite a single example, an American officer who was present attached no significance either to a strong speech by Wurm on German guilt or to the three political declarations but reported to his headquarters that the Evangelical church "had not repented the war of aggression initiated by Germany or the cruelties visited upon other peoples and lands." A second officer present commented that the provisional establishment of the Evangelical Church in Germany, as agreed at the meeting, was possibly for "ulterior motives" or "recruiting for strength." [50]

For such palpably absurd reasons as these, the labels came to be attached. "Nationalistic" presumably referred to the churches' appeals on behalf of refugees, "ultraconservative" to their attitude toward the Soviet Union, "probably reactionary" to their opposition to denazification procedures. Less easy to explain is the bizarre idea of the churches as a potentially subversive force. It might have been thought that this specter, initially conjured up in 1944, would have been recognized as such once American forces were installed in Germany. Instead, Religious Affairs officers meeting over a year after the end of the war were still being cautioned "to be diligent in keeping a close watch on the possible use of church organizations as a cloak for underground activities, as well as on possible nationalist and militarist trends." [51] So seriously was this chimera pursued that the military government maintained a general file labeled "Nazi Activities Under the Cloak of the Churches." It is symptomatic that the contents included at their most "sinister" such documents as reports that Catholic priests in many areas were

---

50. Report of September 6, 1945, from Lt. Lapp to Knappen; "Observations on the Conference of the German Evangelical Church" (undated) by Major Earl Crum; *Fulda Conference–Treysa Conference* Modern Military Records. See Chapter 5, pp. 121 ff. for discussion of the political declarations.

51. Report on Religious Affairs Staff Meeting, June 10–12, 1946, in *Conference*, Modern Military Records.

actively supporting the CDU-CSU and that Protestant clergymen in some places were opposed to denazification procedures. Even Washington's major policy directive of July 1947—the successor to the famous JCS 1067 of 1945—instructed General Clay to "continue to take such action as may be necessary to prevent the revival of National Socialist and militaristic activity under the cloak of a religious program or organization." [52] It was not, in fact, until the winds of the cold war blew away wartime preconceptions that the military government finally put aside this fear of an ecclesiastical Ku Klux Klan. Thereafter, however, some military officials went to the other extreme and began to regard the Evangelical church as an unwitting tool of the Russians and East Germans.

The relationship between the churches and the military government was permanently marred by these initial misunderstandings. Military authorities continued to feel that church leaders should confine themselves to the cure of souls and often sent back rudely phrased responses—or sometimes gave no response at all—to their appeals on social problems. The churches' reaction to all this was perhaps best summed up in one sentence by Bishop Wurm: "The Americans acted not one whit more sensibly after the occupation of Germany than, for example, the Prussians did in Alsace after 1870." [53] Wurm meant that a victorious state, with unquestioning confidence in its own ideals, had sought to impose its way of life upon a conquered area regardless of the wishes of the inhabitants. It was the presence of powerful Russian forces in East Germany and the consequent sense of dependence upon the United States that kept the latent bitterness among church leaders within manageable bounds.

Not suprisingly, General Clay tried to wash his hands of his ecclesiastical problems at an early stage by extricating the military government from ecclesiastical affairs and instead involving American churches. President Truman approved this idea, and in July 1946, the Federal Council of Churches and the Catholic hierarchy each appointed a representative to its German counterpart. The representatives' terms of reference drew a distinction between the clerical and secular activities of the churches and directed them to confine themselves to the former by assisting the German churches in their "problems of spiritual and moral education and reconstruction." Though responsible to the bodies they represented, they were also to act as liaison officials to the

---

52. *Directive to Commander in Chief of United States Forces of Occupation Regarding the Military Government of Germany (JCS 1779, 11 July 1947).*
53. Wurm, *Erinnerungen aus meinem Leben*, p. 174.

military government. The representatives were emphatically abjured from becoming "special pleaders to the Military Government for the German churches." [54] In practice, however, "special pleaders" is exactly what they became; the separation of clerical and secular spheres broke down immediately, particularly on the Catholic side. By the time the Catholic representative arrived, Land constitutions were being drawn up, and the burning problems confronting the Catholic church fell squarely in the realm of church-state relations; these remained his preeminent interest during the remaining period of the occupation.

The Protestant representative was Dr. Julius Bodensieck, a German-born Lutheran. The selection of Bodensieck, an official of an American Lutheran church unaffiliated with the Federal Council of Churches, was made in recognition of the particular responsibility felt by the National Lutheran Council toward German Protestantism and with the intention of avoiding the appointment of a representative of both the Lutheran churches and the Federal Council. Upon his arrival in Germany, Bodensieck was told by General Clay, "Try to be a good brother to the German Evangelicals"— Aesopian advice which Bodensieck followed and which tended to keep him within the bounds of the military terms of reference. But Bodensieck had a good appreciation of the general situation he faced and in the view of at least one Religious Affairs officer improved the military government's understanding of the Evangelical Church. [55] The primary focus of his activities, however, was in organizing charitable assistance; in fact the program of reconstruction and interchurch aid developed by the World Council of Churches received most of its support from American Protestant groups. Despite their generosity, American Protestant churches were slow in taking an interest in the German ecclesiastical situation, and their relationship lacked the closeness that existed between the British and German churches. It is significant that the General Secretary of the Federal Council of Churches at the time, Samuel McCrae Cavert, in a letter of December 18, 1968, was unable to recall a single case in which American Protestant churches intervened in Washington or with the military government on behalf of the German churches.

The Catholic representative, Dr. Alois Muench, Bishop of Fargo, North Dakota, was in a far more powerful position. He was simultaneously ap-

---

54. Memorandum (undated) from General Gailey on "Liaison Representatives from U.S. Churches" in *Bishop Muench*, Modern Military Records.

55. Letter of January 14, 1969, from Bodensieck; letter of December 22, 1968, from Dr. Karl Arndt, former Religious Affairs officer for Württemberg-Baden.

pointed by the American hierarchy to be its liaison official to the military government, by the Pope to be Apostolic Visitator to all of Germany as well as head of the Vatican relief mission, and by Cardinal Spellman (Catholic Military Vicar of the United States) to be Catholic Vicar General to American forces in Germany and Austria. This situation was illustrative of the Vatican's postwar outlook. Now, as in the interwar period, Germany was seen as the great barrier to the spread of communism. Only with full American support would Germany be able to survive. Through Muench a direct and formal channel was opened among the Vatican, the American hierarchy, the German hierarchy, and American Military Government. Following the death in March 1946 of the Papal Nuncio, Archbishop Orsenigo, and in January 1947 of the chargé d'affaires, Monsignor Carlo Colli, Muench further assumed the functions of the Vatican's de facto diplomatic mission in Germany. The Apostolic Mission at Kronberg (near Frankfurt am Main) operated as a quasi-embassy and was, in fact, given by General Clay the privilege of uncensored communication and the right of diplomatic pouch and code in communicating with the Vatican and the American hierarchy.

Muench, a warm-hearted and simple man, was deeply stirred by German suffering, and no epithet better fits him than "special pleader." He appealed unceasingly for material and financial assistance from the American hierarchy. From the military government he demanded countless alterations in policy. He was, however, far from a cautious and subtle Vatican diplomat. His tactics and intellect were crude, and the result was often to aggravate rather than diminish differences between the Catholic church and American officials. From the time of his arrival to the end of the occupation, he caused one row after another. What he did not agree with he randomly characterized as "Nazi," "communistic," "socialist," "undemocratic," or even "un-American," and he otherwise expressed himself in strong and emotive terms. The net effect was to to enrage many military government officials, who were not slow in observing that he was clearly violating his terms of reference. Nevertheless Muench succeeded in presenting his views—and those of his conservative German Catholic friends—to high members of Clay's staff, and these interventions were not without effect.

From his papers it is clear that one of Muench's major crusades was breaking what he perceived as the domination of the American Military Government, at least below the top level, by Jewish émigrés who had fled Germany in the 1930s and had returned in American army uniform. "Jews in control," reads one of his earliest diary entries upon arriving in Germany in 1946. Similar references follow in rapid succession, to the effect that Jews in the military government sought control of education, youth, and press affairs policy in order to condition the minds of the population. He believed that they had also taken over the intelligence services so as to turn denazification into a means of vengeance upon the German nation. All in all, he was convinced that they distorted military policy to the detriment of American national interests. Moreover—or more to the point—in Muench's opinion all Jews were liberal and secularist and as such the natural enemy of the Catholic church. While the churchman's conspiracy theory was high nonsense, his notion about military government personnel was not entirely false. During the early postwar period, there were in fact many German émigrés, including Jews, in the occupation government. Because of their linguistic ability and familiarity with Germany, they were often placed in public affairs activities, such as press and education. Although they were never "in control," there was apparently a not uncommon feeling among the German population shortly after the war that there were "too many" émigrés, including Jews, in the military government. To this extent Muench was registering the privately held view of some Germans—and of some American officers.

From the time when he arrived in Germany, Muench did all that he could to effect a purge of Jews from the military government. He spoke his mind plainly and directly to those who would listen—and those who listened included General Clay, Pope Pius, and President Truman. He also corresponded on the subject with Senator Joseph McCarthy and leading members of the American Catholic hierarchy. Although it is impossible to estimate the overall impact of these interventions, some Bavarians to this day claim that Muench's influence in ridding the Bavarian military government of "Prussian Jewish émigrés" was one of his greatest "accomplishments" during the occupation period.

Apparently the high command did come to believe that the number of émigrés in the military government was excessive, and from about 1947 made a deliberate effort to reduce their number, especially as military officers were replaced by civilian officials. Muench may have contributed to the adoption of this policy; however, his role in this cannot be gauged with any accuracy. There is ample documentation of his other major interventions, and two examples—regarding the press and the schools—illustrate his approach and the relative extent of his influence.

Shortly after his arrival in July 1946 Muench complained to Ambassador Murphy that the military government was discriminating against the Catholic church in its distribution of newsprint. He charged that no paper was made available for Catholic youth publications, almost none for Catholic religious books and very little for Catholic newspapers. In his view this problem was merely a reflection of a deliberate policy of hostility toward the Catholic church. Regarding military officials, he alleged in a typical form of insinuation, "It is widely believed that they try by Hitler methods to extirpate religion, at least such are the comments that are heard." The military government rebutted his charges point for point, observing that 24 percent of the paper available in the American Zone for all purposes, even apart from printing, was being given to the churches, which themselves decided how it was used. Of the 224 magazines published in 1946, 70 were religious, and 36 of these Catholic. In fact, there had been such marked discrimination in this respect to the advantage of the Catholic church that other branches of the military government, certain German groups, and State Department officials had all complained. Muench's charges were all the more questionable, since many Catholic dioceses in Bavaria were, despite warnings, engaged in illegal publishing activities. The official organ of the Regensburg diocese was being issued in 20,000 copies by a publisher who had no license; the official organs of the Passau, Bamberg, and Würzburg dioceses were being published in at least twice the number of copies authorized; several other papers were published in up to three times the authorized circulation, and there were five cases of entirely unauthorized publication. [56]

Muench also criticized the military government for not exercising stricter controls over the contents of nonreligious publications. *Der Ruf* he condemned for having carried "a subtle attack against the free enterprise system" in the United States;[57] *Simplicissimus* he singled out for its "scurrilous cartoons," similar to the "anti-religious cartoons of the Nazi predecessor," and he asked that its editors be given "an order to desist from further caricatures of religious persons or objects".[58] Again the bishop's facts were weak; *Simplicissimus* had been so strongly anti-Nazi that it was one of the first publications banned by the Third Reich. Military government officials accused Muench of wishing to introduce Franco-type clericalism into Germany; they found him "vociferous" in their meetings together and resented being charged with "discourtesy, rudeness and of anti-religious or anti Church attitudes." [59] Muench in turn found their remarks "vicious," "evasive," and "reckless." He considered official reports on press matters to be "so superficial, incomplete

---

56. Memorandum of November 14, 1946, from General McClure to Murphy, Modern Military Records.

57. Memorandum of conversation of December 5, 1946, at residence of Cardinal Faulhaber, *ibid.*

58. Memorandum of April 14, 1947, from Muench to General McClure, *ibid.*

59. *ibid.*

and false" that he had lost all confidence in officials in that branch of the military government. [60] Even in his later years, as Nuncio, Muench kept a critical eye on the press and was especially censorious of the *Süddeutsche Zeitung,* the eminent Munich daily, and *Der Monat,* the sister of the English *Encounter.* The root of the trouble was their leadership: the editor of the former was "a Jew . . . morally corrupt, of course" and that of the latter was—in his often repeated, ultimate pejorative—a "N. Y. Jew." Although he could not interfere with the independent daily, from the moment when he was outraged by *Der Monat's* first issue in 1948, he did everything in his power to close it down or at least to stop the American subsidy for it. He appealed for support both to the American hierarchy and to government officials, and when the grant was finally cut off in 1954, Muench claimed responsibility for the action.

Muench stirred up a much more serious dispute over educational reform; he kept this rancorous disagreement going for over three years. The bishop was passionately opposed to nonconfessional schools even when they provided religious instruction. "Such socialized education, obstructing free enterprise in education," he once complained to the American hierarchy, "bodes ill for the future of democracy" [61]—a statement that, so far as it conveyed any meaning, may well have puzzled the hierarchy, in view of the nonconfessional nature of American public schools, where religious instruction may not be provided. Muench nonetheless felt no reluctance in denouncing American officials as "utterly un-American" for their school policy, by which he presumably if illogically meant their not imposing confessional schools upon the Länder. [62] In the end the Bavarian constitution guaranteed confessional schools, while those of Hesse and Württemberg-Baden adopted nonconfessional schools. Muench's influence was probably superfluous in the former case (where powerful indigenous political forces were working in the same direction) and was clearly inadequate in the latter.

Muench also fought the military government's plans for a reform of the school system, in particular the weakening or replacement of the humanistic Gymnasium. Cardinal Faulhaber initially considered the reform a purely ad-

---

60. Memorandum of conversation of December 5, 1946, at residence of Cardinal Faulhaber, *ibid.*

61. "A Brief Survey—The Church in Germany," *op. cit.*

62. Memorandum of November 4, 1946, from Robert Murphy to J. W. Taylor, in *Bishop Muench,* Modern Military Records.

ministrative and pedagogical matter. Muench persuaded him otherwise, however, and talked him into raising objections to the reform plan. To highly incensed American officials it was "evident that Muench was trying to sow mistrust and suspicion in the minds of the hierarchy rather than achieve harmony." When challenged, the Bishop admitted that no "immediate religious issue" was involved but insisted that anything affecting the German people affected the churches. [63] In January 1948, however, Faulhaber and Monsignor Meixner (chairman of CSU delegation in the Bavarian parliament) assured the military government that their apprehensions had been allayed. A few months later Faulhaber invited the official responsible for religious affairs in the Bavarian Military Government to accompany him to the Vatican and informed the Pope at that time "how deeply he appreciated" the work of the Land Director and the chief of religious affairs. [64] Once the Cardinal was back in Munich, however, Muench again convinced him that the reform plans contained dangers for the church's position. After several rounds, the Land Director for Bavaria, Murray van Wagoner, asked General Clay to recall Muench on the grounds that he had "interfered with the operation of Military Government in a field in which he himself admitted the churches had only indirect responsiblity." [65] General Clay rejected the proposal, and in fact, Muench is widely considered to have saved the humanistic Gymnasium in Bavaria.

Muench's greatest adversary was not the American military but the French. The churchman's Germanophilia carried with it a clear Francophobia, and he was too straightforward to conceal his feelings. The French government was so incensed by his attitude that in February 1947 it instructed its Vatican ambassador, Jacques Maritain, to make a formal protest to the Pope. When Pius XII refused to withdraw Muench, the French appealed to General Clay, who evidently agreed to remove him from Germany—personally and literally. In October 1947 Clay invited Muench to return to the United States with him, ostensibly for a visit, but in fact to be left there. On arriving, the general informed Cardinal Spellman of his decision. Spellman refused to concur in the action, and Clay had no choice but to permit Muench to go back to Germany. Whatever Clay's feelings toward the visitator were after that, the French continued to regard him with profound mistrust and in

---

63. Memorandum of May 7, 1948, from van Wagoner to General Clay, *ibid.*
64. *ibid.*
65. *ibid.*

particular suspected him of assisting the German hierarchy's efforts to preserve the Saar population's loyalty to Germany.

In the end, whatever comfort to the churches Bodensieck and Muench
may have been, they did not succeed in reconciling the churches and the
military government. While they may have contributed to some changes of
approach within policy guidelines, they did not alter the course of Military
Government. "I doubt," General Clay has affirmed, "if there is a specific
instance in which policy decisions were influenced by their voice." [66]

The disagreements between the churches and the military governments
went to the core of the occupation philosophy and illuminate the causes of
Allied failures in Germany. These differences basically stemmed neither from
the often self-pitying, accusatory language of church leaders' appeals and the
often rude responses from military authorities nor from the churches' failure
to understand the enormity of the job confronting the Allies and the military's incomprehension of Christian appeals. The origin of the problem lay in
the belief of the occupation powers that, as total victors and righteous nations, they had a free hand to remake a largely wicked society. But in trying
to reform society without taking into account the society's most important
institution, the occupiers were waging a futile campaign. The Americans especially ignored the fact that, like it or not, the military government was in
competition with the churches for the people's allegiance and that most
Germans would look to the churches rather than to the military government
for guidance. It was a sign of the moral strength of the churches that they
assumed responsibility for the broad social interests of the German people, an
almost unique event in their history. The Americans, by forbidding public
criticism and rejecting private appeals, demanded the very ecclesiastical servil-
ity for which, in the handbook carried by their forces into Germany, they
condemned the churches in the Third Reich. American Military Government
largely ignored the churches' views and thus deprived them of direct influence
on occupation policy. It could not, however, prevent them from influencing
public opinion and in this way depriving cherished occupation programs of
success. The best example is denazification—an issue that not only reveals
much about the churches themselves in the early postwar period but also
offers an illuminating case study of the churches' relationship to the occupation powers.

---

66. Letter of January 13, 1969.

4 | Collective Guilt and Denazification

IN 1945 the great moral issue for the German nation, whether it was faced squarely or not, concerned responsibility for the Third Reich and the crimes carried out in the name of the German people. Although the victorious powers made clear at the Nuremberg trials that they did not in any formal sense charge the German people with collective guilt for these crimes, world opinion—and the occupation armies—in a general sense did so. "World history," as Schiller had observed, "is the world judge." History was now calling an entire nation to judgment. In this moral self-examination, what was the attitude of the churches, the custodians of the nation's morals?

The Catholic church took its cue from the Pope's address on National Socialism in June 1945.[1] In their first joint pastoral message from Fulda after the war, the bishops praised the clergy for having resisted National Socialism, thanked Catholic parents for having clung to Catholic schools, and stressed their own resistance of the state's encroachments on the life of the church. In two sentences, they disposed of the question of guilt:

> We profoundly deplore the fact that many Germans, even in our own ranks, allowed themselves to be deceived by the false teachings of National Socialism, remained indifferent to the crimes against human freedom and human dignity; many by their attitude lent support to the crimes, many became criminals themselves. A heavy responsibility falls upon those who, because of their influence, could have prevented such crimes and did not do so but made these crimes possible and in this way associated themselves with the criminals.[2]

Here was a church of saints, not sinners. Apart from a few black sheep who had gone astray, the whole Third Reich episode was dismissed as some-

---

1. See Chapter 2, pp. 29–30.
2. *Kirchliches Amtsblatt für die Diözese Osnabrück,* November 8, 1945.

89

thing foreign to German Catholicism. "We German Catholics were not National Socialists," Cardinal Frings told the British Catholic hierarchy with stark simplicity during a visit to London in October 1946.[3] Books and pamphlets intended to demonstrate the truth of this statement appeared within months of the war's end and continued to pour forth until the early 1960s.

Not only did the church insist that its behavior before and during the Third Reich was above reproach, it further depicted itself as the single and consistent force of opposition to National Socialism. Here, too, the Pope helped to point the way. "We know very well," he wrote to Cardinal Faulhaber on November 1, 1945, "—and this is here publicly acknowledged to your credit—that in dutiful observance of your office you withstood and resisted with complete conviction the unhealthy teachings and methods of unbridled National Socialism and that you had the better part of your people at your side." In a subsequent letter to the bishops the Pope praised the fact that German Catholics had emerged from "the fiery trial of the recent evil days only strengthened and purified." The church's struggle to maintain Catholic schools, he noted, demonstrated its opposition to the Third Reich. In July of the same year the Pope sent a message of appreciation to Monsignor Alois Natterer for his book, *Der Bayerische Klerus in der Zeit dreier Revolutionen—1918-1933-1945*. This work, along with Vicar General Johann Neuhäusler's *Kreuz und Hakenkreuz*, he wrote, was an "impressive justification of the clergy, its attitude, and its actions during these 23 years.[4]

This appraisal was a classic case of the emperor's new clothes, as church leaders knew better than anyone. They were deeply conscious of their tragic error in having failed to support the Weimar Republic, of having at the very least played into the Nazis' hands by their actions in 1933, and thus of having helped Hitler to consolidate his hold on Germany. They realized that they had misjudged the political situation in 1933 and that the church itself had been innocently drawn into a chain of political events that led directly to disaster. Indeed, it was precisely because the hierarchy felt politically compromised that it revised the church's whole political postwar tactic, as will be discussed in Chapter 6. But publicly the myth of the church as the implacable foe of National Socialism was maintained. This was not difficult since everyone instinctively shied from the subject, perhaps in terror of what the truth

---

3. *Kirchlicher Anzeiger für die Erzdiözese Köln*, October 1, 1946.

4. The Pope's message to Faulhaber, in *Kirchliches Amtsblatt für die Erzdiözese Paderborn*, March 1, 1946; additional messages in *Herder Korrespondenz*, June, December 1947.

might be. Although the Jesuit scholar Max Pribilla in 1950 published a searching account of the church's attitude and actions in the Third Reich, *Deutsche Schicksalsfragen,* it was, paradoxically, the Reichskonkordat litigation in the mid-1950s that forced Catholics, in preparing for the legal proceedings, to cast an objective look at the church's actions in 1933. The publication in London in 1957 of the captured German foreign office documents on the first nine months of the Third Reich accelerated the process. While many Catholic scholars and lawyers continued to defend the church's position, some privately came to the conclusion that the church had exposed itself badly in seeking a modus vivendi with Hitler. In 1960 Rudolf Morsey, a young Catholic historian and expert on the Center party and the Reichskonkordat, openly professed this view, and a year later the taboo on public discussion among Catholics was completely broken with the appearance of an article by Ernst-Wolfgang Böckenförde on the church's behavior in 1933. Soon after this, it was discovered that Neuhäusler had misquoted—to the church's advantage—some of the documents cited in *Kreuz und Hakenkreuz,* and it was increasingly recognized that the entire body of literature on the subject published between 1945 and 1960 was fragmentary, tendentious, and in many cases designed deliberately to create a false impression of the church's position. In 1962 what had been almost a private discussion among German Catholics became a worldwide controversy with the performance of Hochhuth's *The Deputy.* Subsequently two clergymen published books establishing that the German hierarchy had been deeply divided in their reactions to National Socialism. For a decade and a half, however, the facade was carefully preserved.[5]

Not surprisingly under the circumstances, the Catholic church—from the Pope to the parish priest—was utterly emphatic at the end of the war in rejecting the notion of collective guilt. "If anyone today contends that the entire German population and each of us made himself guilty through atrocities committed by members of our population during the war, that is unjust," Bishop von Galen declared in his famous July sermon. "If anyone says that the entire German population and each of us is implicated in the crimes committed in foreign countries and especially in the concentration camps

---

5. Morsey, "Zur Problematik und Geschichte des Reichskonkordats"; Böckenförde, "Der deutsche Katholizimus im Jahre 1933"; the falsification is investigated by Müller, "Zur Behandlung des Kirchenkampftes in der Nachkriegsliteratur". The two clarifying studies are Volk, *Der bayerische Episkopat und der Nationalsozialismus 1930–1934* (1965), and Adolf, *Hirtenamt und Hitlerdiktatur* (1965).

that is an untrue and unjust accusation against many of us." That was the church's first reason for opposition: sociologically it did not fit the facts. The second reason was equally simple: collective guilt is not possible in Catholic theology. Guilt in its deepest sense, the bishops stressed, is an individual matter, to be confessed before God rather than man. "Every German will have to ask himself," Johann Schuster, a Jesuit theologian, wrote, "how great his participation was, by silence or indirect cooperation, in Hitler's election, in the first months of the Third Reich's control to its final consolidation, in the period of open religious persecution, and finally during the war. But this much can be said, an uncritical condemnation of the *entire* populaton cannot be considered justified." Pointing to the final reason why the Catholic bishops opposed collective' guilt, the theologian added, "God does not just pass judgment. What is final and decisive is the word of pardon, of complete forgiveness, of encouragement to the guilty to reform and to those, who sought to the best of their abilities to protect themselves from the guilt of the people's leaders and those leaders gone astray, to have patient forbearance." [6]

The Catholic bishops believed that practically and spiritually the German people needed release from the moral burden of the past and an incentive to reconstruct their lives and their society. A probe of the collective subconscious would lead to despair, not to national or international understanding, and must be resisted. At the investiture of the German cardinals in February 1946 the Pope himself stated: "It is wrong to treat someone as guilty when personal guilt cannot be proved, only because he belonged to a certain community. It is meddling in the prerogatives of God to attribute collective guilt to a whole people and to try to treat it accordingly." Naturally the Catholic bishops rejected the Protestants' Stuttgart declaration. As Archbishop Jäger of Paderborn told a British officer, "I respect the spirit of Bishop Wurm's declaration on the subject of War Guilt, but such statements should not be made in open form in the hearing of youth. In order to influence a man you must acknowledge what was right and straight in him." Less explicitly but more frankly, Cardinal Frings in his 1946 New Year's Eve sermon condemned those "who cannot do enough to proclaim the guilt of their own people to the world and to confess repeatedly before mankind." [7]

The moral questions raised by the Third Reich never engaged the inter-

---

6. Text of von Galen's sermon in File *CR 25/18,* Diocesan Archives, Cologne; Johann B. Schuster, "Kollektivschuld."

7. *Kirchlicher Anzeiger für die Erzdiözese Köln,* March 15, 1946; *British Zone Review,* June 8, 1946; *Kirchenzeitung für das Erzbistum Köln,* January 18, 1947.

est of the Catholic hierarchy. It appears to have felt that what had happened between January 1933 and May 1945 was a closed chapter and that what was needed was the self-confidence to rebuild Germany on a sound basis. The shepherds could, moreover, scarcely demand political as well as religious obedience from their flocks if they admitted that they themselves had once lost the way. And under the postwar circumstances they considered it vital to furnish the faithful with political leadership. Convinced that Germany was a gravely ill nation, the church leaders wanted no hand wringing. They feared that if the German nation were subjected in 1945 to a major moral operation, the patient might easily expire, even if the surgery was a technical success. In this the Catholic church had grasped a point which eluded almost all others. It was also an attitude typical of postwar German Catholicism.

Nor could anything have been more typical of postwar German Protestantism than the reaction of Protestant churchmen. While some Protestants shared the Catholic bishops' viewpoint, most church leaders acknowledged some degree of national responsibility, shared by the church, for the crimes of the Third Reich. There was, in fact, a trend of thought in the Evangelical church going back at least to the end of the 1930s—and most uncompromisingly expressed by Dietrich Bonhoeffer—which held that Germany dare not seek to escape the political and moral punishment due her as a result of the Nazi leaders' actions. With the war's end this sentiment burst into the open with intense passion.

> It is terrible that we find it impossible to escape or suppress the question of guilt. How we wish we knew nothing of all this and could start anew. But the world grants us no rest; she screams at us with questions of guilt, and whether we will or not, we must answer. For that reason it is necessary for the Church to step into the breach. . . . The Church is to blame, the Church of both confessions. Our guilt stretches far into the past.

These words, from a sermon by Pastor Asmussen,[8] might be considered the Protestant contraposition to Bishop von Galen's July sermon. In the Protestant view, to recognize that all Germans were collectively responsible for their state, its historical development, and its acts was simply to recognize a fact. Only such an acknowledgement would make it possible to overcome the past, to face the future with self-respect, to salvage the dignity of Germany and to reconcile Germans with other nations. It was this recognition that led to the Stuttgart declaration which associated the churches with the

---

8. Quoted in Herman, *Rebirth of the German Church*, p. 131.

German people in joint responsibility for the crimes of the nation, even those against itself. The declaration did not mean that there were no gradations of guilt among Germans in a practical sense or that interwar European politics played no role in Hitler's rise to power and in the successes of his foreign policy. Like the Catholic bishops, the Protestant leaders also had practical considerations in mind. They wanted to prevent a split between totally innocent and totally guilty, totally good and totally bad Germans. In addition, they realized that their confession was the price of reconciliation with world Protestantism.

But the issue was too sensitive and the church's implicit (and at times unclear) attempt to distinguish collective responsibility from collective guilt was not generally understood. The Evangelical church appeared to be siding with the occupiers who tended to treat all Germans as Nazis and everyone as equally guilty of Nazi crimes. But when Protestant leaders protested to the Allied Control Council in November 1945 that the Allied concept of collective guilt was "necessarily having the reverse effect of what was intended," [9] occupation officials accused the church of revoking its stand. As a result, the Evangelical church was criticized from all sides, and Protestants themselves were deeply divided. While some pastors and laymen applauded the Stuttgart declaration, other pastors refused to read it to their congregations, and a few laymen even left the church. Angered as he was with the Allies, Bishop Wurm was equally irritated by the complaints of churchmen that the EKD council had gone too far. It was an inescapable fact, he stated at a meeting of the Stuttgart clergy in December 1945, that Germany had caused World War II and had occasioned the death of millions of Jews, Poles, and Russians. Theologically, he insisted, the declaration was thoroughly valid:

> According to today's slogan, not everyone in Israel sinned equally; many kept themselves uncorrupted. But the idea of a collectivity of guilt is a biblical one from A to Z. The Bible views sin not simply in isolation but always in connection with something; it affixes responsibility in an overall context, in all directions. The fathers have eaten grapes and the children's teeth are set on edge; I will visit the sins of the fathers upon the children unto the third and fourth generations. That is one of the rules of life, a divine law which we recognize again and again. One cannot survive without this comprehensive obligation. No married couple can escape the fact that they must assume responsibility for the consequences of their children's behavior, even though in an individual case they may be completely innocent. [10]

---

9. Letter by the council of the Evangelical church to the Allied Control Council in Friedrich Merzyn (editor), *Kundgebungen*, p. 15.

10. Address to the Stuttgart clergy on December 4, 1945, in *File 210, Schuldfrage 1945–1946*, Wurm Papers, Württemberg Church Archives, Stuttgart.

Under Wurm's leadership the Evangelical church held its ground and was the only group to challenge the German people to face the guilt question. While the Catholic bishops refused to lay this moral burden upon their countrymen, Protestant leaders felt that the main hope of avoiding another national catastrophe was to compel each German citizen to recognize an individual responsibility for the acts of his government. It is of interest that German youth today seem to behave in accordance with this precept—at times to a fault—and generally accept the attitude expressed in the Stuttgart declaration. Whether it was the Catholic or the Protestant church that was correct in 1945 in its handling of the guilt question, in the long run Protestant point of view has prevailed.

In a report to the American Army in September 1945, Karl Barth, who had just returned from a two-week trip to Germany, wrote that "National Socialism had totally disgraced itself long before the military collapse in 1945." The claim by Germans, he went on to state, that no one any longer believed in National Socialism accorded with the facts, however incredible this might seem to the Allied officials. [11] There were few persons whose views in this respect deserved to be taken as seriously as those of a man who had been forced to leave Germany under Nazi pressure in 1934 and who was (before as after 1945) anything but complacent or uncritical about the political situation in Germany. But there was probably not a single Allied commander who had ever heard of Barth or who would have paid the slightest attention to his report had he seen it. And yet the Basel theologian put his finger on the central issue of the most controversial problem of the occupation period in the three Western zones: if Nazism was dead, who were the Nazis and what was the purpose of denazification—purification or punishment, social justice or social revolution?

Although denazification guidelines were set down at the Potsdam Conference and subsequently in more detail by the Allied Control Council, in practice each occupation power followed its own policies and procedures. In the American Zone, where denazification was the paramount aim of the military government, an attempt was made to examine the political background of every individual. British policy was somewhat less stringent. The French on the whole did relatively little; considering most Germans to have been sympathetic to National Socialism, they concentrated on punishing the most notorious Nazis. In all four zones from 1946 on, Allied Control Council

---

11. "Bericht über eine Deutschlandreise," September 7, 1945 (copy), in *File 272, Korrespondenz mit der amerikanischen Militärregierung–Allgemeines–1945-1948*, Wurm Papers.

directives, establishing removal categories ranging from war criminals to "Persons who represent Prussian Junker tradition," became the formal basis for denazification procedures. [12] Membership in the NSDAP and related organizations, as well as support for National Socialist philosophy, were the criteria of guilt. Since there were eight million party members and four million members of Nazi organizations, and millions more belonging to other organizations of the ninety-nine proscribed ones, denazification was, to say the least, legal action of historic dimensions. Leaving aside the vindictiveness of the Morgenthaus and the Vansittarts, it is broadly true to say that the desire for justice was as profound as the naiveté of approach.

Leaders of both churches fully supported the Allied aim of removing all National Socialist influences from German life. From the start, however, they were apprehensive of the occupiers' approach. This, in their view, was so impersonal and dogmatic that the essentially innocent would almost inevitably be confused with the genuinely guilty. A purge conducted on the basis of membership in Nazi organizations would, they were convinced, destroy either the denazification program or Germany. Most of all they anticipated—correctly—that the Allies aimed at a sweeping removal of "Nazis" from public life. Churchmen were convinced there were relatively few persons left in office who could fairly be considered such. It was around this issue that the battle between the churches and the occupiers raged.

In addition, the Catholic bishops had very specific reservations of both a theological and a political nature. The theological objections were summed up by Cardinal Frings in his New Year's Eve sermon in 1946 when he stressed "that all guilt is most deeply and ultimately guilt toward the Lord God and that it must be expiated before God, that the Lord God is the final judge of all mankind, that when men judge men—particularly victors, the vanquished—pharisaism very easily results." In keeping with the German legal principle of *nulla poena sine lege,* the Cardinal argued that denazification should be limited to "making judgments upon actions which were previously subject to legal punishment." It would otherwise be thought, he concluded, that full

---

12. During the period of hostilities, denazification guidance for American, British, and French forces was set down in various SHAEF directives. During the occupation period, American Zone regulations were enunciated in JCS 1067 of April 1945 and the later Law for Liberation from National Socialism and Militarism of March 5, 1946. British Zone regulations were set down in Ordinance 79 and 110; French Zone regulations in Ordonnances 79, 133, and 165. Allied Control Council Directives 24 and 38 sought to achieve a basic uniformity in the regulations of all four zones.

justice can be achieved on earth, and this is "at once a pagan and naive optimism." [13] Of no less concern to the Catholic bishops were the potential political consequences of a drastic purge of ex-Nazis from public life. They realized that if denazification swept out everyone who was tainted, virtually only Social Democrats and communists would remain eligible for positions in civil government, industry, and education. This prospect fairly terrified the bishops.

For these reasons the Catholic church took the position that denazification should be applied only to persons who had committed criminal acts which had been illegal in the Third Reich, and the bishops lost no time in publicly warning against a drastic purge. At its Fulda meeting in August 1945 the hierarchy insisted that Nazi party membership was of itself an inadequate basis for punishment. "Many indeed joined in ignorance of the actions and aims of the party, many indeed were forced [to join], many indeed [joined] even with the good intention of preventing evil. It is a demand of justice that everywhere and at all times guilt be judged case by case, so that the innocent need not suffer with the guilty. We bishops have argued for this from the beginning and will insist upon it in the future." [14]

As indeed they did. But any possibility of their directly influencing the military government was reduced to zero within months of the war's end. In consulting ecclesiastical officials on appointments to civil government, military authorities thought they would be directed to impeccable liberal democrats, with immaculate political pasts. Catholic churchmen, on the other hand, had naturally proposed men whom they personally trusted, and these were usually strong conservatives. "They [the priests] recommend persons who are politically questionable but in whom they have confidence because they are good Catholics," a leading Rhineland Catholic politician, Leo Schwering, wrote in his diary on April 13, 1945, about the Rhineland town of Königswinter and the surrounding area. "Many of their candidates had, moreover, been members of anti-Christian parties. In response to American requests, they are recommended, however, because they are repentant sinners, because of indifference, or because other suitable men are lacking. So it happens that a lot of real Nazis are sitting in important positions. . . . But surrounded by the black cassock and its recommendation, they smuggle themselves in." [15] Schwering's diary entry gave an excellent description of

---

13. *Kirchenzeitung für das Erzbistum Köln,* January 18, 1947.
14. *Kirchliches Amtsblatt fur die Diözese Osnabrück,* November 8, 1945.
15. *Fasz I/Sch,* Schwering Papers, Cologne.

what was happening in many places throughout the Western zones in the summer after the war. In the fall, as denazification was stepped up, occupation authorities began to feel that the church had helped saddle them with a lot of very embarrassing civil officials. So keen was the sense of betrayal that British and American military officials reacted like cuckolded lovers, their suspicion knowing no limits. Anyone with a conservative background and clerical ties suddenly appeared sinister. Without difficulty investigations turned up information that could be—and was—interpreted to confirm the worst.

The civil governor of North Rhine Province, Hans Fuchs, who had been recommended· by the Bishop of Trier, was dismissed in October, along with the lord mayor of Cologne, Konrad Adenauer, and the lord mayor of Düsseldorf, Wilhelm Füllenbach. All three were prominent Catholic politicians, and all three were accused of failure to cooperate with British authorities. The real reason was that the British suspected them of having been compromised in the Third Reich. In the American Zone, Cardinal Faulhaber had recommended Fritz Schäffer as minister president of Bavaria. By summer reports began to appear in the American press that Schäffer was a "clerical fascist" and that his appointment had been part of a Vatican plot. Schäffer was dismissed in September on charges of having sabotaged the denazification program, though again the actual reason was the belief that he had been a Nazi collaborator.

As a result of such scandals and the bishops' public stand on denazification, the military government concluded that the Catholic church was an associate and defender of reactionaries. The Catholic bishops, on the other hand, suspected (as did some military authorities) that the military government had deliberately trumped up charges in order to sack conservatives in favor of Social Democrats. Cardinal Faulhaber, for instance, was reported in the Chicago *Daily News* of October 15, 1945, to be furious at the replacement of Schäffer by the Social Democrat Wilhelm Hoegner, and openly charged that this change had undone in one stroke all the "good work" of restoring order to Bavaria. "We can get rid of the Nazis without any trouble at all," Eisenhower's chief of staff, Walter Bedell Smith, was cited in *The New York Times* on November 12, 1945, in reply. "But there is a very strong ultra-conservative party in Bavaria, and I say that advisedly being a Catholic myself." Any chance that the church could support denazification policy or that the military government would trust the church on this issue practically vanished as a result of these incidents.

As denazification was intensified throughout Germany late in 1945 and early in 1946, its severities and injustices became increasingly apparent. By the end of September in the American Zone alone, 120,000 persons had been removed from their positions and 700 persons a day were being arrested. By the end of the year 100,000 persons were under detention, often without the possibility of communicating with relatives. [16] In practice, implementation of denazification regulations tended to vary from severity to leniency, depending on the time and place, the attitude of the local military authority, and occasionally, the usefulness of the accused to the military. The consequent social turmoil and human insecurity were observed by Protestant and Catholic churchmen with growing disquiet; besought by parishioners for help, the bishops and clergy repeatedly appealed to military authorities for relief. Getting nowhere, they went over to a tactic of sabotaging the program.

Since military authorities considered church attendance and other religious activity as evidence of anti-Nazism and therefore a factor in a respondent's favor, clergymen began indiscriminately issuing testimonials for defendants in denazification proceedings. Inevitably these statements were based more closely on the parishioner's relationship, financial or otherwise, to his church than on his political behavior in the Third Reich. Some clergy were not even that scrupulous. "In one community," an American Military Government report states, "almost every person summoned for investigation of his Nazi activity arrived equipped with a certificate from a minister or a priest attesting to his fine Christian character." [17] Cardinal Faulhaber even had forms printed, so that only the name of the respondent had to be filled in. This situation developed into a scandal throughout the Western zones, and the testimonials become known as "Persilscheine." "Persil" being the name of a laundry soap, "Persil certificates" were found to whitewash whiter than white. They cost the churches a good deal of their diminishing balance of respect with military authorities.

Popular discontent with the effects of denazification increased steadily in the early months of 1946. The heart of the concern was the indiscriminate approach based on party membership. "80 percent of today's defendants are innocent," Cardinal Frings once told the Deputy British Military Governor, General Robertson, and in his private conversations with British officials he

---

16. September figures in *Monthly Report of the Military Governor,* October 20, 1945; internment figure in Clay, *Decision in Germany,* p. 69.

17. *Monthly Report of the Military Governor,* November 20, 1945.

often repeated that "the principle that party membership alone is a basis of guilt must be dropped." By leading the opposition to denazification, the churches began to build up pressure against Allied policy. The Catholic church was the first to launch a formal large-scale attack against the whole of the policy when the two archbishops and several bishops in northern Germany under the leadership of Cardinal Frings issued an Easter pastoral letter castigating the Allies for creating misery and chaos. Occupation authorities, the bishops insisted, had not lived in the Third Reich and could not distinguish real from nominal Nazis. As a result, thousands of "adherents of the old regime" were being dismissed from positions in public life and industry and thrown into a situation that was too "reminiscent of the Gestapo, concentration camps, and similar things." Denazification weighed upon the German people "like a nightmare," and the bishops concluded that unless the policy were altered, "an internal poison will be instilled, making moral and religious recovery extremely difficult, if not impossible." [18]

To correct some of the patent defects of denazification procedures and to engage Germans themselves in the denazification process, American Military Government in March 1946 introduced the "Law for Liberation from National Socialism and Militarism," a step followed shortly afterward by the British. This slightly revised approach to the problem required everyone over eighteen to fill out a questionnaire and established German tribunals to examine the results. It was at this point that the Evangelical church entered the picture. Although Protestant leaders had not initially been so opposed in principle to broad denazification as the Catholic church, they had quickly come to share the Catholic bishops' dismay; this unanimity of attitude, incidentally, served to maintain the cooperation between the two churches begun during the Third Reich. The critical attitude was in no way inconsistent with the Evangelical church's acceptance of collective guilt; the notion of collective guilt, in fact, militated against an effective denazification program. The idea that the German people were collectively guilty tended to support an argument for taking legal action against no one, since the whole nation could not be removed from office or punished. Niemöller, for instance, who traveled throughout Germany propagating the church's attitude during the year after the war, complained strongly to a group of Americans in the fall of

---

18. Report of Frings' conversation of September 9, 1946, in File *CR 25/18;* pastoral letter of March 27, 1946, in *Kirchlicher Anzeiger für die Erzdiözese Köln,* May 1, 1946. It was this pastoral message that American and French military officials would not permit to be read in their zones.

1945 that mass internment of Nazi suspects and other denazification methods had not only caused antagonism between the churches and the military government but also made it difficult for Germans to understand the difference between democracy and Nazism. "If the people could really see democracy at work," he argued, "the Church would more easily accomplish its task of moral and spiritual rehabilitation." [19]

In the Protestant view, the Law for Liberation retained many of the worst features of the old policy. Bishop Wurm, in his capacity as chairman of the council of the EKD, lost no time in dispatching a letter to General Clay appealing for fundamental alterations before the law was implemented. The law, he contended, echoing the Catholic bishops, violated fundamental legal concepts by making persons subject to punishment for their association with a legally constituted and internationally recognized regime. This ex post facto approach had already completely undermined respect for judicial order and fair treatment. The Evangelical church was willing to accept a contention that association with National Socialism was morally culpable, but in such a case it was not for occupation authorities to administer punishment. In the Law for Liberation, moreover, the individual was held responsible for his opinions, which were impossible to judge, no less than for his actions, and it was up to the plaintiff to prove his innocence. For these reasons, the bishop warned, "the Christian Church" found that the law "could not be squared with the conscience of the German people," and Protestant leaders were therefore "not in a position to tell the German people that this law and its procedures are in all respects consistent with divine justice and truth." Admitting that he did not anticipate American willingness to rewrite the law, Wurm called as a minimum for a correction of the most blatant injustices implicit in the establishment of presumptive guilt categories. The indictment of individuals because of their office, position, or occupation (as applied for example, to judges and civil servants) was blindly arbitrary and would inevitably weigh most heavily upon those who had been nominal party members and those who had had to join the party to keep their jobs. Similarly, the distinction between those who had joined the NSDAP before 1937 and those who joined afterwards was artificial and ignored all the complexities of life in the Third Reich. The sum result of the new regulation, the bishop predicted, would be to punish the innocent along with the guilty and in this way commit the cardinal error of law. [20]

---

19. Quoted in Herman, p. 121.
20. Merzyn, pp. 27–33.

As in the case of the Catholic bishops, the Protestant leaders' underlying concern about the Law for Liberation was for more than individual injustice; they feared that there could be no stabilization of society, no effective moral, political, or material reconstruction of Germany so long as the country was in the throes of a juridical purge. This apprehension was highlighted in a public declaration, a week after Wurm's letter, by the council of the EKD and representatives of the provincial churches, which stated:

> The message of the Church, which seeks an honest rejection by the people and a destruction of the spirit of National Socialism, is being gravely impeded by many of the current measures. Despair and bitterness are already growing up everywhere in reaction to the disappointed hope of a new beginning for our people. [21]

High military government officials, as previously observed, considered criticism of fundamental policy to be undesirable, and General Clay crisply told Wurm in a letter of May 23, 1946, that his proposed changes were "unnecessary and undesirable." The law had to be ex post facto, he insisted, since otherwise the evils of Nazism would be a bar to their remedy. The new law was not too severe, since individual culpability would be judged on an individual basis and the penalties graded according to the degree of culpability. [22] Clay's comments did not meet the Evangelical church's points, and Protestant bishops individually and collectively continued to criticize the policy and to plead for alterations. None of these representations, Wurm complained publicly several times, even received the courtesy of an acknowledgement from American officials. By the summer of 1946 the atmosphere had become so embittered that in an interview with *The New York Times* on July 28, 1946, Wurm had only caustic words for American policy. Charging that "extreme left elements are using the denazification laws to destroy Germany's leading classes of educated men," he said of denazification, "There is something Bolshevistic about it." While these Protestant attacks were overtly ignored by military officials, they were beginning to make alterations in the law imperative. "The strong and consistent anti-denazification Evangelical agitation," William Griffith, an American expert on denazification, has observed, "had considerable influence in increasing the public demand for basic changes in the Law." [23]

---

21. Merzyn, pp. 35–36.
22. Quoted in Office of Military Government—Württemberg-Baden, *History of Religious Affairs Branch–1 July to 31 December 1947,* Modern Military Records.
23. William Griffith, *Denazification Program in the United States Zone of Germany* (Harvard University doctoral thesis), p. 393.

"Considerable influence" on denazification was being exerted by the churches in another way as well—through something between passive resistance and active sabotage. By guiding the selection of members of the German denazification tribunals and by bringing pressure to bear on the tribunals once they were established, they played an invisible role in the whole administration of denazification policy. Sometimes their public stand alone was enough to interfere with the program. An early example of this occurred in Cologne, when Cardinal Frings in his 1946 Christmas message demanded an end to what he labeled "the Nazi inquisition which will be a shame in the face of history." Within days of the report of this in the *Kölnische Rundschau* on December 3, the chairman of the German Review Board to British Military Government, Friedrich Schilling, resigned because he did not "see any possibility of being active with denazification any longer." Interviewed by British officials, the conversation, according to the British record of the meeting, went as follows:

SCHILLING: While I agree with you on denazification, the church has attacked the whole system and therefore I cannot be associated with it longer. The subcommittee of lawyers . . . told me that I could not reckon with finding any livelihood in Cologne. I have spoken with Frings and he feels too many persons are being dismissed and is disturbed by the moral issue. It will be difficult in Cologne to find any Catholic lawyer who will take the job on.

BRITISH OFFICER: Why?

SCHILLING: Because the Cardinal has spoken thus, therefore no Catholic will take on the job because in Cologne the church is so important. [24]

In the American Zone denazification, a far more thorough and systematic affair than in the other zones, was running into increasing difficulties during the spring and summer of 1947. The Catholic bishops had been as apprehensive as the Protestants about the Law for Liberation, and on July 27, 1947, after the Law had been in force for a year, they submitted their views to General Clay in a memorandum. In a covering letter Bishop Muench explained that the memorandum had been composed by the bishops in reaction to "the increasing resentment and bitterness of the people over the policy and practice of denazification." He went on: "The exploitation of the bitterness by agents of communism, in particular, gives them much con-

---

24. Memorandum dated December 12, 1946, of Headquarters Military Government, City of Cologne in File *CR 25/18.*

cern. The reports they receive from their priests on this point are not at all reassuring." The memorandum itself was probably the most scathingly critical ecclesiastical statement of the entire occupation period. In it the bishops charged that the law, far from reestablishing a sense of legal order in society, had "caused the Germans to lose confidence in the concept of justice of the Americans." Because the law had shown no understanding of the situation facing the individual in the Third Reich, Germans had come to doubt "the formerly so famous tolerance and objectivity of the Americans." The law had been implemented in a way that punished a large number of nominal Nazis but left an equal number of genuine supporters free. Not only was the purge of industrial specialists hindering German economic revival, but communists were using denazification as a political and economic weapon against their enemies. In short, the law had become "the 'legal' basis for compulsion and terror" against the majority of the population. "Denazification," the bishops charged, "has confused the internal political situation almost hopelessly, has made the reeducation of the people to democracy all but impossible and has largely undermined the efforts for legal security and order." Their deepest hope was that the Americans would replace "force, oppression and fear" with "freedom, justice and order." Toward this end they asked for an immediate amnesty for all Nazi party members except the leadership, for a release of all internees, and for stricter provisions in categorizing persons as "major offenders" and "offenders." [25]

The effect of this letter in military government headquarters can easily be imagined; Clay's denazificaton adviser, Walter Dorn, drafted an acid reply for Clay's signature. This draft curtly described the memorandum as "not always easily intelligible" and suggested that the absence of a moral regeneration in Germany was due to the churches' "indifference and lethargy." In icy language the letter rejected as insupportable the bishops' specific points, including the claim that economic reconstruction was impeded by denazification. The letter concluded that no changes in the law would be countenanced and that the Catholic church, instead of asking for alterations, should instruct its clergy actively to support the law. Clay, however, put off signing this letter. Pressure to modify the law was becoming too strong to resist. Trade union leaders, Social Democrats, and even communists were withdrawing their support from it, chiefly because—as the churches had predicted from the very start—the small fry were being caught while the big fish escaped. In the United States itself there was a growing feeling that denazification was indeed

25. In *Cardinal Faulhaber*, Modern Military Records.

undercutting German economic recovery, as the bishops had also long warned. In short, the bishops' intervention came at a critical moment, and Griffith states that it was "extremely influential" in moving matters toward a change. After two months' delay, on September 29, 1947, Clay dispatched a newly drafted letter which conceded "that there is a need for changes in the law which would permit the expedition of procedures." With this undertaking to conclude denazification rapidly, the churches had won half their battle. [26]

The amendments to the law, implemented in October 1947, concentrated attention on major Nazis, negated the significance of party membership prior to 1937, abolished presumptive guilt, permitted lesser offenders to resume their former positions in civilian life, and speeded up the processing of outstanding cases. It therefore met most of the churches' objections. By implying that the original policy had after all been wrong, however, the concessions only redoubled the desire to be finished with the whole business. Niemöller is generally credited with having dealt the coup de grace. In a pastoral letter read in all the churches of Hesse-Nassau on February 1, 1948, the church leader charged that denazification had had disastrous sociological and moral effects. It had given birth to a spirit of revenge and had caused immeasurable injustice. Characterizing denazification tribunals as "arenas for denunciation and battlefields for personal enmities," he called upon Protestants to cease serving as prosecutors, assessors, or witnesses for the prosecution. He declared that members of the clergy were "forbidden for the sake of their own position and the welfare of the community to help justify this scandal any longer by doing any work in connection with denazification." [27]

This was strong language, and American authorities warned that if ecclesiastical officials refused to obey existing instructions, they would be subject to prosecution under German law. General Clay told *The New York Times*, on February 4, 1948, that he found it "distressing . . . that a minister of a religious faith advocates disrespect and violence to a law"—an ironic comment in view of the fact that denazification held persons responsible for having blindly obeyed the legal order of the Third Reich. Less aptly still, the Military Governor of Württemberg-Baden, Charles La Follette, had warned in *The New York Times* of February 3, 1948, "Any German who quits the work of denazification now, or attempts to order or coerce a German to quit now, in

---

26. Draft letter and letter from Clay in *Cardinal Faulhaber,* Modern Military Records; Griffith, p. 393.

27. *Military Government Report for Land Hesse,* 1948, Modern Military Records, p. 19.

the face of the real test—the trial of the hard core Nazi leaders—is rendering a disservice to the cause of Germany." But Germans had already lost confidence in a policy that left most of the main culprits still untried almost three years after the war. By this time neither La Follette nor Clay could hold back the avalanche of antidenazification sentiment set off by Niemöller's pastoral letter. Even newspapers and politicians, until then inhibited from speaking out against Allied policy, joined leaders of the two churches in calling for an end to the whole program. *The New York Times* had reported on February 3, even before the discontent had reached its height, that military government officials were deeply concerned by "the most concentrated wave of resistance to the occupation powers, who are roundly hated by the Germans—the Americans hardly less than the others."

As the organizers and leaders of the popular revolt against the major objective of the occupation, the churches were able to show themselves the prevailing party in this test of strength with the occupation powers. Although, as a result of the first amendments, denazification machinery had churned out hundreds of thousands of "denazified" citizens and released thousands of "serious offenders," nothing could prevent the total collapse of the program. In March a second set of amendments in effect wrote off all but 32,000 of the most deeply incriminated persons, and most of these cases were settled during the summer. For all practical purposes denazification was finished by September 1948. [28]

In the end the churches had been proved right and the military government wrong. Generally speaking, it was the occupation authorities that had been motivated by fuzzy-headed idealism and the churches that had been guided by cold empiricism. Experience demonstrated that denazification aims were ambiguous and its procedures unworkable. To use denazification as an instrument either to establish democracy or to destroy an authoritarian social structure was equivalent to burning down a barn to get rid of the mice. By drawing everyone into the same net, denazification had by and large resulted, not in the disgrace of influential and unrepentant Nazis, but in a sense of solidarity of all Germans against the military government. Instead of confining their action to leading Nazi officials, the Americans, especially, set out to remove every person in public and governmental authority who had been a member of the NSDAP—in effect, almost every person in public and governmental authority. Earlier and more clearly than military officials, the churches recognized both the impracticality and the profound social conse-

---

28. Kormann, *U.S. Denazification Policy in Germany, 1944–1950*, p. 133.

quences of such a policy. They foresaw nothing less than a social revolution and judged that occupation authorities were unaware of the risk they were running, with Germany in ruins and the Russians on the Elbe. And in the end nearly everyone was back in his old position or profession. "Abandoned by the Americans and universally denounced by the disgusted Germans," Griffith summed it all up, "denazification had failed—failed to come near achieving *any* objective ever set forth for it, by Americans or Germans." [29]

Yet considering the deep moral and social consequences of denazification, it was obvious that military authorities should have consulted the churches and sought their cooperation. That the churches should have become the bitterest foe of denazification was surely a situation the occupation powers should have done their utmost to avoid. The two sides might have found it difficult to reach an understanding, but consultation would at least have left the German people with the feeling that moral considerations had been given due weight by military authorities—and it was precisely this that most Germans believed was lacking in Allied policy. Had the churches' arguments been heeded in 1945 rather than at the end of 1947, a swift surgical operation on the body politic might have had a good chance of success. Against the churches' determined opposition, the program was doomed to fail. The churches simply enjoyed a greater hold on the mass of the population than did the military government. They were therefore able not only to give a powerful impetus to an otherwise lethargic public opinion but even to subvert the program. There was no clearer example in the whole of the occupation period of how occupation authorities ignored—to their peril—a basic fact of German society.

The churches, on the other hand, failed to make it clear that they honestly wanted genuine Nazis out of public life. Too often their public statements on denazification did not go beyond an unqualified condemnation of the policy. A case in point was Cardinal Frings' private comments to the British suggesting that 20 percent of the population should be investigated, in contrast to his open execration of the whole program and his demands for its immediate end. "The influence and importance of these clerical attacks on denazification cannot be denied," Griffith has written, "but their correctness and justification is another matter. Certainly much of their individual criticism were [sic] fully justified, as the latter course of events clearly demonstrated. But the spirit in which they were offered, and the basic objectives

---

29. Griffith, "Denazification in the U.S. Zone of Germany" in *The Annals,* January 1950.

behind them, are something else." [30] This verdict is not unfair. Church leaders did not always appreciate the dilemmas facing the occupiers or the pressures on the military governors from their capitals. But military government leaders had largely themselves to blame for the situation. By their scarcely veiled contempt of the churches, their failure to explain their aims carefully, their peremptory responses or refusals to reply to letters from church leaders, they lost the confidence of the churches and left an enduring legacy of bitterness. "No victor was ever more generous to a vanquished nation than was the United States to Germany after the Second World War," the former Bishop of Württemberg, Martin Haug, said in a personal interview over two decades after the war. "We were starving and our cities were in ruins; the Americans gave us food and the materials to begin reconstruction. The French committed atrocities, lived off the land and removed whatever they could get their hands on. But American denazification procedures so poisoned the atmosphere that to this day the people of Württemberg feel friendlier to the French than to the Americans."

The contrast in the Allies' approach to denazification—and to the churches—was even more obvious in the denazification of the clergy. All four occupation powers granted the churches complete independence in matters of organization and dogma. British Military Government followed this policy literally and rigidly, making clear that the principle extended even to denazification and that the churches were to purge themselves of National Socialists without British guidance or interference. The British merely demanded that each provincial church or diocese establish "denazification committees" to investigate its clergy. They did not interfere with these committees and invariably accepted their decisions. The French had no policy directives on denazification of the clergy, though in practice they permitted the churches to deal with the problem in their own way. Occasionally they informed church authorities of the name of a specific clergyman whom they wished removed from his office, but even then they never forced the issue. The Americans exempted only doctors from denazification and held the clergy liable, along with everyone else, to removal from office, to imprisonment or fines, for their political behavior in the Third Reich. However, direct military action to remove a clergyman was usually forbidden in the early period and was later

---

30. Griffith, *Denazification Program in the United States Zone of Germany*, p. 395.

resorted to only in extreme cases, as a result of a policy decision by high military authority. As a rule, local military officials notified diocesan and provincial church authorities of clergymen falling into mandatory removal categories and requested them to take appropriate action.

Denazification of the clergy posed no problem for the Catholic church. However many priests may have been convinced National Socialists at heart, very few—perhaps 150 [31]—had actually joined the party. Those party members whom the church knew about and those subsequently identified by military officials were quietly removed from their parishes. Only a few problems arose. In the summer of 1946 senior British officials publicly complained that the Catholic church in the British Zone was lax in denazifying itself. In reality the bishops saw no point in establishing denazification panels, since the few Nazi priests in their dioceses had already been disciplined. Occasional lapses also came to light, as when twelve seminarians at the Jesuit St. George's College near Frankfurt were found in 1948 to have falsified their denazification questionnaires. [32] But almost invariably removals were promptly carried out, and American authorities were gratified by the Catholic church's cooperation. When denazification in the American Zone was delegated to German authorities under the Law for Liberation, diocesan officials assured the four ministers president that any priest found to be or suspected of being a Nazi would be removed upon notification.

The Evangelical church faced a far different situation. Among the large number of Protestant clergy who were sympathetic to National Socialism, roughly 8-9 percent had actually joined the NSDAP, and at least an equal number had been "German Christians" to the end. Many of the most seriously incriminated churchmen resigned or were discharged immediately at the end of hostilities, when provincial churches reorganized themselves and excluded "German Christians" and other Nazis from ecclesiastical office. But when American military officers began compiling their mandatory removal lists, they found that 15 percent of the Protestant clergy still fell into this category. [33]

In the church's view, a pastor who had supported National Socialism had

---

31. An estimate based on American Military Government reports indicates that an average of five priests in each diocese, as well as some seminarians and members of orders, belonged to the party.

32. *1948 Historical Report; Office of Military Government Hesse.* Volume I: *Narrative* (undated mimeographed manuscript), Modern Military Records; p. 212.

33. McClaskey, *The History of United States Policy,* p. i.

committed a political error, but unless he had violated his spiritual or moral responsibilities, he should not be liable to removal or punishment. Questionable cases would have to be decided on their own merits rather than by mechanical criteria, and the church alone was in a position to make the final judgment. This attitude was not simply a matter of high principle, but in some cases, particularly in the American Zone, the result of a guilty conscience. Certain provincial church leaders, such as Hans Meiser, had willingly tolerated Nazi clergymen in the ranks of their organization and had even appointed some of them to important ecclesiastical positions. They could not now, even if they wished, casually dump these persons. Those who had badly compromised 'themselves—pastors or church officials who were in the category later known as "major offenders" (prominent "German Christians," recipients of party awards, and so on)—were generally removed from their positions with little or no prompting from occupation officials. In the Bavarian Church, for instance, these numbered ten, all of whom were deprived of their positions during the summer of 1945. With this action, church leaders considered the matter more or less closed. [34]

In the British Zone, the churches of Rhineland and Westphalia expeditiously cleansed their ranks on their own initiative. The "German Christian" bishop of the Rhineland Church, for instance, quietly disappeared from the scene and never again exercised his ministry. "German Christian" pastors were normally sent to new parishes. While other provincial churches were less thorough than this, the British refrained from intervening. Similarly, military authorities had seriously considered arresting Bishop Marahrens of Hanover at the end of the war, but ultimately left it to Anglican churchmen to press him—unsuccessfully—to resign.

The French generally accepted the Evangelical church's approach. They gave the provincial churches of their zone over a year and a half to deal with the problem in their own way. In 1947 they established commissions in each of their zonal administrative centers to review and complete the screening process, and they left the commissions effectively in the hands of church officials. These commissions in time examined the entire situation and conveyed their recommendations to the military government, which accepted the commissions' decisions and requested church officials to enforce them.

In the French area of Württemberg, for example, there were at the end

---

34. Diary of Wilhelm Bogner, Fürth. Church Counsellor Bogner, a close friend of Bishop Meiser, handled denazification matters for the Bavarian Church.

of the war 306 pastors, of whom 210 were able to show that they had not been members of any Nazi organization. [35] Of the remaining 96, 32 had temporarily belonged to the SA in their youth. Membership in the SA in the early years of the Third Reich was not normally considered politically compromising, and the commission held these persons to be exonerated. The remaining 64 pastors (members of the NSDAP or an affiliated organization) were examined case by case, with an eventual recommendation of no punishment (in 14 cases), fine (in 16 cases, with an average fine of 400 marks payable to a specified church organization), dismissal (in 2 cases), suspension or probation (in 6 cases), and transfer, early retirement or demotion in the remainder. The judgments—which on balance appear to have been fair—were accepted by provincial church authorities, and in this way the whole issue was settled in a matter of months without friction between the church and French Military Government.

With some notable exceptions, American military officials pursued the matter from the first with martial perseverance and inflexibility. In the Bavarian case again, they considered the church's own purge miserably inadequate, and during the year following the war they provided Bishop Meiser with the names of 170 pastors who were to be removed from their positions. Meiser at first flatly refused to dismiss any of them; the military government reported, "The vast majority of these 170 men were defended by the Bishop along the following lines: 'He joined the party from the noblest motives.' 'He did not realize the true objectives of the Party' or 'he stayed in the Party to fight the party from within.' " A mere 5 of the 170 were dismissed by the summer of 1946; the Bavarian church was so determined to protect the others that it secretly transferred some of them from town to town so as to forestall any action against them by American officials. [36]

The Bremen church, to cite another example, had rid itself of its "German Christian" officials during its reorganization at the end of the war, thus settling the matter in the view of church authorities. In November, however, military officials asked for the immediate removal of three pastors—two for having been Nazi party members and the third for giving alleged Nazi ser-

---

35. *"Französische Militärregierung: Entnazifizierung von Geistlichen,"* in *File 271,* Wurm Papers.

36. Meiser's views in Military Government Land Bavaria, *Cumulative Historical Report* (June 1946) Archives of U.S. Army Europe, Heidelberg, p. 135; for transfers, see Bogner diary.

mons. Three months later, church authorities replied that, after examining the cases, they had decided to retain the men. Negotiations continued until July, when the military government again demanded their removal. Church officials refused to comply on the ground that "an ecclesiastical body is not competent to judge men for their political acts but only for their behavior as churchmen."[37] They further argued that it was pointless to punish a man who had made a political mistake which he now repented. American authorities finally dismissed the lay official responsible for church denazification and compelled his successor to remove the clergymen in question.

In Württemberg-Baden, however, it was the Land military government itself which challenged the whole policy of denazifying the clergy. These officials insisted that the policy was inconsistent with freedom of religion and could never be successful against the church's opposition. Local military personnel were instructed to take no action against any clergyman or church employee until the case had been reviewed by the Land military government and, as appropriate, the bishops of Baden or of Württemberg. Even following this review, Land military officials declared they would "not dismiss or request dismissal of clergymen or church employees for whose dependability the Bishop (or his equivalent) is willing to vouch."[38] In practice, the mandatory-removal cases which were referred to the two provincial churches in the twelve months following the war resulted in some retentions as well as some dismissals, retirements, and transfers. Local American authorities were generally satisfied with the actions taken, though they found Bishop Julius Bender of Baden on the whole more cooperative than Bishop Wurm, who rejected appeals for the dismissal of incriminated persons in the Württemberg Church. They feared, however, that any attempt to force the issue would provoke Wurm to resign in protest and gravely embarrass the military government both in Germany and abroad. But the central military government headquarters in Berlin, deciding to risk a showdown, issued a direct command ordering that the ten most flagrant cases in the church should be selected for prosecution. Stuttgart military authorities asked that the order be reconsidered, arguing that its execution would compromise religious freedom. When Berlin refused to review the matter, the names of ten Württemberg church officials were submitted to denazification officials, and with that Land military au-

---

37. *Functional History of Military Government in the Bremen Enclave;* Part I: *Narrative (1 July-31 August 1946)* (undated typescript), Modern Military Records, p. 53.

38. *History of Military Government for Land Württemberg-Baden to June 1946;* Part I: *General History* (undated typescript), Modern Military Records, p. 50.

thorities washed their hands of the matter. The denazification tribunal eventually exonerated three of the men and fined the others. Since all had been categorized as "mandatory removals," the provincial church considered that it had won a moral victory.

The stalemate between the provincial churches and the military government that marked the first year of the occupation was destroyed with the announcement of the Law for Liberation, which decreed that all persons classified as "mandatory removals" would have to be dismissed from their pastorates by June 1, 1946, after which they could only be employed for common labor. Pastors who were "lesser offenders" could be denied the right to preach for up to ten years. Neither church officials nor religious affairs officers had been consulted in the drafting of this law, and both promptly protested the new regulations. In his letter to General Clay on the Law for Liberation Bishop Wurm pointed out that preaching is the very essence of the ministerial calling for a Protestant pastor and that when the military government claimed the right to determine who might or might not exercise the spiritual office, it was undertaking what the church had resisted the Nazis for attempting. He maintained that ecclesiastical authorities were as intent as the occupation authorities to see the church cleansed of Nazi influences but felt that this had been achieved. In conclusion, Wurm asked that church officials should be given until October 1946 to review the situation and to remove any genuine Nazis; if Land denazification authorities were not then satisfied, the church would review the matter further.

In his response General Clay rejected the significance Bishop Wurm attached to the preaching office and argued that, as pastors were subject to punishment for crimes, so they could be held eligible for the civil sanctions of denazification without any derogation of spiritual authority. General Clay's assertion that a minister's political attitude in the Third Reich was prima facie equivalent to a civil offense, such as robbery or murder, was so incomprehensible to Protestant leaders that they gave up trying to reach the military government on the subject. Instead, they worked out an understanding with Land officials behind the scenes. These German political leaders, considering the church already sufficiently denazified, had every intention, even if the military government did not, of proceeding cautiously.[39] First the Land denazification ministers in Württemberg-Baden and Hesse agreed with church

---

39. A Military Government poll of German political leaders (including fourteen communists) in November 1945 revealed that the large majority felt the churches had already been adequately denazified. Office of Military Government for Germany, *Weekly Information Bulletin,* No. 19.

officials not to deny clergymen the right to preach. Then the minister-president of Württemberg-Baden undertook to act as a liaison between denazification tribunals and the churches in Hesse, Bavaria, and Württemberg-Baden. An unpublicized understanding was thereupon reached which provided that evidence against a pastor would be reported to the minister president, who would in turn notify the appropriate bishop. Provincial church authorities would have four weeks in which to investigate the charge and take action. Should a pastor have to stand trial, another clergyman—"a proven anti-Nazi" —would be one of the assessors of the court. To avoid any embarrassment to the church as a result of these proceedings, it was further understood that no publicity would be given to the trials.[40] Subsequent decisions by General Clay (in response to appeals by Religious Affairs officers) to drop the automatic dismissal provision for "mandatory removals" but to retain the ban on preaching by lesser offenders were thus left far behind by events. As a report of the Württemberg-Baden Military Government aptly remarked, denazification appeared

> doomed to failure as far as the Church is concerned because of the dictatorial manner in which the law was written and because of the complete disregard with which the Religious Affairs Office and the Evangelical Church of Germany were treated in the writing of the law. The process of Denazification . . . has been handled so mechanically and has become so tedious, especially for those not having strong political backing, that both autochthons and Americans are showing signs of nervous exhaustion. The Evangelical Church has and will continue to play with Military Government on this point as the cat with the mouse because the law has proved to be unsound and because the Bishops feel that their message is both older and more permanent than the voice of Denazification.[41]

Once a modus vivendi had been reached with Land officials, church authorities rapidly took action on the majority of the outstanding cases. In connection with the Law for Liberation, American Military Government had turned over to German authorities the names of 156 persons in mandatory removal categories who still occupied ecclesiastical positions. Of these cases, 91 were in Bavaria, and by mid-October 1946, 15 of these had been classified

---

40. Text of agreement in Kormann, pp. 80–81.
41. Office of Military Government-Württemberg-Baden, *History of Religious Affairs Branch July 1 to December 31, 1947* (undated typescript), Modern Military Records, p. 27.

"lesser offenders," fined, and prohibited from preaching for specified periods; 44 were classified as "followers" and fined, 19 were exonerated, and 5 were considered not liable to denazification. "The remainder," an official American report dryly noted, "could not be located" [42] —demonstrating the Bavarian church's success in helping its pastors evade detection. Probably no provincial church was so badly ravaged as that in Bremen, where the military government reported in June 1947 that denazification was finally complete, with the result that "to date, approximately 25% of the total Protestant clergymen in the Bremen area have either been pensioned or dismissed." Although action of some sort was eventually taken on almost all unsettled cases, Niemöller once again signaled the effective end of the affair by announcing that the Hessian church "did not intend to comply with sanctions prohibiting clergymen classified as 'offenders' from preaching." [43]

The basic issue in this dispute between American and Protestant officials was that the two sides could not agree on what the basic issue was. To the military government it was the question of whether or not the church was to be purified of National Socialist influences. But in claiming the right to remove clergymen who had been party members, American officials were at once contradicting their policy of full freedom for the churches in their internal affairs and imposing what amounted to a political test upon the clergy. The decision as to who may hold spiritual office is one that any church or sect always views as exclusively its own, a sine qua non of a religious body's existence. For the military government to participate in and enforce a purge of the clergy was therefore a totalitarian act beyond any Hitler himself had tried. The American handling of the problem had the effect of shifting the issue from denazification as such to one of the liberty of the church. In a battle of this sort it was proper and inevitable that the church would oppose the military tooth and nail. As an intact institution headed by persons who had never been National Socialists, the church considered itself competent to cleanse its own ranks. For this reason it insisted that clergymen should in effect be treated as exceptions to general denazification procedures.

---

42. Kormann, p. 111.

43. Military government statement in *Functional History of Military Government in Land Bremen, 1 July* 1946–30 June 1947, Part I: Narrative (undated typescript), Modern Military Records, p. 129; Niemöller quoted in Office of Military Government Hesse, *1948 Historical Report,* Volume I: *Narrative* (undated manuscript), Modern Military Records.

But was the line which the church wanted to draw between the spiritual office and a pastor's political behavior really so clear? Was it ever—even in 1933—possible to have been a convinced Nazi and at the same time true to Christian teachings? These were the central questions. However they were to be answered, the responses came better from the church than from the military government. As a result, although the dispute over denazification of the Protestant clergy ended in a draw, American Military Government had even less to be proud of than did the Evangelical church.

In sum, the record makes clear that denazification was less the price exacted of the German people for the Third Reich than the tribute which the Allies, particularly the Americans, had to pay to public opinion at home. Not surprisingly, the program had little relation to the facts of the situation or the political needs of German society. It was dedicated to rooting out Nazism through an elaborate system of legal punishments. But Nazism had died with the Third Reich. And a political trial is too difficult and delicate an operation to impose upon a whole population. Political punishment would have been legitimate and workable—and useful—had it managed in practice to distinguish between political criminals and political comformists, assigning the former to the courts and leaving the latter to the moral judgment of their fellow citizens. But because they failed to understand the sociological and moral problems of a nation under·a totalitarian dictatorship, the policy-makers developed a program that failed both to achieve its aims and to do the job that was needed.

THE CHURCHES' POLITICAL AIMS AND TACTICS

5 | *The Political Ethic of German Protestantism*

DIETRICH BONHOEFFER once said that when one was on a train headed for the wrong destination, there was no point in running through the train in the opposite direction; one had to jump off. In the German political context, the train might be likened to the deep-seated authoritarianism which pervaded German society and which went completely out of control after 1933. Protestant churchmen had always been among the most comfortably installed passengers. Over the centuries almost none of them had run along the corridor and even during the Third Reich few had actually jumped off. It was not until 1945 that the great majority got out. "This is what today we have to say to our people and to Christianity," Martin Niemöller told his fellow churchmen at Treysa in August 1945: "We do not come and stand before you as the righteous and the just; rather, we are guilty and want in the future to see clearly and act loyally. . . . We have been an Erastian church, and this circumstance has made it easy for us to do only the traditionally conventional and not to question further what our real responsibility was. The church of the future must never again be an Erastian church." [1]

These words must have fallen hard on the ears of such leaders as Wurm, Dibelius, Meiser, and Marahrens, who were basically neither liberal nor democratic. The third Reich and the collapse of 1945 had left them more bewildered than changed. When in May 1945, for instance, Provost Grüber recalled in an interview, he had told Dibelius of his possible appointment by the Russians to the Berlin civil administration, the latter had responded, "Let's leave politics to the Catholics." Some weeks later Dibelius told American military officers, "Democracy will not take root in Germany because . . . it is a foreign ideology." He maintained that "because of Germany's experience with the weak Weimar Republic, democracy is associated in the German mind with unemployment and ineffective foreign policy." And

---

1. *Kirchliches Jahrbuch,* 1945–1948, pp. 12–13.

he concluded that, "in order to prevent the revival of Nazism, the Occupying Powers should assist the Church which offers its supporters traditional ideology rooted in Germany which will fill the vacuum left by the collapse of the Hitler movement." [2]

This same state of mind had held German Protestantism captive since the Reformation. By instilling a sense of the inwardness of religion and the vanity of human effort in its adherents, Lutheranism had given rise over the centuries to a political passivity that in turn led to a deification of the state, whose agents were entrusted with responsibility for all public affairs. In this way Lutheranism—inherently without specific political content—not only pliantly accommodated itself to any form of government, but even became the central foundation of the prevailing political philosophy. As a result, Lutheranism in most of Germany became thoroughly conservative, patriarchal, and authoritarian. For four hundred years Luther's catechism and his commentary on the thirteenth chapter of the Epistle to the Romans were instruments of political no less than religious indoctrination, the effect of which was to inspire a submissive political temper.

The practical consequence, as Troeltsch has observed, was both the political emasculation of Lutheranism and the inculcation in the German character of deep contradictions—the linking of Christianity with conservatism, piety with love of power, freedom of conscience with fanatical nationalism. Far from being a politically neutral element in society, German Protestantism was the main buttress of a patriarchal, militarist Prussia as she expanded her dominance over the rest of Germany. Since it was bound to the status quo and against democracy and progress, Troeltsch fairly concluded that "Lutheranism opposed the modern development of the State only one degree less ardently than Catholicism." Written at the beginning of the twentieth century, Troeltsch's words were a terrible prophecy of the disaster to which German Protestantism was helping to lead the nation. [3]

It was, however, a mark of the intellectual vigor of German Protestantism that this error was recognized, not just after the apocalypse of 1945, but eleven years earlier, at the Barmen synod. The theological declaration adopted there raised a new political standard, and after the collapse of the Third Reich active members of the Confessing church were determined to make this the guiding principle of the Protestant political outlook.

> We went wrong when we began to dream the dream of a special German mission as if the world could be restored through the German

---

2. Report dated June 28, 1945, on conversation with Dibelius by Major Marshall Knappen, in *Evangelical Church, Lutheran,* Modern Military Records.

3. Troeltsch, *The Social Teachings of the Christian Churches,* Vol. II, p. 573.

genius. As a result we opened the way to the unlimited use of political power and placed our nation on the throne of God. Once we founded our state internally on a strong government alone and externally on a display of military power alone, disaster followed.

We went wrong when we began to build up a "Christian front" against a reform that had become necessary in the social sphere. The alliance of the church with the old and conventional conservative powers has taken heavy revenge upon us. We betrayed the Christian freedom which offered us the opportunity of altering the way of life where social life required such changes. We rejected the right of revolution and tolerated and justified the evolution toward absolute dictatorship.[4]

This was part of a statement entitled "On the Political Course of Our Nation," issued by the council of the Confessional church in August 1947. Two years earlier, at their meeting in Treysa, Protestant leaders had already acknowledged the church's responsibility for the German catastrophe and had recognized—if at first dimly—that the Evangelical church would have to strike out on an entirely new political course. In a "Declaration Regarding the Responsibility of the Church in Public Life" churchmen made a complete break with the traditional Lutheran attitude of passive obedience to civil authority. "The terrible experience of the past twelve years," they stated, "has made many persons both inside and outside the German churches realize that only when the fundamentals of the Christian way of life are applied in public affairs is the political community protected from the danger of demonic corruption." The declaration went on: "In recognition of this, the Evangelical Churches of Germany have to assume the enormous and difficult duty of playing a much greater part than before in influencing public life and especially the political community." In spelling out this aim, the statement made it clear that the overriding objective was to be the opening of a dialogue between church and politicians, so that Christian principles might be applied in "all areas of public affairs." While the church would have to strive for cooperation with "all political and social groups," the declaration warned that the church might "associate itself neither with the objectives of an individual party nor be in the slightest influenced in its public statements and its political attitude by party interests."[5]

---

4. Heidtmann (editor), *Kirche im Kampf der Zeit*, pp. 37–38.

5. Merzyn (editor), *Kundgebungen,* pp. 3–4. Whether this declaration was ever officially promulgated by the EKD is a matter of dispute. In any event, the sections quoted here caught the mood prevailing in the church at the time and were symptomatic of the revolutionary rethinking taking place among Protestants. A favorable reference to political cooperation with Catholics in a party based on Christian principles is discussed in Chapter 11, p. 000.

That was the first aim of the majority of church leaders after the war: to destroy the "Obrigkeit"—authority—of the past and to become a force on behalf of Christian principles in public life. Political power—gaining it, using it—was clearly not in the Protestant church's scheme of things. But how can a church be coresponsible for society without exerting direct political influence? There was the rub.

In committing themselves to a clean break with the authoritarianism, illiberalism, and ultraconservatism of the past, Protestant leaders were taking a historic step. The Social Democratic leader, Carlo Schmid, stated in a personal interview that in his view this change, along with Franco-German reconciliation, was the most important salutary development of the postwar period. Of course the pledge was far from the accomplishment. Many Protestants, clergy and lay, still could not grasp that, as Karl Barth once put it, "there is not a single problem harassing the State by which the Church is not also affected in some way or other." Moreover, the early political statements of the church were all combined with such flat declarations of ecclesiastical (and German) guilt as to make the whole notion of church engagement in political affairs widely unpalatable. "A widely-held point of view maintains that the church must be silent on political issues," Bishop Lilje found it necessary as late as 1956 to comment. "But it is not in the least possible to go along with this assertion. For whoever maintains that the Church has to be silent in politics lacks both a correct understanding of politics and a correct understanding of Church." If, however, some of the Protestant rank and file had— and have—qualms, there was no turning back for the leadership. Like it or not, they were thrust into direct political engagement during the occupation period. With the establishment of rival governments in Bonn and Pankow in 1949, the Evangelical church saw itself increasingly touched by the cold war. As a consequence, all of the main issues that have faced the Federal Republic —reunification, Western alliance, rearmament, nuclear weapons—became matters of direct concern to the church. By 1968 the Evangelical church's annual report could note as a matter of course that the council and the church conference had "been frequently and sometimes continuously occupied during each of their sessions with the major domestic and foreign policy questions and controversies," of which "the Vietnam war, emergency legislation, student unrest, and the nuclear non-proliferation treaty naturally figured the most prominently." [6]

---

6. Barth, *Christengemeinde und Bürgergemeinde* (this essay along with some of Barth's other shorter writings referred to in this chapter have been well translated and compiled in R. G. Smith, editor, *Against the Stream*); Lilje, *Kirche und Welt* p. 44; annual report in Evangelische Kirche in Deutschland, *Rechenschaftsbericht 1968,* p. 83.

Individual church leaders, provincial churches, and the central bodies of the EKD have time and again spoken out publicly on such issues. Both the EKD synod and the provincial church synods have at times been virtual forums for political debate. The great majority of the church leadership, no matter how conservative they had been in the past, have participated in these discussions and over the years have moved in a gradual but marked leftward political direction. In its first three council chairmen—Wurm, Dibelius and Scharf—the Evangelical church had three men who were personally convinced that their church held an important political responsibility. However, the current council chairman, Bishop Dietzfelbinger, believing that the Evangelical church has been politically overextended, has sought to withdraw it somewhat from open political controversy. His silence on political affairs at the 1968 session of the EKD synod was so deafening that he came in for strong criticism from many younger theologians. This disagreement highlights the fact that, while there is no longer any question that the church has a political role to play, the extent of this role is still very much disputed. In the words of the annual report for 1968: "There is no less criticism from those who demand a stronger political engagement on the part of the church leadership than from those who accuse it of too much zeal." Here, however, the Evangelical church is grappling with a problem that faces every church. Determining what is Caesar's and what is God's is one of the central problems of Christianity. The problem can only be debated; it can never be solved.

A dilemma that is equally difficult in theory but far more troublesome in practice is finding an acceptable form of political engagement. How can the church be politically engaged without becoming politically committed—or, to phrase it another way, how can the church take action on a concrete political situation without prejudging the technical decisions of the government? The problem is especially acute in Germany where, alone of the countries that are not overwhelmingly Catholic, the church has been a key factor in any political equation simply because of its historic position in society.

As far as the mechanics of politics are concerned, the churches have only the same means of exercising political power as has any other group in society: by establishing a partnership with a political party—through close institutional links and the ability to guarantee political support at and between elections—by influencing parliamentary and government leaders, and finally, by swaying public opinion. Traditionally, Protestant leaders have never really thought in such terms; as a consequence, at the end of the war they had no tradition of political activity. The Evangelical church also has no real "power base," since Protestant group consciousness is weak. But most of all, the Evangelical church simply lacks a "will to power." In this it is far from unique. Protestants of all major traditions—Anglican, Lutheran, and Calvinist—are in full theoretical agreement that the mission of the church is to profess, teach, and appeal, but not to tie itself to a specific political program or a political party. In his famous essay, *Christengemeinde und Bürgergemeinde,* Karl Barth wrote:

> In making itself jointly responsible for the civil community, the Christian community has no exclusive theory of its own to advocate in the face of the various forms and realities of political life. . . .
> In the political sphere the Church will not be fighting for itself and its own concerns. Its own position, influence and power in the State are not the goal which will determine the trend of its political decisions. (p. 18)

Referring to the specific postwar German situation, Professor Ernst Wolf a Göttingen University theologian, in effect spelled out what Barth was driving at:

> The [Evangelical Church] has no political program at all because it has no interests at all of its own to pursue.
> The Church cannot be associated with a political program even to the extent of moral legitimation without losing something of itself.
> I know also of no contemporary program of "Christian policy" whose Christianity can be clearly and convincingly formulated without contradictions, at least from the Protestant side.[7]

In short, according to the Protestant approach, there cannot be and ought not to be a monolithic Christian bloc or single Christian course of action in the political sphere. As the Treysa declaration emphasized, the church must never compromise its political neutrality by associating itself with a particular political party or group. It should seek to have good relations with all parties and should welcome Protestant activity in all parties loyal to the democratic order. There can consequently be no "Christian" political parties and no "Christian" political policies. When the Christian addresses himself to public affairs, he may never claim that his views have divine sanction or that his position alone is Christian. Though Protestants are a social group they can never be a political bloc.

But in practice the situation has never worked out so neatly. Anyone who might have turned in the postwar period to Barth for guidance in "the political service of God" was, indeed, first assured that the Church "must refuse absolutely to be tied down to a political line" but quickly found

---

7. "Kirche and Öffentlichkeit," in Arndt & others, *Christlicher Glaube und politische Entscheidung,* pp. 121, 123.

himself being fitted into a political straitjacket—forbidden to join the CDU, admonished to be actively neutral in the East-West confrontation, told to oppose German rearmament, and so on. The disciple was further assured that in holding these views, he might with complete propriety "act and speak proleptically for the whole church."[8] How did Barth and his German students shift so easily from the principle of political tolerance to the practice of political dogmatism? Barth outlined the intellectual process in the essay *Politische Entscheidung in der Einheit des Glaubens.* Here he sketched out how the Christian should weigh the arguments and counterarguments of a specific course of action:

> As he looks at the backgrounds of the two sets of arguments the Christian confronts the mystery of history and of his own life, in the conflict between the God who rules the world and the chaos that resists him. This is a case where it becomes impossible to say: "Perhaps—or perhaps not!" He has to listen to God's commandment; he has to choose aright not only between a better and a worse, but in accordance with his Christian faith ("as far as the measure will let him": Rom. 12.6), and therefore, in the meaning of Deuteronomy, he has to choose between life and death, God and idols. In the midst of problems of reason and evaluation, the Christian faces the problem of obedience. Since (and the salvation of his soul is at stake!) he can only do justice to the problem in one absolutely definite direction and can answer it in one way only and in no other, he finds himself called and constrained to make a concrete political decision and to stand by his decision, to defend it publicly and to summon other Christians (and non-Christians!) at all costs to take the same decision. (pp. 8-9)

By means of this—not easily comprehensible—theological alchemy, Barth and his followers transformed Christian political responsibility into a rigid political doctrine, so that some Protestant theologians could declare in 1958 that the Christian *must* oppose the nuclear armament of the Bundeswehr and *must* refuse to serve in the Bundeswehr and in 1968 that the Christian *must* support the Viet Cong. In the 1950s Niemöller advised Protestants to vote for one specific party or another and in the 1960s not to go to the polls because none of the parties deserved their votes. In 1950 Heinemann opposed rearmament and in 1958 condemned nuclear weapons for the Bundeswehr with the argument that "God has struck weapons from our hands."

This group of Protestants, moreover, often recognized no limits upon

---

8. *Politische Entscheidung in der Einheit des Glaubens,* pp. 6, 9–10; *Christliche Gemeinde im Wechsel der Staatsordnungen,* p. 44.

political engagement. In 1950 Niemöller (under circumstances described below) met with SPD leaders to discuss ways of preventing German rearmament. During the parliamentary debates on this topic and, subsequently, on conscription, some pastors and theologians took to the streets to demonstrate against government policy. On the other hand, those who did not agree with their views were accused of being theologically soft and politically feckless. In fact, Barth in *Politische Entscheidung* taunted his opponents with the charge that "they have hardly ever pleaded the word of God as the basis of their decision. Why," he asked, "is not the Niemöller who is anti-Adenauer confronted by a Niemöller who is pro-Adenauer?" (p. 10).

The question was not only rhetorical but also loaded, since the contention of the others, particularly the Lutherans, was that there is no unique theologically sound course of action in the political sphere. This point of view was most vigorously argued by the Hamburg University theologian, Helmut Thielicke. Firm in the belief that the church has an obligation to keep abreast of political developments, Thielicke insisted that church leaders had to combat political apathy among Protestants and help the laity to apply Christian principles to practical political and social situations. However, the very complexity of contemporary issues means, he maintained, that the church must on the one hand go beyond enunciating abstract, unexceptionable principles and on the other make no flat assertions that ignore critical facts and beg pertinent questions. Like Barth, Thielicke outlined a decision process, though significantly, his starting point was the church rather than the individual:

> Much as the church must confront the proponents of the two political concepts with questions and admonitions and summon them to take a stand, it may not as a church take a position on the two concepts. . . . It is not the duty of the church to determine which of these two ways is the right one and thereby decide something that is a matter of political judgment. It can only place the responsibility for a decision upon the conscience of the Christians for whom it is responsible, the decision to be made as a Christian. But it cannot give ecclesiastical legitimacy to a specific solution and in that way discredit as heretics those Christians who decided otherwise.[9]

Regarding a 1950 declaration by the Rhineland synod that Germany should not rearm—because rearmament would interfere with social progress, revive nationalism, deepen the division of the country, and psychologically harm the German people—Thielicke commented that the group had used

---

9. *Die Evangelische Kirche und die Politik*, p. 29.

arguments for which it was "patently incompetent" and that "a Protestant theologian could only be ashamed" over such theological irresponsibility (p. 36). Moreover, Heinemann's apothegm, "God has struck weapons from our hands," was, in his view, not only theologically untenable but essentially a political argument dressed up in religious finery. The Christian political duty, to Thielicke, included the obligation to shun sloppy thinking hidden behind a tricky phrase.

Bishop Dibelius, whose years as chairman of the EKD council saw this dispute in its most critical phase, had somehow, in the interests of church unity, to reconcile these two positions. He did so in a way that avoided the arrogance of the one and the restrictiveness of the other. A new chapter in the history of German Protestantism had begun in 1945, he once said to the All-German synod, in the belief that the church had a definite responsibility to the people for the condition of the society in which they lived. But the church had gone as far as it could and must not appear to wish to assume the responsibility belonging to the nation's elected political leaders. The council and the synod, he observed on another occasion, issued pronouncements from time to time on political matters; that, if anyone wondered, was the "official" position of the church. But these statements were in no way binding upon the clergy or the laity. It had never been a Protestant ideal to mold the faithful into a unified political bloc. "An alliance between Protestant church groups and a political party for the purpose of political action," he remarked of Niemöller's meeting with Social Democrats, "contradicts all I have learned to think about the purpose and methods of the church." [10] Despite the political dissension within the church, he commented in an article in *Christ und Welt* in 1951, there was complete agreement on all the important matters. For example, though the church could not but be fully aware of the tragic situation in East Germany, it passionately wanted peace and was therefore opposed to any idea of an anticommunist crusade. Furthermore, while it might be theologically argued that God is indifferent to whether the German people live in one state or five, the Evangelical church ardently favored reunification. Until it was achieved, the church was eager to act as a bond between the two parts of the nation and hoped that an offer to negotiate by one German government would not be rejected by the other. Dibelius always insisted that such questions as whether the Russians planned aggression against the West and whether they would tolerate the creation of a West German army were matters of purely political judgment and therefore ones to

---

10. In *Kirchliches Jahrbuch* 1951, p. 10.

which the church would not address itself. Statements by individual clergymen on these matters were nothing more than personal opinions. For himself
he found it impossible to say that a neutral Germany was more or less
Christian than a rearmed Germany in the Atlantic Alliance. A church based
on the priesthood of the believer had to leave such matters to each individual.

Clearly the Evangelical church has been deeply split on its whole approach to political affairs. On the one hand most of the leadership was more
deeply engaged and more left of center than many of the clergy and laity and
on the other hand it was less committed and more conservative than the
Barth-Niemöller-Heinemann group demanded. The more difficult the problems facing the Federal Republic—and they could scarcely have been more
agonizing—the deeper the church was riven, to the point that in the early
1950s ecclesiastical unity itself was several times threatened. "I can only seek
understanding for my—I might say, desperate—resistance to our Evangelical
Church's being torn apart by political differences," Dibelius wrote privately
to a friend on January 18, 1952. ' I can only hope and pray that the unity of
our church, which we have maintained in spite of everything, does not break
up over these grave difficulties. . . . The divisions which we are experiencing
in our inner-most circles go far deeper than the public realizes." [11] The majority of the church leadership and laity shared Dibelius' apprehension and felt
increasingly uncomfortable with the presence of Niemöller and Heinemann in
their ranks. In their judgment, the Evangelical church was being drawn directly into a political battle that threatened to damage its spiritual mission. As a
result, in 1955 Heinemann was not reelected president of the synod, and
Niemöller lost his seat on the council—a political purge in the view of some.

The repudiation of the two leaders in effect marked the formal rejection
of any attempt to transform German Protestantism into an active, partisan
political force. The vast majority had never wanted this in any case. And the
Barthians, by dividing the church, had destroyed any chance that the chairman of the council of the Evangelical church would be able to speak with the
same authority as the chairman of the Fulda Bishops' Conference. Now the
official course of the EKD was fixed. There would be no political crusades
and certainly no Protestant political army. The church would speak out on
political and social issues. It would even intervene to influence government
policy. But it would appeal, not threaten. In this way the leadership itself
narrowed the margins of the church's political role. Protestant political activi-

---

11. Letter to Dr. Reinhold Saenger, *File Dr. Tillmanns,* Archives of the Evangelical Committee of the CDU/CSU, Bonn.

ty was consequently reduced to rather meek lobbying on the one hand and attempts to influence public opinion at large on the other.

In any event, ridding the council of the "troublemakers" did not settle the point of principle. Disputed again and again, it reached particular virulence in 1958, for instance, when some theologians and clergymen demanded that the church officially make it an article of faith that the Christian must refuse to particiate in preparations for a nuclear war—that is, that a German Protestant must not serve in the Bundeswehr if it were equipped with nuclear weapons. More recently nothing has done more to keep the dispute alive than the "theology of revolution." According to this ideology, the church has a legitimate and necessary responsibility to foster a radical change in the social and economic order. Though the general concept originated in the United States with particular reference to the problems of the Third World and Latin America, it has enjoyed considerable vogue in Germany, especially among theologians anxious to keep up with the youth revolt. While such theologians as Helmut Gollwitzer have grafted this approach on an essentially religious ethic, a larger number tend to see the Second Coming in terms of the destruction of the capitalist system, with the church, helping to bring down the status quo, as a part of a grand millenial process. With some, indeed, the religious aspect of the "theology of revolution" is negligible at best. "Oh, I don't believe in God," one of them put it. "And religion isn't important. But it *is* important that we live together peacefully in a civilized world, and here the church can help."

Painful though they have been, these disputes have over the years served in themselves to fulfill one of the major aims the church set for itself in 1945—to encourage Protestants to face up to invidious political issues and to try to find a solution compatible with Christian principles. Thus, far from attempting to keep their differences "in the family," Protestant leaders have frankly argued them out before the laity. The disagreement over rearmament, for example, had no sooner become a public issue than Dibelius, Niemöller, and Heinemann appeared before a meeting of men's lay organizations to present their contrasting points of view. The pattern has remained the same right down to the present—at synodal meetings, before lay groups, and even in special parish meetings. Churchmen have therefore been more in the public spotlight than some of them liked, and the situation has at times focused attention on matters dividing Protestants rather than those elements that united them. The laity may at times have been as much confused as helped. Throughout the 1950s this impression of an argumentative, divided church contrasted starkly with the outward serenity of German Catholicism, and this situation in itself distressed many Protestants. Although it was difficult to perceive in those years, however, the very freedom to dissent kept intact a subtler, broader unity. The Evangelical church was one of the few institutions in postwar Germany where dissenters, even violent dissenters, were as much a part of the organization as anyone else. This was not only good training for democracy but spared the Evangelical church the grave crisis of confidence that struck the Catholic church in the following decade.

Encouraging Protestants to participate actively in political affairs was another of the outstanding aims which the Evangelical bishops set for themselves at Treysa and which they have followed ever since. At the end of the war the political apathy of the Protestant laity was substantial. From a religious point of view, it is broadly true that Protestantism everywhere, but German Lutheranism in particular, laid such emphasis on religion as a private spiritual matter that the individual layman felt little impetus either to relate his religious ethos to the community's problems or actively to participate in political life. There was a deep strain of thinking among German Protestants that regarded politics as a dirty business. Power, like the ring of the Nibelungen which symbolized it, was thought to bring all who touched it to grief in the end. It was better to be the passive Gutrune than Wotan struggling to influence the course of events. Presumably as a broad consequence, Protestant laymen as a rule went into business or the professions or, at most, the Prussian civil service, but rarely into party politics. This long-standing tendency was reinforced in 1945 by a widespread popular disillusionment with politics, strengthened by denazification, and a lack of confidence in the new parties. Moreover, a relatively high number of politically inclined Protestants were banned from politics because of their National Socialist past. Not only did the CDU/CSU therefore have a problem in recruiting enough Protestant support to make itself genuinely interconfessional, but the Land and federal governments, when they were reconstructed, were also faced with the difficulty of finding suitable persons.

A few Protestant churchmen, such as Bishop Meiser, gave fleeting thought at the war's end to founding a Protestant political party. Several tiny Protestant parties did, in fact, grow up here and there in 1946 and 1947, but they had no ecclesiastical and virtually no popular support and quickly vanished. It was almost instinctively clear that an indirect approach was all that was philosophically feasible in the Protestant camp. Interestingly enough, it was several of the most conservative of the bishops who made the greatest effort in 1945 to encourage lay participation in politics. Meiser, for instance, induced Deacon Langenfass, the head of the Protestant church in Munich, and a number of influential laymen to help organize the CSU. Langenfass traveled around Protestant areas of Bavaria in 1945 and 1946 on the party's behalf and, curiously, had greater success in gaining the support of Protestant clergy and laity than had his Catholic counterpart, Monsignor Emil Muhler, among the Catholic clergy. Marahrens followed a similar course in Hanover, and the clergyman in that case, Church Counsellor Adolf Cillien, was not only a cofounder of the CDU but later a CDU member of the Bundestag. While ecclesiastical leaders have since then discouraged clergymen from participating in partisan politics, the synod and the council of the EKD, provincial church synods, and individual church leaders have repeatedly called upon Protestant laymen to make themselves available for public office in a sense of Christian political responsibility.

It was for just this reason that four prominent laymen entered federal politics after 1949 and took on important positions in the federal government. Hermann Ehlers, a member of the council of the provincial church of Oldenburg, a director of the Hilfswerk, a member of the EKD synod, and a delegate to the 1948 meeting of the World Council of Churches was Bundestag president from 1949 to 1954. Eugen Gerstenmaier, the founder and head of the Hilfswerk and a member of the EKD synod, was president of the Bundestag from 1954 until 1969. Robert Tillmanns, head of the central office of the Hilfswerk in East Germany and a member of the EKD synod, became minister without portfolio in 1953. Gustav Heinemann, the president of the EKD synod and a member of the EKD council, was appointed minister of interior in the first Adenauer cabinet. The four men were anxious to strengthen Protestant influence in the CDU, and Adenauer was delighted to have leading Protestants as important members of his government. Ehlers, Gerstenmaier, and Tillmanns took leaves of absence from their ecclesiastical positions. Heinemann, however, did not; he explained his decision in a letter of November 12, 1949, to Bishop Wurm, in his capacity as chairman of the EKD council:

> It is precisely at this time that I am anxious not to loose my ecclesiastical roots. I should therefore like very much to remain president of the Synod and a member of the Council.
> It appears, however, that reservations arise for several brothers in the Soviet Zone now that two German states exist and the Council of the EKD must of course stay out of any political collusion. [12]

---

12. In *Evangelische Kirche in Deutschland 1949–1951* in *File 220,* Wurm Papers, Württemberg Church Archives, Stuttgart.

The church approved Heinemann's request. The decision was soon seen to have been a mistake, however, both because it tended to compromise the church's fundamental neutrality in the eyes of East German authorities and because his subsequent resignation from the cabinet illustrated the problems the church risked when an important church official became party to a sensational and bitter political dispute. For this reason the EKD has since then not permitted—and probably will never permit—a high government official to be president of the synod or member of the council. When Heinemann became minister of justice in 1966, for instance, he resigned his position in the council. When elected federal president in 1969, he also resigned from his remaining church offices, including membership in the synod. On the other hand, simple membership in the synod by government ministers and political leaders is, if anything, still welcomed.

A variety of institutions have grown up since 1945 to encourage lay involvement in public affairs and to bring churchmen into contact with groups outside the church. The very spontaneity of their development and the fact that they originated with the laity were signs of the new mood in postwar German Protestantism. Most notable among these institutions are the various Protestant academies and related organizations. The first academy was set up at Bad Boll (near Stuttgart) in 1945 by Eberhard Müller and Helmut Thielicke, both theologians and adherents of the Confessional church, as a means of combating the political apathy of Protestants and of relating Christian ideals to the social problems of contemporary life. They chose the term "academy"—in its platonic sense, as a place for a free exchange of views in the search for truth—to emphasize the breadth and nonconfessional nature of the meetings. The academy, novel and daring as it was under postwar conditions, was exactly what Germans needed psychologically and politically after thirteen years of National Socialism. So successful were the first Bad Boll sessions that thirteen similar Protestant academies were founded in the following ten years, and the Catholics unabashedly copied the idea on a more limited scale. Five academies were also established in East Germany and somehow have managed to survive. The academies together hold about a thousand meetings a year with an average attendance of sixty persons at each; altogether about half a million people have attended since 1945. The sessions, completely nonreligious in tone, have dealt with an extraordinary range of topics, a catholicity that has been matched by the variety of persons who have participated—from housewives, workers, and industrialists to doctors, professors, and politicians, including the two federal presidents and the three chancellors up to 1969, as well as a number of foreign notables.

The academy at Tutzing (Bavaria) alone has been attended in recent years by musicians, cabaret artists, ambassadors, most government leaders, Cardinal Döpfner, and the leading German humanist, Gerhard Szczesny. It has on occasion been used as a forum for important political initiatives, such as the formulation in 1966 of Social Democratic policy toward Eastern Europe by Egon Bahr, Willy Brandt's foreign affairs advisor. More American congressmen seem to find their way to Tutzing than to Bonn. The academies have developed far beyond their original purpose, and by wide agreement they are possibly the single most efficacious means of adult political education to have developed in postwar Germany.

A number of specialized academies represent new approaches in German Protestantism and healthy influences in German society. The Social Academy at Friedewald in the Ruhr, founded in 1949, has become a center for meetings on outstanding social issues. Its activities have primarily focused on developing a critical understanding of Marxism and a Christian concept of a democratic social and economic order. Its 25,000 participants over the years have included business executives, civil servants, and industrial workers.

Academy leaders have jointly established a permanent "study group" to organize detailed studies of important problems of contemporary German life. Almost two hundred scholars and experts have participated in this work, and the reports of the group circulate not only in the Evangelical church bodies but in government offices as well. On the whole, activities of this sort and the academies have, in the judgment of one observer, "contributed greatly to some of the most controversial of contemporary problems being approached in a positive and conciliatory spirit." [13]

The success of the academies has led to related ventures in the social sphere. A Protestant Committee for Labor Questions was founded in 1951, followed by the establishment of similar committees for family problems and for agriculture. All the provincial churches have experts on social problems, and in many cities there are "social pastors." The man who has pioneered in Protestant social work, particularly in the labor sphere, is Klaus von Bismarck, the grandnephew of the Iron Chancellor. In 1949 von Bismarck founded "Haus Villigst" in the Ruhr to provide a site for discussions of labor problems and as a place for workers to live together with Protestant laymen. The project has enjoyed the support of the Trade Union Federation, and the meetings at "Haus Villigst" have been attended by several thousand trade union officials and workers from nearby industries. For his work in this field,

13. Hiscocks, *Democracy in Western Germany*, p. 267.

von Bismarck was in 1954 given the University of Hamburg's Freiherr vom Stein prize, an award for persons who have made an outstanding contribution toward improving social relations.

The church assembly (Kirchentag) is another instrument through which the Evangelical church has tried to stimulate lay interest in political, social, and economic affairs. As in the case of the academies, these biennial sessions were enormously successful from the start—200,000 persons attended the 1951 meeting in Essen—and quickly broadened into something far beyond their founders' dreams. In an interview, the late Professor James Pollock, a civil affairs advisor to the American Military Government, expressed the view that the meetings fulfilled better than anything else the craving of the German people in the first postwar years for fresh, liberal, and humane political ideals. For this reason they became, he felt, the Evangelical church's most important channel of political influence in the decade after 1945. A centerpiece of the discussions at the assemblies has always been the discussion group on political questions in which both theologians and laymen participate. These are the best attended and most spirited of all the various groups, and over the years they have given Protestants a unique opportunity to argue out their differences face to face. They have been a useful national forum for airing controversial and unconventional ideas. At the 1956 session, to cite a single example, the German Ambassador to Yugoslavia, Kurt Pfleiderer, discussed a strategy of movement in the German attitude toward eastern Europe; this was at the height of the Adenauer era, and a full decade before this idea became policy. In ways such as this, a *Manchester Guardian* correspondent observed on August 6, 1956, the church assembly came to embody "within itself many of the burning questions to which every responsible German must find his own answer, and to an outsider at least it seems that only good can come of public discussion of them on a theological, and not merely a political, basis." It is as such that they were intended by their founder, Reinnold von Thadden-Trieglaff, who always stressed that a continuing process of education in the fundamentals of Protestantism and liberal democracy were necessary to assure a healthy German state.

As a more direct expression of the church's sense of social and political responsibility, the council, the synod and the church conference have made official pronouncements on the entire range of important national issues since 1945. The aim of these statements has been both to influence political leaders in a direction church leaders consider to be wise and to arouse popular thinking about major public issues. This is the church in its capacity as the nation's conscience. More than 175 statements, declarations, and open letters have been promulgated over the years. In the early postwar period a dozen or so of these contained acknowledgments of guilt for the Third Reich, along with advice and encouragement regarding the material and spiritual difficulties then being experienced. Another twenty-two statements concerned occupation policies—denazification, land reform in the Soviet Zone, the return of prisoners of war, and so on. Over the years there have been five declarations on the problems of German expellees from the Oder-Neisse territories, seventeen on social issues (such as industrial codetermination, lotteries, and compensation to victims of Nazism), thirty-eight on the difficulties of the church in East Germany, and twelve on schools and education. In addition, there have been one or more statements on such topics as German guilt for anti-Semitic atrocities, trade unions, sports, reparations, war crimes, Marxism, the press, housing, elections, and human rights. But the most passionate declarations of all were the thirty concerning peace and reunification and the effects on these of German rearmament.

With the passage of time it was increasingly felt, both inside and outside the church, that ecclesiastical declarations were simply ecclesiastical declamations. There had been no national spiritual renaissance. The more appeals launched on behalf of reunification, the further the two parts of the country moved apart, it was argued. There is some Teutonic overcriticism in this attitude—exaggerated disillusionment following unwarranted expectations. In fact, through its declarations the Evangelical church over the years has built up a corpus of viewpoints that made it a clearly progressive social force. Moreover, its recommendations on the relationship that should be established between the two German governments were fifteen years ahead of their time. (This is discussed in Chapter 9, pp. 254–256.) If a church can establish this sort of record, its views deserve to be taken very seriously by any government. In any case, churchmen were increasingly of the view that general statements, keyed to Biblical or theological arguments, offered an inadequate basis for a public discussion of important issues. For this reason by the 1960s the church came to make fewer declarations and to sanction instead brief, tightly written, expert studies of certain social and political problems.

So far there have been five such memoranda, as these are called: on property ownership, on part-time employment of married women, on the reorganization of German agriculture, on the Oder-Neisse question, and on what the German people can do to maintain peace. Although the first three sought to break new ground in important social problems, it was the "Memorandum on Expellees and the Relationship of the German People to Their Eastern Neighbors" that created the greatest public stir when it was issued in

1966. By arguing on theological, historical and political grounds that Germany has no right to reclaim the Oder-Neisse territories, the memorandum provoked widespread discussion of the issue and had thereby precisely the effect intended. The theory of the new approach is that the memoranda, not representing ex cathedra pronouncements, can therefore be more concrete, specific, and daring in substance. Church leaders appear to believe that in this way they can promote a specific and, if necessary, controversial political course of action without assuming full responsibility for these views. Only time will tell if this ambiguous approach will work.

To advise the EKD council and to assist in the preparation of reports and ecclesiastical declarations, a variety of commissions, study groups, and bureaus have been established; the most important of these are the Commission for Public Affairs, the Commission for Social Affairs, the Commission for Family Legislation, the Commission for Questions of Sexual Ethics, the Committee for Traffic and Transportation Matters, the Commission for Public Media, and the Commission for Education, Training, and Instruction. There is also a permanent study group, headquartered in Heidelberg, under the direction of a Tübingen University political scientist, Professor Ludwig Raiser (who also assumed the presidency of the synod in 1970). The study group has issued a number of formidable monographs, the most recent of which concerned the nonproliferation treaty. In 1965 it issued a three-volume study of the Bundeswehr which was the most penetrating sociological study of that topic that has so far been published.

What all this adds up to is a church consciously struggling to show some responsibility to society, a church at the same time striving to keep itself in touch with the variety of forces in this society. As the *Süddeutsche Zeitung* remarked on October 28, 1968, the man on the street has the general impression that the main function of the two churches is to propound in sermons and on television a conservative view on sexual morals. "Or put colloquially: we pay church taxes so we can be given a bad conscience. Against this general view, the annual report of the EKD for 1969 makes highly surprising reading." As indeed it does. For almost 270 pages the report reviews the church's activities in fields as diverse as the underdeveloped countries, the penal code, education, family problems, foreign and defense affairs, disarmament, the continuing problems of refugees and expellees, the complexities of copyright law, computers, and criminal law. It is impossible to measure the interacting influences of church and society or to quantify the value of such efforts. But in style and aim they clearly place the Evangelical church among the important forces serving to fortify liberal democracy in Germany.

Clearly the essence of the Evangelical Church's political approach has been one of indirect influence on behalf of a general objective. Unwavering neutrality toward the political parties was a central principle. Not only was this a logical consequence of Protestant philosophy, it was a practical necessity in view both of the political disagreements among church leaders and of the Protestant lack of cohesiveness. The church could not lead in a partisan direction and the laity would not have followed had it tried. Moreover, the Protestant bishops, whatever their personal political views, wanted to have active laymen in all the parties and were determined to establish a confident relationship between the church and these parties. Only once did the church qualify this rule. That was in the latter half of the 1960's when it quietly requested pastors to discourage, as appropriate and as discreetly as possible, Protestant support for the neo-Nazi National Democratic Party (NPD). The NPD was receiving most of its support from Protestants and the church leadership, concerned by the party's deleterious impact on German politics and the Federal Republic's international standing, sought to cut off the party's major source of strength.

In short, Protestants were politically on their own. The church spoke out on major postwar issues and encouraged a debate of them—in ecclesiastical publications, at its academies as well as at synodal meetings and the church assemblies—but it was up to the laity to draw their own conclusions. As a consequence church ties had no direct effect on Protestant voting behavior. Public opinion polls,[14] it is true, suggest that regular Protestant churchgoers (generally estimated at 10-20 percent of all Protestants) were in the early postwar years more inclined to support the Christian Democrats than those attending infrequently or never, who strongly favored the Social Democrats. This, however, necessarily resulted from social rather than ecclesiastical considerations and in time moderated so that by 1961 the CDU enjoyed among church-goers no appreciable preference over the SPD.

More important than such estimates is the actual voting behavior of Protestants as a whole and this is unambiguous. In stark contrast to Catholics, Protestants voted for the party that appeared best to serve their economic

---

14. See, for instance, Erich Reigrotzki, *Soziale Verflechtungen in der Bundesrepublik; Elemente der sozialen Teilnahme in Kirche, Politik, Organisationen und Freizeit* (1959), especially pp. 130–134; DIVO, *Undersuchung der Wählerschaft und Wahlentscheidung, 1957* (1959), especially p. 162; and Karl-Heinz Diekershoff, *Das Wahlverhalten von Mitgliedern organisierter Interessengruppen; Dargestellt am Beispiel der Bundestagswahlen 1961*, especially pp. 75, 191, 219, 225, 227.

Table 1
Voting preference of Protestants (1961) [15]

frequency of church attendance	number of respondents	CDU	SPD	other	no information
weekly	44	34%	30%	25%	11%
monthly	112	40%	29%	17%	14%
several times a year	167	32%	37%	13%	18%
seldom; never	188	24%	46%	11%	19%

and social interests. Religious considerations and ecclesiastical loyalty were minor motivational factors at most and on the whole worked negatively rather than positively. This can best be observed in relatively "pure" Protestant areas, even though, for reasons to be explained, the CDU's strength in strongly Protestant areas is disproportionately larger than in mixed and Catholic areas. Similarly, in Protestant areas there was no ecclesiastical or social pressure on behalf of a specific political party. For these reasons electoral results in Protestant areas varied little with the normally-assumed indexes of such influences—age, sex, and the size of the community. Even against the general assumption that women, especially older women in rural areas, tend to be more conservative than men and younger persons especially in urban areas, Protestant women showed a remarkable independence. In the 1953 election 32% voted for the CDU, 32% for the SPD and the remaining 35% for other parties. Furthermore, in the 1961 election, Protestant women over sixty in small towns "voted about evenly for the CDU/CSU and for the SPD." [16] Urban, small town and rural Protestants displayed a great similarity in the way they voted, as is clear from Table 2.

But Protestant independence of political judgment was not new in German politics. Nor was the other outstanding characteristic of Protestant voting behavior: the absence, at least in the early postwar period, of a firm political commitment. This was reflected in the drastic fissiperation of the Protestant vote. Until about the mid-1950s Protestants were dispersed in

---

15. Karl-Heinz Diekershoff, op. cit., p. 219.

16. Statistiches Bundesamt, *Band 100, Die Wahl zum 2. Deutschen Bundestag am 6.9.1953*, Heft 2 *(1955)*, pp. 70–71 (The available figures do not include Rhineland-Palatinate and Bavaria.); *ibid., Fachserie A, Bevölkerung und Kultur, Reihe 8, Wahl zum 4. Deutschen Bundestag am 17. September 1961*, Heft 4 (1965), p. 46. It is, however, true that the CDU enjoyed the support of a somewhat higher percentage of Protestant women than men and the SPD of Protestant men than women.

Table 2
Voting pattern in Protestant
communities by size (1961) [17]

| percentage | communities with fewer than 3,000 inhabitants | | |
of Protestants	CDU/CSU	SPD	other
over 90%	35%	34%	31%
80%-90%	31%	41%	28%
	communities with 3,000 to 50,000 inhabitants		
over 90%	32%	45%	23%
80%-90%	34%	43%	23%
	communities with more than 50,000 inhabitants		
over 90%	—	—	—
80%-90%	36%	40%	24%

roughly equal portions across the political spectrum, from the neutralist parties and the SPD on the left, to the CDU in the center and the various small, arch-conservative parties on the right. It is not suprising that Protestantism, which because of its very nature gave birth to a variety of radical fringe groups—sects—should have produced a similar phenomenon of radicalism and protest in politics. This took shape over the years in the Protestant backing for one or another of the several anti-establishment "political sects" of which Heinenmann's All-German People's party (GVP) was the most notable. Appropriately this party reached its peak of strength (following sorry failure on the national level in the 1953 federal election) in Württemberg, precisely the area of Germany in which Protestant sects had for centuries been strongest, where the overwhelmingly Protestant constituency of Freudenstadt gave the GVP 18% of the vote in the March 1956 Land election. Heinemann's own political peregrination—from being a founder and prominent member of the CDU, to a period of political uncertainty, followed by his organizing the GVP and concluding with membership and rising to unprecedented prominence in the SPD—was symptomatic of the political development of those Protestants, typified by the brotherhoods of the Confessing church, who were uncomfortable with established institutions and who were motivated by deep moral conviction rather than practical political considerations.

Another and more significant cause of the Protestant lack of political commitment sprang from a fundamentally different situation. This was the

17. ibid., p. 45.

long-standing *Heimatlosigkeit* or political "homelessness" of Protestants which for understandable reasons took extreme form in the political conditions of the immediate postwar period. Those of the Protestant bourgeoisie who had been anti-Nazi and who favored, or could accept, a new approach in political affairs, including political cooperation with Catholics, went into the CDU. Those who were socialists—especially Protestant workers—returned to the SPD. But in the early postwar years these together were a minority. For the other Protestants, especially those of the national-conservative tradition who were generally antipathetic to Catholics and socialists, there was no real political home and no alternatives. It was in this milieu that there grew up a great variety of regional and special interest parties, such as the South Schleswig Voters' League in Schleswig, the German party of the Right, the Socialist Reich party and the German party in the north; the Economic Reconstruction League, the German Community and the Bavarian party in Bavaria; and the National Concentration in the far north and far south. Except for the Bavarian party these parties were for all practical purposes entirely Protestant in membership and support and to the right of center, the Socialist Reich party being manifestly neo-Nazi. Even the Free Democrat party, though unquestionably founded on the German liberal tradition, deliberately cultivated this ground and owed its early successes, at least outside Württemberg, to Protestant right wing, in part ex-National Socialist, in part anti-clerical support.

As a result, in the 1949 federal election the predominantly Protestant constituencies throughout Germany, with remarkably few exceptions, gave a plurality to parties other than the CDU and the SPD. In the case of Flensburg, for instance, no fewer than 85 percent of the votes cast were for small, special interest parties, parties which in every case eventually disappeared from the political scene. Furthermore, in the strongly Protestant districts of Waldeck, Kassel, Fritzlar, Marburg, Wetzlar, Giessen, Wiesbaden, Darmstadt, Salzgitter, Stuttgart (south), Heilbronn and Waiblingen, the FDP alone received more votes than either the CDU or the SPD.

Nothing could better have illustrated the political rootlessness of these Protestants than their response to the establishment, shortly after the 1949 election when occupation licensing requirements lapsed, of a party for expellees and refugees—the Bloc of those Driven from their Homes and Deprived of their Rights (BHE). The party was designed, as its name suggested, to appeal not only to expellees and refugees but to those who had temporarily lost their civil rights as a result of denazification. As such it had an obvious attraction to conservative Protestants and drew roughly twice as much support from Protestants as Catholics. Within six months of being founded, the BHE secured 23 percent of the vote in the Schleswig-Holstein Land election, taking voters at once from the CDU (which lost 11 percent of its 1949 vote) and from the small parties of the right (which dropped by 9 percent) while, significantly, leaving the SPD essentially unscathed. This result was repeated in Land after Land in subsequent months. In short, the BHE was not merely a party of and for refugees and expellees but a rallying-point for those conservatives who had no firm attachment to another party—that is, it was one more temporary home for Protestants of the right. But naturally enough, the BHE was vulnerable to the same lack of political commitment that it had initially turned to its advantage. From the time of the 1953 election campaign the Christian Democrats made a more determined effort than ever to spread out from the Catholic-oriented center to embrace Protestant conservatives. So, after having fed on the right, the BHE soon found that most of its substance was being swallowed whole by the CDU. It could not compensate by absorbing fresh refugees from East Germany since to them "the right" as such had little attraction and they therefore went directly into either the CDU because of its anti-communism or the SPD because of its social policy. The BHE's decline and, with the 1957 election, disappearance from the Bundestag was paralleled by the parties explicitly of the right as well.

The general characteristics of Protestant voting behavior can be gauged from the outcome of the seven postwar federal elections in two strongly Protestant constituencies, Eschwege and Kassel, both in the same area of northern Hesse. Eschwege, 82 percent Protestant and 15 percent Catholic, is a rural constituency with the largest portion of the population engaged in small-scale manufacturing. Kassel, a city of approximately 240,000 inhabitants, with 37 percent of its population workers, is 82 percent Protestant and 16 percent Catholic [Table 3]. These two constituencies illustrate how Protestants on the whole voted in the postwar period. From the first, the SPD clearly enjoyed the loyalty of a substantial percentage of Protestants, receiving a far larger proportion of Protestant support than any other single party, with this support steadily increasing as the Social Democrats broke further and further into the Protestant middle class. Typically, of the ten electoral districts where the Social Democrats did best in the 1961 election, all were predominantly Protestant with the two marginal exceptions of Essen and Duisburg, industrial centers with a slight Catholic preponderance. By contrast, Protestant support for the CDU was in 1949 so modest that the CDU in some Protestant areas was merely one of a number of minor parties and in a few districts the Christian Democrats did not even put up a candidate in the first federal election. However, by 1953 Protestant support for the CDU had virtually doubled and, apart from the 1961 election this support has steadily if gradually expanded. By contrast, the vote for the FDP and the splinter parties has generally varied inversely to the CDU's success with Protestant voters.

Table 3
Eschwege

	CDU	SPD	other
1949	11%	41%	48%
1953	23%	44%	33%
1957	28%	49%	23%
1961	24%	54%	22%
1965	28%	56%	15%
1969	30%	59%	11%
1972	31%	61%	8%

Kassel

	CDU	SPD	other
1949	12%	39%	49%
1953	28%	40%	32%
1957	34%	46%	20%
1961	30%	48%	22%
1965	37%	51%	17%
1969	32%	55%	13%
1972	33%	55%	12%

Although there has been a slow but dramatic increase in the Protestant political commitment, a Protestant political bloc has never developed. However, substantial numbers of Protestants could be and at times were actuated by a vague confessional "self-defense" instinct. This is not immediately apparent from voting statistics since it is a state of mind that tends to operate negatively rather than positively. The crude confessional appeals of the All-German People's party in the 1953 election, for example, failed because of the practical impossibility of rallying Protestants on behalf of a specific political cause. Heinemann's experiment was the acid test of Protestant solidarity and when it failed no further attempts were ever again made to form a Protestant party even though the GVP did not dissolve itself until 1957. But if Protestants could not be mobilized *for* a cause, many were animated by a desire to defend themselves from putative external threat. It was this that in the early postwar period inhibited some Protestants from supporting the SPD because of its anti-clericalism and Marxism. By the same token the CDU's claim to be a Christian party which protected the interests of the churches attracted few Protestants, while the belief that the CDU was a Catholic-dominated party which worked against the interests of German Protestantism frightened many away from it. This residual mistrust of the Catholic role in the CDU was a highly significant factor in the voting behavior of some Protestants and explains a number of important and otherwise puzzling electoral phenomena.

In all postwar federal elections since 1953 the CDU vote has been inverse to the proportion of Protestants in the population, up to the point where Protestants are a majority of the population when the decline in CDU vote either levels off (as in 1953 and 1957) or is reversed (as in 1961, 1965 and 1969). The SPD vote shows an opposite trend: rising directly with the percentage of Protestants, again to the point where they become a majority when it declines. The FDP vote consistently rises with the proportion of Protestants though the extent of the increase has varied from one election to another. Moreover, in 1961 and 1965 the party did as well in confessionally-mixed areas as in strongly Protestants ones and in 1953 actually had its greatest successes in the former. Its huge gain in 1961 at the expense of the Christian Democrats may have reflected—since the CDU vote in strongly Catholic communities in fact increased in that year—a largely, or purely, Protestant shift from the CDU to the FDP and some extent the SPD. These various developments can be clearly seen in the diagram on page 144, which shows the results of the elections of 1961 and 1965.

What appears to have lain behind these electoral pheneomena was a residue of suspicion on the part of politically uncommitted Protestants toward Catholic control of the CDU. Because of this the Protestant vote for the CDU tended to fluctuate from election to election and area to area, depending upon the Protestant perception of the confessional condition of the CDU. Where the CDU fell under suspicion of being a crypto-Catholic organization, some Protestants voted for another party. This occurred in every election in constituencies that were predominantly Catholic or confessionally-mixed where the CDU was in Catholic hands. It was here that the SPD and FDP tended to do their best. In strongly Protestant constituencies the CDU was an essentially Protestant party and as a result received a high proportion of Protestant votes. Suspicions also fluctuated in time. What changed between 1961 and 1965, for example, was not the CDU's policies, which had not altered in the slightest, but the party's leadership which came into Protestant hands in 1963. The consequence was a nearly 10 percent increase in the CDU vote in predominantly Protestant areas in the federal election two years later. On the whole, as will be further discussed later, Protestant support for the CDU has been relatively volatile, declining and rising with the confession-

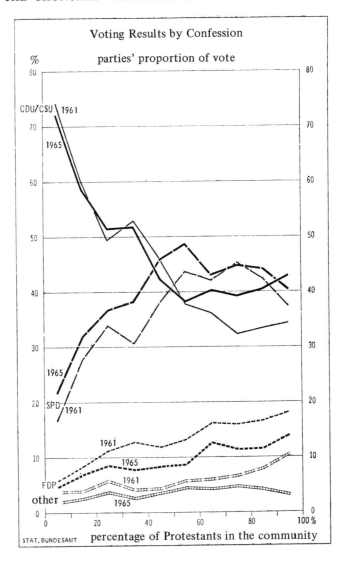

Voting Results by Confession

parties' proportion of vote

percentage of Protestants in the community

STAT. BUNDESAMT

al tone of the party. This contrasts with the relatively smooth growth of Protestant support for the SPD, since, for reasons explained, Protestant CDU voters are less committed to their party than are Protestant SPD voters to theirs.

In summary, Protestants have been a dynamic and somewhat destabiliz- ing force in politics. As will become clear in subsequent chapters, this has had far-reaching consequences. Briefly, Protestants have constituted a powerful inducement to the two major parties to move to the right in an attempt to pick up uncommitted Protestant voters. At the same time Protestant political behavior effectively forestalled those persons and those tendencies which would have confessionalized politics. By downgrading the political relevance of confessional issues, Protestants could not be swayed by religious considerations or appealed to on a confessional basis. While they could neither be tempted to follow Catholics into the CDU to form a "Christian front" against the other parties nor be prodded into the SPD to combat the "Catholic policies" of the CDU, they forced the SPD to be ideologically neutral and the CDU confessionally so. In these ways Protestants, despite the unpredictable element which·they injected into politics, had a strongly secularizing influence on the parties. This in turn reinforced the already narrow limits of the Evangelical church's own political role.

Only secondarily has the Evangelical church sought to influence political affairs through direct intervention with the government. Significantly these approaches have almost always concerned policies with far-reaching political and social consequences rather than matters affecting the more immediate interests of the Evangelical church itself. Its major appeals have addressed themselves not only to such broad issues as reunification, codetermination in industry, and the establishment of a nonconfessional trade union movement, but to rearmament, conscription, broader rights for conscientious objectors to military service, and equipping the Bundeswehr with tactical nuclear weapons. The council of the Evangelical church has devoted much of its sessions to a discussion of political and social problems and, on the basis of these discussions, has often conveyed its views privately to the chancellor or a particular government minister. Bishops have also interceded by calling upon or writing to political officials.

The church's outright lobbying activities are conducted by the council's official representative to the federal government. This position, the first of its kind in the history of the Evangelical church, was created by the council in March 1950 and has been held since its establishment by Bishop Hermann Kunst. Kunst's terms of reference instruct him "to keep in continuing touch with the principal officials of the federal government, the Bundestag and its Protestant members. In particular he has the responsibility of informing the Church Chancellery of the Council of the EKD about the political situation and [of informing] the principal officials of the Federal Republic about the general views and current interests of the EKD. He is, moreover, to assume responsibility for the spiritual affairs of Protestant members of federal agencies and offices."[18] A branch of the church chancellery was established at the

---

18. Directive of the EKD Council, March 8, 1950; archives of the Representative of the EKD Council to the Federal Government, Bonn.

same time in Bonn. Its staff keeps informed about and makes suggestions regarding legislation being drafted in the various ministries.

Kunst's role and influence have grown considerably over the years. His office and the branch church chancellery have developed from a channel of formal church-to-government contact into a powerful influence throughout the government. By means of contact with political leaders and thanks to confidential "contact men" in every ministry and bureau of the government, the office is probably better informed than any other in Bonn, apart from its Catholic counterpart and the chancellor's office.

Kunst's office (supported by the branch church chancellery) has three functions, broadly speaking. It works as an open pressure group regarding matters of legislation and executive policy affecting either direct church interests or what are considered the broad moral interests of the nation. For example, it played a decisive role in the drafting of family, marriage, and divorce legislation and brought strong influence to bear in the drafting of military-conscription legislation on behalf of conscientious objectors. It was also involved in the major penal law reform of 1969. Kunst has also had discussions with government leaders regarding outstanding political issues—in 1968 alone, for example, emergency legislation, the nonproliferation treaty, Vietnam, Biafra, and German policy in Eastern Europe and toward East Germany. A second function is to defend general Protestant interests in the government. "Personalpolitik," for instance, was of much concern in the mid-1950s, and while confessional competition for government jobs has since then become much less acute, Personalpolitik is still the object of a watchful eye by the office and its ministerial "contact men." The final of the office's functions is to offer sympathy and counsel to anyone who seeks it—as many do. Ministers and other government officials with personal or professional problems have often turned to Kunst as someone from whom they can expect, not bland Christian generalities, but sophisticated political and moral judgments. Kunst himself sees this as by far the most important aspect of his work. In short, the main intent and method of Kunst's and the church chancellery's activity are dissimilar from the normal form of lobbying in America and Britain, where paid agents protect and promote an organization's interests. The former are rather a standing channel of communication, by which government officials and church leaders can be sure they understand the viewpoints and objectives of the other.

The style of operation has been rigorously set by Kunst himself. While receiving his directives from the council of the EKD, whose meetings he regularly attends, he has enjoyed wide independence of action. From the first he threw himself into the work with vigor and imagination but at the same time with marked outward reserve and discretion. He has often stressed that the principal value of the office to the church and to the government is less as a lobby to influence the government and the Bundestag than as a channel through which the church can receive full and accurate information about what is occurring in political circles and vice versa. In this sense his approach has consistently been more passive than active: on the whole keeping himself available if called upon, without aggressively pushing for specific political objectives. In the early 1950s, however, he did cooperate with Hermann Ehlers, the Protestant CDU leader, in organizing periodic informal meetings of all Protestant parliamentarians and civil servants. While the purpose of these sessions was to discuss either a political issue of moment or a problem facing the Evangelical church, an intended side effect was to increase the cohesiveness of Protestants, at least the Christian Democrats among them. By the mid-1950s, after Ehlers' death, the meetings were only rarely held; they were, however, revived in the early 1960s and have occurred fairly regularly since that time. Similar sessions were organized in 1953 for civil servants. These are held twice a year and are generally attended by a total of about 700 officials. The discussion topics are sometimes political and sometimes ecclesiastical. Recent sessions have concerned such issues as student unrest and the nonproliferation treaty.

Kunst has always cast *his* net wide, seeking to reach not just Protestants and not only government leaders. In the 1950s his patient cultivation of Social Democrats gained him such confidence in party circles that he was invited to address the SPD party congress in 1958, the first ecclesiastical figure to have done so in the party's history. In the process of forging contacts with the Social Democrats, Kunst became close to the man who has called the tune for the party during the last decade, Herbert Wehner. But Kunst's closest contact in the government is probably Gerhard Schröder, former defense minister and chairman of the Evangelical committee of the CDU/CSU.

Kunst's personal role has probably increased more over the years than has his political influence as the offical representative of the EKD. Universally respected, he is generally reckoned in Bonn to have all the skill of a natural politician—according to a local pun, *ein geborener Künstler* (a true artist). On the scene since the founding of the Federal Republic, he has known everyone of political influence and has been a well-informed observer of every event of importance. Thanks to his outstanding discretion in a notoriously indiscreet capital, as well as to his general political impartiality (though he is well known to be a practicing Christian Democrat), he is consulted by high government leaders and from time to time is asked to conduct highly delicate missions. He was also one of the very few persons trusted by President Lübke in his last years of agony in office. As a result, Kunst was one of the persons to whom the Christian Democrats turned in seeking to persuade the President to resign his office before the end of the term.

Kunst, an official of the Westphalian provincial church prior to his appointment to the present position was also the Protestant military bishop from 1956 to 1972. In 1958 he was given the rank and styling of bishop, a unique honor in the Evangelical church and a mark of the council's judgment of his performance. The council's very confidence in him and the willingness of the provincial churches to entrust him entirely with the handling of government operations, has placed Kunst in a stronger position than his Catholic counterpart, who often finds himself in the cross fire of intrachurch dissension and competition from the central committee of German Catholics.

"Not everything that is black in Bonn is Catholic," a Catholic church official once remarked in an interview. Certainly Kunst and the Evangelical chancellery in Bonn have not been shy about advancing Protestant interests in the government. Yet the fundamental political approach of the Evangelical church since 1945 has been both different and more ambitious than the simple pursuit of ecclesiastical advantage. Protestant leaders wanted influence rather than power, but the influence that they sought was to change the political course of German Protestantism and the political values of German society. This was the church in its "prophetic" role, a role accepted by the conservatives no less than by the progressives in the church. The dispute among them has largely concerned whether the church should direct its efforts primarily inward upon itself or outward upon society. Here the orthodox Lutheran response was bound to differ from that inspired by Calvin and Barth. At present it is the conservative Lutherans, Bishop Dietzfelbinger and more recently the new head of the VELKD, Bishop Hans-Otto Wölber of Hamburg, whose approach prevails. These are not the men of Stuttgart and Treysa. As a result, the political debates in the church are dying down, and the church is falling into silence. While this could be the silence of internal accord, it may be the more ominous silence of a group whose two extremes are so far apart that they have nothing to say to one another and have given up the attempt to communicate. Can German Protestantism find a middle way between its antipodal tendencies of quiescence and revolt? The answer appears as remote as ever.

6 | The Political Ethic of German Catholicism

IF Protestant churchmen were convinced at the war's end that their mistake prior to 1933 had been a lack of political responsibility, the Catholic hierarchy saw its error as too close an implication in the events leading up to the Third Reich. To avoid ever again running such a risk, the bishops were determined to keep their church and clergy out of active politics. To the bishops, one of the most telling arguments after the war in support of a new, interconfessional party was that a reestablishment of the Center party would inevitably revive "political prelates"—priests who were not only party officials, but also members of parliamentary bodies from the municipal to the national level. Moreover, despite the uncertainty of the status of the Reichskonkordat and its political articles, it was widely assumed that clerical participation in politics would be at least unwise and possibly illegal. By the same token, most Catholic political and lay leaders believed that the church had so badly compromised itself in 1933, especially in concluding the Reichskonkordat, that they had little or no respect for the bishops' political judgment and no intention of further political cooperation with the hierarchy. The great majority of Catholic political leaders and bishops therefore found themselves in agreement in 1945 that the church itself should avoid direct participation in political affairs.

Important as it was, however, the change was a tactical one on the church's part. In turning away from open political activity, the bishops had no intention of surrendering their influence over issues which they considered vital to society and the church's own interests. They also undoubtedly took it for granted that "political Catholicism" in Germany would be revived—that is, the faithful would form themselves into a solid rank and march together toward specific political goals. Politics would be left in the hands of the laity, but those hands would need ecclesiastical guidance—no more and no less.

Consequently, while a visitor to postwar Germany might easily be more impressed by the church's deep political involvement than by its distance

149

from politics, as compared to the situation before 1933 there has been a marked withdrawal from direct clerical participation in political affairs. Although the church has never wavered in its support for the CDU both at and between election times, it always made a point—indeed, a fine art—of not mentioning the party by name and of leaving direct support activities to the lay organizations. Priests have rarely appeared at election-campaign rallies and have not openly canvassed for votes. With very few exceptions, they have not sat in local councils or Land parliaments, and when Father Franz Ott was elected to the Bundestag as a member of the Refugee party in 1949, he was defrocked by the Bishop of Rottenburg.[1] In its political pronouncements and its lobbying activities, the church has deliberately sought to be as discreet as possible. This led on the one hand to an extravagant secretiveness about the dabbling in politics that it in fact engaged in and on the other to one of its strongest differences over the years with such Christian Democratic leaders as Adenauer, Josef Müller, and Franz-Josef Strauss, who wanted the unreserved and undisguised support of the clergy.

The extent of this disengagement has, however, been both limited and characterized by sharp contradictions. On the philosophical plane alone, Catholicism, in contrast to Protestantism, rejects the notion that church and state are separate spheres and claims an important place for the church in political and social life. This central part of Catholicism was in no way altered even at the height of the generally liberal reign of Pope John XXIII, who stated in his Encyclical *Mater et Magistra* (as quoted in *The New York Times* on July 15, 1961), "The Church has the right and obligation not merely to guard ethical and religious principles but also to intervene authoritatively in the temporal sphere where it is a matter of judging the application of these principles to concrete cases." Consequently the Catholic church in Germany (as in some other European countries) has considered its temporal aims to be

---

1. In Ott's case the CDU, which was unwilling to suffer the humiliation of a priest active in another party, strongly encouraged the bishop to make this decision. The two exceptions in Land parliaments were Monsignor Georg Meixner, chairman of the CSU in the Bavarian parliament, and Monsignor Franz Hermann, chairman of the CDU in the Baden-Württemberg parliament. Cardinal Wendel of Munich, however, once forbade a priest to stand in a Land election while Cardinal Frings by contrast pressed the CDU in Münster to put up a priest, Monsignor Schreiber, in the Bundestag election of 1949. The party declined the archbishop's request on the ground that "it is certainly out of the question that under present circumstances clergymen could be elected to the federal parliament." Letter, undated, from Paul Steup (Manager of Westphalian CDU) to Voss (Chairman of Münster CDU), *File 322–33 Münster Stadt*, Archives of the Westphalia-Lippe CDU, Dortmund.

"Christian policies" and the party supporting them to be a "Christian party." To a hierarchy, moreover, accustomed since the Kulturkampf to a Catholic population that was psychologically and politically largely united and under the bishops' direction, it was difficult to make a clean break with tradition. Although this unity had begun to unravel during the Weimar Republic, at the end of the war the bishops were obsessed with the dangers of the postwar period, and as an automatic reflex, did everything in their power to mold Catholics into a monolithic bloc. In 1946 Cardinal Frings, for instance, said to a British church group (which he had nearly refused to receive because it was interconfessional), "The work of reconstruction should be done by Catholics and Protestants in alliance but each acting separately." [2] He and the other bishops wanted Catholic secondary schools, a comprehensive range of Catholic lay and professional organizations, a Catholic trade union, a Catholic press and radio station, a Catholic university, and a Catholic political party— in short, an organizational infrastructure to encompass Catholics from the cradle to the grave.

> We want a concentration and activation of Catholic forces. We want to put an end to the crippling division and dispersion of our forces. We want to fight against the old deadly evil of pusillanimity and division of our forces, of irresolution and apathy, of feelings of inferiority and of lack of daring.
> Neither democracy in itself nor a state formally based on the rule of law offers Catholics . . . enough guarantees. Therefore the necessity of banding together exists as much today as in the time of our fathers.[3]

These were the themes, repeated over and over, of German Catholicism in the two decades after the war.

This attitude had profound sociological and political consequences. For twenty years German Catholicism was inclined to self-isolation and within its own world had no room for dissent or dissenters. The Catholic assemblies, academies, lay organizations, and press were organized so as to prevent non-conformists from having a voice or position of authority. Lay groups made little or no provision for an exchange of views at their meetings; the leaders (rarely elected in any truly democratic sense) laid down the line, and the

---

2. Report on meeting between Frings, Bishop of Chichester, and Bishop of Nottingham on November 19, 1946, File *CR25/18*, Diocesan Archives, Cologne.

3. *Kirchenzeitung für das Erzbistum Köln,* February 11, 1951; Kafka, "Christliche Parteien und katholische Kräfte" in *Die neue Ordnung,* March-April 1958. Kafka was at that time the political expert of the central committee of German Catholics.

members could accept it or resign. In 1949, before the full authoritarian weight had descended, a group of laymen slipped through the Bochum Catholic assembly a resolution supporting industrial codetermination. The hierarchy's response was to decree that in future sessions no announcements might be made until church authorities had reviewed them. Ten years later an unprecedented invitation to Social Democrats to participate in a meeting of the Catholic academy in Bavaria was enough to set off a bitter row in clerical and lay circles. On the other hand, an eminent Jesuit economist, Oswald von Nell-Breuning, was sharply criticized, not for bringing political heretics into the ranks, but for taking his message to them by publishing an article in the Social Democratic monthly, *Die neue Gesellschaft.* Such prominent Catholic laymen as Walter Dirks, Helene Wessel, Heinrich Böll, Reinhold Schneider, Carl Amery, and Klara Fassbinder, who did not fall in with the church's approach, were rigorously shut out of Catholic life. They were largely boycotted by the lay movement and church press and, to cite merely one but a typical example, were excluded in 1958 from contributing to *Die Katholiken vor der Politik,* a volume of Catholic political views edited by an official of the central committee of German Catholics, Gustav Kafka, on the ground that they were "not representative" of Catholic thought (p. 6). When they spoke out against rearmament in the early 1950s they were shamefully abused by church leaders and the church press (see Chapter 9, pp. 249–250). Their principal outlet, Walter Dirks' monthly *Frankfurter Hefte,* was denounced at the 1956 Catholic assembly as an example of the "nihilistic journalism" especially enjoyed by "intellectual mugs."[4]

Nothing better illustrates the hierarchy's abhorrence of political division in the ranks—and one of the ways it became deeply involved in politics after 1945—than its efforts to destroy the various Catholic splinter parties that grew up following the war, chief of which were the Center party and the Bavarian party. On October 1945 the Zentrum was refounded, despite Archbishop Frings' emphatic appeal that the name and organization of the old party be abandoned in favor of the CDU. From that moment on, the church worked hand in hand with CDU officials to effect a merger of the Zentrum with the CDU. In the Rhineland and Westphalia, where the party was strongest, Cardinal Frings, Monsignor Robert Grosche (dean of the Catholic Church in Cologne), and Monsignor Wilhelm Böhler (Frings' principal political advis-

---

4. *Die Kirche, das Zeichen Gottes unter den Völkern; der 77. Deutsche Katholikentag* (1957), p. 366.

er) invited Adenauer and the other party officials to their residences to discuss a party fusion. "Repeated references were made," a typical report of the time ran, "to everyone's heavy responsibility to the Catholic population to save it from being divided between two separate political parties."[5] Center party leaders were unmoved by these appeals, principally because they considered the CDU too far to the right (in large part because of Protestant influence) to offer a basis for unity, and they increasingly resented the ecclesiastical pressure on them to disband their party.

By 1948, when it was clear that these mediatory efforts were getting nowhere, church leaders began attacking the Zentrum outright. To suppress sympathy among the clergy of his diocese, Bishop Bornewasser of Trier privately warned his clergy in a letter in July 1948: "When such important matters as divine right, natural rights, human rights, and human worth are at stake, the complete unity of a party invariably supporting these rights is more important than an aberrant private opinion. To work for this unity is one of the highest political objectives of the priest." In a press interview a few months later, Bishop van der Velden of Aachen characterized the political division among Catholics as a "catastrophe" and prophesied that it would ultimately cause the downfall not only of Christianity but of "the whole of western culture"—a theme he repeated in his sermons.[6] About the same time, Böhler stepped up his campaign to destroy clerical support for the party, speaking at dozens of meetings of priests and arranging for groups of clergymen to be addressed by CDU officials. Cooperative clergymen were encouraged to follow the bishops' example and bring local CDU and Zentrum leaders together to discuss a party merger. To cap these efforts, Cardinal Frings demonstratively joined the CDU on December 2, 1948. In this public explanation he said that with the Communist, Social Democratic, and Free Democratic parties out of the question, his choice lay between the CDU and the Zentrum; he chose the former simply because in Cologne it was the larger. His private explanation, as recorded by Richard Muckermann, a prominent Zentrum convert to the CDU, was more frank: "The Cardinal declared that it was deeply painful to him to see how the energies of the Christian-Catholic camp could not be fully realized because the two groups [CDU and Zentrum] could conduct a discussion together up to a certain point but then parted ways because the one was in the CDU and the other in the Zentrum. . . . He

---

5. Report by Father Schreiber of meeting on February 5, 1946, in *Akte Zentrum—1945–1950,* Archives of the Rhineland CDU, Cologne.
6. Report (undated) entitled "Kirchliche Mahnungen," ibid.

said of his joining the CDU that the future alone would tell whether this step was justified. But, in view of the tragic situation in North Rhine-Westphalia, he had taken the odium upon himself to present an example to others." [7]

The steady episcopal pressure, Frings' example and Böhler's negotiations (which included securing positions in the CDU for Center party defectors) eventually cracked the unity of the Center party executive. In January 1949, when a number of important Center party leaders, led by Richard Muckermann and Karl Spiecker, went over to the CDU, they promptly arranged meetings of CDU and Catholic lay officials to map out a strategy to deal the Center the final blow. It was agreed that the Catholic clergy and lay groups were in the best position to apply pressure. "In many cities," Muckermann noted in the same report "as, for example, Essen, the entire clergy is prepared to do so." This is what then occurred throughout North Rhine-Westphalia, and by the spring of 1949 the results were apparent. One local CDU organization reported in a letter of March 22, 1949:

> An open battle against the Zentrum in every form is now being conducted by the clergy here. On Sunday a religious retreat was held . . . and, to the deep distress of the Zentrum people present, the priest stated:
> "If Christ were alive today, he would certainly be in the CDU."
> . . . On Sunday almost every sermon in the church concerned political unity in the Christian camp. [8]

In the town of Uckerath the local priest, as the Rhineland CDU manager reported to Adenauer, for a time "simply would not permit any party in the community other than the Center party." The priest eventually went over to the CDU and thereupon decreed "that in the future in his community it would only be possible to vote CDU." [9] When the CDU could not win over pro-Zentrum priests, it asked church officials to transfer them from the locality.

Despite this intense pressure, the Center party still had a sizable organization as the 1949 federal elections approached. To minimize political stress among Catholics, Böhler tried to get the two parties to agree on a catalogue of fair campaign practices. To the churchman's annoyance, Adenauer refused. In the election the CDU did better than anticipated in almost every area. In

---

7. Report of February 23, 1949, by Richard Muckermann, ibid.

8. Letter from CDU Dinslaken to Hans Schreiber (Manager of Rhineland CDU), ibid.

9. Memorandum of May 21, 1949, from Schreiber to Konrad Adenauer, in *Akte Dr. Adenauer*, Archives of the Rhineland CDU, Cologne.

regions of strong Zentrum tradition, however, it generally did worse. In North Rhine-Westphalia and Lower Saxony, the Center party received almost three-quarters of a million votes, an increase of 125,000 over the 1947 Land elections, and sent ten representatives to the Bundestag. In the 1950 North Rhine-Westphalian election, it slipped only slightly (still winning sixteen seats in the Land parliament and two seats in the cabinet), and in the 1951 Lower Saxony election it held its own. There were several remarkable paradoxes in this situation. The Zentrum did so well because it had been able to argue that it was a better defender of Catholic interests than the CDU, which had refused to insist on a constitutional guarantee of confessional schools in the Basic Law (discussed in Chapter 7, pp. 186–188), despite the fact that the CDU was actively supported and the Zentrum actively opposed by the Catholic church. On the other hand, the main focus of the Center party's appeal was directed toward Ruhr workers, the party claiming that it was better able than the "rightist" CDU to keep them out of the hands of the Social Democrats. "However," as the annual report for 1949 of the Westphalian CDU stated, "the election results clearly disprove this. In areas where workers were strong, the Zentrum was insignificant; in fact it declined there. This can be credited to the attitude of the Catholic workers' and men's groups which aligned themselves with the CDU." [10]

The relative success of the Center party in 1949 and 1950 caused Böhler, diocesan officials, local clergy, Catholic lay groups, and the CDU to redouble their efforts to bring about either the party's merger with the CDU or its elimination. By 1952 it was clear that the Center party was markedly on the decline. But in a few areas it was still strong enough to split the Catholic vote almost evenly. Church officials therefore decided to work for an electoral arrangement between the two parties, to dampen political controversy among Catholics and to prevent the Social Democrats from benefitting from a divided Catholic vote. The provost of the diocese of Münster arranged a meeting at his residence in September 1952 among Johannes Brockmann (Zentrum chairman), Karl Arnold (CDU minister-president of North Rhine-Westphalia), and Catholic lay leaders. Here an agreement was reached on an electoral alliance for the local elections in 1952, leaving certain constituencies uncontested by one or the other party. An accord was later worked out for the 1953 federal election, giving the Center party the constituency of Oberhausen (which would otherwise have been lost to the SPD) in return for a CDU candidate in the top place on the Zentrum Land list. This arrangement

---

10. "Jahresbericht 1949," in *Akte 314–3, Lensing Persönl. Parteiakten,* Archives of Westphalia-Lippe CDU, Dortmund.

took the Center back into the Bundestag with two seats. By 1956, however, the party—which continued its decline—moved into opposition to the CDU and entered into a electoral alliance with the SPD, capturing one seat in the 1957 Bundestag. In the North Rhine-Westphalian election the following year, it lost all its seats and ceased to be a factor on the political scene. (The Zentrum has never actually been dissolved and maintains a headquarters in Münster. It put up a Land list in North Rhine-Westphalia in the 1969 federal election).

The Zentrum was probably destined to vanish along with the other small parties that grew up in the early postwar period. But the Catholic church's decision to destroy it was decisive; it weakened the party from the start and greatly hastened its demise. By its action the church not only became directly involved in politics but came very close to exerting religious compulsion on behalf of its own narrow political objective. No Center party leader was permitted to speak at a church assembly, was given access to the Catholic press, or was permitted to play a role in the lay movement. The party was attacked by priests in and out of church, at and between elections. A report of July 13, 1950, in the files of the Rhineland CDU records the feelings of Zentrum leaders at that time: "Absolute amazement has been expressed by Zentrum authorities that church circles have particularly opposed the Zentrum in the new elections to the NRW [North Rhine-Westphalian] Land parliament. . . . There appear to be blind CDU fanatics in church circles." Center party leaders were increasingly embittered by the church's blatant discrimination against them. The mayor of one town in Baden complained of cases in his area "where priests prevented persons from being candidates for the Center party but permitted them to be candidates for the CDU." *Unsere Linie*, a Center party newspaper, repeatedly charged Catholic clergy and lay leaders with intimidating Zentrum supporters into switching to the CDU. At the 1953 party congress in Cologne, Brockmann warned the Catholic church against further "pressure against the existence and freedom of the party." He and other leaders repeatedly accused the church of suggesting that the Catholic was obliged in conscience to vote for the CDU rather than the Zentrum. [11]

Most Center party leaders recognized—some sooner, some later—that the church's attitude had condemned their party to death and that it was senseless to try to swim against the ecclesiastical tide, which they felt flowed against them more strongly than the political tide. Many, such as Spiecker and Muckermann, went over to the CDU. Others, like Frau Wessel, went into

---

11. Report in *Akte Zentrums-Partei (1952-)* in Archives of the Rhineland CDU, Cologne; the Baden mayor's complaint reported in *General-Anzeiger* (Bonn).

the All-German People's party and eventually into the SPD. Still others dropped out of politics entirely. Almost all of them were bitterly resentful of their church. They were convinced that it wanted to be a dominant influence in Germany and to this end was willing to sacrifice the political independence of the faithful and to jeopardize the establishment of an effective democracy in Germany. And, indeed, the lesson of the Zentrum was well learned. The Catholic left wing never even made an attempt to organize itself into bodies like the Protestant "brotherhoods" or into a Catholic equivalent of the All-German People's party. "Political realism," Walter Dirks has commented, "is in fact what kept these [left] Catholics from founding an action committee or a party (left of both the CDU and the SPD)." [12] Not until 1966 was even the loosest form of left-Catholic association formed—the so-called Bensberg circle, a group whose most radical pronouncement to date has advocated German recognition of the Oder-Neisse line.

Strength through unity—this was the hierarchy's political formula after 1945, as it had been after the Kulturkampf. It deeply marked the face of German society. Pluralism held little meaning for the bishops and had no place in their scheme of things. Social institutions and groups were regarded as essentially either hostile or friendly to the church's mission and, if hostile, were to be fought into submission. It was consequently central to the church's tactic that the Catholic layman should adopt this attitude for himself and act politically first as a Catholic and only secondarily in keeping with his own political preferences, social ideals, and material aspirations. The founding of an interconfessional rather than a Catholic party after the war made this cohesion appear all the more urgent so that Catholic dominance in the party could be maintained. In this way the ideal of Catholic solidarity became indistinguishable from a policy of keeping Catholics in the CDU and the CDU in power.

All the weight of the hierarchy's authority was thus brought to bear upon Catholics to give automatic and unquestioning support to the Christian Democrats and their policies even when these had nothing to do with Catholicism as such and no direct bearing on the church's ecclesiastical interests. The bishops, assisted by the lay movement, were highly successful. They made Catholic political unity and concern for the political protection of Catholic interests as potent considerations to the average Catholic voter after 1945 as they had been before 1933. The church, no less than the CDU, played on these sentiments, the tactic of both being to arouse confessional sensitivity and establish the CDU as the defender of Catholic interests. In Catholic

---

12. "Ein 'anderer' Katholizismus?" p. 299.

communities ecclesiastical influence was reinforced by a popular drive toward conformity with the church's viewpoints. The strength both of church ties and social pressure therefore had a distinct influence on the individual Catholic's a political outlook. Not surprisingly, the difference in party preference between regular church-goers (generally estimated at roughly 60 percent of all Catholics in the two decades after the war) and other Catholics was enormous, as can be seen in Table 4.

Similarly, the firmer the religious and social constraints, the greater the preference for the CDU. Since church ties were generally stronger among

Table 4
Voting preference of Catholics (1961) [13]

frequency of church attendance	number of respondents	CDU	SPD	other	no information
several times a week	73	82%	7%	4%	7%
weekly	315	76%	13%	2%	9%
monthly	84	61%	26%	1%	12%
several times a year	73	37%	42%	11%	10%
seldom; never	110	27%	49%	4%	20%

Table 5
Voting pattern in Catholic
communities by size (1961) [14]

percentage of Catholics	communities with fewer than 3,000 inhabitants		
	CDU/CSU	SPD	other
over 90%	76%	15%	9%
80%-90%	64%	24%	12%
	communities with 3,000 to 50,000 inhabitants		
over 90%	65%	25%	10%
80%-90%	61%	27%	12%
	communities with more than 50,000 inhabitants		
over 90%	—	—	—
80%-90%	48%	38%	14%

13. Karl-Heinz Diekershoff, *op.cit.*, p. 219

14. Statistisches Bundesamt, *Fachserie A, Bevölkerung und Kultur, Reihe 8, Wahl zum 4. Deutschen Bundestag am 17. September 1961*, Heft 4 (1965), p. 45.

women, the old and residents of small towns, voting behavior varied markedly with age, sex and the size of the community. This is proved by actual voting results (Table 5). The Catholic support for the CDU reached its apogee, logically enough, with women in small towns. In the 1953 election, for example, 78% of them voted for the CDU, a mere 11% for the SPD and 11% for other parties. [15] Exceeding even this, no fewer than 85% of Catholic women over sixty in predominantly Catholic small towns voted for the CDU and a mere 9% for the SPD in the 1961 election. [16] (That this extraordinarily high vote for the Christian Democrats was due to confessional considerations and not primarily to a tendency of women in rural areas to be more conservative than men and urban women is evident from a comparison of these figures with those cited above for Protestant women.) In fact, Adenauer himself considered this the key to the CDU's election victories. When, for instance, party officials voiced their concern to him about the reliability of Catholic voters in the 1965 election, he responded: "But you have forgotten the most

Table 6

Ahrweiler

	CDU	SPD	other
1949	68%	19%	13%
1953	72%	19%	9%
1957	74%	20%	6%
1961	68%	21%	11%
1965	66%	26%	9%
1969	62%	31%	7%
1972	57%	37%	6%

Koblenz

	CDU	SPD	other
1949	58%	25%	17%
1953	62%	23%	15%
1957	61%	27%	12%
1961	56%	28%	16%
1965	56%	34%	11%
1969	52%	39%	9%
1972	49%	43%	8%

15. *Ibid., Band 100, Die Wahl zum 2. Deutschen Bundestag am 6.9.1953*, Heft (1955), pp. 70–71. (The available figures do not include Rhineland-Palatinate and Bavaria.)

16. *Ibid., Fachserie A, Bevölkerung und Kultur, Reihe 8, Wahl zum 4. Deutschen Bundestag am 17. September 1961, Heft* 4 (1965), p. 46.

important thing. The good Catholic housewives will never forget us when the chips are down." [17]

The general characteristics of Catholic electoral behavior are most clearly illustrated by the results of the seven postwar federal elections in two predominantly Catholic upper Rhineland constituencies, Ahrweiler and Koblenz, similar in their way to the Protestant constituencies referred to earlier. Ahrweiler, a rural area with much of the population engaged in small-scale manufacturing, is 89% Catholic and 10% Protestant. Koblenz, a city of over 200,000 people, 36% of whom are workers, is 77% Catholic and 22% Protestant.

There are constituencies with a higher CDU and a lower SPD vote than these two examples. In 1961, for example, in the ten constituencies where the Christian Democrats did best—all strongly Catholic—the CDU received from 70% to 81% of the vote while the ten constituencies where the SPD did worst—again predominantly Catholic—gave the Social Democrats as little as 12% to 20%. But Ahrweiler and Koblenz offer a generally good picture of how Catholics have voted in federal elections since the war. They illustrate how Catholic support for the CDU was large and solid, expanding steadily until 1961. (The Koblenz result is aberrant in showing a decline in the CDU vote between 1953 and 1957). Catholic electoral behavior in 1961 is difficult to analyze. Support for the CDU actually increased in that year in communities which were 80% or more Catholic. It is therefore possible that the general decline in the CDU vote in 1961 reflected primarily—or even entirely—the defection of Protestants. Not until 1965 did it become clear that Catholics were actually abandoning the CDU. By the same token Catholic support for the SPD was repressed to about one-fifth of the voting population until 1965 when it increased sharply with the laity's assertion of independence of ecclesiastical guidance, the church's own tendency toward political neutrality and the SPD's friendlier attitude to the Catholic church. For the splinter parties and the FDP, Catholic support was clearly modest at best and much of this was concentrated in the two Catholic parties, the Zentrum and the Bavarian party. Apart from a slight increase in the vote for the FDP in 1961, when the Christian Democrats suffered general reversal, Catholic support for the minor parties steadily declined from an initially low level.

In summary, Catholic voting behavior was — in comparison with that of Protestants—committed, calculable and stable. Generally, it varied less with the normal sociological motivations (such as occupation, education, class

---

17. Quoted in Friedhelm Baukloh, "Deutsche Katholiken vor der Wahl" in *Der Monat*, March 1965.

background, income and so on) than with the strength of allegiance to the church and the pressures of the Catholic social environment. Only as these changed in the mid-1960s did the Catholic commitment to the CDU lessen. But for most of the post-war period there was a high degree of Catholic political unity and this bloc was highly responsive to church direction and confessional appeals. "The principle of Catholic political unity," an official of the central committee of German Catholics could write (at the height of the Adenauer era) with understandable pride, "has been turned to the advantage of the CDU/CSU in the same degree as to that of the Zentrum and the Bavarian People's Party in Imperial Germany and the Weimar Republic. [18]

However, this unqualified commitment clashed directly with the church's principle of staying out of politics. To escape from this dilemma, the hierarchy was drawn into its most peculiar stance during the whole postwar period: it tried to legitimize its political engagement by depicting German politics as an ideological struggle, a clash between spiritual values rather than political viewpoints. This approach so permeated German Catholicism in the two decades after the war that the foreign observer was less aware of having crossed the Rhine than of having moved centuries back in history, to a time when Christian civilization was being defended from barbarian and infidel— which was exactly the terminology sometimes used in Catholic circles. While only the full text of a document, such as the 1958 report of the central committee of German Catholics, can adequately convey the full flavor of German Catholic thinking in this period, the mood comes through in a passage by Anton Böhm, an editor of the *Rheinischer Merkur* (an arch-conservative weekly which claimed—with some justice—to speak for German Catholicism in those years):

> It would indeed be good if political differences concerned merely practical matters. But this struggle over ideologies between two parties is only a symptom of the fact that there is no agreement on the basic issues of the form of the State, and these basic issues are all of an ideological nature.
> ... The situation in Federal Germany is characterized by a large amount of parliamentary work touching on ideological issues. This is not simply because we Germans are more doctrinaire but because the state is unfinished, because its foundation and structure must be discussed, and because the principles of the construction itself are matters of debate. [19]

---

18. Gustav Kafka, "Christliche Parteien und katholische Kräfte in *Die neue Ordnung*, March/April 1958.

19. "Voraussetzungslose Politik" in *Wort und Wahrheit*, July 1957.

The fundamental issue at stake in this ideological contest was presented as one of Christianity versus liberalism and individualism. The theologian Hans Pfeil expressed this in a typical way:

> Certainly life under the dominion of collectivism and totalitarianism is far more dangerous, the destruction of man and culture far more obvious; basically, however, collectivism and totalitarianism are not more inconsistent with reality or more harmful to ethics, religion, and Christianity than are individualism and liberalism.
>
> The powerful influences of individualism and liberalism today to a large extent shape and govern science and art, economics and politics, education and the whole of public life. It belongs to the current duties of the Catholic not to allow himself to be influenced in such a way that his own Catholic life is harmed. [20]

The idea that liberalism, individualism, and collectivism were the poisonous fruits of the Reformation and a menace to society was probably the most pervasive theme of German Catholicism in the twenty years after the war. "A God-removed or Godless world in the spirit of liberalism and materialism," Cardinal Frings once told a group of religious pilgrims, "stands opposed to the kingdom of God." In a speech to a group of Social Democratic leaders in January 1958, Professor Gustav Gundlach, the Jesuit adviser to Pius XI and Pius XII, stressed that Catholics "regard the freeing of democratic socialism from Marxism as not primarily the problem of breaking from materialism but rather of breaking from the liberal way of thought and the liberal heritage." Gundlach went on to remark that the reason socialism was declared to be incompatible with Catholicism in the Encyclical *Quadragesimo anno* (which Gundlach, along with Nell-Breuning, is credited with having drafted) was that it is "a laicizing, secularizing form of proletarian liberalism." The theologian's thrust, which was directed as much against trends within Christian Democracy as against Social Democratic philosophy, did not go over well with CDU Protestants. Bundestag President Gerstenmaier, for instance, told the CDU party congress in September 1958 that liberalism was being misrepresented and that his party would do well to follow the liberal tradition of Alexander von Humboldt and Friedrich Naumann—a comment which earned him a stiff rebuke in turn from some of his Catholic colleagues. [21]

---

20. "Individualismus und Liberalismus" in *Die neue Ordnung*, September-October 1955.

21. Frings in *Kirchenzeitung für das Erzbistum Köln,* March 23, 1952; Gundlach, "Katholizismus und Sozialismus" in Forster (editor) *Christentum und Demokratischer Sozialismus*, pp. 22–23.

Church and lay officials applied this ideological approach to the gamut of practical politics. Political parties were portrayed as disagreeing over the very ends of society, rather than over mere political tactics. Elections were presented as a clash over ultimate values and legislation as a matter of the recognition or rejection of divine mandates. With the issue drawn in this way, the Catholic voter and the Catholic politician had little or no independence of his church. Moreover, the bishops exploited Catholic religious discipline for their own political purposes by encouraging the same obedience in the public as in the ecclesiastical sphere. In fact, they deliberately blurred the boundary between the two. Their views on elections and the school question, as well as a great variety of political and social issues, were set out in pastoral letters and sermons, and these were in turn echoed in sermons by the parish clergy. To deepen the confusion, the churchmen admonished the laity to make its political decisions on "grounds of conscience," but then advised what that conscience should say. An ingenuous and rather harmless example was the priest who at election time used to remark to his congregation in the Christian Social Union's homeland of Bavaria: "It is not for me to tell you how to vote. But I do say: Vote Christian! Vote Social!" More serious were the election appeals in the Rhineland and in Westphalia, where a handbill regularly passed out in the 1950s by Catholic lay groups stated:

> Everyone must vote according to his conscience. But it is clear that every true Catholic's voice of conscience recommends giving his vote to the candidate or the list which offers really adequate guarantees for the protection of the rights of God and the soul, for the true good of the individual, the family and society, in keeping with the law of God and Christian ethical teachings.

For a good twenty years after the war, Catholic ecclesiastical and lay group leaders expounded similar guidance regarding federal, Land, and local elections and on a variety of political issues at other times. In this way the German bishops in effect destroyed any practical distinction between politics, where a Catholic may make independent decisions, and moral issues, where theologically the church's advice is normally accorded priority over "private judgment."

This situation exasperated most non-Catholics and the national press, which had caustic remarks at every election for the way it felt the Catholic church was inhibiting parliamentary democracy by appearing to make it a religious duty for Catholics to vote for the CDU. No one was more angered than the handful of Catholic nonconformists, such as Walter Dirks, who argued that while the hierarchy could have a legitimate political preference for the CDU, it was intolerable that "voters who have good reasons in their own minds not to vote for the CDU are subjected to the pressure of conscience." This was precisely the reason why Helene Wessel, in drafting with Heinemann a program for the All-German People's party, referred to the "misuse of Christianity for political purposes" and wrote into the program the further statement: "We call for a complete end to all racial, religious, and ideological prejudices. We condemn in particular the debasement of Christianity into an instrument of political utility and the establishment of a Christian front directed against another part of the population." [22]

For about twenty years the Catholic church and its lay groups succeeded in assembling the majority of Catholics in a bloc, tied them to the CDU, inposed upon them the party's policies, muzzled its own dissidents, and conducted an ideological war against the Free Democrats and Social Democrats. The political consequences of this course can scarcely be exaggerated. At the most difficult moment in the Federal Republic's history the Catholic church more than any other institution contributed to stability and calm. Heinrich Köppler, a prominent Catholic lay leader and CDU politician, in an interview summed it up in one sentence: "Without the political conformity of German Catholics, the Adenauer era as it was would not have been conceivable." It is, indeed, difficult to see how Adenauer could have successfully launched his foreign and defense policies against the formidable opposition that existed in non-Catholic circles had he not been able to count on what Köppler further characterized as the "automatic and unquestioning" support of Catholics. But this enormous contribution to the Federal Republic—and to Europe—was achieved at a terrible cost. While the Evangelical church was doing its best to fight authoritarianism and strengthen liberal democracy, the Catholic bishops rested their whole position on authoritarianism and represented politics almost as a choice between good and evil, defying the very premise of liberal democracy. As the Evangelical church was shedding its Erastianism, the Catholic bishops were making an unqualified commitment to the party in power. Where the Protestant bishops were motivated by the desire to build up a tolerant society, the Catholic church was guided by narrow self-interest. A New York Times correspondent saw signs of this at the very outset of the postwar period and in the issue of August 25, 1946, observed, "If the German Catholic Church lost little in the war, it learned little that is new. It may help to preserve Germany from communism, but it offers little promise of yanking

---

22. Dirks, "Die Kirchen und die CDU;" interview with Helene Wessel; text in Treue (editor), *Deutsche Parteiprogramme*, p. 293.

Germans out of their old follow-the-Führer complex of solving their problems."

And what was the point of it all? Far from plotting to undo the Reformation or manipulating the laity in an attempt to hinder the development of parliamentary democracy, the bishops were acting in accordance with an automatic reflex. While as a matter of course they wanted a society in Germany that was based on "Christian moral principles," their immediate aim was simply what they had struggled for since 1871: full guarantees, as they saw them, for the church's security. As they had in the past, they regarded the laity as a political army that could protect church prerogatives when these were challenged from the left or the right and defend German society against liberalism and Marxism. Having witnessed the way Catholics went over to National Socialism, the bishops no doubt also believed that it was their duty to give the laity sound political guidance. Their aims were, in short, essentially defensive. Indeed, the greatest weakness of postwar Catholicism is its lack of a positive approach except in the matter of confessional education and a few dated, ambiguous social concepts.

Consequently even the broad Catholic principles that, after much Catholic lobbying, were enshrined in the postwar constitutions of Catholic Länder did not so much vivify as petrify the church's position in the state. In subsequent years any fresh thinking on the problems of German society was precluded by the church's unconditional commitment to the CDU. If Protestant church leaders circumscribed their influence by declining to adopt a specific political course, the Catholic bishops undercut theirs for going too far in the opposite direction. The political prisoner of the CDU, the Catholic church had no practical alternative but to sacrifice any views of its own to the Christian Democrats' policies.

Not only was the church's whole approach out of step with the pragmatic and pluralist trend of postwar German society, it paradoxically grew out of a notion of confessional imbalance that no longer existed. A group that is 50 percent of the population, but merely 50 percent, cannot be kept politically united either in fear of Protestants, liberals, and Marxists or in the dream of "Catholicizing" German society. It was the greatest of ironies that the isolation of Catholics, begun by Bismarck, was maintained by the hierarchy. By the mid-1960s, however, the church's approach was becoming untenable. The Catholic laity woke up to the fact that its political unity, however well it was serving the church and the CDU, meant isolation rather than integration. The laymen suddenly realized that they were hardly any better off socially under the Catholic-dominated Federal Republic than they had been under a Protestant-controlled empire. The evolution of the CDU into a frankly unideological party headed by a liberal Protestant, paralleled by the Social Democrats' campaign for rapprochement with the churches, swept the ground from under the bishops. Even they began to recognize the situation for themselves. "We sacrificed to the CDU the chance of a purely Catholic party," declared Bishop Johannes Pohlschneider of Aachen in evident anguish in 1965; "we sacrificed to it the possibility of a Catholic daily press; and we sacrificed to it many of our desires in the educational field—for example, the establishment of a Catholic university. And what have we gotten out of this mixed marriage? A liberal party in power and now even a liberal Chancellor." [23]

Paradoxically, the most devastating blow to the bishops' political approach was dealt by the second Vatican Council. The Council's pastoral constitution on "the Church and the Contemporary World" gave formal Catholic acceptance to democratic, pluralist society. It recognized that there are legitimate differences of political and social viewpoint and just disagreements among political parties. "That," commented Karl Rahner, "is nothing other than a clear rejection of the still widespread 'monolithic' unanimity—oriented toward power rather than nonpartisan politics and tinged with ideology—that has been maintained by Catholics in political questions." [24] And so it was considered by much of the laity. Throughout the world the Catholic church was undergoing a revolution, but only in Germany did it take the form of ecclesiastical *and* political revolt—in both spheres against Catholic isolation and episcopal authoritarianism.

These various trends came to a head simultaneously with the bitterest church-state clash of the postwar period—the controversy over confessional schools between 1965 and 1969. The bishops who tried to fight the battle along old lines found themselves repudiated by the laity and, even more humiliatingly, by much of the younger clergy. On May 17, 1967, the *Frankfurter Allgemeine* reprinted the text of a letter to Cardinal Jäger by fifty-seven priests in the diocese of Paderborn. It read in part:

> Catholic Christians should also have the freedom to hold differing views on the school question. We do not contest the bishops' right to present their position on the school issue. But there must be no ecclesiastical *dirigisme* by which the Catholic citizen's political decision is directed from above, as was the case in earlier pastoral letters on elec-

---

23. Quoted in Baukloh.
24. Rahner and Vorgrimler, *Kleines Konzilskompendium,* p. 442.

tions. . . . Episcopal pronouncements on political questions should contribute to the outlook of the faithful but may not use the Catholics' religious bonds and their confidence in the pastorate for the church's own purposes.

This challenge, publicly raised by priests in other parts of the country as well, signaled the end of nearly a century of Catholic political solidarity.

In a situation characterized for two decades by Catholic unity and ecclesiastical commitment, the church's lobbying activities were on a different scale, were conducted in a different way, and were directed toward a different end than those of the Evangelical church. The instruments created for this purpose and the way they were used were the accomplishment of Monsignor Wilhelm Böhler. Böhler, the political advisor to Cardinal Frings and the Fulda Bishops' Conference after 1945, was by the time of the establishment of the Federal Republic already the undisputed political expert of the Catholic church. He had participated in the founding of the Rhineland CDU in 1945, had been the principal mediator between the CDU and the Center party, had negotiated with the British Military Government on a variety of issues, and was the representative of the hierarchy to the Parliamentary Council which drew up the Basic Law (as the constitution of the Federal Republic was known). It was inevitable that Cardinal Frings, as chairman of the Fulda Bishops' Conference, should appoint him to represent Catholic interests in Bonn. The man, the job, and the moment fitted well together. With the Federal Republic being constructed from the foundations up, the possibilities of influencing the personnel, structure, and direction of the government were enormous. Böhler enjoyed Cardinal Frings' full confidence, knew what he wanted, and set about getting it with boundless enthusiasm—and as much as possible behind the scenes.

Catholic leaders keenly recognized the unprecedented opportunities open to the Catholic church in a confessionally balanced state, and they tended to look to the CDU as the means of achieving them. But the CDU was not, as they thought, a kind of neo-Zentrum plus a few sympathetic Protestants; it was the most pragmatic and least ideological party in German history. It was not the instrument of any single group or institution. Böhler's main tactic was to try to circumvent this reality by creating a Catholic core within the CDU which could be closely linked to the hierarchy and the Catholic lay movement. To this end he immediately set about organizing groups within his own liaison agency—which, with disarming simplicity, he called the Catholic Office—to bring ecclesiastical, lay, and governmental officials together to advise him and to support his work. Gradually he built up an extraordinary system of "interlocking directorates" which became a masterpiece of coordination to the admirer and a system of naked clericalism to the critic. First he organized the so-called Tuesday Circle as a social and political center for important ministerial officials, Bundestag members, journalists, professors, and a few church officials. It met on Tuesdays, following the regular Bundestag caucus held on that day in preparation for Wednesday's plenary session, and was to foster personal and professional contacts in a social atmosphere where business could also be conducted.

Another body he founded was the ecclesiastical-political group (Kirchenpolitisches Gremium), a body whose existence has never been publicly acknowledged. It was, in fact, established to be Böhler's main advisory body and channel to the bishops. Originally it had fifteen members, most of whom were political advisers to various bishops (while not every diocese was represented, and no one from East Germany belonged, there was at least one person from each Church Province) and the remainder was made up of a number of leading theologians. To its sessions, held four times a year, Böhler invited a few top government officials. Government policy and ecclesiastical interests in the political sphere were reviewed. As such there was nothing sinister about the group. Each side went away better informed on the thinking of the other. The group, like the Catholic Office itself, was designed to keep the bishops politically informed and thereby to fill the informational void resulting from the tacit ban on "political prelates" after 1945. But the ecclesiastical official no doubt also went home with a political line to sell, and the ministerial official no doubt went back to his office with some concrete political suggestions in his pocket.

Böhler also set up a number of "working groups," committees responsible for the detailed study of important political issues or pending legislation. There were generally about ten such groups, the topics and membership changing with current issues. Each group had an average membership of thirty, consisting of a few church officials and theologians, representatives of Catholic lay organizations, ministerial officals and Bundestag members, as well as various other experts on the topic under consideration. On occasion the minister or state secretary and all of the Catholic members of the Bundestag committee involved were invited to attend its sessions. It went without saying that all participants were Christian Democrats.

Böhler was fortunate in being able to take advantage of the relatively unorganized state of the Catholic lay movement after 1945 and to shape it so as to enhance his own influence. He was the moving force behind the establishment of the Catholic news agency, the central committee of German Catholics, and the political working group of Catholic organizations. The central committee not only coordinated and guided the political activities of Catholic lay groups, it also directly assisted Böhler by maintaining a staff of permanent experts, housed in its headquarters near Bonn, to keep themselves informed of ministerial and parliamentary activity. As circumstances warranted, ad hoc working groups similar to those of the Catholic Office were established, bringing together lay and clerical officials, CDU Bundestag members, and CDU ministerial officials. The central committee afforded an excellent channel to the lay organizations and from time to time called together representatives of the important lay groups whose interests were touched by a pending government action. In that way the committee alerted the lay movement and elicited views on how the committee itself should handle the matter. The central committee also played a role in Personalpolitik and the distribution of government funds to lay groups, not only in securing as much money as possible, but also in making sure that the lay groups did not thereby fall under government control or interference.

The political working group of Catholic organizations, a large committee of the sort described above, was established at Böhler's initiative in 1952 to propagate the church's political views among lay groups and to build support for his lobbying activities by mobilizing Catholic opinion behind him. Böhler also wanted still another instrument through which the church could directly intervene with the government. The political working group was comprised of representatives of sixty major lay organizations (eighteen of the largest of which had a total membership of three million and the press organs of which had a combined circulation of about two million). Its meetings were attended by ministerial officials, parliamentarians, lay group representatives, and church officials. Böhler was the director of the political working group; other officials were members of the central committee and the ecclesiastical-political group. In this way the coordination of the various activities of the three bodies was assured.

The political working group met irregularly, but at least every two months. Its discussions were considered so confidential that no minutes were kept. At the sessions Böhler outlined the general issues facing the church and then asked the ministerial officials and Bundestag members about the "political possibilities" of achieving the church's aim. The representatives of the lay groups then expressed their views, after which there was general discussion culminating in a decision. Each participant at the meeting was expected to carry out the agreed program in his individual area of responsibility. The political working group rarely made public pronouncements. On occasion it interceded directly with the Chancellor, the Bundestag, or a particular ministry. However, Böhler frequently used the group for a reverse purpose—to communicate the government's view directly to the lay organizations, which were then expected to propagate this policy at their meetings and in their press organs.

Thanks to Böhler's organizational creativeness, government and church met on three levels: government and hierarchy in the Catholic Office; government and Catholic laity in the central committee; and government and Catholic lay movement in the political working group. In all three cases the essence of Böhler's approach was less that of church versus government than one of churchmen and government officials working together. His greatest success in this regard was at the very top of the government, in the Chancellery. Adenauer had recognized that the Catholic church would be one of the main pillars of Christian Democratic political strength and wanted to be sure that the government's relationship with the hierarchy was smooth. A Protestant would have been incapable of keeping the channel open; an arch-Catholic such as Franz-Josef Wuermeling (who was one of the earliest candidates for state secretary in the Chancellery) would have pushed Catholic interests so far that the Chancellor's position and the interconfessional viability of the CDU would have been jeopardized. Adenauer therefore entrusted the Chancellery to Otto Lenz (a Catholic, like all other candidates for the state secretaryship), assisted by Hans Globke, who had responsibility for the civil service and who succeeded Lenz as state secretary in 1953.

From the start Globke handled church relations. He fully shared Böhler's intention of destroying Protestant dominance of the civil service and had full understanding for the hierarchy's general point of view. Böhler therefore had a sympathetic ear at the highest level of government. His immediate, tangible objectives were full government support for the Reichskonkordat, the appointment of a Catholic ambassador to the Vatican, the adoption of the Catholic view in a great range of legislative issues, support in Personalpolitik, and the prevention of a majority voting system since this would enlarge the CDU and thereby weaken Catholic influence in it. (Each of these points is discussed in subsequent chapters.) Although Globke had his own Personalpolitik and would often refuse to support Böhler's candidate unless he were a member of the CV,[25] Böhler generally got all the traffic would

---

25. CV (Cartellverband der Katholischen Deutschen Studentenverbindungen) is one of three Catholic student organizations, the others being KV, Kartellverband katholischer deutscher Studentenvereine, Unitas and UV, Verband der wissenschaftlichen katholischen Studentenvereine Unitas. These organizations were established in the mid-nineteenth century to further the careers of Catholics in the Protestant-dominated civil service. The loyalties of the members have always been extraordinarily strong. Because their ranks were relatively free of National Socialists and as a result of the confessional

bear, even though he often wanted more. Asked in an interview years later what Böhler had sought that he did not get, all Globke could recall off-hand was the church representative's request that the religious marriage ceremony should be considered as valid as the civil ceremony. Globke remarked that he had repeatedly to explain to Böhler, that, however desirable this might be from the Catholic view, it was not politically possible, given the attitude of Protestants generally and the SPD and FDP specifically. Although Böhler undoubtedly had many other failures, the comment underscores the limits on their cooperation. Globke went as far as he could without sacrificing his first responsibility of maintaining an efficient executive administration. Globke often had to say no to Böhler, and at times the relationship between the two apparently became cool.

Böhler was by no means only a *demandeur* at the Chancellery. He was exceedingly useful to Adenauer because of his excellent contacts in Rome. Thanks to Pius XII's intense interest in German affairs, direct contacts had been established between the Pope and Böhler in 1948 over the drafting of the Basic Law; this unusual arrangement ended only with Böhler's death in 1958. More important still to Adenauer was Böhler's political influence in German church circles and his ability to secure the active support of the bishops, clergy, and lay movement for the government's policies. Böhler did what Adenauer could not do as Chancellor and would not do as Adenauer.

Adenauer's relationship to the Catholic church has sometimes been misunderstood as a result of several confusions, of which he himself was never guilty. Adenauer's deep religious feelings did not mean that he applied his religion to his politics in any pragmatic sense. Similarly, his reliance on the Catholic church's political support did not translate into concern for its public interests. He was, indeed, a classic example of the secularist political leader who regarded the churches in a coldly objective light. They were important forces in society and politics and, like all such institutions, were of interest only to the extent that they supported or opposed him. Like many other

---

balance in the Federal Republic, the corporations' patrons, such as Hans Globke and Heinrich Krone, were in an excellent position to place large numbers of members in the government after 1949. (They were an important factor on the Land level as well; for instance, between 1946 and 1950 virtually every CSU member of the Bavarian cabinet belonged to KV.) This situation gave rise to suspicions—not limited to Protestants alone—of a Catholic underground. An anecdote of the early 1950s was symptomatic. "Was ist der Unterschied zwischen CV und Mau Mau? Es gibt keinen Unterschied; sie sind beide gut organisierte, schwarze Untergrundbewegungen." ("What's the difference between the CV and the Mau Mau? There is no difference; both are highly organized black underground movements.")

Catholic leaders from Charles V on, he developed and pursued his policies with scant regard for ecclesiastical considerations. "Although a religious man," Golo Mann has put it epigramatically, "he distinguished between the things of this world and the next like a Lutheran." [26]

Despite his formally strict Catholicism, it appears clear that Adenauer viewed religion primarily in sociological terms. He regarded it as a force of the utmost importance in molding a nation's character and by that means its political life. His devotion to Catholicism seems to have been primarily stimulated by its historic humanistic influence. For this reason he was inclined to have greater confidence in the Catholic church and in Catholics than in other institutions and non-Catholics, though not on doctrinal grounds but because he believed Catholicism's western roots went deeper and were more firmly embedded than those of other institutions. Typically, in his first meeting with an American official after the war, Adenauer spoke not of his own political plans or the revival of political parties but of the general moral-religious condition of the German people and the significance of this for the country's political future. After expressing fear that Germany would be divided in two as a result of the "iron curtain" (his actual term) which the Russians had let down at the Elbe, Adenauer maintained that Germany in any case fell into two parts culturally. He observed that Germany west of the Elbe and south of the Weser had been civilized by the Romans and by Christianity a thousand years earlier than the remainder of the country, while central and eastern Germany had still been pagan as late as the fourteenth century. No sooner was this latter part of the country Christianized a hundred years later than the Reformation occurred, leaving Christianity in that area without a firm foundation. In this milieu developed the Prussian ideal of the state, of which Nazism was merely an exaggerated form. [27] In subsequent years Adenauer apparently never wavered in this belief that the Russians intended to divide Germany but that the requisite moral force for German recovery would in any event have to come from its western portion. Although it superficially appeared to be confessionally oriented, Adenauer's almost mystical devotion to a *christliches Abendland*—a Roman but not necessarily a Roman Catholic Europe—was ultimately an intellectual and cultural but above all a political rather than a religious matter.

---

26. *The History of Germany since 1789*, p. 507.

27. An account of this conversation which took place between Adenauer and an official of the Office of Strategic Services on June 22, 1945, is attached to a letter by Ambassador Murphy to the Department of State; letter No. 722 of July 30, 1945 in 740.00119 Control (Germany) 7–3045; General Records of the Department of State, National Archives, Washington.

This subtle form of secularism was reinforced by a more orthodox secularist approach. For Adenauer, the Catholic church was an institution which, properly handled, could serve his political ends. In return, he would grant the church an occasional concession, but he was otherwise indifferent to its institutional objectives. "Adenauer used the church, but the church used Adenauer, especially in the school issue," Heinrich Krone put it in an interview. However, in balancing Catholic ecclesiastical claims against the nation's political interests, Adenauer never hesitated to decide for the latter. This position he made unmistakably clear in the early postwar period when, as chairman of the Parliamentary Council, he refused to give the Catholic church the support it desperately sought from him in drafting the new constitution. Later, as Chancellor, he demonstrated that his attention was focused on broad policy matters and that the Catholic church would have to fight its own battles.

His treatment of the Papal Nuncio on one occasion in 1954 is illustrative. Calling upon Adenauer with instructions from the Holy See to make a formal request that the federal government should appeal to the federal constitutional court for a judgment on whether the school law of Lower Saxony was consistent with the Reichskonkordat—a matter of absolutely paramount interest to the German hierarchy and the Pope—Archbishop Muench found the chancellor "quite excited." The cause of this excitement, however, was not the purported anti-Catholic school law. Quite the contrary, it was a series of recent Catholic church activities which Adenauer considered susceptible of the charge of "clericalism and confessionalism." He first expressed high indignation over the church's attempts during that period to alter the law holding Catholic priests liable to severe punishment for performing a religious marriage prior to the civil ceremony. Even though the statute was one of Bismarck's original pieces of Kulturkampf legislation, Adenauer showed no patience with the episcopat's feelings and railed against their efforts to have it dropped. The Nuncio further found him "angry" with Bishop Döpfner and "annoyed" with Cardinal Wendel because of their treatment of Protestants. When Muench succeeded in shifting the conversation back to the point of his official call, Adenauer brushed aside the démarche with a spare comment that the time was not "opportune" for an appeal to the court. Muench saw through this and commented in his diary that Adenauer was in fact "using dilatory tactics to appease Protestants so as not to lose them for the CDU." A confessionally viable CDU, a popular government, and a western-oriented foreign policy—these and not the desires of the German hierarchy or the Pope himself—were of importance to Adenauer.

Not surprisingly, the relationship between Adenauer and the Catholic bishops lacked a basis for confidence and cooperation. Already in the inter-war period Adenauer had the reputation of being a liberal in church-state questions. After 1945, indeed, many bishops had not forgotten or forgiven his public clash with Cardinal Faulhaber at the Munich Catholic assembly in 1922, when he had warned against ecclesiastical disloyalty to the Weimar Republic. For this reason he was neither especially trusted nor liked by most of the hierarchy when he became chancellor in 1949. The disdain evident in Cardinal Faulhaber's remark that "this of all men became the first Chancellor of the Federal Republic" [28] was shared by other bishops. It was primarily Adenauer's stand on Western alignment and Western defense that finally led the bishops, in their stark anticommunist mood, to develop real confidence in him and to honor him as a great Catholic statesman.

Even had Adenauer been inclined to consult Catholic church leaders, he would have been unable to find a bishop with anything approaching a sophis-ticated knowledge of the affairs of state. Frings, the obvious person to consti-tute a link to the hierarchy, was interested in social policy, which Adenauer left to others, and had no grasp of international politics. There were other obstacles. Although both men knew one another from their early middle age, came from the same social background in the same city, and possessed a similar conservative political temperament, they were never close friends. Immediately after the war they shared a deep mistrust of British policy and worked together to try to modify it. But when Adenauer gave up the fight for confessional schools in the Parliamentary Council, the relationship between the two was irremediably torn, and they subsequently found themselves at odds more often than not. "If the Catholic Church exerts influence on Ade-nauer," Bishop Kunst claimed in an interview during Adenauer's chancel-lorship, "it is certainly not through Cardinal Frings." The personal gap be-tween them was wide. In general Frings thought Adenauer cynical and unreli-able, while Adenauer considered Frings naive and narrow-minded. Indeed, Frings' approach to politics was more pastoral than practical. This approach suited Adenauer well, since it spared him from the Catholic side the trou-blesome political kibitzing to which he was continuously subjected from many Protestant church and lay leaders. In later years, when he wanted to know the hierarchy's view on a matter of public policy or when he was interested in the Catholic theological position on some particular issue, he generally turned to his son, Monsignor Paul Adenauer, who lived with him at

---

28. Quoted in von Aretin, "Kardinal Faulhaber–Kämpfer oder Mitläufer?" in *Frankfurter Hefte*, May 1966.

Rhöndorf. Monsignor Adenauer not only knew all the important persons in German Catholic life, but also maintained close touch with Father Robert Leiber in Rome and through him enjoyed a direct link to the Vatican.

But to the end of his chancellorship, Adenauer maintained a cool relationship to the hierarchy. "Excellent Catholic . . . but critical of Church authorities—'too demanding,' " as Muench once remarked. Adenauer's treatment of the bishops could often be peremptory to the point of brutishness. "Blackmailer's methods again," Ivo Zeiger complained to Muench regarding the chancellor's mode of dealing with the Catholic church—in this particular case, Adenauer's threat to treat the Reichskonkordat as invalid unless the Nunciatur were moved from Bavaria to Bonn. While Adenauer always considered it a political necessity to receive Catholic lay group delegations, to hear their requests, and after each election to thank them for their help in the CDU's campaign, he was in private appalled by their clericalism. His concessions to them were minimal and, even then, worried him later. Significantly enough, the papal award—the order of the gold spur—which Adenauer was granted in 1956, was far from being a token of a grateful church's thanks to a loyal son. Rather, according to Muench's diary, it was a concession to Adenauer's own demand, as he himself put it, for an addition to his collection of "decorations from other governments." He deserved this, he claimed with disarming cynicism, as "the outstanding Catholic European statesman" and because it "would raise my prestige in European affairs."

It was against this general background that Böhler carried out his liaison function. He never lost sight of the fact that cooperation had to work both ways and that the hierarchy had to do its best to keep the CDU in power. From Adenauer, who was not inclined to give the church much, he extracted support for Catholic interests in the social sphere; in the church, which wanted to minimize its direct political involvement, he encouraged active support for Adenauer's defense and foreign policies. The coordination of these interests was a far deeper process than could be set in motion by any individual alone, but it was Böhler who did more than anyone else to bring the two sides together and to give practical effect to this coincidence of interests.

Böhler's greatest obstacle was Böhler himself. A thoroughly pre-Vatican II man, he regarded the mass of Catholics as a docile flock which should obediently follow its shepherds' advice. He had no patience with dissenters in the Catholic camp or with those, like Social Democrats and Free Democrats, who did not share his philosophy. While he had occasional contact with Social Democrats and FDP ministers—characteristically in secret—he largely cut himself off from all but politically orthodox Catholics. At the same time he was regarded as such a clericalist that President Theodor Heuss and some other officials would have nothing to do with him. It was widely felt that he pushed too much, too fast, too far. Bonn was not Weimar, and the CDU was not the Zentrum. By the mid-1950s the mood in the CDU and in German politics generally had greatly narrowed the scope for a church representative in making specific demands of ministerial officials and legislators. Each victory increased resentment, and Böhler's influence gradually declined, particularly as the potential for Personalpolitik, one of his main weapons, diminished.

Ironically, Böhler nowhere evoked more suspicion than in the Vatican itself. Even there he came to be regarded as too uncompromising and too aggressive. When given in 1956 the styling "excellency"—with the implied rank of bishop—this was not a Vatican acknowledgment of his services to the church, as it was put about at the time, but was in fact to raise him to the equivalent status of his Protestant counterpart Bishop Kunst. Only a short time later, as Muench's diary reveals, Pius XII complained to Cardinal Frings with papal understatement: "Boehler seems to have pushed himself forward too much." In Pius' view, Böhler had taken over many of the functions of the nunciature, damaging its mission and prestige. For nearly two years the controversy over Böhler ensued among the Vatican, Cardinal Frings and the Nuncio, leaving the object of the imbroglio a deeply wounded man. While it is tempting to speculate—and Böhler succumbed to the temptation—that Adenauer was behind the Pope's dissatisfaction, Pius' concern over the German hierarchy's assertion of political independence was no doubt genuine.

Böhler died suddenly in 1958. His successor was Father Wilhelm Wissing, religious counsellor of the Catholic Farm Youth Movement. Wissing faced two formidable difficulties. The organizations that Böhler had built up were largely his personal instruments and could not be handled in the same way by others. The central committee of German Catholics, for instance, was created in part to reinforce the work of the Catholic Office but by that very fact shared much of its area of responsibility. After Böhler's death the central committee asserted a more independent role, and its religious adviser, Monsignor Bernard Hanssler, often intervened directly with the government. Wissing's second problem was the fast changing political climate as the twilight of the Adenauer era approached. Recognizing that Böhler's tactics had become in many ways self-defeating, he had to feel his way toward a new approach. This he accomplished with some success. He reduced the obsessive secrecy of the Catholic Office. He extended cautious feelers to the SPD, the trade union movement, and other groups that had been virtually boycotted by the Catholic Office. He was more inclined to make general suggestions than to raise specific demands. It was indicative that his relations with Adenauer were warmer and with Globke cooler than Böhler's had been.

Wissing, who retired because of illness in 1966, was succeeded by Wilhelm Tenhumberg, Auxiliary Bishop of Münster, who himself left the position three years later upon being appointed Bishop of Münster. He was followed in turn by Wilhelm Wöste, an ecclesiastical backwoodsman, whose appointment clearly signified that the bishops preferred someone less politically active and ambitious in the position. Tenhumberg and Wöste followed the general tactical course of their predecessor, with the result that the substantive work of the Catholic Office during the past fourteen years is marked by a number of clear trends. Considerable attention has been given since 1962 to a church role in development aid projects in backward countries. The Catholic Office has acted as an intermediary between the government and church agencies in negotiations over funds and projects. Increasing interest has also been shown in humanitarian assistance (through legislation or executive policy) to groups and causes which have no spokesman or pressure group representing their interests. The Catholic Office has intervened on behalf of groups as diverse as foreign workers in Germany and the victims of the war in Biafra. Some cynics say that this is merely diversification by a company whose old line of trade is on the decline. But the fact remains that, for whatever reasons, the church is assisting persons often forgotten by the politicians. Another major development has been the cultivation of Social Democrats and trade union officials. Between 1966 and 1969 meetings were held once a month among Tenhumberg; Carlo Schmid, minister for Bundesrat affairs; Herbert Wehner, minister for all-German affairs; and Georg Leber, minister of transport. Although these contacts were later less cordial and frequent, as the relationship between the church and the SPD froze up again after 1969, the Catholic Office remains the church's sole channel to the SPD and FDP leadership.

Tenhumberg's period of office also coincided with a period of unprecedented stress in German Catholicism in the wake of the Vatican Council and a steady secularization of German society. Between 1965 and 1968 the controversies over schools, church taxes, and birth control exploded. Tenhumberg, sensitive to the feelings of the mass of the laity and to public opinion generally, did his best to move the hierarchy in a progressive direction—appealing to the bishops to compromise on confessional schools, to reveal information on church income, and to show some understanding of the laity's view on birth control. He moved them only slightly, but the fact that relations between the hierarchy and the faithful are no worse than they are is in fair measure due to his mediating influence.

But the main purpose of the Catholic Office remains as it was originally: to enunciate the Catholic theological position and the hierarchy's attitude on issues under consideration by the government and the Bundestag. During the past decade these have included, in addition to the school problem and development aid, virtually the entire range of social legislation—family, marriage, and divorce legislation; penal reform; wartime compensation matters; legislation concerning youth and education; conscription legislation; old-age insurance; and so on. As in Böhler's time, the church's views are conveyed through official approaches to parliamentarians, ministries, and the Chancellery as well as through the institutions maintained by the Catholic Office.

The groups founded by Böhler still exist in slightly altered form. The Tuesday Circle, which became the Catholic Club, is now the Wilhelm Böhler Club. It has 300 members (ministerial officials, parliamentarians, churchmen, and a variety of others, including journalists) who, with their guests, meet every two weeks. The ecclesiastical-political group now has roughly 35 members—the vicars general of the West German dioceses along with a handful of church officials, theologians, and lay experts. It meets every three months for two days and remains the principal channel of contact with the dioceses. Finally, the Catholic Office maintains ten working groups, the topics and membership of which change with the political issues facing the church. A working group generally has about 30 members, all of whom serve voluntarily but whose names are never divulged. One of the oldest groups, that on penal reform, has included among its members professors, judges of various instances, ministerial officials, parliamentarians, lawyers, prison chaplains, theologians, and church officials. The approach at these meetings—and in the work. of the Catholic Office generally—is not, as in Böhler's time, one of making specific demands, but of laying out the church's general standpoint and then exchanging views on whether and to what extent the law can be written to take account of this position. However, since the CDU's fall from power in 1969, the whole point of the operation has become conspicuously academic. For the great weakness of these committees, epitomizing the essential flaw of the church's whole political approach, has been their restriction to Christian Democrats and, even at that, the party's staunchest conservatives rather than its younger or more intellectual members.

Catholic political interests continue to be fostered by a number of other groups. The central committee of German Catholics broadly represents the Catholic lay movement vis-à-vis the government and at the same time tries to influence public opinion through resolutions, appeals, speeches and so on. The central committee continues to maintain working groups, though it has reduced the number from twenty to five—for marriage and family affairs, agricultural problems, German policy in Eastern Europe, and "economic development and peace" (the German chapter of the international Catholic movement, Justitia et Pax). Since 1965 the central committee has also had advisory councils both to assist in its normal activities and to advise the bishops' conference in its work. There are four such bodies—for educational affairs, political affairs, press and public relations, and ecclesiastical responsibilities of the laity. Although the advisory councils, with 40 to 70 members, are much larger than the working groups, the membership is similar, each comprising parliamentarians, ministerial officials, journalists, professors, trade unionists, lay experts, church officials, and theologians. The political working group of Catholic organizations was transformed in 1969 into the association of Catholic organizations so as, in the general postconciliar atmosphere, to give laymen more independence and to remove the stigma of the organization's function as agent of the Catholic Office for propagating government policy. The new body will be more independent of the Catholic Office and will probably withdraw somewhat from political activity. Coordination of Catholic political activities remains a difficult task and further reorganization is currently under active consideration.

In these ways the postwar period witnessed the establishment by Catholics of an elaborate extraparliamentary political structure. Designed as a substitute for the Center party, it was to act as ultimate defender of Catholic interests. In practice this arrangement served neither the church nor the political process well. The church became hostage to the Christian Democrats, and they victim to complacency. Yet even by the end of the 1960s, few bishops recognized that this strategy had put the church in a political cul de sac and had so compromised its pastoral responsibilities that some young Catholics now consider it only logical in shifting from the CDU and to the SPD to abandon their church at the same time.

Little or nothing, in short, has changed over the years in the church's political approach. At the beginning of the 1970s most Catholic lay organizations are as intimately and as exclusively linked to the CDU as they were in the late 1940s. They continue to discourage their members from joining the SPD, while such important lay groups as the Catholic worker's movement and the Catholic artisan's Kolping Family still forbid their officials from affiliating themselves with the party. The central committee of German Catholics, which had the daring to permit Georg Leber membership from 1968 to 1971, now has Bundestag vice-president Hermann Schmidt-Vockenhausen as its sole Social Democratic member. Like the Catholic news agency, the central committee is regarded on all sides as little more than a propaganda instrument for the Christian Democrats. *Publik,* the Catholic weekly newspaper, which tried to bring fresh intellectual air into the Catholic world and foster a dialogue between the church and the SPD, was liquidated by the bishops in 1971 after three years of publication. Even the Catholic Office, which at the end of the 1960s had begun leading the church toward a modus vivendi with the Social Democrats, remains dominated by backward-looking Christian Democrats.

Whatever the pastoral damage the church may have done by this, its great political sin was not clericalism as such. It had as much right to close contact with the CDU as the trade unions with the SPD or the Federation of German Industry with the FDP. Its supreme error was rather that of total partisanship. After 1969 this left the church with no firm links to the parties in power and the two sides consequently ignorant of the views and aspirations of the other, to the disadvantage of effective parliamentary government. Committed to the most conservative brand of Christian Democracy at a time when German society is in a decidedly progressive mood, the hierarchy now finds itself increasingly challenged and ignored. The 1972 election demonstrated that, to a degree unprecedented since the Kulturkampf, Catholics are politically independent of their church. In the course of a quarter of a century, the church's overriding objective of Catholic unity had undermined its political power. Currently it has little of either.

THE CHURCH-STATE RELATIONSHIP

The Legal Relationship between Church and State

IN contrast to German political development, which has been marked by sharp breaks and fresh starts, the church-state relationship has been characterized by a relatively continuous flow, with the result that contemporary German civil and constitutional law in this field bear the traces of centuries of development. The close association between church and state that resulted from the Reformation was taken so much for granted over the centuries that Germany never experienced the violent outbursts of popular anticlericalism that occurred in most of Western Europe in the late nineteenth and early twentieth centuries. The various waves of secularism—even those forcibly imposed by Napoleon and Bismarck—had remarkably little social impact. Politics and religion, church and state, were caught up in such an epiphenomenal relationship that it appeared impossible in the public mind to disentangle them. It was the collapse of the Second Reich itself rather than popular feeling or deep-seated social trends which destroyed the long throne-altar connection. Even so, the Weimar constitution, which in most aspects represented a new and thoroughly liberal course, kept intact most of the traditional legal and psychological ties between church and state.

In 1948, when German political representatives met to draw up the Basic Law—as the constitution pending reunification was to be called—they had a tacit but deliberate desire to steer clear of the church-state issue. The Herrenchiemsee conference, which prepared the first draft of the Basic Law, did not mention the topic at all. In the Parliamentary Council, as the constitutional assembly was known, the prevailing opinion—shared by the Christian Democratic leader Adenauer no less than by the Social Democratic leader Schumacher—was that the work would be arduous enough without being complicated by this problem. It was considered a Pandora's box and best left to the Länder to grapple with.

Leaders of both churches, on the other hand, were still under the trauma of the Third Reich and wanted categorical safeguards protecting the churches from any future totalitarian threat. They considered it vital that constitutional provisions be made to "recognize" the churches' essential independence of the state and to guarantee their freedom to carry out their mission. They also sought clear assurances with respect to certain basic human rights; to freedom of religion and conscience; to special protection for the family; to a recognition of the right of parents to have their children educated in confessional schools and to a guarantee of religious education in schools; and to the continued validity of all treaties and concordats in the church-state sphere. While the churches did not call for a radical revision of their pre-1933 relationship to the state, they were in fact—by asking for complete legal autonomy coupled with broad responsibilities in the educational and social sphere—demanding a privileged position and an unprecedented influence in public life. To this extent their requests amounted to a desire for a significant revision of their status.

Probably at no other time in German history did the churches find themselves so united over such a broad range of political and social issues.[1] But while the Evangelical church was content to make its position known and to accept general provisions incorporating its views, the Catholic approach was—as in 1933 with respect to the Reichskonkordat—compulsively legalistic. The church's technique was to exert the utmost pressure to secure specific legal guarantees which it could then insist upon, despite any change of government, despite any shift in public opinion, and despite any novel social trends. This approach reflected not only the personal inclination of the Catholic church's liaison representative to the Parliamentary Council, Monsignor Wilhelm Böhler, but also the attitude of Pope Pius XII, with whom Böhler was in close touch over the Parliamentary Council's deliberations.

By contrast, the Evangelical representative, Heinrich Held, President of the Rhineland provincial church, played almost no role in the work on the Basic Law.[2] In the Council itself the main spokesmen for the Catholic church

---

1. The main differences were within the Catholic hierarchy itself and concerned not only ecclesiastical matters but such questions as how strongly federalist the new state should be. Böhler had to work hard to hammer out a common position. As Lambert Lensing, the CDU chairman in Westphalia, once wrote to a CDU member of the Council: "Böhler repeatedly stated that it had taken a long time in church circles to reach a clear decision on what demands should be made to anchor church and educational matters in the Basic Law. Monsignor Böhler referred to the long negotiations which he personally had conducted in Munich." Letter of August 6, 1949, to Helene Weber, *File 314–3, Lensing Persönl. Parteiakten*, Archives of the Westphalian CDU, Dortmund.

2. It is difficult today to find anyone in ecclesiastical or political circles who recalls any activity by Held in the Parliamentary Council and the Rhineland Church can find nothing in its archives that can shed any light on the Church President's role.

were Adolf Süsterhenn (CDU), zealously assisted by Helene Weber (CDU), and the two representatives of the Center party, Johannes Brockmann and Helene Wessel. Protestant interests on the other hand were represented, not by Protestant Christian Democrats, but by the two representatives of the German party, a purely Protestant group with historic connections to the Zentrum. While the Catholic representatives were under the control of Böhler, the German party officials not only acted independently, but had much closer contact with Böhler than with Held and were at one point indirectly admonished by Bishop Lilje against resting their argumentation so much on (Catholic) natural-rights concepts.

Initially the churches hoped that their aims would be included in the fundamental-rights section of the Basic Law. These points touched sensitive emotional and political nerves, however, and encountered immediate resistance from the Social Democrats and the Free Democrats, who argued that church-state matters were too complicated to be opened up to examination and were in any case better left entirely to the Länder, as the Western occupation powers had demanded in a memorandum of November 22, 1948 to the Council. They pointed out that the Council's preeminent objective was to create a state where the churches, along with other social institutions, would ex hypothesi be free, without needing the protection of a catalog of special rights. Theodor Heuss, the Free Democratic leader and later German president, openly complained at one point that the churches were concentrating too much on protecting themselves from a past menace. In no time a schism developed within the Council, aligning the Christian Democrats, the Center party, and the German party against the Social Democrats, the Free Democrats, and the Communists. Although the latter three parties together held a tiny majority, the Free Democrats were often willing, when it came to pragmatic issues, to meet the churches part way, making possible a number of important compromises.

The church-state issue first formally reached the Council in November 1948 with the German party's tabling of a letter from Bishop Wurm to Adenauer (as Council chairman) which generally set out the views already summarized. This was followed by a formal proposal of the CDU, Zentrum, and German party for church-state provisions recognizing the churches' autonomy, their traditional property and taxing rights, and existing church-state treaties. The Council as a whole eventually agreed that while a discussion of ecclesiastical affairs should be postponed, it would be appropriate to include freedom of religion among the basic rights. This eventually became Article 4 of the Basic Law. The right, also contained in this article, of conscientious objection to military service was, however, added at the initiative of the

Social Democrats and, though a majority of Catholic Christian Democrats were against the provision, the church representatives neither opposed nor supported it.

Wurm, who during the Third Reich had openly condemned euthanasia, medical experiments on human beings, and compulsory sterilization, also asked in his letter for a specific prohibition of such practices. This proposal found wide support and was eventually incorporated in Article 2, which guaranteed "the right to life and the inviolability of the person." For its part the Catholic church was especially anxious to have constitutional recognition given to "family rights." In reaction to the removal of children from their homes during the Third Reich, both churches further asked for guarantees against the separation of children from their parents. The Social Democrats resisted bringing such matters into the Basic Law. They maintained that the constitution should confine itself to the classic civil rights and pointed out that they had resisted trade-union requests for a guarantee of specific "social rights." Against the votes of the Social Democrats and Communists, the Council nevertheless adopted Article 6, giving "marriage and family" the "special protection of the state" and declaring "care and education of children" to be "the natural right of the parents." In response to the churches' view, the article also prohibited the "separation of children from the family" unless the child was "threatened with neglect."

In all the Council's work no issue was so strongly or lengthily contested as that of "parents' rights"—that is, the Catholic notion that parents possess a God-given right to have their children educated in state-financed schools where they could be taught by Catholic teachers and given instruction in history, literature, and so on, in a "Catholic spirit." The Free Democrats and Social Democrats were at first not even willing to discuss the subject. They pointed out that education was among the topics which the occupation powers wanted reserved to the Länder, and they insisted that the basic rights section be a simple list of fundamental rights. However, securing a guarantee of publicly financed confessional schools was the supreme social aim of the Catholic church, and supporters of "parents' rights" made themselves, as John Golay has written, "the most pertinacious minority in the Parliamentary Council." [3]

Again and again, in the face of the arguments of the Free Democrats and Social Democrats that confessional schools would be a financial burden and a

---

3. The background of the school issue prior to the Basic Law's promulgation is sketched in Chapter 8, pp. 208–213; Golay, *The Founding of the Federal Republic of Germany*, p. 196.

divisive rather than an integrating force in a society faced with digesting millions of refugees, Catholic representatives iterated and reiterated their arguments. Finally, a majority of the Council agreed to an insubstantial school article (Article 7) which, lifting a sentence directly from Bishop Wurm's letter to the Council, made religious instruction a normal part of the secondary-school curriculum. At the suggestion of the Free Democrats the article further stipulated that it was up to parents to decide whether their children should attend religious instruction and that teachers had the right to decline to provide such instruction.

But neither the direct interventions of Cardinal Frings and Bishop Michael Keller of Münster nor all of Böhler's negotiating skill—nor the chorus of public threats and appeals by Catholic lay groups—succeeded in persuading the Free Democrats and Social Democrats to go further than this. Even Theodor Heuss, who had emerged as the intellectual leader of the Parliamentary Council and who was the particular object of Böhler's attempt to split the opposition, could not be swayed. This impasse on the issue threatened the whole of the Council's work. What role, if any, the occupation authorities—who were increasingly impatient over the delay in completing the Basic Law—played in breaking the deadlock is not entirely clear. It does, however, emerge from Cardinal Frings' papers that General Robertson sought at this moment to confer with the Archbishop. To Robertson's extreme annoyance, Frings refused to meet with him so as, in the words of his response to the Military Governor, "to avoid giving the impression of wishing to interfere in high policy matters." [4]

In any event, in early February 1949 the representatives of the CDU, FDP, and SPD, under strong pressure to complete the work, privately reached a compromise on outstanding differences. Adenauer, who considered it more important to have a solidly established liberal state without confessional schools than to have confessional schools against the convictions of two major parties, promised to drop the school issue. Böhler and Frings were profoundly shocked, and both wrote to Adenauer, reproaching him for having sacrificed the Catholic church's most important constitutional objective. The Catholic bishops were so vexed that they met in special session and agreed "under no circumstances" to give up their demand for confessional schools. Even the Pope intervened (almost certainly at Böhler's instigation) with a sharply phrased letter of February 20, 1949, to the German hierarchy

---

4. Letter to General Bishop of February 12, 1949, *File CR 25/18,* Diocesan Archives, Cologne.

which Cardinal Frings promptly forwarded to the Council. In this letter Pius XII criticized the "meaningless explanations" given by the opponents of "parents' rights" and the Reichskonkordat. He added that nothing would cause him, a true friend of Germany, more pain than to witness the adoption of church-state arrangements in effect similar to those of the Third Reich.[5] Böhler, in his letter to Adenauer, and the Catholic bishops, in their Lenten pastoral messages, had appealed for a national referendum to decide the issue. When this proposal was formally presented to the Council, the SPD leader, Kurt Schumacher, privately agreed to it provided there were also a referendum on the nationalization of industry. Adenauer would have none of this. Not only did he care little about "parents' rights," he also showed the virtually unanimous distaste in the Council for anything savoring of Nazi plebiscitary government. And the idea of a referendum on nationalization was to him unthinkable.

The remaining issue, the legal church-state relationship, also ran into trouble when it was officially raised with the Social Democrats and the Free Democrats. Heuss insisted that the issues were too intricate to touch and warned that if they were opened to full examination, the churches might lose some of the advantages (as in the financial sphere) which they had enjoyed in the past. As a compromise, he offered his party's support for a simple adoption of the church-state provisions of the Weimar constitution. The SPD at first resisted Heuss' proposal on the ground that it would give the churches a privileged position over other groups, such as the trade unions. But in the end Article 140, which incorporated the "church articles" of the Weimar constitution, was accepted without debate. Although the churches would have liked in addition an explicit declaration of their legal autonomy and recognition of their "importance for the maintenance and strengthening of the religious and ethical foundations of human life,"[6] they accepted the Council's decision.

This solution still left the question of the continued validity of the various church-state treaties—the Reichskonkordat, the concordats with Bavaria (1924), Prussia (1929), and Baden (1932), as well as the Protestant provincial church treaties with Bavaria (1924), the Palatinate (1924), Prussia (1931) and Baden (1932). While the Council had no reluctance in accepting the Land concordats and treaties, which were all pre-Third Reich, the proposal to recognize the Reichskonkordat raised an immediate storm. "I believe we

---

5. Catholic bishops quoted in *Herder Korrespondenz,* April 1949; Pope's letter in *Kirchlicher Anzeiger für die Erzdiözese Köln,* May 15, 1949.

6. This was the wording of the original CDU/CSU, Center party, and German party proposal; "Antrag vom 29. November 1948" in *Artikel 123,* Bundestag Archives.

are all generally clear on the fact," Heuss remarked, "that this concordat was, from a legal standpoint, concluded in a thoroughly deceitful way and that it received no ratification by any sort of parliamentary body." To this his party colleague and later president of the Federal Constitutional Court, Thomas Höpker-Aschoff, added, "The so-called Reichskonkordat was concluded by a band of criminals with the deliberate intention of not honoring it. We cannot be expected explicitly to recognize this Reichskonkordat here in the Basic Law. That we will never on any account do." [7] But in making provision for the status of prewar international treaties, the Council in effect provided (in Article 123) that all laws not repealed by the occupation authorities would remain in force unless they were incompatible with the Basic Law. This covered the Reichskonkordat beneath several layers of ambiguity.

Although the Basic Law contained clear traces of the churches' views, it fell far short of their optimum desires, particularly on the school issue. As a consequence, some Catholics and a few Protestants were reluctant to accept the new constitution. The Center party and German party representatives in fact abstained in the final vote, partly for this reason. Böhler, however, recognized that the churches had achieved some significant concessions and feared that a large number of abstentions could prevent the Allies from proceeding with the establishment of the Federal Republic. He successfully prevailed upon wavering Christian Democrats to vote for adoption, and the Basic Law was approved by an overwhelming majority.

The Evangelical church made no comment on the new constitution.[8] The Catholic bishops were, as usual, divided in spite of their outward unity.

---

7. *Parlamentarischer Rat, Verhandlungen des Hauptausschusses,* 22nd session (December 8, 1948); the background of the Reichskonkordat is described in Chapter 8, pp. 209 ff.

8. The council of the Evangelical church apparently never discussed the matter; no record of a meeting on the topic can be found in the EKD archives in Hanover, and none of the surviving members of the council at the time (Lilje, Niemöller, and Wilhelm Niesel) can recall a discussion of it. However, in a letter to Robert Lehr, a prominent Protestant CDU political leader, President Held expressed satisfaction at the inclusion in the Basic Law of the Weimar "church articles" and Article 7 on the family. He regretted the failure of the Parliamentary Council to accept "parents' rights" and feared that, since Catholic schools were guaranteed in the Reichskonkordat, Protestants might as a result be at a disadvantage. (Letter of February 12, 1949, Archives of the Rhineland provincial church.) Held's view can probably be considered indicative of the attitude of most Protestant church leaders. Despite the disappointment expressed in it. Held's letter to Lehr implicitly disproves an assertion by Adolf Süsterhenn that the church president favored a rejection of the Basic Law because it inadequately protected the churches' interests. See Adolf Süsterhenn, "Mitgestalter des Grundgesetzes" in Bernhard Bergmann and Josef Steinberg, *In Memoriam Wilhelm Böhler.*

Some believed that federalism had been taken too far, others that it did not go far enough. Some were dissatisfied with the basic-rights section, others with the provisions on marriage and family. All disapproved in varying degrees of the school provision and the lack of an explicit recognition of the Reichskonkordat. In a long official pronouncement regarding the Basic Law, the bishops decried these weaknesses and went so far as to declare that they consequently regarded the constitution "only as a temporary one which requires alteration as soon as possible." [9] At the same time they were deliberately very careful not to repeat their church's mistake during the Weimar Republic, when the hierarchy and many Catholics withheld support of the constitution and in that way weakened the democratic order; this time they were determined to preserve the republic. But reckoning that the Basic Law could be interpreted generously or stringently, and that with a friendly parliament and executive they would make the best of an unsatisfactory situation, the bishops encouraged loyal Catholics to enter the government. The CDU being the channel of this political engagement, the effect of this policy was to reinforce the Catholic church's commitment to the Christian Democrats. To this extent the church's position in the Federal Republic was more a function of politics than of law.

From an ecclesiastical point of view, the Basic Law represents little legal change from the Weimar Constitution. The only essential difference is that while the latter gave the Reich and the Länder concurrent authority to legislate on church-state matters, now the Länder, with their reserved powers, have exclusive authority to do so within the guidelines established in the Basic Law. These guidelines, moreover, set the minimum standards; the Länder may endow the churches with greater privileges and a higher status; many Lander have, in fact, done so. In the guidelines alone the churches enjoy a favored position in the state that is probably unique in the world, while admitting no political authority over themselves in return. The churches regard this arrangement, moreover, not as a *concession,* but as a *recognition* of their rightful status in society.

From a legal point of view, however, the Basic Law incorporates the Weimar constitution's fundamental ambiguity on the church-state relationship. Although the "church articles" declared that there is no state church, they left the precise relation between church and state unclear and, as a result, particularly susceptible to public attitudes and political circumstances

---

9. Quoted in *Herder Korrespondenz,* July 1949.

(and expediency). Exactly how, in what way, and to what degree the two spheres are separated is consequently a matter of legal and scholarly debate. It is in a state of flux as new treaties and concordats are concluded, old ones altered, existing ones reinterpreted by the courts, governments change, and public opinion shifts. Symptomatically, at the most recent symposium of German experts on church-state relations, the discussion was disconcertingly reminiscent of the medieval controversy over the delineation between *sacerdotium* and *imperium*—and was similarly indecisive. [10] It is on this uncertain foundation that a vast structure of ecclesiastical privileges has been developed.

By the terms of the Basic Law the churches have an unrestricted right to regulate and administer their affairs independently of the state. This means that the churches alone determine who may hold office even when this involves political factors (such as a Nazi past). The Reichskonkordat further expressly gives the Holy See complete freedom in its relations with the German hierarchy. Churches—in practice, Protestant provincial churches—have an unqualified right to unite or confederate without the approval of the state and may establish new ecclesiastical jurisdictions at will. In 1965 a Protestant parish in Hesse appealed to the federal constitutional court to invalidate a provincial church decision affecting parish borders. The court rejected the case on the ground that the state had no authority to review such ecclesiastical matters. The Reichskonkordat, however, requires the Catholic church to secure state approval for the establishment of a new diocese or for changes in existing diocesan borders.

In various Land concordats and in the Reichskonkordat the Catholic church has agreed to a degree of negative influence by the state in its appointment of bishops. Both the Reichskonkordat and Land concordats require that they be of German nationality, have had their higher education in Germany, and have had at least three years of theological training. The Reichskonkordat also gives the state a right to raise "objections of a general political nature" before the appointment of a bishop is made and requires the bishop to take an oath of loyalty to the minister president of the Land concerned or to the head of state. (An emendation in the appendix, however, declared that this provision did not imply a "state veto," and presumably any objections may therefore be disregarded by the church.) In certain areas of southern Germany a few aristocratic families and the mayors of some towns still retain

---

10. Veröffentlichungen der Vereinigung der Deutschen Staatsrechtslehrer, *Die Kirchen unter dem Grundgesetz*.

their medieval right to select the local parish priest; in practice nowadays the head of the family and the mayor give the bishop a choice of three names from which to choose. Some Protestant provincial churches have in postwar agreements given the state some slight influence over the appointment of their leaders; in Bavaria the Land synod must ascertain whether the Land government has any political objection to the proposed appointee. By contrast, the churches have the right to appoint such state officials as military, hospital, and prison chaplains and to approve the appointment of religious instructors in public schools. Normally all ecclesiastical officials appointed by or with the concurrence of the state—from bishops to prison chaplains—are considered civil servants and are paid by the state. There is also a graduated salary scale, extending from archbishop and bishop downward. The state also pays in part for the construction and upkeep of a bishop's residence and even some of his entertainment allowance.

One of the most remarkable features of the church-state relationship is the obligation of the state to provide for the education of the clergy in university theology faculties. On the one hand this compels the state to pay the members of the faculty and to secure church agreement before either opening a new faculty or closing an existing one. [11] On the other hand, it frees the faculty of church influence, since the state rather than the church appoints the teaching staff. It is the faculty itself which nominates the candidate and, while the church is consulted and may express a "reservation," the state almost always accepts the nominee. In practice the churches are extremely reluctant to raise any objection; since 1945 the Catholic church has done so rarely and the Evangelical church only once—in the case of an instructor who has since risen to be a full professor. As in the case of other professors in Germany, once installed, a theology professor can be dislodged by almost nothing short of death. Whatever his theological views, even if these are not consonant with the accepted doctrines of his church, the state will not dismiss him. Should he become a professed atheist or change his religion entirely, the state leaves him his professorial status and merely moves him to the philosophy faculty. The most negative action the churches can take on a professor whom they consider heretical is to warn their theology students not to study under him.

---

11. At the present time only the universities of Cologne, Düsseldorf, Giessen, and Constance have no theological faculty. The universities of Bochum, Bonn, Mainz, Münster, Munich, and Tübingen have both Catholic and Protestant faculties. There are only Protestant faculties at Berlin, Erlangen, Frankfurt, Göttingen, Heidelberg, Kiel, Marburg, and Saarbrücken (as well as at Jena, Halle, Greifswald, Leipzig, Rostock and East Berlin), and only Catholic faculties at Freiburg, Regensburg, and Würzburg.

No doubt tradition and other factors are responsible for the fact that the theological "brains" of both Protestantism and Catholicism have long been centered in Germany. But the total intellectual freedom which results from these constitutional arrangements undoubtedly plays a role as well. One of the most famous theologians of the nineteenth century, Adolf von Harnack, was appointed theology professor at Berlin by the Prussian government over Protestant church objections that he was too liberal. Successors have enjoyed similar professional security whether—as Bultmann, Käsemann and Braun— they were theologically heterodox or—as Gollwitzer and Bartsch—they were politically nonconformist. This is no less the case on the Catholic side, and it is because liberal theologians such as Küng, Metz, Rahner, Karl Lehmann, and Walter Kasper could thrive in Germany that German theologians led the liberal reform in the Vatican Council.

The "church articles" further guaranteed the churches the right freely to possess, administer, and dispose of property. While church officials are willing to divulge little information about their capital holdings, indications are that such wealth is relatively modest by the reputed standards of many American churches and the Church of England. In addition to urban real estate and stocks of undetermined value, the Catholic church owns a total of 1400 square miles of agricultural land and the Evangelical church (which suffered grievously through the Soviet land reform in East Germany and the loss of the Oder-Neisse territories) 500 square miles. [12] Property is owned by the diocese and provincial church and sometimes reflects local character. The diocese of Regensburg owns seventeen breweries, and the diocese of Trier can boast of several Mosel vinyards. (The unfortunate Protestants have only an inferior Rhine-Hesse Sylvaner.) The annual income from these capital assets is roughly estimated to be about twenty to thirty million marks for the Evangel- ical church; while no authoritative estimate is available for the Catholic church, its capital income is widely thought to be somewhat larger. This works out to about 2-3 percent of the total income of the two churches.

What makes the German ecclesiastical scene unusual and probably unique in the world is the constitutional guarantee of annual cash grants and

---

12. Letter of March 1969 from Paul Zieger, chief of the statistics office of the Evangelical Church Chancellory, Hanover. Except where indicated otherwise, all facts regarding Evangelical church income are from this source. The German press has been remarkably uninquisitive about the capital holdings of the churches. One journalist, Klaus Martens, in his book *Wie reich ist die Kirche?*, estimates that the churches own over six billion marks worth of negotiable property and a like amount in their charitable infrastructure (hospitals, kindergartens, and such). These figures obviously exclude the value of cathedrals, churches, and church treasures of incalculable worth.

the authority of the churches to levy taxes. The state grants, in a few cases traceable to customs and agreements of the immediate post-Reformation situation, are principally a consequence of the secularization of 1803. In that year the Imperial Reichstag (in the decree formidably entitled "Reichsdeputationshauptschluss") gave monasteries, church treasures, and church lands to the state but in compensation ordered the state (in practice the ruling house, the province, or the town) to cover the churches' expenses with annual payments. Elsewhere in Europe the church was normally reimbursed for its loss of property or privileges by a one-time cash settlement. The 1803 arrangement was guaranteed in the Weimar constitution, was honored by the National Socialists as well as by the four occupation powers, and is maintained in the Basic Law. Some of the original donations in kind—firewood and agricultural produce, for instance—are still made to parishes by many South German towns. The financial payments have gradually increased over the past fifty years; in 1965 they amounted to 241 million marks. Small grants are also made for the upkeep of church property. Protestant provincial churches and parishes receive about 60 percent of such grants, and the Catholic dioceses and parishes collect the remainder. This generally represents about 7-8 percent of the church's total income. The size of the payments varies substantially from Land to Land and, though fixed by law, depends largely upon the attitude of the government to the church—as a result of which Bremen gives nothing and Rhineland-Palatinate pays, per capita, over twenty times as much at Hamburg (see Table 7).

Tabie 7
State Funds to Churches for Ecclesiastical Purposes in 1965 (in marks)

	Free Grants	Property Grants	Total
Schleswig-Holstein	5,662,000	26,000	6,049,000
Lower Saxony	16,764,000	15,000	16,779,000
North Rhine-Westphalia	34,454,000	2,117,000	37,046,000
Hesse	18,641,000	66,000	18,707,000
Rhineland-Palatinate	33,610,000	310,000	33,931,000
Baden-Württemberg	52,672,000	9,212,000	62,379,000
Bavaria	50,511,000	8,400,000	58,984,000
Saarland	3,470,000	–	3,470,000
Hamburg	807,000	8,000	815,000
Bremen	–	–	–
Berlin (West)	9,296,000	–	9,296,000
Federal Government	15,107,000	–	15,107,000
Total	240,994,000	20,154,000	262,563,000

Report of 19 April 1968 of Statistics Office of the Evangelical Church Chancellory

By the mid-nineteenth century the level of these grants had already fallen short of the churches' expenses. The state was unwilling to increase the sums but permitted the churches instead to levy a tax on their members. This understanding was incorporated in the Weimar constitution and thence into the Basic Law; it is further guaranteed for the Catholic church in the Reichskonkordat. Actual taxing arrangements have always been worked out on a Land basis (dioceses and provincial churches crossing Land borders in some cases have different tax rates in the two Länder), and since 1955 state authorities have collected the tax at a charge of 3-4 percent of the receipts. The churches themselves determine the level of the tax and whether it is to be on income, property, or some other basis. Before the war the tax was about 3-4 percent of the income tax paid by an individual; with the establishment of the Federal Republic, it was put at 10 percent. (Protestant churches have negotiated agreements with the very rich limiting the church tax paid to the state.) Some parishes also levy a tax on property. The churches decide whether the tax is to be collected by the Land for the diocese/provincial church or by the community for the local parish. Since there is almost no provision for sharing income, the local arrangement often causes particular inequities. With parishes rich in some communities and poor in others, the local tax has varied on occasion from nothing to 26 percent. [13]

The sweeping authority of the churches to raise taxes as they wish has always been fully upheld by the courts. Astonishingly enough, only since 1965 have the churches even been restricted to taxing their own members. Prior to that time, by a strange but deliberate provision of the "church articles" of the Weimar constitution, they were permitted to tax juridical persons. As late as 1958, for example, the federal administrative court upheld a tax imposed by Catholic parishes in Heidelberg upon the German Shell Oil Company to cover the costs of a church construction program. Two textile manufacturers similarly assessed by another Catholic parish, however, managed in 1965 to bring their case to the federal constitutional court, which found that while such taxation was clearly permitted by the "church articles," it is inconsistent with the ideological neutrality of the state as guaranteed by the Basic Law. On the same ground the constitutional court shortly thereafter struck down both the taxation of individuals whose spouses only are church members and the splitting of the tax between the churches when husband and wife are of different confessions. The last decision has been highly unpopular with the churches.

---

13. Flatten, *Fort mit Kirchensteuer?*, p. 19.

These decisions have not, however, perceptibly slowed down the steady rise in the churches' income. Although figures for the two churches throughout the whole postwar period are not available, enough of a picture can be constructed to show the striking increase in church income. In Hesse, for instance, the churches' income from taxes went up 800 percent in the first fifteen years of the Federal Republic's history (see Table 8). The increase for all Protestant provincial churches was, as Table 9 shows, almost as great in the fifteen years from 1953.

All that is known about Catholic dioceses in the Federal Republic is that together they collected a total of 700 million marks in church taxes in 1961, a figure that rose to 1,300 million in 1968. (The smaller share of church taxes going to the Catholic church is due not only to the smaller Catholic population, but to the fact that Catholics tend to be somewhat poorer than Protestants.) With an annual tax income of this order—and rising—the churches are clearly in a solid financial condition. "Nowhere else in the world," one Catholic writer crisply put it, "can bishops rest assured that church funds will rise in direct proportion to the national income and that everyone who is baptized—whether he participates in the life of the parish or not—will make his contribution." [14]

Table 8
Church Income from Taxes for Hesse

| | Tax income in millions of marks | | | |
	1949	1954	1958	1963
Evangelical Church	17.8	37.1	59.3	149.1
Catholic Church	7.4	16.0	27.7	75.0
Total	25.2	53.1	87.0	224.1

Der Spiegel, May 27, 1964.

Table 9
Evangelical Church Income From Church Taxes
and Church Dues (Excluding West Berlin)
Tax income in millions of marks

	Income tax	Other tax	Church dues	Total
1953	336,019	14,999	8,562	359,580
1963	1,245,744	37,585	29,530	1,312,860
1968	1,719,875	19,337	30,440	1,769,652

EKD Chancellory, Hanover

---

14. Volker Schmidt, "Was macht die Kirche mit dem vielen Geld?" in Greinacher and Risse (editors), *Bilanz des deutschen Katholizismus*, p. 248.

On the basis of the above figures, along with estimates of other church income, Table 10 provides a rough outline of the churches' total income at the present time. These figures—and they are supplemented by special government funds, to be described later—suggest that the German churches are among the richest in the world. The idea, in T. S. Eliot's words, that "the True Church need never stir/To gather in its dividends" has, however, become a major issue of public controversy. The impression of churches choking on money, combined with an almost total lack, until recently, of any hard information on church income and expenditure, led to increasingly widespread criticism in the press, radio, and television of the whole system of church finance. The public media's treatment of the matter, based on the premise that it is wrong in principle for churches to be well off, was generally one of breathless exposé. Critics made much of the fact that thousands of churches were constructed in the two decades after the war—more than in the four centuries since the Reformation—and that church taxes had gone up far more than the cost of living, wages, and similar indexes.

Church officials were embarrassed, if not worried, by the growing criticism and began removing the secrecy in which the whole subject of church finance had unwisely been wrapped. By 1965 the Evangelical church had fully accounted for its income from taxes and state grants, remaining discreet only about its capital holdings. Since 1964 a few Catholic dioceses have given varying amounts of information about their income; the dioceses of Cologne and Essen have been particularly candid, with the incidental intent of embarrassing other dioceses into similar frankness. In parrying the criticism by the public media, church officials have stressed that what they take in, they

Table 10
Estimated Church Income in 1968 (in Marks)

	Evangelical Church	Catholic Church
Church taxes and dues	1,769,000,000	1,300,000,000
Income from capital	20,000,000	not available
State grants	180,000,000	120,000,000
Offerings	100,000,000	100,000,000[a]
Special collections[b]	25,000,000	100,000,000
Total	2,074,000,000	1,620,000,000

a. Rough estimate of church sources.

b. Here are given merely the collections for assistance to underdeveloped areas: the Protestant "Brot für die Welt" and the Catholic "Misereor" and "Adventiat." In addition large sums were given in this year for humanitarian aid to Biafra.

spend—saving nothing, even for pastors' pensions—and that 80 percent of their income goes out in wages for their several hundred thousand church workers, who range from hospital attendants to clergymen. Although the criticism of church taxes has become steadily more strident, it has had little or no impact on the church member. "The taxpayers themselves have, indeed, scarcely reacted, either through protests against having to pay church tax or through leaving the church," a Protestant authority, has written. [15] Catholic officials are of a similar opinion. Although resignations have increased since 1969, their total number is insignificant and not demonstrably the result of the church tax.

In several respects, however, the churches are vulnerable to criticism. The evident relish with which they have amassed and spent their income has created the impression that money is a paramount interest. Recent tax negotiations with Lower Saxony and Hesse, for example, demonstrated no diffidence on the churches' part about putting their hands into the taxpayers' pockets. As a result "Church & Co." has become a popular gibe and ecclesiastical prestige has certainly not been enhanced. The deepest cause of popular cynicism—the suspicion that "the Church can sleep and feed at once,"—to cite Eliot once again—was well summed up in a *Simplicissimus* cartoon which pictured a Protestant pastor telling his youthful congregation on their confirmation day: "Should many of you find yourselves today in a house of God for the last time, we will still remain closely united through the church tax." This, however, is less a social than a pastoral problem, and the feeling has been spreading among churchmen that the existing system may be bad both for the churches and their members.

In fact, the church tax issue goes to the very core of the church-state relationship as it most directly affects the individual. At birth each person is registered with the state by religion. As soon as he earns an income, the church tax is automatically deducted for the church of which he is officially a member. He can stop paying the tax only by officially notifying the state of his wish to leave the church, after which he may not turn to the clergy for marriage, baptism, burial, or any other services. Both churches have insisted that every adherent either pay his tax or resign. This has provoked strong resentment among some laymen. One of them is Heinrich Böll, who in 1970 tried to call both the church's and the state's bluff by refusing to pay his church tax while declining to leave the Catholic church. The diocese of Cologne eventually filed suit against Böll, won the case and in 1972, not long

---

15. Zieger, "Die Kirchensteuer in Deutschland." In a letter of March 1969, Zieger stated that this continues to be the case.

before being awarded the Nobel prize for literature, the author was forced to pay his accumulated church tax.

By the terms of the Basic Law the churches clearly enjoy a body of important de jure privileges. In addition, they have secured many de facto prerogatives since 1949. The favored status, which they unsuccessfully sought from the Parliamentary Council, was gained in practice from the federal government and many Länder. The determination of the churchs to prevent the new German republic from going the way of the Weimar Republic, to intervene on behalf of the moral interests of the nation, and to influence the ultimate social aims of the people made the churches a strong force. The German people, aware of the churches' role during the occupation and skeptical at first of the political parties, invested the churches more than any other institution with their confidence. For the first ten years or so of the Federal Republic's history the churches occupied a position of broad social and political influence—an influence to which the succession of Christian Democratic governments was particularly susceptible.

The gap between this situation on the one hand and constitutional law on the other was glaring. The Basic Law had scarcely been adopted, however, when a leading authority on church-state law, Professor Rudolf Smend of Göttingen University, published a provocative and ingenious legal theory to bridge the gulf. Though the Basic Law reverts formally to the Weimar constitution in ecclesiastical matters, "when two constitutions say the same thing, that does not imply they mean the same thing," Smend argued. Although the letter of the law remains the same—indifference on the state's part toward the church and its mission—the Basic Law contains a tacit recognition that church and state must now cooperate in sustaining the Christian basis of life in Germany and that to this end the church has a right of "help, admonition, and intervention." In contrast to the Weimar system, "that means a new closeness to the state." This is often called the church's "public claim" ("Öffentlichkeitsanspruch"), but by whatever term, it represents the church's most important demand upon the state. As a result, he concluded, the "church articles" mean "something entirely different than in the Weimar Constitution." Smend's interpretation of the Basic Law set the tone for legal theory in the church-state field for over a decade. [16]

Interestingly enough, it has been the Evangelical church which has sought to codify this new situation through treaties with various Länder. The first and model treaty was signed at Loccum in 1955 between Lower Saxony

---

16. "Staat und Kirche nach dem Bonner Grundgesetz," pp. 4–14.

and the five provincial churches of the Land. In contrast to the Weimar "church articles," this treaty speaks of "joint responsibility" and "friendly relations" between church and state and makes practical provision for active cooperation between the two "partners." The church is no longer merely a "body of public law," but becomes an institution with a recognized mission in the life of the state. [11] The Loccum Treaty was followed by similar agreements between provincial churches and Schleswig-Holstein (1957), Hesse (1959), Rhineland-Palatinate (1962), and the Lippe provincial church with North Rhine-Westphalia (1958). In latter case the Rhineland and Westphalian provincial churches themselves, perhaps as a result of the Calvinist influences there, declined to enter into a treaty arrangement. This inclination toward treaty-making was largely a continuing reaction to the experience of the Third Reich and signifies a definite withdrawal from the general Protestant notion of keeping a fairly clear separation between church and state. Symptomatically, the phraseology of the treaties echoes at once the Barmen declaration and the Reichskonkordat. To complete the paradox, the Catholic church, which took the lead during the Weimar period in negotiating Länder concordats, has tended to shun such agreements, and it has entered into one postwar concordat, that with Lower Saxony, only as a result of extreme pressure from the Land government.

On a practical level as well, one of the distinguishing characteristics of the postwar German political landscape has been the privileged position in the state and the fixed role in public affairs which the churches have come to occupy. The churches' role in social and political life extends from the pressure-group activities discussed in Chapters 5 and 6 to institutionalized practices that amount to the de facto partnership between church and state referred to by Smend. The clearest example of the churches' position as an accepted partner of the state is the systematic role they play in social, educational, cultural, and youth affairs. On the local and Land level the churches have an important and often decisive voice in the appointment of officials whose duties touch on these matters. This is also the case with radio and television, where the churches (with fixed representation on the networks' boards of directors) not only influence the appointment of the top personnel but insist on a confessional parity at lower levels, with results that have been described as "like a virus which weakens the vitality of speech." [18]

---

17. Text in Weber, *Die deutschen Konkordate und Kirchenverträge der Gegenwart* (1962), pp. 212 ff.

18. Peter von Zahn, quoted in *Süddeutsche Zeitung,* March 25, 1969.

More importantly, the churches bear responsibility for much of what would otherwise be left to the state and which in most other countries does in fact fall to state or voluntary charitable agencies. Their activities extend from maintaining homes for the blind, training places for school drop-outs, and insane asylums to travelers'-aid offices in railroad stations, seamen's homes, and emigrant advisory bureaus. The two churches together maintain almost nine thousand establishments of various sorts. In addition, they operate over 11,500 kindergartens, with places for more than three-quarters of a million children; 1100 hospitals, with over 200,000 beds; 2500 old people's homes; 1000 rest and vacation homes; 1000 children's homes; and 2000 student and youth hostels. [19] On the federal level the churches carry out programs in conjunction with the family ministry, the foreign office, the ministry for economic cooperation, and the federal center for political education.

As a related aspect of this partnership, the churches receive funds for their social and political activities from local, Land, and federal governments. While the churches themselves bear virtually the entire running costs of their various charitable establishments, Land and local governments contribute handsomely to the construction and renovation costs involved. They generally pay at least 95 percent of the cost of building a hospital, 50-70 percent of a kindergarten, and about 50 percent of youth hostels, children's homes, and so on. Activities contributing to political education and international understanding also receive state support, ranging from funds for the Catholic and Protestant academies and church assemblies to support for youth exchange programs in foreign countries. On the federal level, there is, as one church official noted, scarcely a ministry the churches do not tap for some funds. While there was jesting hyperbole in the remark, the churches and their organizations do in fact receive money from a great variety of federal bodies, of which four are the most significant.

The ministry for family and youth implements most of its programs through private organizations, of which church groups are the most important. The federal youth plan, which was established in 1950 to cope with the material and social problems of youth in postwar conditions and which more recently has been designed to help "youth to develop in a healthy way and to measure up to their responsibility to family, society, and state," [20] has spent altogether one billion marks up to 1969. Church organizations have received

---

19. "Zahlen aus der Arbeit des Diakonischen Werkes und des Deutschen Caritasverbandes," in *Die Innere Mission,* No. 8/9, 1968.

20. Federal Press and Information Office, *Deutsche Politik 1965*, p. 302.

between a third and half of this amount. In 1969, of a budget of 75 million marks, they presumably received 25-30 million marks. Protestant and Catholic organizations also receive on an annual basis about 3 million marks for political education programs; 2.5 million for various youth programs; 1 million for the charitable programs of Caritas and the Diakonisches Werk, and several millions more in connection with various other ministerial projects. Church groups thus probably receive a total of about 35-38 million marks, or roughly a third of the ministry's total budget, excluding children's subsidies, for its regular programs, as was estimated by Peter Flor of the ministry in an interview. The sum is evenly divided between the two confessions even though Protestant organizations are smaller than Catholic ones. The organizations have almost complete freedom in using the monies they receive.

The federal center for political education has an annual budget of 2.5 million marks for meetings organized by private, political, and religious groups. Protestant and Catholic academies and lay groups together receive about one-third of this amount for programs, approved by the center, for discussions of political topics. According to Manfried Klein, an official of the center, in 1968 Protestant academies and lay groups received 350,000 marks and Catholic academies and lay groups 406,000 marks. These funds cover about half the costs of the various meetings.

The foreign office gives each of the churches annual grants of 2.5 million marks for religious activities with guest workers in Germany, for German churches and their activities in foreign countries, and for chaplains for students abroad. In addition, the Evangelical church annually receives 3 million marks and the Catholic church 2 million marks for missionary work overseas. [21]

The ministry for economic cooperation has since 1962 given an average of 55 million marks annually to church development aid agencies for their programs in underdeveloped areas. [22] The idea of drawing the churches into this work was developed by Adenauer personally and was accepted with alacrity by the Church Office. The Evangelical church, because of its East German provincial churches, only went along with some reluctance. Although each program is approved by the government, the churches can ignore official German foreign policy precepts in their proposed projects. Despite the fact, for instance, that German government aid programs were for policy reasons terminated in Tanzania in 1965, church programs have continued.

---

21. These figures, for 1968, were provided by a source who prefers to remain anonymous. The foreign office budget (*Einzelplan 05*) states that funds are provided to the churches but does not indicate the amount.

22. Karl Osner, *Kirchen und Entwicklungshilfe*, p. 60.

While church organizations are not in principle favored by the government, they receive the lion's share of these various grants because of the multitude of their organizations and activities. It is difficult to estimate the total amount of all such government funds reaching the churches, their lay groups and charitable agencies. On the local level little or no record is kept, and neither church is fully informed of all the sources of income of the parishes, dioceses and provincial churches. But, allowing for this uncertainty, Church Councellor Hermann Kalinna, of the Evangelical church chancellery in Bonn, has suggested that such grants together are probably on the order of 800 million marks per year for the two churches.

In the dark territory between these de facto changes in the church-state relationship and outright ecclesiastical pressure-group activities lies the strange terrain of "Personalpolitik"—that is, the confessional topography of government and civil service personnel. When the Federal Republic was founded and the government had to be rebuilt from bottom to top, Catholics felt that in a state where the confessions were of roughly equal strength, they deserved approximate equality with Protestants. To achieve this end it was necessary radically to alter a traditional, deeply entrenched system. The German Reich had been not only Protestant in spirit but Protestant in practice, with its two pillars—the Army and the civil service—both manned almost exclusively by Protestants. This situation was not significantly altered during the Weimar Republic. But in 1949 Catholics formed a majority of the dominant party for the first time in German history, and they were determined to have their way. For Protestants this was a bitter pill to swallow.

Confessional parity at the top level was relatively easy to establish and was popularly accepted with little difficulty. The chancellor was of one confession and the president of another; the cabinet was evenly balanced, and a minister of one confession had a state secretary of another. The presidents of the eleven federal courts and the judges of the federal constitutional court were kept in confessional near-balance. On the executive side, this parity began to break down as early as 1959, when Heinrich Lübke was elected President, so that both the head of state and the head of government were Catholics. Many Protestants were angered, and Lübke had to be persuaded not to make matters worse by carrying out his plan to make the Vatican the place of his first state visit. Following Heinrich Lübke's retirement in 1969, it was generally taken for granted that his successor should be a Protestant. The Christian Democrats had only Protestants on their short list of candidates, including Richard von Weizsäcker, the president of the Protestant church assembly; the Social Democrats also nominated their best-known Protestant layman, Gustav Heinemann. Cabinets, including that of the grand coalition established in 1966, have continued to be confessionally balanced, except for a short period in 1968–1969, though the rule on state secretaries has conspicuously lapsed. When the SPD-FDP coalition ousted the CDU from power in 1969, confessional considerations necessarily played no role in cabinet formation, since there are few Catholics prominent in either party. The 1972 cabinet has only two Catholic members—Minister of Agriculture Josef Ertl (FDP) and Minister of Transport Georg Leber (SPD).

Far more problematic was the manning of the permanent civil service positions in the ministries. When such traditional ministries as justice and interior, as well as the foreign office, reassembled their old members, they turned out to be once again as much as 90 percent Protestant. In other cases the initial minister himself influenced the confessional character of his office. The ministries of labor and finance and, later, the defense agency (the forerunner of the ministry of defense), for instance, were headed by Catholics and, largely as a result, contained a predominance of Catholics, especially at the high levels. The same was true of Protestants in, for example, the ministries of economics and transport.

One of the principal interests of the church liaison officials was to keep watch on this situation; centers of Catholic predominance were particular targets of Bishop Kunst, the Evangelical church representative, and centers of Protestant predominance were those of Böhler. Both officials maintained a file with the names of persons suitable for certain types of positions. Sometimes they proposed a specific name for a position; more often, however, they sought to put a confessional tag on a job without specifying the actual person who should occupy it. The heads of the foreign office personnel section, for instance, had until 1968 (with two brief exceptions) been Catholics.

If Protestants had the initial advantage because of their traditional predominance in the civil service, Catholics were favored by the fact that the effective head of the civil service, Adenauer's state secretary, Hans Globke, was Catholic and took it as one of his aims of office to establish a greater confessional balance in the government. While he found it relatively difficult to establish Catholics in the foreign office, one of his favorite targets, and in the ministries of justice and interior, he had a much freer hand in newer agencies, such as the press and information office (itself a branch of the chancellery) where in the early 1950s whole divisions were reputedly staffed with Catholics. The family ministry was given a rigid fifty-fifty confessional balance, which has been firmly maintained. Globke also sought to have only Catholics appointed as ambassadors to important Catholic countries. He and the Catholic hierarchy furthermore insisted that the ambassador to the Vatican be a Catholic. This, however, was more than Protestants, from Bishop

Dibelius to President Heuss, would accept. So obdurate were the two sides that three full years passed before a compromise could be worked out. According to the settlement, a Catholic and a Protestant would alternate as ambassador to the Holy See and the ambassador to Italy would be of the other confession. However, the arrangement did not last for long, and three successive ambassadors to the Vatican were Catholics.

The activities of Globke and Böhler enraged many Protestants. Bishop Lilje, for instance, who was—and still is—a strong supporter of CDU policies, broke with Adenauer as a result. The contretemps over the Vatican ambassadorship, moreover, marked the only occasion in the postwar period when leaders of the two churches—Dibelius and Frings—publicly attacked one another. The CDU itself underwent serious confessional strain during the early years of the Federal Republic, and in 1952 Protestants in the party formed the Protestant committee of the CDU/CSU (Evangelischer Arbeitskreis der CDU/CSU), mainly to be in a position more effectively to resist Catholic influence, especially in Personalpolitik. By the early 1960s, however, the problem had largely resolved itself. Catholics had won a larger place in the civil service, and the bureaucracy had become so stabilized there was little scope for further "confessionalization." The competition largely ceased and church representatives disengaged themselves from the matter. By the mid-1960s the church liaison representatives were no longer consulted on such of their old prerogatives as appointments to the cultural sections of the foreign office and ministry of interior.

Confessionalism is one of the skeletons in the closet of German politics. But any state, finding itself with Catholics and Protestants roughly equal in strength, would probably have gone through an experience similar to that of the Federal Republic in its early years. Even in the United States and Great Britain, where Catholics are small minorities, a silent religious test for the presidency in the former and the lord chancellorship in the latter have at least until recently prevailed. But the way in which Catholics and Protestants fought for what they considered their proper share in the body politic was one of the great scandals in the early history of the Federal Republic. In discussing the matter some years after leaving office, Globke in an interview maintained that his aim had not been a strict confessional balance, but merely a greater equality between Catholics and Protestants. Even this aim, however, was too much for many Protestants, who were accustomed to the prewar situation and wanted to preserve it. While some ministries or divisions of some ministries may have been heavily Catholic, on a government-wide basis the balance never went beyond three-to-two relationship in the Protestant favor, he insisted. Protestants focused on pockets of Catholic dominance and ignored the general situation. They complained, for instance, that Catholics initially held all the top positions in the ministry of defense but passed over the fact that virtually the entire officer corps of the three military services was composed of Protestants. To clarify the situation, Globke had a classified survey prepared in the mid-1950s on the confessional balance throughout the government. This demonstrated such over-all Protestant predominance that Protestant circles thereafter tended to drop the matter.

As understandable as Catholic feelings in the matter are, the controversy over Personalpolitik injected a lasting poison into governmental operations in Bonn. Although a struggle over the issue may have been inevitable because of the confessional balance of the new state, it is difficult to defend the direct intervention of church officials. This tampering with the civil service was unheard of in the German bureaucratic tradition and compromised good and just government administration. Moreover, the recruitment and placement of government officals for confessional reasons is both unconstitutional and in violation of civil service regulations. Article 3 (3) of the Basic Law states that "No one may be prejudiced or favored because of . . . his faith or his religious . . . opinions." Even more explicitly, Article 33 (3) proclaims that "Enjoyment of civil and civic rights, eligibility to public office, and rights acquired in the public service are independent of religious denomination. No one may suffer disadvantage by reason of his adherence or nonadherence to a denomination or ideology."

If the churches had insisted that requests for information regarding religious affillition be removed from civil service questionnaires, they would have supported not only religious freedom and confessional equality but also the legal order. In the long run the confessional balance would probably have worked out naturally about the way it has artificially. President Heuss no doubt spoke for millions of Germans when in 1957, at the end of his period in office, he said, "Nothing is so distasteful to me as confessional statistics in the civil service." [23] For this situation, church officials bear as much responsibility as anyone.

In these various ways—through participation in the political and social activities of municipal, Land and federal governments—the churches have successfully asserted a claim to a significant role in public affairs. To this extent Smend's ingenious legal theory was correct. And yet it was less a description of an objective legal situation than a shrewd prognostication of a

---

23. Quoted in Eschenburg, *Ämterpatronage,* p. 56.

practical one. The church-state partnership after 1949 was due, not to an esoteric transformation of the "church articles," but to the exceptionally high public tolerance of ecclesiastical participation in public life and to the control of the federal government and certain Land governments by the Christian Democrats, who were bound to be as cooperative as possible with the churches. In strongly Christian Democratic Länder, whether the population was Catholics or Protestant, church-state ties were especially close. In Länder where the Social Democrats and Free Democrats were in power, Land constitutions and the tone of government were much more inclined toward a separation of church and state. Here, the situation was much less profitable for the churches—even literally so, as already noted in the case of monetary grants.

By the beginning of the 1960s trends toward a "deideologization" of political life and a secularization of society had reached a new threshold. There were ever louder calls for the state to be "religiously neutral." The general mood of the country made it increasingly difficult for the churches to stand on tradition or legal rights or de facto privileges. The churches' privileged position in the state had to be justified on pragmatic grounds. At the same time many church leaders themselves began to feel that the existing church-state relationship entailed too much ecclesiastical dependence upon the state. By the mid-1960s there was a steady shift from the ideal of the church as a political power and a privileged institution in the state to the concept of the church as an institution with certain unique qualifications to carry out certain public functions in service to the state. This new approach coincided with an unprecedented readiness of the Social Democrats no less than the Christian Democrats to work with the churches in the public sphere. The approach on both sides is no longer, as it was in the 1950s, one of paying off favors, but one of joint partnership for broad social objectives without regard for narrow church interests. The sum result has been an intensification of the partnership between church and state despite the deepening secularization of German society.

8 | *The Schools and Other Problems of the Reichskonkordat*

PROBABLY no single question has so bedeviled domestic German politics as the school problem. After the Reformation as much as before, education was in the hands of the church, and it by and large remained there until 1918. Disagreements arose in the early nineteenth century and continued with growing intensity until 1968. At issue was not only whether church or state should control elementary education but also whether schools should be confessional or interconfessional and, following national unification, whether the Reich or Land government should decide such matters. (Never disputed, even during the Kulturkampf or the Third Reich, was religious instruction as a regular part of the curriculum.) The school system varied from area to area. In Prussia, for instance, the state assumed formal responsibility for schooling early in the nineteenth century but left confessional schools intact and allowed the clergy to remain in charge of school supervision. Baden, on the other hand, established interconfessional schools in 1876 and was one of the very few Länder to do so, but it gave the church a controlling influence over them. Under the imperial constitution of 1871 the Länder retained their exclusive authority over education. Significantly enough, church and school matters were—and continue down to the present to be—handled by the same agency, the so-called Kultus ministry.

Not until the collapse of the empire in 1918 was there a serious effort to break the churches' hold on elementary education. This move reflected the desire of the left and the liberals both to separate church and state and to establish a school system in keeping with their own ideology (just as confessional schools were a means by which Catholics and conservative Protestants contributed to their social goals). But in drafting the Weimar constitution, the national assembly found it could agree only to disagree, and the result was what came to be known as the Weimar school compromise. While this recognized "parents' rights" (Article 146), it prohibited turning interconfessional schools into confessional schools (Article 174). Apart from these provisions, only the most general educational principles could be agreed upon, and since a Reich school law, as foreseen in the constitution, could never find the necessary Reichstag majority for enactment, educational decisions were effectively left to the Länder. In short, the status quo remained essentially intact after 1918, although a number of Protestant Länder with Social Democratic (or liberal) majorities later adopted interconfessional schools. Even so, on the eve of the Third Reich no less than 83 percent of the elementary schools in Germany were confessional.[1]

With the vast majority of Catholic children in Catholic schools, the Catholic church had reason to be content. But as Pope Pius XII noted after the war: "In fact, neither the special concordats already concluded with certain Länder nor the Weimar constitution seemed to them [Catholics] to offer adequate protection and guarantees of respect for their convictions, their beliefs, their rights and their liberty of action. Under such circumstances these protections could only be achieved by an agreement with the government of the Reich in the solemn form of a concordat."[2] The Pope was seeking to explain why the Vatican had jumped at Hitler's offer in the spring of 1933 of a Reichskonkordat, and his reference to legal guarantees was both sincere and symptomatic. Pacelli loved neat legal arrangements and saw the concordat as a device for securing and fixing the best possible position for the Catholic church. As Nuncio in Germany from 1920 to 1929, he had negotiated concordats with Bavaria, Prussia, and Baden. A concordat for the Reich itself was to crown his work and permanently assure a solid legal position for the church throughout Germany. Various Weimar governments had also wanted to tidy up the church-state situation, and work on a draft Reichskonkordat went on intermittently from 1920 to 1932. Upon coming to power, Hitler revived the negotiations which both sides pushed to a hasty conclusion —Hitler in the desire for domestic and foreign respectability and the Vatican with the intent of at once taking advantage of and thwarting the possible dangers of the National Socialist revolution. The treaty was signed at the Vatican on July 20, 1933, by Pacelli, then Cardinal Secretary of State, and von Papen, German Vice Chancellor.

Stripped to its barest essentials, the Reichskonkordat had two key points, each a concession to the other side. Article 23 guaranteed confessional schools everywhere in Germany; it was the provision of supreme, practically of sole, importance to the church. By the same token it was Hitler's bait. The

---

1. Samuel and Thomas, *Education and Society in Modern Germany,* p. 103.
2. "The Church and National Socialism," an address to the College of Cardinals on June 2, 1945, in Schäufele (editor), *Zur Neuordnung im Staats- und Völkerleben.*

other central feature was the "political neutralization" of the clergy achieved in the so-called political articles. These banned party membership and political activity by the clergy (Article 32), made the appointment of a bishop contingent upon the state's raising no "objection of a general political nature" to the nominee (Article 14), and required a bishop to swear an oath of loyalty to the government, to "honor" the government, and to have his clergy do so as well (Article 16). These three provisions were Hitler's greatest success and were teased out of the Vatican only with difficulty. Other provisions, while not unimportant at the time, were of marginal significance. The article requiring government approval for any change in diocesan organization, gained real relevance only after 1945 in connection with the Oder-Neisse issue.

Inasmuch as the Enabling Act had nullified the requirement for parliamentary approval of treaties, German ratification was accomplished simply with President Hindenburg's signature. This fact is of importance, since no genuinely democratic Reichstag would have approved the Reichskonkordat, as Pacelli himself privately admitted at the time.[3] The Vatican's gamble was, in any event, a total failure. The German government blatantly violated the treaty within weeks of its ratification. By the spring of 1941 all confessional schools had been turned into nonconfessional schools. Though both the Vatican and the German government were at one time or another on the point of denouncing the treaty, neither side ever took this step.

After the war the German hierarchy and the Vatican at first took opposite positions on maintaining the Reichskonkordat. At their Fulda conference in August 1945 the bishops decided, as Ambassador Murphy reported to Washington, that while the matter ultimately rested with the Allied Control Council, they did not themselves "favor" the treaty. In their view it should be "suspended in effect" with the church's legal position resting instead upon the earlier Länder concordats.[4] Presumably the bishops felt that the Reichskonkordat was tainted and best forgotten. In any case their conclusion was reached before contact had been reestablished with the Vatican. It was some weeks later that Father Zeiger reached Germany with Pius XII's message

---

3. The British Minister at the Holy See, Ivone Kirkpatrick, reporting on August 19, 1933, that he found Pacelli apologetic about having signed the concordat with the Nazi government, cites the explanation he gave: "The German government had offered him concessions, concessions, it must be admitted, wider than any previous government would have agreed to." E. L. Woodward and Rohan Butler (editors), *Documents on British Foreign Policy*, Second Series, vol. 5: *1933* (1956), p. 524.

4. Despatch 907 of August 28, 1945; 862.404/8–2845 in Box C–729; General Records of the Department of State, National Archives, Washington.

(referred to earlier) insisting upon the continuance of the Reichskonkordat.

For the Vatican the status of the Reichskonkordat after 1945 was completely caught up in the emotions and complex personality of Pius XII. Pacelli evidently regarded the treaty as his greatest secular triumph. In his eyes it had an aura of veritable sanctity. Glimpses of his attitude have been recorded by Cardinal Muench. According to Father Zeiger, for Pacelli the "past is enshrined in a halo." Sister Pasqualina Lehnert once wrote: "I was in the Nunciatur all those years when His Holiness was Apostolic Nuncio in Germany and I know with what concern and devotion the Holy Father worked for the well-being of the church in Germany. I also know how much sacrifice and labor the concordats in Germany cost him and therefore I can understand full well today his concern and great interest about all these matters." The psychological importance to Pius of the Reichskonkordat was reinforced by his continuing fascination with Germany. "He thinks he is still Nuncio of Germany," Muench was told by a member of the curia in 1946. The "Holy Father [is] more interested in the affairs of the church in Germany," Montini and Tardini commented to Muench, "than that in any other part of the church; [he] looks back to his experiences in G[ermany]; [he] admits changes but does not seem to grasp fully the implications of changes. . . ." To Pacelli, maintanence of the Reichskonkordat was therefore an end in itself, and enjoyed a priority over all other secular church interests in Germany. The German concordats were the "Holy Father's principal concern," Muench noted in his diary after his first meeting as Apostolic Visitator with the Pope, and this was the central topic of all their subsequent discussions.

But it is clear from the Muench papers that Pius did not allow wishful thinking to lull him into the misapprehension that the Reichskonkordat was valid because he wanted it to be. Rather he anticipated that its validity would be challenged, and he moved with determination to do everything in his power to blunt these thrusts. On the one hand the state must be pressed, cajoled, and if necessary bluffed into adhering to it. As reported to Muench early in 1947, the Pope told his closest advisors on Germany, Leiber, Zeiger, Kaas, and Montini, "The juridically very ambiguous situation in Germany suggests only *one* mode of dealing—that is, establishing as many legal faits accomplis as possible." And that is precisely what the church from then on bent every effort to do. Acting in public as though the treaty were unquestionably valid, clerical officials reacted in private with delighted near-surprise whenever a Land government observed its provisions. The deception was all the more remarkable since even church authorities were uncertain how some of the treaty's provisions would apply in the post-Nazi state. As late as 1953

Muench himself commented in evident frustration: "we are at sea on a number of . . . questions touching on [the] Concordat."

On the other hand the German hierarchy should do nothing that would call a single sentence, word, or comma of the concordat into question. When Cardinal Frings joined the CDU—risking the charge that he had broken the Reichskonkordat's ban on membership by the clergy in a political party—the Pope insisted that he should resign from the party and find, as Muench recorded, "some appropriate way of 'repairing [the] damage.' " Why was Pius so inflexible in holding to a treaty that the German bishops evidently considered a moral if not a political liability? At his meetings with Muench the Pope laid no stress on any particular feature of the agreement as justifying the need to preserve the treaty. It therefore seems probable that he considered maintanence of the Reichskonkordat necessary to his vindication, by showing that the treaty was in fact a workable one whose connection with the Third Reich was only incidental. At the very least, however, he must have regarded it as the legal foundation—as in fact it was—of the confessional school system in Germany.

Certainly the desire of the Pope and the German hierarchy for confessional schools after the war can only be described as obsessive. It was considered not merely a doctrinal ideal to have all Catholic children in Catholic schools, but also an urgent practical matter both to counteract Nazi indoctrination and to prevent youth from succumbing to communism as a result of postwar conditions. They also doubtless took it for granted that by strengthening the ties of the faithful to the church, the church's position in society would be fortified. Protestant leaders, while lacking a clear theological justification for confessional schools, also felt that the postwar situation demanded a Christian influence in education. Most of them considered nonconfessional schools that included religious instruction in the required curriculum adequate to the social emergency. In Catholic areas Protestants saw no choice, however, but to support confessional schools, though only the Bavarian church did so with any conviction. The great majority of Catholic and Protestant parents followed the lead of their churches. Indeed, Catholic parents were told by their church that they had, in Cardinal Frings' words printed in the *Kirchlicher Anzeiger für die Erzdiözese Köln* on February 18, 1946, "a serious and heavy obligation in conscience" to support confessional schools. Wherever plebiscites on the issue were held in 1946 and 1947, Catholics voted overwhelmingly for confessional schools and Protestants (except in Catholic Länder) for nonconfessional ones.

Obviously the Evangelical church as a whole found a federal solution ideal. For this very reason the Catholic church did not. Recognizing that

Protestant Länder, whatever political party governed, would establish non-confessional schools, Catholic church officials worked unceasingly after 1945 for a national school settlement. During the occupation period the three Western military governments adamantly refused either to make zonewide regulations or to accede to the requests of Catholic bishops and impose confessional schools upon the Länder as they were drawing up their constitutions in 1947. As a consequence, only in three Catholic Länder—Bavaria, Rhineland-Palatinate, and North Rhine-Westphalia—did confessional schools become the norm. Baden and all the Protestant Länder decided in favor of nonconfessional schools including religious instruction as part of the curriculum.[5] Catholic officials then made their equally unsuccessful attempt to retrieve the situation by securing a guarantee in the Basic Law for confessional schools throughout the Federal Republic. Subsequent negotiations with the Länder as school legislation was revised in the early 1950s achieved liberal financial support in some cases for private Catholic schools but no fundamental revision in the system. With all its political ammunition exhausted, the Catholic church had only one other weapon in trying to force the recalcitrant Länder to establish confessional schools—the Reichskonkordat.

Immediately after the Basic Law had been adopted, Cardinal Frings resigned from the CDU, which he had joined with some fanfare less than a year before. Seeking to "repair the damage," as instructed by the Vatican, he publicly explained that he had resigned "not in view of recent political events" (that is, Adenauer's abandonment of "parents' rights" in the Parliamentary Council), but to remove any doubt that he was violating the Reichskonkordat's ban on party membership by the clergy. While maintaining that this particular provision never came into force because a similar agreement with "non-Catholic confessions," as called for in the treaty, was never made, the Archbishop sought to avoid the slightest chance of misunderstanding and to emphasize that the Catholic church took the treaty's validity for granted. With a clear conscience—though in fact with less than total conviction—he declared (as reported in *The New York Times* of November 8, 1949) shortly after the establishment of the Federal Republic that the Reichskonkordat was "once more in lawful being." Whether this was so became a matter of wide

---

5. The Saar, upon becoming part of Germany in 1957, also made provision for confessional schools; in fact it was the sole Land to permit only confessional schools. Bremen is an exception to the rule for nonconfessional schools. It has nonconfessional schools of "Christian character" which provide courses in Biblical history but no religious education. This has been recognized in Article 141 (the "Bremen clause") of the Basic Law.

public controversy. The Social Democrats and Free Democrats considered the treaty morally and legally dubious. The Evangelical church made no statements, though most of its leaders privately inclined to the same view. Those Länder which did not want to establish confessional schools ignored it.

For the Vatican, even after the death of Pius XII, it was a point of honor that the Reichskonkordat be maintained in force. Abrogation would have implied an admission that the treaty had been opportunistically concluded. Moreover, the Reichskonkordat was—leaving aside the Lateran Treaty, which was virtually an internal Italian affair—the most important international agreement concluded by the Vatican in a century. In the view of the curia, the agreement demonstrated better than any other concordat (which were otherwise concluded with small, Catholic countries) the international legal status of the Holy See. For the German government the diplomatic angle was even more important. In requiring German government approval for any change in diocesan borders, as well as for the appointment of new bishops, the treaty gave Bonn a firm legal basis for preventing for as long as it wished any formal ecclesiastical acceptance of the Oder-Neisse line. The refusal of noncommunist states officially to recognize the Oder-Neisse line had minor practical significance at most. The refusal of the Holy See to do so affected Poland directly and visibly. The Reichskonkordat also constituted an important link between East and West Germany; it could be—and was—used in a way to support the federal government's claim to be the successor to the German Reich and the sole representative of the German people.

But what was advantageous to the federal government was problematic to the church. The Reichskonkordat's applicability to East Germany has, for instance, placed the Papal Nuncio in a delicate position. When diplomatic relations were established between the federal government and the Vatican in 1951, the then Nuncio, Bishop Muench, told President Heuss that he was presenting the credentials by which the Pope accredited him "as Apostolic Nuncio to the German people." [6] (When, however, the Federal Republic appointed its ambassador to the Vatican in 1954, Papal officials declined, according to the *Frankfurter Allgemeine* of March 10, 1954, to make any statement on whether he was considered the ambassador of the Federal Republic or of the German people.) Despite this claim, neither Muench nor his successor, Corrado Bafile, ever had personal contact with the East German government, and Muench was the only one of the two to visit East Germany— once in 1947 (in his capacity as Apostolic Visitor) and again in 1954. Arch-

---

6. Text in Archives of Bundespresseamt, Bonn.

bishop Bafile attempted to attend a religious ceremony in East Berlin in 1960 (shortly after becoming Nuncio), but was denied entry by the East Germans. He has never made another attempt to visit there.

In order to emphasize the continuing validity of the Reichskonkordat throughout Germany, the Vatican has generally honored its concordatary obligations to the East German government. Once a churchman has been nominated for a See wholly or partly in East Germany, the church has asked the appropriate East German authorities whether they have any political objection to the nominee. The oath of allegiance also required by the Reichs-konkordat was, however, considered politically objectionable, and the church has asked the East German authorities either to waive the requirement or to accept the oath by letter. For their part, East German officials, as Muench once summed it up, "expect [the] Church to honor the C[oncordat] but they themselves do not recognize it." Obviously East German authorities have welcomed any form of legal obeisance by the church to the state, such as the church's clear acknowledgement of an East German veto over a candidate for bishop. They also sought a further degree of international recognition when they could. Before permitting Muench to visit East Germany in 1954, they required a written statement from him that he was Nuncio for all of Germany (and presumably thus accredited to them). Beyond that, however, they have not observed any provision of either the Prussian or the Reichskonkordat. The Vatican has never protested this but when it sees practical advantage in doing so, the church invokes the terms of the treaty. For instance, it has successfully protected its priests from pressure to join communist organizations by treating Article 32, banning political activity by the clergy, as still being in force.

If the Reichskonkordat's applicability to the Oder-Neisse question gave the Federal Republic its greatest advantage from the treaty, this same point caused the Vatican its biggest diplomatic headache since the war. The Holy See has had to balance its desire to support the Federal Republic, as the West's main anticommunist bastion, against its need to care for Polish Catholics in the detached areas and to encourage one of the most vital churches in the world. At issue was the diocesan structure, established by the Prussian concordat of 1929 and implicity reaffirmed by the Reichskonkordat, in the former German territory east of the Oder-Neisse line. The diocese of Ermland (in East Prussia) and the free prelature of Schneidemühl (a strip along the corridor) came entirely under Polish control. Most of the diocese of Breslau (in Silesia; now Wroclaw), the Pomeranian and West Prussian parts of the diocese of Berlin, and a tiny portion of the diocese of Meissen also fell to Poland. In July 1945 Cardinal August Hlond, the Polish Primate, returning by

way of Rome from exile, claimed papal authority to administer these areas.[7]
He persuaded Bishop Maximilian Kaller of Ermland and Prelate Hartz of
Schneidemühl (Cardinal Adolf Bertram of Breslau died just after the war) to
leave their dioceses; he then divided the entire territory into four administrative areas to which he appointed apostolic administrators, purportedly with
the rights of resident bishops, though with no formal connection to the Polish
hierarchy. Ecclesiastical possession of the dioceses remained with the German
church heads; Kaller, for instance, was characterized in the *Annuario Pontificio* as an "impeded" bishop. The German diocesan structure remained intact;
church heads, their canons, and so on, simply moved into "exile" as explained above.

The Vatican always explained its stand by pointing out that changes in
diocesan borders must await a de jure settlement, that the Reichskonkordat
ruled out any change in the "East German Church Province," and that a
unilateral step on the Oder-Neisse issue would be a political act prejudicial to
negotiations for a final political settlement. While each of these arguments had
extrinsic legitimacy, none of them was completely persuasive. The absence of a
de jure settlement did not prevent the Vatican from eventually incorporating
Danzig into the Polish church under a Polish bishop. The requirements of the
Reichskonkordat that priests and other church officials be German citizens
and German-educated (Article 14) and that they "honor" the German government (Article 16) have been ignored since August 1945. Finally, given postwar circumstances, the Vatican's "neutrality" on the Oder-Neisse issue
amounted to a highly partisan stand.

Indeed, political considerations were of the essence of the Vatican's
position, and it was upon these that the German government always played—
stressing the need to support the Federal Republic in the East-West struggle
while also predicting electoral disaster for Adenauer (or Erhard or Kiesinger)
and the Christian Democrats generally should the Vatican "sell out" the
refugees and undermine the German position vis-à-vis the East. To this the
German hierarchy in later years added the threat of stopping its financial

---

7. In German church circles it is suspected that Hlond's authority did not extend
to these German dioceses but merely to those areas which had been incorporated into
Germany after 1939; Pope Pius is quoted as having said words to the effect: "I never
wanted that to happen." Given the Pope's critical attitude toward the Oder-Neisse line
and the impossibility in the summer of 1945 for the Vatican to know what was going on
in the area, this claim could be true.

contributions to the Vatican which, according to *The New York Times* (July 21, 1970) are the largest in the Catholic world after the United States. The Poles, gloating over the "recatholicization" of Eastern Germany, found it difficult to grasp that Rome could give long-range political considerations priority over immediate ecclesiastical interests. Cardinal Wyszynski never tired of reminding the Vatican that the Catholic church had, after all, returned "hand in hand with the Polish people into provinces from which she was ejected as a result of the Lutheran reformation," as he put it in a statement to the press in Rome late in 1951, as quoted in the *Frankfurter Allgemeine* on December 18, 1956. But just as frequently it was noted—as, for example, on June 21, 1957, by *The New York Times*—that "the Roman hierarchy appeared to be painstakingly and deliberately cool in its recent reception of Wyszynski . . . in order not to affront the Germans." In short, the views of the German government and the German hierarchy—though no doubt sincerely shared by the curia, particularly in the time of Pius XII, which coincided with the worst period of the cold war—carried sufficient weight in Rome to restrain the Vatican from making a formal, final change in the status quo. From the end of the war until June 1972, therefore, the Polish church had to be content with minor variations in the 1945 arrangement.

For these different reasons, and despite the countervailing pressures, the Vatican, the German hierarchy, and the German government saw it as very much in their own interests to preserve the Reichskonkordat. For the second time in the treaty's history, however, the Vatican soon found that the treaty's "guarantees" assured nothing. This, its principal device for securing "parents' rights" throughout Germany, proved to be as ineffective after 1945 as it had before. After the founding of the Federal Republic, Catholic church officials were evidently too uncertain of the school article's constitutional enforceability in the Federal Republic to rush into a juridical test. Instead they used the treaty as an instrument of political suasion upon the Länder at least to protect existing Catholic schools. Although this tactic helped to stave off a school reform in Baden-Württemberg in 1952, it had no influence on the governments of Berlin, Bremen, Hamburg, Schleswig-Holstein, and Hesse, all of which kept their nonconfessional school systems. However, the passage of a new school law in Lower Saxony in 1954 for the first time involved the actual closing of some confessional schools. This action was precisely what the hierarchy and the Vatican would not tolerate. Consequently, following an official démarche by the Holy See to the foreign office, the federal government appealed in March 1955 to the federal constitutional court for a ruling that the Reichskonkordat was in all parts still legally valid, that it was binding upon the Länder, and that the Lower Saxony school law prevented compliance with Germany's international obligations.

Neither the Pope's decision to request the German government to take the matter to the highest court, nor Adenauer's agreement to do so were easily reached. The Pope was aware of the treaty's possible incompatibility with the Basic Law and was not anxious for a legal showdown. At the time of the Baden-Württemberg school controversy, Tardini had warned Muench against pushing any challenge to the Land government as far as the constitutional court on the ground that the "Holy Father does not trust Höpker-Aschoff, a liberal and anti-Catholic, Chief Justice—as Nuncio crossed swords with him in Berlin." Now, however, the point had been reached where the church had little or nothing to lose from an appeal. For Adenauer a Reichskonkordat litigation was a nuisance from which little good and much trouble could result. To appeal would annoy Protestants in his party and liberals in his government coalition. Lawyers, including half the Catholic legal community, were dubious that the Reichskonkordat would emerge from the constitutional court unscathed. If the treaty were struck down, nothing would stand in the way of the Holy See's acceptance of the Oder-Neisse border. But not to appeal would shock and anger the mass of German Catholics—as one delegation of them after another made plain to him. Adenauer's difficulty in reconciling the conflicting pressures can be gauged from the fact that he delayed for more than two years from the time when the Nuncio conveyed the Holy See's formal request for action in May 1954 until he reached the final decision to initiate legal action in the court.

The case, which was heard in June 1956, was not decided until March 1957, when the court in effect turned aside the federal government's appeal.[8] The court found that, though the Reichskonkordat had come into force through the illegal Enabling Act of 1933, it was valid and had not lost its legality. However, the Basic Law had clearly granted the Länder sovereignty over educational affairs, and neither the articles—Article 123, concerning the continued validity of state treaties, nor Article 7, concerning state supervision

---

8. Muench's diary reveals that there was secret collusion in the case between the Nunciatur and at least two of the Catholic judges hearing the case, Willi Geiger and Ernst Friesenhahn. Father Bernhard Hack, the Nuncio's concordat specialist, made several furtive visits to Karlsruhe to discuss the case. After the trial, Friesenhahn, contrary to the constitutional court's regulations, gave Muench a copy of the dissenting opinion, which was written by the four Catholic members of the nine-member court who had heard the case. When some of the other judges learned of this gross impropriety, they demanded that Muench should return the document forthwith.

of education—nor general constitutional principles required the Länder to honor the school provisions of the Reichskonkordat. Since the concordat was not with the Länder, which were now solely responsible for education, they were not bound to obey its provisions, even though these continued to be in principle valid. To decide otherwise, the court concluded, would be to destroy the federal system as established in the Basic Law and to deprive the Länder of their most important area of autonomy.[9]

The outcome of the Reichskonkordat litigation thus left the federal solution untouched—and untouchable. As a result, five types of schools have existed throughout Germany: public schools for Catholics, public schools for Protestants, public schools for other ideological groups, nonconfessional public schools, and private schools. As of 1961, in a tabulation in the *Frankfurter Allgemeine* of February 15, 1967, of the 30,320 schools in the Federal Republic, about 40 percent were Catholic, 17 percent Protestant, and 40 percent nonconfessional, with the final 3 percent a mixture of others. In Berlin, Bremen, Hamburg, Hesse, Schleswig-Holstein, and Lower Saxony (except in Oldenburg) all public schools have been nonconfessional, while in some Länder virtually the full cost of maintaining Catholic schools on a private basis has been borne by the Land. In Bavaria, Rhineland-Palatinate, Baden-Württemberg, and Saarland, where "parents' rights" prevailed, the picture was mixed. In Saarland there were only confessional schools; in Bavaria schools were confessional except in a few large cities; in Rhineland-Palatinate two-thirds and in Baden-Württemberg one-fifth of the schools were confessional. Thus, despite the federal arrangement, the large majority of Catholic children were in Catholic public schools and an additional number were in publicly supported Catholic private schools. Although this situation did not meet the Catholic church's ideal of having every Catholic child in a Catholic public school, it gave Catholic schools a financial and legal status superior to those obtaining anywhere else in the world.

Then suddenly the whole confessional school system began to crumble. Educators, politicians, and parents became increasingly conscious during the 1960s that the quality of German primary education was significantly below that in other Western countries and that the country faced what was widely labeled an "educational catastrophe." The confessional school system, with

---

9. *2 BvG 1/55*. The court injected an element of ambiguity, however, by also stating in the decision that the Basic Law "gave the federation [Bund] no means that would enable it either to fulfill the school articles by itself or to secure their fulfillment." This wording suggests that the Länder have an obligation to honor the Reichskonkordat but cannot be forced by the federal government to do so.

its proliferation of one-room schoolhouses scattered across the countryside to meet Catholic "parents' rights," was as ill-suited to the demands of a highly technological era as the horse and buggy. With the rapid growth of suburbs, parents had to face the decision of establishing either duplicating confessional school systems at great expense or a single confessional school to be attended by children of both confessions. To Catholic parents, who had always been the claimants for confessional schools, the arguments for confessional schools had already worn thin when the Vatican Council's pronouncement on religious tolerance dealt them a further blow. By the mid-1960s the great majority of Catholics wanted nonconfessional schools.

In reality this process was merely the outward sign of one of the most revolutionary transformations in German Catholicism since the Reformation. The school issue ultimately epitomized the Catholics' attitude to society no less than to their church; it was therefore bound to be caught up in the general crisis of authority in the Catholic church. But there was also something more pragmatic.

By the mid-1960s, beginning with the end of the Adenauer era, Catholics had awakened to the fact that after roughly a decade of "never having had it so good"—being numerically equal to Protestants, controlling the party that had governed the Federal Republic from the beginning, and so on—they were socially little better off than they had been at any time since 1871. One young Catholic sociologist made a devastating comparison of the two periods: "Just as twenty years after the founding of the German Reich, in which Catholics were a disadvantaged minority, and after the 'economic miracle' of the founding years, so twenty years after the collapse of the National Socialist regime and similarly after an 'economic miracle,' educational problems again became a topic of daily conversation, and Catholics once again discovered their inferiority." [10]

The central committee of German Catholics was sufficiently concerned about the growing evidence of the "educational backwardness" of Catholics to commission an analysis by vocation and religion of the 1961 census statistics. [11] The study confirmed the fact that Catholics were behind in all fields of highly trained, professional, and academic endeavor and that by and large

---

10. Wolfgang Zapf, "Angst vor der wissenschaftlichen Frage," in Greinacher and Risse (editors), *Bilanz des Katholizismus,* p. 407.

11. Nellessen-Schumacher, *Sozialstruktur und Ausbildung der deutschen Katholiken.*

the longer the training and the older the profession, the wider the gap. Only where politics governed, as in the cabinet, the Bundestag, and the top of the ministries did the confessional balance conform to that of the population as a whole. Business, banking and industry, academic life, law, the military officer corps, and even the civil service were in the hands of Protestants almost to the same extent as before. These results combined with similar data from other sources are schematized in Table 11.

Unlike the situation that prevailed in the two decades after unification, there were after 1945 no objective disabilities upon Catholics, and they had to face the fact that their inferior position was their own fault, though social and historical factors were naturally part of the cause. A higher proportion of Catholics has always been farmers and workers and lacked the means or incentive to rise. Modern German universities were Protestant foundations, where Catholics felt (and sometimes were) unwelcome. Academics and particularly the natural sciences were considered modern, rational and Protestant and as such a danger to religious faith. While these and many other factors contributed to the overall situation, poor secondary education was widely

Table 11
Vocational Distribution and Confessional
Distribution in Germany (1961)[a]

	Catholic	Protestant
Population of the Federal Republic (1961)	44%	51%
government ministers (1949–1963)	44%	50%
division directors of federal government	41%	59%
Bundestag members (1961–1965)	50%	50%
federal judges (1963)	27%	56%
two- and three-star generals (1965)	18%	78%
business managers (1964)	18%	72%
university students	35%	61%
teaching staff of Tübingen University (1964)	15%	77%
mathematicians and physicists (1961)	28%	62%
civil servants and trained staff (1961)	38%	55%
agronomists and foresters (1961)	37%	60%
physicians (1961)	40%	52%
actors and actresses (1961)	33%	53%

a. The number of governmental division directors is approximate; the source is a qualified agency wishing to remain anonymous. The figure for Bundestag members also represents an approximation—unlike the CDU and FDP, the SPD does not keep a record of the religious affiliation of its Bundestag members; this estimate is based on private SPD calculations regarding 1965 Bundestag candidates as reported by a Katholische Nachrichten-Agentur dispatch 30/31 of July 25, 1965. The bottom five categories are taken from Nellessen-Schumacher. All others are given in Zapf.

seen as the main cause of Catholic inferiority in society. To Catholic parents in the mid-1960s it was the quality of this education, not its religious environment, that was of overriding importance. The desire to break out of the old isolation converged with the desire to raise educational standards through a rationalization of the school system. With this decision the confessional school was doomed.

The Evangelical church, which had previously left the issue open, formally announced its support for interconfessional schools in 1958. The position of the Catholic church, on the other hand, had not changed at all. As in 1949 with the Parliamentary Council, in 1946 with Land constitutional assemblies, in 1945 with the Allies and in 1933 with Hitler, the bishops wanted confessional schools at all costs and at whatever political and social impact in Germany. "The old positions of strength and vapid legalities are still often trundled out," wrote the *Frankfurter Allgemeine* despairingly on March 1, 1967. "But a new concordat litigation can help no one. If its pedagogy, its teaching materials are unconvincing, then the confessional school will not be saved by pastoral letters, advertising campaigns, or state guarantees." In fact, the Catholic hierarchy was becoming deeply divided on the issue. For the older bishops, who still thought defensively in terms of a Catholicism menaced by Protestantism, socialism, and liberalism, Catholic schools were sacrosanct. To some of the younger bishops, such as Cardinal Döpfner, the traditional position was no longer in keeping with the needs or the mood of the times. In their view, while school reform need not leave every Catholic child in a Catholic school, it must not rule out Catholic schools altogether. The Vatican was not out of sympathy with this general posture but was insistent that the legalities required by the Reichskonkordat be observed—in other words, that any legislation affecting existing confessional schools should be made only after agreement with the Holy See and should keep intact the principle of "parents' rights" in some general form.

The issue came to a head as the Free Democrats and the Social Democrats, who had always opposed confessional schools as educationally inadequate and socially divisive, began in the mid-1960s to campaign for school reform and the establishment of larger nonconfessional schools. The CDU was caught in a dilemma. Protestant Christian Democrats favored school reform; Catholic Christian Democrats had either to make a painful break with their church or an even more painful break with their voters. In the end they decided in favor of reform.

Baden-Württemberg was the first of the Länder with confessional schools to go to the brink. As minister president, Kurt Georg Kiesinger had shown particular interest in raising the educational standards of the Land and in putting an end to the three different educational systems which helped keep alive traditional provincial divisiveness in Baden-Württemberg. Archbishop Hermann Schäufele of Freiburg and Bishop Carl Leiprecht of Rottenburg, however, would hear of absolutely no changes affecting Catholic schools, and from 1964 to 1966 they rejected all the suggestions put to them by Kiesinger. When Kiesinger became chancellor in December 1966 and the Baden-Württemberg government was reformed, the Social Democrats made it a condition of entering a coalition with the Christian Democrats that a school reform bill should be enacted. The CDU agreed, and in January 1967 school legislation was drafted, providing for nonconfessional schools throughout Baden-Württemberg after 1973. The government at no time entered into negotiations with the Papal Nuncio, Archbishop Bafile. Apparently it assumed that the Vatican would take the same uncompromising line as the two bishops and in effect veto any school reform.

Recognizing that Baden-Württemberg's decision could undermine the confessional school system and the Reichskonkordat with it, the Catholic hierarchy and the Nuncio swiftly intervened. Bafile called upon Chancellor Kiesinger and Foreign Minister Brandt; Döpfner saw the Chancellor; Bafile and Minister President Hans Filbinger met secretly; stories were leaked to the press that a violation of the Reichskonkordat could provoke the Vatican into recognizing the Oder-Neisse line; officials of the two dioceses appealed to Filbinger and Land parliamentarians, and *L'Osservatore Romano* published a front-page editorial bitterly attacking the proposed law. Although many Christian Democrats were shaken, all but six CDU Landtag deputies voted for the legislation, which was passed by a large majority. The parliamentary action, which was a clear violation of the Reichskonkordat, released a flood of clerical reproach. The Bishop of Rottenburg vented his fury in a pastoral letter which was so sharply phrased that it touched off open protests during some church services. Vicar General Föhr of Freiburg compared the action to the German violation of Belgium in 1914. The two dioceses also appealed to the administrative court to declare the law invalid. In a decision that eliminated some of the ambiguities of the 1957 decision of the constitutional court, the administrative court threw out the case. The judge observed that confessional schools existed for the benefit of parents, not that of the Catholic church, and that the Reichskonkordat concerned the Holy See and not German dioceses. For both reasons therefore, he ruled, no German ecclesiastical authority had any basis of appeal, and it was a matter for each Land to decide how to interpret "parents' rights." Up to then it had been argued that the Reichskonkordat was valid but could not be enforced by the federal government. This decision suggested that the Länder themselves had broad authority to interpret the treaty's provisions.

Far more grave was the reaction of the Vatican, which came within an ace of denouncing the Reichskonkordat or at least of declaring that it considered itself free to alter existing diocesan borders in East Germany and Poland. Some German bishops, in equal anger, supported the Vatican's impulse. The Holy See was, as already noted, under extreme pressure during that period from Cardinal Wyszynski and the Polish government to appoint Polish bishops to the Oder-Neisse territories. German church circles and the German government, however, managed to persuade Rome to be content with a rebuke conveyed by letter from Bafile to Foreign Minister Brandt.

At one point in 1967 the grand coalition government considered proposing the negotiation of a "Bundeskonkordat" applicable only to the Federal Republic. The Vatican was willing to discuss the approach, but the government soon realized that through the arrangement would be much tidier than a treaty now in shambles, it would hold advantages for neither side. The Bundestag was no more inclined than the Parliamentary Council to force confessional schools upon the Länder and a treaty restricted to the Federal Republic would have sacrificed the government's position on the Oder-Neisse issue.

In March 1967 the Catholic Office in Bonn publicly lamented the fact that the Catholic church's "relatively restrained reaction" toward the Baden-Württemberg government had apparently been misunderstood by other Land governments where school reform was under consideration. This moved the *Süddeutsche Zeitung* to remark that it was difficult, after the onslaught in the southwest German state, to conceive quite how ecclesiastical opposition could in the future be escalated. The paper and the German public were soon to find out, for the battle in Baden-Württemberg was a mere prelude to an engagement in North Rhine-Westphalia whose outcome would mark a watershed in modern German Catholicism.

Following their victory in the 1966 North Rhine-Westphalian election, the Social Democrats began work on a school-modernization program with their FDP coalition partners. Nowhere in Germany was the SPD's campaign at that time to improve relations with the Catholic church more vital than here, and the party moved with extreme caution, allowing more than a year to pass before acting. While the Land government was still developing its plans, the Catholic bishops decided to go onto the barricades and, without even waiting for the enemy to appear, fired a sharp warning salvo. An article in the *Kirchenzeitung für das Erzbistum Köln* in November completely ruled out any sort of school reform. It demanded the full support of the Christian Democrats in defeating any reform legislation and threatened to establish a "truly

Christian party" if they did not do so. Instead of drawing Christian Democrats to the church's side, this extraordinary statement, which was undoubtedly approved by Cardinal Frings, sent them scurrying off the government camp. "We are a Christian but not a Catholic party," *Die Welt* reported on November 14, 1966, as the typical CDU parliamentarian's reaction. As the government's plans began to crystallize on the basis of nonconfessional schools for the fifth through ninth school years (leaving confessional schools for the first four years intact), the bishops condemned the proposal as a violation of human rights, a violation of "parents' rights," a violation of the Reichskonkordat, a violation of the Prussian concordat, and finally, an imitation of the policies of Hitler and Ulbricht. They claimed that a majority of Catholic parents were determined to keep Catholic schools. The argument that nonconfessional schools were more efficient, the vicar general of Paderborn countered with the statement, reported in the *Frankfurter Allgemeine* of January 27, 1967: "It cannot be denied that persons like Himmler and Goebbels were efficient." Cardinal Jäger, the Catholic leader responsible for ecumenical relations, brushed aside the Protestant bishops' support for school reform. In the same newspaper on February 15 he was credited with the remark, "It appears that Protestants are more afraid of Catholicism than of atheism."

All this agitation might have been a case of verbal overkill had it not missed the target. When the smoke of the verbal barrage cleared, it was clear that the bishops stood alone. No independent group and scarcely any Catholic group supported them. They were, in fact, demonstratively abandoned in subsequent weeks by the CDU, the Junge Union (the CDU youth group), the teachers' union, many Catholic teachers, Catholic pedagogical-school professors and students, several groups of priests, and the entire national press. Public opinion polls, moreover, left no doubt of the side taken by parents. As of March 1967 these investigations suggested that 82 percent of the population wanted nonconfessional schools, and only 11 percent preferred confessional schools; of practicing Catholics alone, only 22 percent spoke out for confessional schools. Less than a year later the support for nonconfessional schools rose to 88 percent. [12] The bishops reacted by organizing a mass advertising campaign. Catholic teachers were offered 40 marks an evening to canvass parents on behalf of Catholic schools; pamphlets and handbills were circulated; and priests were asked to give prayers and sermons in support of confessional education. Some priests ignored the instruction; others publicly

---

12. *Bonner Rundschau,* March 30, 1967; *Frankfurter Allgemeine,* January 22, 1968.

protested. In an open and widely publicized letter, reprinted in the *Frankfurter Allgemeine* on May 11, 1967, to Bishop Hengsbach of Essen, a group of priests condemned the bishops' brazen disregard of the feelings of the large majority of Catholics. They went on to say:

> We know that a growing proportion not only of parents but also of the clergy do not approve the actions of our bishops on the school question. The position of the bishops on the school issue has no dogmatic significance. For this reason it should not be set forth during religious services and in that way related to the spiritual authority of the sermon. Should this happen, we would then see the credibility of our spiritual office endangered.
>
> We see how, with the increasing flow of declarations, appeals, and publications, the credibility of the Church is declining because our alert fellow citizens are inclined to see behind these efforts an interest in group consolidation rather than in the pastorate. Indeed, the actions of the bishops, in our opinion, impede the true work of the Church, the pastorate. The ecclesiastical argumentation is widely considered to be merely a delaying action, and it is regrettable that the time, energy, and goodwill of priests and faithful are unnecessarily absorbed in what is now a secondary issue.
>
> The public confessional school cannot be saved; its collapse can only be postponed. The current idealization and dogmatization of the public confessional school—soon legally and long actually dead—also make it more difficult for the faithful to accommodate to the new school situation.

These views, according to a Catholic authority not in sympathy with them, were shared by a clear majority of younger priests, if not by the clergy as a whole. This open defection of the clergy was without precedent in German Catholicism. The bishops were demonstrably isolated. The school dispute had become virtually a disagreement between five ecclesiastics and a Land government backed by nearly four-fifths of the population. The worst of it was that even then the bishops were unwilling to give an inch. They resolutely rejected the pleas of certain other bishops, as well as those of the Nuncio, to show some willingness to compromise. Instead they fought on, drawing themselves and their church into deeper humiliation. The Nuncio's letter to Foreign Minister Brandt (concerning the Baden-Württemberg dispute) was leaked to the press and played up as a sharp protest. Churchmen even spread the rumour that the Holy See's attitude on the Oder-Neisse issue depended on the outcome of the school dispute in North Rhine-Westphalia. Minister-President Kühn, who had maintained that the Reichskonkordat was not affected by his school plan, was stung into remarking that if the treaty were law in North Rhine-Westphalia, the law would have to be changed. "It is not appropriate," the *Frankfurter Allegemeine* summarized his comment on May 9, 1967, "that the Pope become a factor in German school policy. The Catholic Church will have to face the question whether it is well advised to stand on a treaty that carries the signature of Papen, and that was only concluded by Hitler so as to secure the first recognition in international law for his criminal regime."

This was a revealing case of overreaction. The Vatican and the cooler heads in the hierarchy sought substantive discussions and a willingness to permit confessional schools under reasonable circumstances. In his meeting with Chancellor Kiesinger in June 1967, for example, the Pope advocated (as Kiesinger later put it to *Bonner Rundschau* for June 2) "joint practicable solutions"—in other words, a compromise settlement. But the North Rhine-Westphalian bishops, literally more papal than the Pope, would not yield. The Nuncio was consequently in an impossible position. He met and exchanged correspondence with the Land government but was unable to negotiate a compromise. This left the Land government free to proceed more or less as it wished. Against the background of a full-scale ecclesiastical publicity campaign, with the theme that school reform was a "destructive blow to freedom of conscience," the government and the CDU opposition in February 1968 approved a school-reform bill, Kühn's greatest political success to that time. The legislation, which left confessional schools at the primary level more or less intact, provided for a referendum on junior high schools. This was held in July 1968 and the result, as reported in *Die Zeit* on July 5, 1968, was that of the 1307 junior high schools, there was support for the maintenance of only 71 of them on a confessional basis. For the first time since the Kulturkampf, Catholic parents had demonstratively abandoned their bishops.

In Bavaria and Rhineland-Palatinate, in the meantime, educational reforms had also been enacted. In Rhineland-Palatinate the provisions in effect made confessional schools possible only in highly Catholic areas. In Bavaria, following an FDP initiative in February 1967, the CSU government put all its weight behind an abolition of confessional schools. By ruling out even the option of "parents' rights," the government ran into trouble with Cardinal Döpfner. However, Franz-Josef Strauss, Bavaria's political boss, persuaded the Cardinal that any other school reform would be impolitic and unpopular. Somehow Döpfner managed to persuade the other members of the Bavarian hierarchy. The government quickly worked out draft legislation with the two churches and thereupon secured the concurrence of the Free Democrats and Social Democrats. The final legislation proposed transforming all Bavarian elementary shcools into "Christian schools"—that is, schools attended by persons of all confessions, with some instruction given on a confessional basis. Allowance was also made for confessional schools on a private basis with full government financing. A public referendum, held in July 1968, on whether the Bavarian constitution should be amended to permit this move, was overwhelmingly approved. The Bavarian concordat and the treaty with the Protestant provincial church were then altered accordingly. The smooth Bavarian solution made the North Rhine-Westphalian bishops appear all the more dogmatic, narrow, and outmoded.

The quarrel over school reform had a significance far surpassing the character of elementary education. For Catholics it marked the clear end of a century-long chapter in their history. The group consciousness, the closed psychological world of German Catholicism was shattered. For a majority of the clergy and for most of the laity and politicians, it occasioned the first clear break with the most traditional of Catholic public interests. For the bishops it represented probably the most severe crisis of confidence between the hierarchy and the faithful since the Reformation. Catholic bishops and theologians had often been contemptuous of Protestant flexibility and willingness to compromise—"lack of principle," they called it. But the Evangelical church had been able to move with the times and was applauded on all sides for its position, while the majority of Catholic bishops made themselves look like so many King Canutes ignoring, railing against, and resisting the tide of progress. So obscurantist were the arguments, so fanatical was the manner of some bishops that, as some Catholic officials remarked privately afterward, almost any episcopal appeal nowadays would have the reverse effect of that intended. Cardinal Döpfner salvaged some of the church's prestige, even though his acceptance of the extreme Bavarian solution did not go down at all well with the Vatican, where he was felt to have gone too far too fast. In this way the school problem highlighted the current dilemma facing Catholic bishops in a number of countries: to keep the loyalty of their flocks, they must risk obloquy at the Vatican.

With the conclusion of the school controversy, there was little left of the Reichskonkordat. The article banning political activity by the clergy had never come into effect (in the absence of a parallel agreement with Protestants) and was officially declared void through an exchange of notes between the foreign office and the Holy See in 1951 and 1952. The loyalty oath was antiquated, not to say pointless, and the government of Hesse has declined to accept it. Much of the remainder of the treaty consists of provisions—such as the guarantees of freedom of religion, the freedom of the religious orders to engage in pastoral work, the protection of Catholic organizations, and so on—which are superfluous in a liberal democratic state such as the Federal Republic. A number of other provisions—such as the legal rights, privileges, and protection of the clergy—are also covered in German civil law. Apart from the provision establishing military chaplains, the only remaining articles of practical significance are those guaranteeing the maintenance of theological faculties and training institutions, as well as the payment of state subsidies and the collection of church taxes. But since these provisions cannot be enforced by the federal government, it is up to Land governments to decide whether to honor them. Moreover, the school dispute had already clearly shown that if Land parliaments and the majority of the population do not want to maintain these provisions, the Reichskonkordat can not save them.

By the late 1960s, in sum, the main import of the Reichskonkordat was no longer its anchoring of church privileges in German law. Rather it was the legal constraint upon the Vatican to accept Bonn's position both on East Germany and the Polish border issue. The treaty's significance was its application outside rather than within the Federal Republic. In retrospect, it is clear that the Reichskonkordat—in exact reverse of Cardinal Pacelli's intention—far from providing the church immunity from political involvement had over the years hopelessly entangled it first in domestic and then in international politics.

Now, in addition, the Reichskonkordat had become an object of increasing dispute within the curia itself, as sympathy for the Polish position on the Oder-Neisse issue and a desire to normalize the ecclesiastical situation in the area began to grow. Interestingly enough, this was only secondarily for pastoral reasons. Although there were now more than eight million Catholics in the area, the four apostolic administrators appointed in 1967 had proved equal to the ecclesiastical task, and, directly subordinate to Rome, were less susceptible to government manipulation than if they had been normal bishops. Rather it was the political status quo that the Vatican was beginning to question. Already under Pope John XXIII the Vatican had begun to edge away from its stance of total ideological war against communist governments. Under the guidance of Archbishop Agostino Casaroli, secretary for special affairs in the curia (in effect foreign minister), its cautious support for East-West détente was becoming more pronounced and visible. For Rome no less than for Bonn the Oder-Neisse problem had become an obstacle to conciliation in central Europe and a modus vivendi with the Polish government. Moreover, the Pope himself, an admirer of Catholicism in Poland ever since a visit to the country in 1921, not only had been prevented from participating in the Polish church's millenial celebration in 1966, but would also remain inhibited from visiting Poland as long as the diocesan issue was unsettled. At the same time it was recognized that a German peace treaty, opening the way to a formal adjustment of church borders, was as remote as ever. While the Vatican did not waver in its support for the West German position and continued to give the German hierarchy assurances to this effect, the feeling that the ecclesiastical anomoly must somehow soon be rectified became strong in Rome.

Ironically, it was the advent of the SPD-FDP coalition in 1969 that finally offered the Vatican what appeared to be a way out of its dilemma. As a central element of its Ostpolitik, the new German government sought a political settlement with Poland that would include acceptance but, because of four-power reserved rights over Germany as a whole, would stop short of granting de jure recognition to the Oder-Neisse border. To prepare German public opinion for even this concession, Bonn now in fact began to encourage the Holy See to transfer the dioceses in question from the "East German Church Province" to the Polish hierarchy. This was one of the principal messages conveyed to the Pope by Herbert Wehner, SPD Bundestag floor leader, and Transport Minister Georg Leber during a visit to Rome in November 1969.

Curial officials had no intention of taking the first step. Casaroli was fond of saying that the time had long passed when the Pope could let his hand fall on a map and determine a state border. But during the year between this approach and the signature of the German-Polish treaty they, or at least Casaroli, had virtually decided the issue in favor of the Poles. At the same time the curia was well aware that the prospective agreement would not be the final German peace treaty of the sort up to that time envisioned in the church's policy of awaiting a de jure settlement before adjusting diocesan borders. As a consequence, the Vatican began to disengage from its centuries-old legal position. Accordingly, the 1971 edition of the *Annuario Pontificio*, which went to press a few weeks after the Warsaw treaty had been signed in December 1970, dropped its traditional statement that diocesan borders in the Oder-Neisse area could be changed only in consequence of fully recognized treaties. Although the Papal Nuncio in Bonn denied that it had any significance, this deletion was a clear signal that, in so far as the Holy See was concerned, the German-Polish agreement would, upon ratification, be an adequate basis for appointing full bishops and redrawing ecclesiastical borders. It was a highly risky approach, but one in which Paul VI had apparently concurred by early 1971.

In effect, this decision had the extraordinary result of ranging the Vatican, the social-liberal German government, German Catholic non-conformists, such as the Bensberg circle, the Polish hierarchy, and the communist government of Poland against the German hierarchy and the Christian Democrats. During the year and a half between the signature and the ratification of the treaty, the curia was naturally under sharply conflicting pressures. On the one extreme were the Polish bishops who wanted Rome to move before Bonn did so that the church rather than the Polish government could claim credit for the first decisive step toward normalization. At the other extreme were, in addition to one or two members of the curia itself, the German hierarchy and the CDU. Although the German bishops fully supported German-Polish reconciliation and, as a church official stated in an interview, had decided by 1970 not to retaliate by cutting off their financial contributions to Rome because of any alteration in the eastern dioceses, they adamantly opposed formal acceptance, political or ecclesiastical, of the Oder-Neisse border.

The stark rigidity of the episcopat's position was undoubtedly accentuated by the Catholic Office, which itself was almost completely under the influence of conservative members of the central committee of German Catholics and such refractory Catholic refugee leaders as Herbert Czaja and Clemens Riedel (both CDU Bundestag members), who staunchly resisted acceptance of the Oder-Neisse border either by church or state. Consequently German Catholic leaders—clerical and lay—appealed to curial officials not to act prior to a final peace treaty and not to "recognize" the unjust expulsion of millions of German Catholics from their homeland. They argued that the Vatican's acceptance of the Oder-Neisse border could shake the fidelity to the church of many Catholic refugees, perhaps provoking some of them to shift their political support from the Christian Democrats to the Social Democrats as well. Furthermore, they warned that the SPD-FDP coalition was an interregnum, which would only briefly interrupt Christian Democratic rule in Germany, after which the Ostpolitik would lapse. These points were conveyed to Casaroli not only by officials of the German church and emissaries of the Christian Democrats, but also by the German ambassador to the Vatican, Hans Berger, who heartily disliked the new government and its eastern policy. (As a result of his egregious contumacy Berger, a conservative Catholic and Christian Democrat, was recalled from Rome and dismissed from government service in the middle of 1971.) Such arguments had little or no effect on Casaroli, who apparently created the impression that the matter was still open merely to minimize the anguish north of the Alps. German church officials, however, deceived themselves into believing that only the Poles had the archbishop's ear and redoubled their efforts to press their own views more forcefully.

In fact, the German hierarchy had fallen politically out of step with the Vatican. Casaroli had his own Ostpolitik and his own plan for a modus vivendi in eastern Europe, and, like Brandt, he left the Catholic bishops and the CDU conceptually far behind. In any case the time had passed when those in command in the curia viewed Christian Democratic rule in Bonn as the summum bonum. Leading curial officials were also convinced—if the German hierarchy were not—that the sharp East-West confrontation of the postwar years was over and that Europe was moving into an era of negotiation, reconciliation, and détente. It was no doubt a bitter blow to the leaders of the German church and the CDU when Casaroli publicly articulated such views in a speech in Milan in January 1972. It was undoubtedly a still greater humiliation to them when the Vatican's press spokesman declared—on the eve of the Bundestag ratification debate in May 1972—that the Ostpolitik was in fact Realpolitik, deserving support on that ground.

The yawning gap between the Vatican and the Christian Democrats became even wider with the CDU-sponsored resolution adopted by the Bundestag during the ratification proceedings of the Warsaw treaty, which declared that the agreement established no legal basis for existing borders. This was merely a political declaration of the German government's consistent legal position, which had already been formally stated in letters to the three western Allies and the Polish government. But it threatened to expose the Vatican's strategem of treating a political settlement as though it were a final legal one. Curial officials nonetheless quickly convinced themselves that the resolution was inconsistent with the treaty itself, which, in their view, provided them sufficient authority to act. Accordingly, on June 28, some three weeks after the treaty went into effect, the Holy See announced that it had decided to construct new dioceses in the Oder-Neisse area and to appoint bishops to govern them.

The announcement—or at least its timing—came almost as a shock to the German hierarchy, as Monsignor Wöste admitted to the press. The curia, to avoid pointless controversy, had in fact not strictly kept its promise to consult Cardinal Döpfner before acting. Predictably, German refugee groups denounced the decision and expressed dismay that the Holy See should, as it was phrased, in this way have placed might before right. Reinforcing the irony that had characterized the situation since 1969, the SPD formally welcomed the decision while the CDU expressed regret. For its part the foreign office, when asked whether the Vatican had violated the Reichskonkordat, replied evasively.

This was not surprising since the foreign office no doubt realized that the Vatican's action had two dangerous consequences, one following directly from the other. Altering the church structure in the Oder-Neisse area directly impinged upon the Reichskonkordat, in particular articles 11 and 14, which require the agreement of the German government to changes in diocesan borders and the appointment of bishops. However, since the Vatican did not secure the German government's concurrence, the conclusion appears inescapable that the Vatican violated the treaty. In the Vatican's view, by contrast, Bonn's agreement was unnecessary—and the Reichskonkordat remained inviolate—because the Warsaw treaty placed the Oder-Neisse area outside Germany, thereby removing it from the provisions of the Reichskonkordat and annulling the requirement for negotiations. Despite the internal logic, this line of argument is fallacious, because it necessarily assumes that the settlement was a de jure one and that four-power reserved rights over the area of the German Reich of 1937 are no longer valid. This, however, is a position that neither the two parties to the agreement nor the Soviets and the western Allies held. The rights reserved by Britain, France, the United States, and the Soviet Union, as victors over Germany, to determine final German borders have been consistently reasserted in treaty form, most recently in the Berlin agreement of 1972. It was therefore untenable for the Vatican to maintain that there had been a change in the international legal status of the area. The Vatican obviously had every right—and in this case excellent reason—to alter unilaterally its own policy on borders; it could not alter unilaterally its treaty obligations in this regard. For understandable reasons the German government was extremely uncomfortable with the Vatican's legal approach and reportedly let this be known through diplomatic channels. Since government leaders had encouraged the Vatican to take this step, however, the foreign office clearly could not protest its having done so and could only convey a word of caution about the legal implications of the Holy See's position.

Moreover, in treating the Reichskonkordat as no longer valid in the Oder-Neisse area and in implying that quadripartite rights over Germany are no longer relevant to the issue, the Vatican has fallen into a potentially far more serious legal trap. The two positions together raise the important question as to where in fact the Reichskonkordat does apply. For though the Holy See continues to regard the Federal Republic as the "Germany" of the Reichskonkordat, its legal approach implies that this "Germany" is no more than the Federal Republic—that is, the area where the Bonn goverment claims sovereignty and has legal authority. On this basis the validity of the Reichskonkordat in East Germany obviously collapses. It was certainly no mere coincidence that soon after the Vatican's action the East German official in charge of ecclesiastical affairs, Hans Seigewasser, summoned Cardinal Bengsch for a discussion of the normalization of East German diocesan borders.

Upon concluding the Reichskonkordat in 1933, the German government presented the Holy See with a Meissen statue of the Blessed Virgin. The statue can be seen today—broken and in an out-of-the-way corner of the Vatican museum. It is an apt symbol of the Reichskonkordat in 1973.

KEY ISSUES OF CHURCH INTEREST

9 | Reunification, Rearmament Conscription and Nuclear Arms

IN July 1948, four months after the Berlin blockade had begun and the iron curtain had rung down through the center of Europe, Protestant leaders came together in Eisenach (in the Russian Zone) and founded the Evangelical Church in Germany. Day and night during the five-day meeting American aircraft flew overhead on their way to and from the isolated former capital. Despite the grave and unprecedented tension between the Russians and Americans, a representative of General Clay freely crossed the zonal border to attend the meeting and, as an American report at the time stated, "the delegates to the conference were probably surprised in this critical political situation to find a US Military Government representative in the Russian zone and appearing on the same program with the representative of the Soviet Military Government."[1] In a sense this was the finest hour of the Evangelical church in the postwar period: the church was demonstrating that, despite the separation of Germany into two bitterly hostile parts, some all-German ties still existed; the German people remained spiritually united; at a deeper level national unity was intact.

For nearly a quarter-century—until the Evangelical church was itself geographically torn asunder in 1969—maintaining national unity and working for political reunification was the double mission the Evangelical church set for itself. This task infused the church with a vigor and sense of purpose which went far to negate the severe blow to the church resulting from the political consequences of the war. The church's objectives touched every aspect of the central issue of postwar German politics: "Deutschland-politik"—the conditions under which Germany could be reunified and, until then, the relationship West Germany should maintain with the Western Allies and the Soviet Union.

---

1. Military Government Land Württemberg-Baden, *Monthly Report* (July 1948), Modern Military Records, p. 2.

German politicians and intellectuals lost little time after the war in speculating on Germany's future place in Europe. But few of them were as fast off the mark as was Karl Barth. In a series of talks given throughout the Western zones in the summer of 1946, the theologian made an impassioned plea for Europe to pull herself together and determine her own future, so that "at least a remnant of the Western spirit might be preserved." He stressed that there was nothing for Europe to choose between the Americans and the Russians and added:

> Europe today is being ground between two millstones. It has become the country of a people seriously threatened from the West and from the East. . . . Must we then really pay for our sins by ceasing to be ourselves in our own home, but have our way of life determined for us by others?[2]

With the growing tension of the cold war, this prefiguration of Gaullism became an increasingly explicit philosophy of neutralism. Of the East-West confrontation, Barth advised "not to take part in the conflict. As Christians it is not our conflict at all. It is not a genuine, not a necessary, not an interesting conflict." And in one of his frequent rhetorical questions he drove the point home by asking, "Will not the way of the community of Jesus Christ have to be another, a *third* way, its *own* way?"[3]

Barth was less than frank in explaining exactly why Western Europe should opt out, why fear of communism was so laughable and why he, the most categorical of opponents of National Socialism, could tell Eastern European Protestants after the war to be loyal to the totalitarian regimes under which they lived. Probably the deepest impulse setting him off in this direction was his long attachment to socialism, making him well disposed to "What has been tackled in Soviet Russia—albeit with very dirty and bloody hands" and leaving him critical of America as the citadel of capitalism. He found it "quite absurd to mention in the same breath the philosophy of Marxism and the 'ideology' of the Third Reich, to mention a man of the stature of Joseph Stalin in the same breath as such charlatans as Hitler, Göring . . . etc." From this point it was a short step to an out-and-out apology for the Soviet Union. The Russians were judged to have better grounds than the West to feel threatened "if one notes on a map in how many places [America] —directly or indirectly through her British ally—has blocked Russia's access to the open sea." And in the religious sphere, he found that communism never sought

---

2. *Die christliche Verkündigung im heutigen Europa*, p. 11.
3. *Die Kirche zwischen Ost und West*, pp. 9, 10-11.

"the removal and replacement of the real Christ by a national Jesus, and it has never committed the crime of anti-Semitism. There is nothing of the false prophet about it. It is not anti-Christian. It is coldly non-Christian." [4]

Another influence in Barth's political outlook was his antipathy toward Catholicism. His sly digs about "Mr. Truman and the Pope" and "America and the Vatican," intended to establish guilt by association, demonstrated, rather, the intermingling of his own religious and political prejudices. The Swiss theologian Emil Brunner once challenged him on this point, asking why the Catholic church's opposition to communism required Protestants "to stand aside merely because the truth is spoken by the Catholic Church?" [5] Barth gave no clear response. An additional impulse was anti-anticommunism. Barth's explanation for failing to speak out against the communist governments in Eastern Europe was that condemnation was already so widespread that any word from him (or other Christians) was unnecessary. Fairly or not this stance gave rise to the feeling that Barth was begging the question of principle and was applying a double standard to the policies of the Soviet Union and those of the Western governments.

Barth's themes—antipathy toward America, suspicion of the Catholic church, and sympathy for the political left—had an immediate attraction in certain Protestant circles in Germany and left a mark that endures, particularly in Protestant theological faculties. This impact was due both to Barth's enormous prestige and to the fertile ground on which his ideas fell. The strengthened position of the Catholic church in comparison with the Evangelical church and the general orientation of Protestant churchmen toward central and Eastern Europe (where a high proportion of them had been born and educated) gave Barth's ideas a great appeal, especially among those Protestants who had been connected with the Confessing church and who stood outside a strong Lutheran discipline. As in the years of the Third Reich, it was Barth who provided the intellectual nourishment for a coterie of churchmen who found themselves increasingly out of sympathy with dominant political trends in Germany.

With the establishment of the Federal Republic in the fall of 1949, and with the inauguration of Adenauer's policy of West European integration—"a German and European policy, with the Cologne cathedral as center," as it has been impressionistically described[6]—which appeared to downgrade the provi-

---

4. Ibid., pp. 7, 22, 24.

5. Barth and Brunner quotes in *Christliche Gemeinde im Wechsel der Staatsordnungen*, pp. 65, 69.

6. Schwarz, *Vom Reich zur Bundesrepublik*, p. 435.

sional nature of the West German state and the importance of reunification, this dissatisfaction exploded. The man who led the opposition to the new state was a man who had been an archcritic of the Weimar Republic and who was one of the most renowned opponents of the Third Reich: Martin Niemöller, president of the church of Hesse and Nassau. His declaration of war came in an interview with the *New York Herald Tribune* on December 13, 1949, when he stated that he would consider a Russian dictatorship over a reunified Germany preferable to the continued division of the country. He suggested that if the four powers could not reunite the country, the armed forces of several neutral states should replace the occupation armies under the auspices of the United Nations and then unify the nation. He went on to complain that there were too many Catholics in the German cabinet and asserted that the Federal Republic had been "conceived in the Vatican and born in Washington." Three days later he repeated most of these views to the *Wiesbadener Kurier* and added that the war had been a devastating blow to German Protestantism. East Germany was now Polish and Catholic, central Germany was neutralized by the Russians, and West Germany had become a Catholic state. The recent federal election (for the first Bundestag) had been dishonest, he claimed, since it had not given voters the opportunity of indicating whether they had wanted the new state at all.

Niemöller's malediction caused a great commotion—or, as Adenauer wrote in a letter to the church president, "pained embarrassment" in Germany among the high commissioners as well as abroad.[7] This was no less true in church circles. That reunification was in the ecclesiastical interest of German Protestantism was clear to everyone. The question Niemöller was posing was whether—in the ultimate hope of reunifying the country and restoring Protestant dominance—the Evangelical church should fight Adenauer tooth and nail, try to force Protestants out of the CDU, and move Western Germany toward neutralism. This challenge was as provocative to conservative Lutherans, who considered politics none of the church's business, as it was to the government and the CDU, which were dependent on Protestant backing. So sensitive were these issues and so great was the public hubbub that the church was forced to take a stand. Meeting in November, the council declared that reunification could not be purchased at the price of political freedom and that Protestants and Catholics must continue to cooperate. However, the

---

7. Weymar, *Konrad Adenauer*, p. 361. Lord Robertson, British High Commissioner at the time, recalled in an interview that he was so infuriated by Niemöller's remarks that he arranged a meeting with the churchman to express his feelings.

church leaders at the same time denounced the occupation powers for having divided Germany, warning that this division was a threat to the peace, and declared that they intended to keep a watchful eye on the consequences of the country's confessional balance upon the personnel structure of the federal government. The council's appeal for an end to the division of Germany was repeated in April 1950 by the synod of the EKD which called upon the four powers promptly to draw up a peace treaty.

These declarations showed that the church leadership supported neither the neutralism advocated by Barth and Niemöller nor the Western alignment policy of Adenauer but would seek, for itself at least, a middle way. When the two German states had been founded in 1949, the church "recognized" them both and dealt with them as equals through official representatives in Bonn and Pankow. On the other hand, it declared that it considered both states to be only provisional. Throughout the most frigid of the cold-war years it struggled to keep itself ideologically and politically unaligned with either state or power bloc. To some extent this tactic was intended to strengthen the church's position as an East-West link and to maintain some acceptability to the East German regime and so reduce pressure on East German congregations. But the attitude was born equally of the conviction that the church had a political mission—to work for compromise rather than confrontation, for East-West contact rather than ideological isolation, and for reconciliation rather than deepening division. The Evangelical church could not therefore be Adenauer's ideological ally, and it would oppose those of his policies which might deepen the gulf between the two parts of the country.

The silence of the Catholic church during this period was as shrill in its way as was Niemöller's invective. But this was more the quiescence of anxiety than of contentment. Throughout the postwar period the prevailing mood of the Catholic bishops was defensive. They looked inward, not outward; they desired consolidation, not risks. They thought above all of fending off the danger of the left and the threat from the East. As in 1933, when the establishment of a barrier to bolshevism was their main objective, so after 1945 they considered the establishment of an East-West balance to be of first priority. Beyond this, however, their views were probably less definite than those of the more passive Protestant church heads. Traditionally Catholic bishops concentrated on social issues, and it was Adenauer who molded their ideological anticommunism into a political commitment to Western alliance and European integration. That the division of Germany involved fewer psychological and ecclesiastical difficulties for the Catholic church than for the Evangelical church is clear. The Catholic church was a western and southern German institution; Protestant strength was in the northern and eastern parts.

Protestants traditionally looked eastward; Catholics gazed toward the west and south. The views of the Catholic bishops therefore coincided in an entirely natural way with the outlook of Adenauer and the CDU, and the hierarchy could support his policies with genuine conviction.

However, it does not follow that the bishops were opposed to reunification, still less that Adenauer was motivated by a combination of confessional and political factors to prefer a "neo-Carolingian empire" to a reunified Germany.[8] Adenauer had little cause to fear the political consequences of reunification. Prior to 1933 only 34 percent of the population east of the Elbe voted for the SPD—hardly enough to frighten the CDU. Most of the SPD support was centered in Berlin, Saxony and areas of Thuringia. In the other parts of East Germany the CDU might very well have become a Protestant party, dominating politics in those traditionally conservative areas as it did in Schleswig-Holstein. Finally, had Adenauer succeeded in bringing the two parts of the country together, he would probably have evoked tremendous enthusiasm for himself and his party throughout East and West Germany. Similarly, the Catholic bishops—even attributing to them the most cynical motives—must have seen more to their advantage in reunification than in the status quo. Indeed, perhaps the gravest political sin of the Catholic bishops in Germany after 1871 was their excess of nationalism. This nationalist ardor by no means evaporated after 1945. Moreover, the bishops' very dread of communism would have led them to welcome the withdrawal of the Russians to the Oder-Neisse line (with the consequent impact upon eastern Europe) and full religious freedom for the two million East German Catholics. But until then, acquiescence in the division of Germany was the price, and they saw no alternative to paying it. Had the federal government started off in a neutralist direction in 1949, there would have been a Catholic outcry as anguished as that of Niemöller's—but for political, not ecclesiastical, reasons. As it was, the Catholic bishops sat back and let the CDU, actively supported by Catholic lay organizations and the Catholic press, carry on the campaign for Western security.

---

8. In Britain and the United States assertions to this effect were more widespread and longer in dying than in Germany. Typically, a leading article in *The Economist* on November 15, 1958, for instance, maintained: "Dr. Adenauer, whose political position is built on the Catholic predominance in western Germany, still bases his policies on the concept of a Carolingian Europe centered on the Rhine and the unquestionable necessity not to weaken its defences. He, too, like Mr. Khruschev, wishes to maintain a *status quo*." Articulating a similar view in some American circles, Walter Lippmann wrote in the *Manchester Guardian* of November 28, 1958: "few responsible West Germans wish to have integration in a unified state. For integration would change radically the balance of religious forces and political parties."

By the end of 1949 the Federal Republic was on the road to Western alignment with the full support of the Catholic church, despite the misgiving of the Evangelical church and in the face of furious opposition by significant numbers of Protestants. The only question concerned the number of further steps down this road that could be taken without leaving reunification behind. German rearmament, a subject of widening speculation at this time, posed this question in its most acute form. Protestant leaders were in a pacifist mood, and their instinctive reaction was as much moral and emotional as it was political, and in all three respects it was strongly negative. At the April 1950 session of the synod Bishop Lilje was emphatic in his opposition, declaring:

> The question of German rearmament need not be answered on the basis of abstract principles. A remilitarization of Germany can only serve to increase world tensions without contributing to a political settlement. Whoever takes up arms today without having decisively contributed to the political reconstruction of Europe commits a political act which, taken in isolation, is senseless and sterile. Christian political realism can therefore in this case only say no.[9]

The outbreak of the Korean war a few weeks later only strengthened Protestant leaders in this belief. The EKD council declared that the situation in Asia had clearly demonstrated that peace was threatened by national division, and it called upon the United Nations to end such division wherever it existed. "We consider German remilitarization out of the question," the Protestant leaders went on, "either in the west or in the east. . . . That Germans should ever fire on Germans must remain unthinkable."[10]

To Adenauer, however, the Far Eastern crisis held a quite different meaning. He had already perceived in rearmament a means of achieving sovereignty and equality for the Federal Republic within the Western community; the Korean war gave him an opportunity of putting his policy in high gear. On August 29, two days after the EKD council had condemned rearmament, he despatched a memorandum to the three Western High Commissioners asking that additional Allied forces be stationed in the Federal Republic and proposing both the creation of a European army with German units and the establishment of a West German security police force. Although this recommendation directly involved the interior ministry, which was responsible for internal security matters, Adenauer had not discussed the issue with the

---

9. *Sonntagsblatt,* May 14, 1950.
10. *Kirchliches Jahrbuch,* 1950, pp. 165–166.

minister, Gustav Heinemann. Heinemann was so angered as a result that he immediately submitted his resignation—the first German minister in history to do so on the ground of principle alone. He wished, he said, to force a showdown, not only on procedures in the government, but also on whether West German citizens would, like the cabinet, be confronted with a fait accompli or be given an opportunity of democratically deciding the issue. The decision should further take into consideration the "brothers in the East." For himself, as one 'guided by Christian responsibility," he believed that God had taken arms away from the German people, and he was therefore convinced that rearmament was wrong. [11] Adenauer, who was no more inclined to filter his politics through religious ideals than to accept ecclesiastical advice on a political question, had only contempt for this line of thought. In his view, God gave man reason with which to reach political conclusions, but He did not provide political guidance. To mix religion and politics, to attempt to divine a political policy from spiritual precepts or to claim religious sanction for a political view, in Adenauer's judgment, resulted in addled religion and addled politics. However, the Chancellor hesitated for more than a month to accept Heinemann's resignation because of the confessional repercussions. Eventually, as Heinemann, though wavering and confused, moved further into the Niemöller camp, Adenauer concluded that he had no choice but to accept the minister's resignation.

Heinemann's defection put the Chancellor on the spot. The Western Allies were unable to reach a prompt decision on rearmament and, as Adenauer's friends warned the American High Commissioner, John J. McCloy, this risked making it possible for Heinemann to argue that the Allies understood German interests better than did the Chancellor. At the same time Heinemann's action had a profound effect upon Protestants, even in those Evangelical church circles that had been left cold by Niemöller's outburst against the Federal Republic. Bishop Lilje's *Sonntagsblatt* on September 22, 1950, complimented the minister for his attempt at occupying both an ecclesiastical and a political post and complained that "of all the arguments in this affair, one angers us most: Heinemann has shown too much concern for East German Protestants." Bishop Dibelius, writing in the Berlin church newspaper, *Die Kirche,* stated that Heinemann "had only raised his standing by what he had done." [12]

---

11. Heinemann set out his position in a statement entitled "Deutsche Sicherheit," originally published as a handbill and later reprinted in *Kirchliches Jahrbuch,* 1950, pp. 179–186. He further elaborated his views in "Was Dr. Adenauer vergisst," in *Frankfurter Hefte,* July 1956.

12. Quoted in *Kirchliches Jahrbuch,* 1950 p. 212.

The Niemöller group of course pounced on the affair and transformed it, not merely into an attack on rearmament but into a massive campaign against the entire foundation of Adenauer's policy. Even before Heinemann's resignation had been accepted, Niemöller launched a devastating public attack on Adenauer, accusing him of having already begun to organize an army and to produce armaments behind the backs and against the wishes of the German people. Adenauer's biographer, Paul Weymar, who devotes an entire chapter to these differences between Niemöller and Adenauer, comments that Niemöller's attack "aroused Adenauer's wrath to a degree seldom experienced by him." He states that the Chancellor, "in a mood of profound and violent agitation" denounced Niemöller to the cabinet as "an enemy of the State" and characterized his actions as "nothing less than high treason" [13] Unfortunately the Chancellor made similar remarks in a radio address in reply to Niemöller. With Germany's best-known Protestant and the German Chancellor publicly at one another's throats, the question was whom the majority of Protestants would side with. If with Niemöller and Heinemann, not only Adenauer's whole foreign policy, but even the viability of the CDU itself, would be endangered. Such was the aim of Niemöller and his friends who, within two weeks of Heinemann's resignation, met with a group of Social Democratic leaders headed by the party's chairman, Kurt Schumacher, and demonstratively issued a communique stating that only a newly elected Bundestag could legitimately decide the rearmament issue. A wing of the Evangelical church was now allied with the opposition with no less an objective than the downfall of the government.

This course of events demonstrated the depth of the hostility between the government and the most dynamic segment of the Evangelical church at a time when the Federal Republic was scarcely more than a year old. At the same time, however, dangerous rifts were developing in the church. Differences of view divided provincial churches both internally and from one another, with the synod of the Rhineland church almost unanimously supporting Niemöller's view and the synod of his own church declining to do so. The disagreement was so grave by mid-November that the council and church conference of the EKD had to hold a special session in Berlin. At this meeting a majority of the church leadership was against Niemöller and Heinemann, and abandoning its previous position, the council declared that "the community of faith does not imply a unity of political judgment" and so "whether rearmament is unavoidable can be differently answered on the basis of belief." [14]

---

13. Weymar, p. 370.
14. *Kirchliches Jahrbuch,* 1950, pp. 223–234.

Was the shift a result of the old "Obrigkeitsdenken," the traditional Protestant acceptance of government authority? Apart from a few churchmen who wanted to take the easy way out, this is doubtful. Paradoxically, it was Heinemann's resignation that had provoked the change by arousing a counterattack on theological grounds by such Lutherans as Meiser and Thielicke and on political grounds by others such as Lilje and Kunst. Kunst, convinced by the Korean war that a German defense contribution was necessary, threatened to resign his position rather than represent a church opposed to Adenauer's policy. Since no one at this point argued that an ultimate moral principle was involved, the issue amounted to a political one and, since church leaders were deeply divided on this matter, the council could do no more than refuse either to support or oppose government policy. While it remained to be seen how the majority of Protestants would divide on the issue, Adenauer could be confident by the end of 1950 that he would at least not have the Evangelical church officially against him.

By contrast, the Catholic church gave the Chancellor its complete and unswerving support from the first—in fact, well before. Over a month prior to Adenauer's memorandum to the High Commissioners and long before the Western governments agreed to a German defense contribution, Cardinal Frings stated to a diocesan church assembly in Bonn (in the words of the dispatch in *The Times* of July 25, 1950):

> True peace would be based only on an order which was founded essentially on God. Wherever this divine order was threatened and attacked in its most vital fundamentals, then the peoples in their unity under God had not only the right but also even the duty, when other means failed and there was justified prospect of success, to reestablish by force of arms the right which had been broken and the order which had been upset. To start a war lightheartedly was a gross wickedness, but it would show lack of responsibility not to bring the law-breaker to account, or to stand outside in selfish neutrality, instead of hurrying to help one who had been unjustly attacked.

He further stated, as reported in *Der Tagesspiegel* of July 25, 1950:

> The Holy Father leaves no doubt that it would be reprehensible sentimentality and falsely directed humanitarianism if, out of fear for the suffering of war, one permits every kind of injustice to occur. If, in the opinion of the Holy Father, going to war can be not only a right but also an obligation of states, so it follows that propaganda for an unlimited and absolute conscientious objection to military service is not compatible with Christian thinking.

This was church militant indeed. The Cardinal's statement was re-markable not only in placing the Catholic hierarchy well ahead of any other group in German society in favoring rearmament but also in propounding a doctrine precisely the opposite of Niemöller's: it was a Christian duty to support German rearmament. At the time the speech shocked many Germans, Catholic and Protestant alike, and provoked a sharp retort from the president of the Protestant church assembly, von Thadden-Trieglaff, who stated in the same paper: "The Evangelical Church would never have spoken as Cardinal Frings has done. No one should speak so frivolously and glibly of a war between brothers." But in a pastoral letter read in all the churches of the Cologne diocese on the following Sunday, Frings stressed that he had spoken in complete accord with the views of the Pope. [15] The Cardinal's statements presaged the hierarchy's consistent support for the entire range of the govern-ment's defense policies and its opposition to neutralism, pacifism, and broad legal guarantees for conscientious objectors. These views were repeated in sermons and pastoral letters as the debate over rearmament grew in intensity. "Those who love freedom must let it be clear that they are ready to make every necessary sacrifice for the defense of freedom and human worth," Cardinal Frings stated, for instance, in a pastoral letter in February 1951. [16] Official diocesan newspapers joined in the chorus, of which the following excerpt, under the headline "Soldiering—In the Christian View," is an exam-ple:

> Yes, it is time that we learn to see soldiering in the right light. There is absolutely nothing dishonorable about being a soldier or having been a soldier. St. Sebastian would not otherwise have come into our church. He who fights in good faith for his nation and his homeland has no need to be ashamed of that. [17]

Even religious gatherings became propaganda forums. As the Bonn correspon-dent of *Le Monde* reported with sharp irony on February 28, 1952, in "the religious conferences of the various dioceses, the principal subject being raised at these inspirational meetings is 'the Christian and military service,' 'the right

---

15. As was the case. Pius XII, well ahead of Western foreign ministries, declared in his Christmas message of 1948 that a strong Western defense arrangement was the best guarantee of peace.

16. *Kirchenzeitung für das Erzbistum Köln,* February 18, 1951. The entire hier-archy echoed this view in a joint message in November 1953.

17. *Kirchenzeitung für das Erzbistum Köln,* January 6, 1952.

to defend one's homeland,' etc." But it was the Catholic lay press (such weeklies as the *Rheinischer Merkur* and *Echo der Zeit*) and above all the Catholic lay organizations that led the campaign on behalf of rearmament. Lay group leaders began as early as the fall of 1951 to work out a position. They established contact with the government defense agency and began discussion in their own ranks over strategy. They found a line without difficulty: if the Bundestag should vote for a German defense contribution, Catholics would give their full support to rearmament. Adenauer could not have asked for more than that.

The debate over reunification and rearmament rose to a crescendo in early 1952. In February agreement was reached on a draft treaty for the European Defense Community, and the Lisbon session of the North Atlantic Council settled the relationship between the European Defense Community, (EDC) and the North Atlantic Treaty Organization (NATO). In the same month the Bundestag held its first debate on a German defense contribution, and a few weeks later the Russians made new proposals for a German peace treaty. At the time many Germans felt that they were faced with a final choice between Western alliance through rearmament and eventual reunification through neutrality. This was the critical moment, and the Catholic lay movement promptly went into action on behalf of the government's policies. In March the participants at the annual meeting of the Catholic Workers' Movement (Katholische Arbeiterbewegung: KAB) gave their full support to an appeal by Theodor Blank, the Chancellor's advisor on security affairs and a member of the KAB, for a German defense effort. The following month the Federation of German Catholic Youth approved a declaration rejecting neutralism and describing rearmament as an inescapable necessity—an amazing endorsement in view of the strength of the opposition of German young people and the fact that virtually every non-Catholic German youth organization opposed, refused to support, or declined to take a position on rearmament. In the same month the Association of Catholic Men's Organizations of Germany called for a German defense contribution and—in an appeal that might almost have been issued by a Holy Roman Emperor—besought Christians "in rejection of liberalism and collectivism, to contribute to the strengthening of the spiritual-ethical stability of the international community on the basis of the rich treasure of the centuries-old Christian western culture." [18] In all three cases the members themselves had little voice in deciding upon these pledges; the leaders laid down the policy, and the members had to

---

18. Quoted in Institut für europäische Politik und Wirtschaft, *Der deutsche Soldat in der Armee von morgen*, pp. 65–66.

like it or leave it. The relatively high proportion of Catholics who belonged to lay groups, read Catholic newspapers, and attended church services heard one message: support the government's defense policy. Adenauer had known from the first that public opinion would require careful cultivation before it would go along with rearmament. No single body helped him so decisively as the Catholic church and its lay movement.

Opposition to rearmament in Catholic circles was crushed by the hierarchy's massive authority. The clergy were instructed to stay out of the debate but to defend the government position on theological grounds if necessary. Those few priests and theologians who were against rearmament either kept their views to themselves or risked being removed to a small country parish or other remote spot. Laymen who were pronounced opponents—such as Walter Dirks, Helene Wessel, and Klara Fassbender—obviously could not be rusticated, but they were deprived of access to the laity through Catholic activities and were denigrated in the Catholic press. The Catholic historian and poet Reinhold Schneider, for instance, was bitterly attacked in the spring of 1951 by almost every diocesan newspaper for an article he published in an East German publication condemning rearmament in both parts of Germany. The West Berlin *Petrusblatt* even suggested that he deserved to be excommunicated for what it considered his implied support for communism. President Heuss was appalled by the ecclesiastical and political intimidation of Schneider and personally saw to his political rehabilitation by giving him Germany's foremost award for science and the arts, Pour le Mérite, in 1952. The hierarchy, however, never forgave Schneider. In 1956, when German publishers awarded him their peace prize (held by such persons as Albert Schweizer, Martin Buber, and Hermann Hesse), the seat reserved for a Catholic church representative at the ceremony in the Paulskirche at Frankfurt remained unoccupied. A short time later Schneider lectured on Shakespeare at the German Shakespeare Society headquarters in Bochum; following the lecture Cardinal Frings, as president of the society, hosted a reception from which Schneider was deliberately excluded.

In the lay movement itself dissidents were silenced by the simple argument that their viewpoint was not in keeping with Catholic theology. This maneuver was successful because, as Josef Rommerskirchen (head of the Catholic Youth Movement from 1950 to 1953) could claim in an interview from his own experience, "German Catholics accepted their leaders' pronouncements on public issues with virtually the same unquestioning fidelity as they gave to those on religious matters." A small group of recalcitrants in the youth movement, who quoted scripture against scripture, maintaining that a political decision was being forced upon them by theological ratiocination, were arbitrarily declared to be no longer members of the youth organization. "Die Schar," a tiny youth group and the only one in the movement not subscribing to the government policy, was all but summarily read out of the youth movement by the leadership. Official declarations of the Catholic youth movement during 1952 and 1953 made no mention of any opposition in the ranks, and it was not until 1954 that the organization's newspaper, *Die Wacht,* would even publish letters disagreeing with the official line. Those were the days of the closed Catholic world; the hierarchy stated its position, the majority of the faithful accepted it, and the matter was settled. If the Protestant layman had to bear the scandal of a church in theological and ecclesiastical disarray, the Catholic layman was the victim of a church engaged in political thought control.

In an article published at the height of the Heinemann-Adenauer affair in *Unterwegs* on November 1, 1950, Karl Barth left open the question of whether Protestant opponents of rearmament should break away from the Evangelical church and engage in a new Kirchenkampf as "confessing" churchmen had done in the Third Reich. Heinemann and Niemöller were unwilling to commit themselves to that extent, as they made clear at the meeting of the EKD council in November 1950. Instead, they took their opposition directly into the political arena. They would probably have liked to have joined ranks with Social Democratic leaders, but they soon realized that there was little or no common ground in their points of view. Essentially the Protestant antirearmament case, particularly as argued by Barth, Niemöller, and Heinemann, rested on five points: since the Germans had been disarmed and psychologically demilitarized, it would be wrong for them to rearm; the Allies would use German forces as cannon fodder and Germany as a battleground; rearmament would be at the expense of social justice and democratic development; the Russians would regard rearmament as a provocation; and a situation in which Germans would have to kill other Germans was instinctively repugnant. [19] Although these ideas did not lack sympathizers in the Social Democratic ranks, Schumacher and the party leadership

---

19. Probably the two best expositions of this viewpoint are Heinemann's *Deutsche Sicherheit* and Barth's *Unterwegs* article. Both were written within two weeks of one another and used identical arguments, with two exceptions. Barth did not make Heinemann's point that rearmament might reduce the possibility of reunification, and Heinemann did not argue, as Barth had, that it was "one thing when an Englishman or a Swiss put on a uniform and took a weapon in hand, but quite another when a German does the same thing." The most striking difference between the two documents is Barth's self-assurance and Heinemann's equivocation.

had no more patience with them than had Adenauer. While Schumacher disagreed with Adenauer's mode of rearmament and feared that it would deepen the division of Germany, he was not opposed to rearmament in principle and repudiated both pacifism and neutralism. Moral arguments against a defense effort he regarded as well-intentioned but misguided. Military security was not inconsistent with a healthy social order, in his view, but was a premise for its achievement. An alliance between the SPD and the Protestant dissidents was consequently out of the question, and a marriage of convenience apparently never tempted Schumacher, who had little sympathy with the churches and even less with churchmen in politics.

The SPD could offer no home to the clerical antirearmers and, after their tactical agreement in 1950 that a decision on rearmament should be postponed (which Schumacher intended as a step to political power, not to prevent rearmament), the SPD kept the Protestant group at arm's length. In 1952 an SPD pamphlet in fact attacked a group of Protestant pacifists headed by Pastor Herbert Mochalski as a communist front. This publication greatly agitated left-wing Protestants, and in September 1952, on the occasion of the SPD party congress in Dortmund, at their initiative a meeting was arranged between Heinrich Held and Ernst Wilm, respectively heads of the provincial churches of the Rhineland and Westphalia, and a number of Social Democratic leaders, including Pastor Heinrich Albertz, subsequently the mayor of Berlin. The church leaders wanted to reach an agreement with the SPD to fight the EDC and the Bonn contractual accords and to avoid attacks on one another in federal and local elections. This was further than the SPD would go, and party leaders continued to reject any form of cooperation with Mochalski's and similar Protestant groups.

It was therefore clear to Niemöller and Heinemann from the earliest stage of the rearmament controversy that they would have to go their own way. This realization did not diminish their political enthusiasm nor, apparently, their political effectiveness. In January 1951 Niemöller founded the Emergency League for the Peace of Europe, an antigovernment neutralist and pacifist movement. The following year Heinemann left the CDU, and Helene Wessel left the Center party. Together they established the All-German People's party which transformed the Emergency League's ideas into a political program aimed at creating an independent, reunited, demilitarized, and neutral Germany. At the same time Niemöller pressed for a popular referendum on rearmament and wrote to Jakob Kaiser, minister for all-German questions, as well as to President Heuss, asking for their intervention on behalf of the proposal. Kaiser did not respond, and the President merely pointed out that the Basic Law makes no provision for referenda except in the case of redefining Land borders. Niemöller's proposal never really caught on; the Social Democrats were opposed to it, and the idea quickly fizzled out. Toward the end of 1951, however, the church-president caused another public storm when he announced that he was going to Moscow at the invitation of the Patriarch of the Russian Orthodox Church. He said he planned to discuss the relations of the Russian church to the World Council of Churches (which had been broken off in 1948) as well as the release of German prisoners of war. He may have hoped that this action would lead to political talks with Russian leaders as well. Adenauer was infuriated and publicly commented that it was deeply regrettable that Niemöller "should choose to stab his own government in the back in this fashion and at this time." [20] This was not just a matter of personal enmity; Niemöller's position as head of the Evangelical church's foreign bureau worried the Chancellor. To Adenauer—and to a good many Protestants—it was intolerable that Niemöller, the "foreign minister" of German Protestantism, should spread the impression abroad that his views were those of the Evangelical church and should take advantage of his position to deliberately embarrass the federal government. Adenauer could have spared himself the worry—at least in the case of the Moscow visit. The Russians would neither return the prisoners nor permit Niemöller to remain as their pastor, and it was Adenauer himself who finally secured the prisoners' release in 1955 in connection with the establishment of diplomatic relations. [21]

Niemöller and his allies managed in this way to keep the initiative on rearmament and related issues largely in their own hands. For two years (after October 1950) support for rearmament steadily declined, and opposition was soon the prevailing viewpoint. The role of Niemöller and Heinemann in this development seems clear. Public opinion polls taken by the office of the U.S. High Commissioner found that the grounds for opposition during most of this period were based, not on the Social Democrats' arguments, but on the Protestant antirearmers' line, in particular on "an inclination to remain neu-

---

20. Quoted in Schmidt, *Pastor Niemöller*, p. 182.

21. Dissatisfaction within the church with Niemöller as head of the foreign bureau steadily increased. In February 1952 Niemöller's remarks on rearmament during a tour of the United States provoked "a highly placed official" of the church to give an interview to *The New York Times* to make clear that Niemöller spoke only for himself and did not accurately reflect the Evangelical church's viewpoint. Attacks on Niemöller (and on the foreign bureau itself by arch-Lutherans) finally led to the EKD council's replacing Niemöller in 1956.

tral in the East-West struggle." [22] This was a desperate worry to the CDU for political reasons and to the government for practical reasons. Two letters illustrate what was occurring throughout the Federal Republic during this period. On October 30, 1951, the chairman of the Westphalian CDU, Lambert Lensing, wrote to Adenauer:

> As I have been informed by reliable Catholic and Protestant circles, Dr. Heinemann is giving speeches to intellectual circles in industrial areas that are having a very *destructive* and *confusing* result. He maintains that the Federal Government, the press and other public-opinion media are completely dependent upon the Americans.
>
> I am of the opinion that something must be done about this and done as soon as possible. In my view well-known Protestants, above all Bundestag President Dr. Ehlers, must appear at counter-meetings. . . . Bundestag member Dr. Gerstenmaier is ruled out on the ground that he strongly supported National Socialism from 1936 to the outbreak of the war. [23]

The other side of the coin was the explanation to a CDU official by church counsellor Erwin Wissmann on September 13, 1952, of his disenchantment with the CDU:

> In foreign affairs I have long been unable to support or approve its course. This must, in my opinion, lead either to war or to a complete break with East Germany. Domestically, Catholics are completely dominant. [24]

It was against this tide that Theodor Blank had to struggle as he began to rebuild a German defense contribution. As he recalled in an interview, he found the Protestant antirearmament effort to be the most difficult influence against which he had to contend. The Social Democrats were not opposed to rearmament in principle, and Blank had an open channel to Schumacher. The Protestant group, however, was dogmatically against rearmament, and Blank's decision to bring Count Baudissin (who had contacts with this group) into his agency in order to deflect some of their hostility and establish a channel to it had only limited success.

To go from the microcosmic to the macrocosmic, the contrasting effects of Protestant opposition to and Catholic support for rearmament became

---

22. Office of the U.S. High Commissioner for Germany, Report No. 48, Series No. 2, "An Analysis of Possible Determinants of Opposition to German Participation in the Defense of Europe" (November 22, 1950). These polls were the most detailed public-opinion studies made by any group in Germany on rearmament and related issues.

23. *File Dr. Tillmanns*, Archives of the Evangelical Committee of the CDU/CSU, Bonn.

24. Letter to W. Jansen, in *File Dr. Tillmanns*.

Table 12
Attitudes on Rearmament By Confessions: 1950–1951

		Oct. '50	March '51	June '51
in favor of rearmament	Protestants	64%	50%	48%
	Catholics	60%	47%	43%
opposed to rearmament	Protestants	29%	39%	32%
	Catholics	33%	39%	34%

Source: Office of the High Commissioner for Germany. For October 1950: Report No. 46, Series No. 2, "Germans View the Remilitarization Issue" (November 10, 1950). For March 1951: Report No. 69, Series No. 2, "The West German People View Defense Participation, Neutrality and Related Issues" (March 29, 1951). For June 1951: Report No. 88, Series No. 2, "Current Thinking on West German Defense Participation" (July 6, 1951).

Table 13
Attitudes on Rearmament by Confession: 1952

		Feb. '52
in favor of rearmament	Protestants	47%
	Catholics	52%
opposed to rearmament	Protestants	35%
	Catholics	28%

Source: Office of the High Commissioner for Germany, Report No. 130, Series No. 2, "West German Opinion on Defense Participation" (March 31, 1952)

increasingly apparent. It is noteworthy that both Catholics and Protestants at first reacted similarly to the rearmament controversy (see Table 12). But once the Catholic church, its lay organizations, and its press launched their campaign on behalf of rearmament at the end of 1951 and early in 1952, the confessional reactions began to diverge, with Catholic support taking a substantial swing upward and the opposition dropping. Protestant antirearmament groups were having a reverse effect upon Protestants (see Table 13).

It was not simply over the rearmament issue that Adenauer had difficulty securing Protestant support; he also ran into problems over his policy concerning East Germany and Eastern Europe. This was not only because Protestant churchmen were generally more inclined to believe that rearmament was at the expense of reunification, but also because they thought more in terms of reconciliation with the East than of defending "the Christian West" against communism. The EKD synod's "Appeal for Peace" in 1950, at a moment of particular virulence in the cold war, mirrored the church's desire to find—without equating the policy motivations of communist and noncommunist governments—some middle position in the escalating confrontation between East and West. Less remarkably but perhaps more effectively, pastors, laymen, and whole parishes worked throughout the 1950s to establish contact with Protestant groups in Eastern Europe. In their unwillingness to concentrate on Western integration and Western defense to the virtual exclusion of approaches to the East, Protestants differed fundamentally from Adenauer and most Catholics.

As a result, many Protestant church officials believed that if the West German government sought to bring the East Germans into negotiations, it would stand a better chance of moving toward reunification than if it tried to fight it into submission. This was a daring, not to say scandalous idea in the 1950s, and one that remains an object of disagreement. Not long after the establishment of the two German states, Bishop Dibelius' office, for instance, began launching proposals on how the bishop personally or the Evangelical church as an all-German institution might facilitate steps leading toward reunification.

In December 1950, Provost Heinrich Grüber, writing anonymously in *Die Kirche,* proposed that Adenauer and Otto Grotewohl, the East German Minister-President, meet in Dibelius' West Berlin residence. Then, in April 1952, Dibelius appealed for all-German elections leading to reunification. He pointed out that the Evangelical church, with reliable officials in the smallest villages, could help arrange these elections. While the approach may have been somewhat naive, the fact that it was ignored on both sides is perhaps the best evidence that neither government was by then even thinking in terms of how the two parts of the country might be brought together in the foreseeable future. With a trace of bitterness, Dibelius commented in the *Sonntagsblatt* on May 25, 1952:

> We will not become mixed up in political affairs. But we will never stop saying: you politicians owe our people reunification. Do what you think you must, but do it always in the thought and with the aim that Germany must once again be united. That remains your task, and you may have no rest until you have fulfilled this task.
>
> . . . There should be discussions on this side [of the iron curtain] and on that. There should be agreements and understandings. Not to want to conduct negotiations because they are not certain of success is a weak excuse. Only during negotiations themselves will it become clear whether anything like success can be achieved. It would not require persons of the highest level to conduct such negotiations; there are thousands of other ways and means to get things started.

Dibelius' appeal was significant for two reasons. It demonstrated that though popular attention was focused on the rearmament debate, the Evangelical church leaders were less concerned about Western defense than about approaches to the East. It was also remarkable for its independence of approach. The bishop's suggestion amounted to the general course followed after 1966 by the grand coalition and later by Brandt's SPD-FDP coalition. At the time the bishop's proposal was regarded in Bonn as political heresy. Fifteen years later it became official government policy.

As long as it could, the Evangelical church practiced what it preached in the one way open to it—that is, by holding meetings of its own bodies as often in the East as in the West. Indeed, the greatest popular manifestations of unity from the end of the war to the present time were the church lay assemblies, which brought together at regular intervals hundreds of thousands of laymen from the two parts of the country. "What seemed impossible from a political standpoint," the president of the assembly, von Thadden-Trieglaff, commented of the 1951 session, "became fact during the Protestant church assembly in Berlin: the barriers fell, the wall collapsed, and the divided people streamed across the border, pushing aside all obstacles and spanning the gulf. It was as though there were no longer any differences. Simply through the occurrence of this elementary reunification, the church assembly succeeded in achieving something that was obviously completely impossible on the political level." [25] Such was even more dramatically the case in 1954, at the Leipzig session, when 650,000 East and West Germans, among them laymen prominent in the two governments, met and in that way brought about, as *The Times* reported on July 10, 1954, "the hitherto unthinkable achievement of bringing leading politicians of East and West Germany together." When Hermann Ehlers (Bundestag president), Robert Tillmanns (minister without portfolio), and Walter Strauss (state secretary in the ministry of justice dined with Johannes Dieckmann (president of the East German parliament), Johannes Becher (East German minister for culture), and Otto Nuschke (chairman of the East German CDU), the occasion marked the first meeting of officials of the two governments. Although it soon became clear that the event had no lasting political significance, the importance of the assemblies in maintaining the psychological ties between the German people was perhaps best demonstrated by the refusal of the East German government to permit the 1957 session from being held in Erfurt and its subsequent refusal to allow its citizens to attend the meetings in the West.

As the 1953 national election approached, the strains in the Evangelical church reached such intensity that it was judged best to hold no meeting of the synod that year. All the accumulated Protestant dissatisfaction with Adenauer reached its climax in the GVP's campaign. Indeed, the formation of the

---

25. *Kirchliches Jahrbuch*, 1951. pp. 38–39.

GVP marked an attempt to do in the Protestant camp what the Catholic bishops had achieved in theirs: to create a political-religious bloc which would follow a certain political party and support a certain political program. The appeal of the GVP was directed particularly at Protestants and was no less specifically anti-Catholic and anti-CDU. A typical GVP campaign poster first quoted Cardinal Frings ("The realization of the ideal of reestablishing the empire of Charlemagne, in which the great people of Europe—Germans, Frenchmen, and Italians—lived together, has never been so close as now.") and then went on to point out that Charlemagne's empire had extended only to Magdeburg; that the leaders of France, Italy, and Germany were all Catholics; that the CDU and the German government were overwhelmingly Catholic; that Protestants in the government and the party were "without political influence" and followed a Catholic political course which had no interest in reunification "with the sixteen million Protestant brothers and sisters behind the iron curtain." The appeal concluded:

Therefore: no Protestant vote for the few and
uninfluential followers of political Catholicism
NO PROTESTANT VOTE FOR THE CATHOLIC CDU

Don't make the 16 million Protestants in the
heartland of the Reformation, with Wittenberg
and the Wartburg, wait still longer for the
PEACEFUL REUNIFICATION OF GERMANY

Although the official church bodies maintained their neutrality, in July 1953 Niemöller issued an appeal to "Save the Peace Today" and declared that the coming election might be the last chance for West Germans to stop a political course leading to total commitment to the West and the final division of Germany. He urged everyone who was in favor of reunification through neutrality to unite to bring the Adenauer government down. This statement not only produced a revolt in his own provincial church, where a special session of the synod disassociated itself from him, but provoked Bundestag president Gerstenmaier to charge that Niemöller had "politically nothing better to offer than the formula of Moscow." [26]

The election on September 6, 1953, resulted in a stunning victory for the Christian Democrats. Adenauer turned the SPD's flank by fighting the

---

26. Quoted in *Kirchliches Jahrbuch*, 1953, p. 43.

election, not on rearmament as such, but on German security. This was the principal reason for his electoral success. Rather than flocking to the polls to turn the Christian Democrats out of power, Protestants voted for the CDU in such numbers that they helped to give it an unprecedented absolute parliamentary majority. The All-German People's party received only 318,000 votes (1.2 percent of the total vote). In Frankfurt—Niemöller's "parish"—it gained less than 5 percent of the vote, and in its best constituency (in the town of Siegen in Westphalia) it polled just over 8 percent. [27] Even more humiliating was the fact that, so far as can be told from an analysis of the results, support for the GVP came not from Protestants as such but from persons who had previously voted for the communists or Social Democrats. In the end, therefore, Niemöller and Heinemann had hurt the Social Democrats more than the Christian Democrats.

The result was especially crushing, since in the early days of the Federal Republic there were many persons politically adrift and looking for leadership outside the established political parties. But the Protestant neutralists had waited too long to organize a political movement, and by the time the All-German People's party was founded, much of the latent opposition to Adenauer had dissipated or gone to the Social Democrats. Heinemann struck most Germans as politically confused. His party's acceptance of money from East German sources reinforced the feeling, particularly in SPD circles, that left-wing Protestants were naive if not reckless. Niemöller, for all his dash and self-assurance, gave the impression of doing what he did *pour épater le bourgeois*. Shocking the bourgeoisie with wild charges may, as he wished, have shaken them from political lethargy, but it did not lead them to take him or his cause seriously. The group's political message, which amounted to neutralism and pacifism, might have struck a deep responsive chord among many Germans had it not been explicitly based on a view of Soviet policy that most Germans were emotionally and politically unable to accept. The uprisings in East Germany in June 1953 proved to doubting West Germans that Niemöller and Heinemann were deliberately shutting their eyes to facts and that their arguments were politically bankrupt. While the antirearmers continued to appeal to pacifists and neutralists, as a political force they were finished. This they realized, and by the time of the next federal election Heinemann and Wessel had dissolved their party and advised their followers to throw in their lot with the Social Democrats, which they themselves then joined.

However, Niemöller and Mochalski, with a group of younger pastors and

---

27. Grosser, *Western Germany from Defeat to Rearmament* (1955), pp. 217–218.

theologians, carried on the fight. Their basic argument—that the state did not have the moral right to enact rearmament legislation—was repeated so often during the critical Bundestag debates in 1954 and 1955 on the EDC and the subsequent Paris agreements that the EKD council had to reassert its position. Complaining that the entirely false impression had been created that "the Evangelical Church as such and in fulfillment of its ecclesiastical mission had to come to some specific decision on the Paris Accords," the council insisted that Scripture alone was not a sufficient guide on such an issue. [28] In short, the official stand of the Evangelical church from the time German rearmament became a matter of official government policy to the moment of its approval by the Bundestag was that the decision to rearm was not a moral, theological, or ecclesiastical issue and therefore was not one for the church to make. Unlike the Catholic church, it did not support, and unlike the Niemöller-Heinemann group, it did not oppose rearmament. The majority of Protestant church leaders personally had strong reservations about rearmament but felt that, if it were politically and militarily necessary for the common Western defense effort, it was on balance a sacrifice worth making.

At the next stage of the defense controversy—whether the Bundeswehr should be a volunteer or a conscripted force—the Evangelical church formally opposed the government. In insisting that rearmament was a matter for individual decision, the Evangelical church adopted the corollary that no one should be required to serve in the armed forces. This view marked a revolutionary change in Protestant thinking. Two world wars and the invention of nuclear weapons had set off a fundamental reevaluation of the traditional Protestant position on war. This first became apparent at the 1950 meeting of the synod which, at Heinemann's direction and in response to intensified East-West tension along with the growing speculation about German rearmament, was to be devoted to the church's role in preserving the peace. Heinemann, as head of the synod, had asked Bishop Wurm to give the principal address and received a response which illustrated the rethinking going on among Protestant church leaders:

> I doubt whether I am in a position to deal with so difficult a question. Certainly the Lutheran concept of war as an indispensable police action against the criminal is no longer adequate for the current type of weapons; certainly the question can be quite seriously raised whether Germany in particular should propagate the idea of passive resistance which

---

28. *Kirchliches Jahrbuch* (1955), p. 15.

Gandhi applied to internal situations. However, are those who proclaim conscientious objection in the name of Christ aware of the responsibility they bear for the women and children of their nation?. . . As someone who is striving to arrive at the correct solution to this problem, who sees on the one hand the justification for pacifism but on the other does not believe in the possibility of the eradication of war through the Holy Scriptures, I cannot risk going before the public, which wants a clear, unequivocal formula and will not be satisfied with a simple exposition of the problems. If I am asked what the church can do on behalf of peace, I can answer: It must make a radical break with the justification, indeed, the glorification, of war which all began with us Germans in 1813 and 1870; with respect to the current division of Germany between West and East, it will have to follow the policy of the Prophet Isaiah, who condemned an alliance both with Egypt and with Assyria and advised instead the watchword, "in quietness and in confidence shall be your strength," and it will work devotedly with the churches of all the other states concerned for a "United States of Europe." [29]

One can only read with sympathy the record of this eighty-two-year-old man, conservative and nationalist to the marrow, struggling at the end of his life to think a difficult theological and political problem through to a new solution.

Wurm's inability either to accept the orthodox Christian concept of war or to embrace pacifism was so widely shared by Protestant churchmen that the 1950 synod in Berlin propounded an entirely new doctrine for the Evangelical church. It declared that, should Germany become involved in a war, it would be up to each individual to decide "whether he could take a weapon in hand." [30] The Evangelical church called for a volunteer force and made clear that, if conscription were judged necessary, it would demand broad guarantees for conscientious objectors. The Catholic bishops did not waver from the traditional Catholic position (which the Pope restated, perhaps with Germany in mind, in his Christmas message of 1956) that ruled out conscientious objection. The hierarchy and the lay organizations also supported conscription on practical grounds, since a professional army would have meant that the "old Prussian-officer type" would have been back in command and an old-style, exclusive Protestant institution would have been reestablished. That was the situation when the Bundestag in 1955 began to consider conscription legislation.

Bishop Dibelius, as chairman of the council of the Evangelical church,

---

29. Letter dated February 22, 1950, from Wurm to Heinemann in *File 220, "Evangelische Kirche in Deutschland 1949–1951"* in Wurm Papers.

30. *Kirchliches Jahrbuch*, 1950, pp. 223–234.

transmitted to the federal government in December 1955 a request that anyone (not simply members of certain religious or ideological groups) who could not in good conscience serve in the armed forces, either in peace or war, be exempted from conscription and permitted to serve instead in some nonmilitary capacity. This appeal was followed by the decision of the EKD synod in June 1956 to send a delegation to Bonn to express "concern" over the conscription legislation then in its final reading in the Bundestag. This move was sufficient in itself to raise some question of how the Protestants in the CDU would vote and to cast some doubt on the passage of the bill. As the Bonn correspondent of *The Times* reported on July 2, 1956, "The proposal of the synod, which amounts to a vote against compulsory military service, is the heaviest blow the conscription bill has yet received. It will supply moral support for the SPD which has led the opposition to conscription and probably enhance the differences among Adenauer's followers, who are not all Roman Catholic." The delegation, which was headed by an East German church leader (Bishop Krummacher of Pomerania), in the event went beyond expressing concern and appealed to CDU leaders to drop the legislation entirely. An important consideration to both the council and the synod, as the delegation pointed out, was the fear that East Germany would also adopt a conscription system and give no recognition to conscientious objectors (as in fact occurred). However, the government not only went ahead with the legislation (which CDU Protestants, in some cases only after much heart-searching, supported) but failed to provide the strong guarantees requested by the council. The Social Democrats were not slow to point to the paradox of the country's professed Christian party having rejected the official view of the church to which a majority of the population belonged.

The Christian Democratic election victory in 1957 was the high-water mark of the Adenauer era, and not long thereafter the Chancellor began to have more and more trouble both with his party and with his policies. His foreign and defense concepts in particular came under mounting criticism. This was the initial period of East-West detente, characterized by calls for "flexibility" in foreign policy, proposals for disengagement, schemes for nuclear free zones, and pleas for a unilateral nuclear test ban. These issues were in turn caught up in the debate over nuclear weapons following the American decision in 1957 to equip certain Allied forces with them. The question whether Germany should participate in such an arrangement touched off a controversy almost as impassioned as that over rearmament itself. Once again the contrast in the reaction of the two churches was striking.

Among Protestants generally, there was a conspicuous willingness, as there was during the entire period after 1949, to consider new foreign policy approaches. Concepts of disengagement, the Rapacki and Gaitskell plans, and a new policy in Eastern Europe had a receptive hearing in Protestant circles and were exhaustively discussed in the Protestant academies and press. Even in the CDU Bundestag delegation, Gerstenmaier and other Protestants began to stand out because of their desire to inject fresh ideas into German policy. [31] President Heuss, the country's leading Protestant, perhaps best expressed the general mood in his 1958 New Year's message. In that he not only made a general appeal for a foreign policy free of "ideological shackles" and subordination to "military-technical considerations" (as reported in *The Observer* on January 5, 1958), but also praised George Kennan, who was at that time in the course of his Reith lectures which, in advocating disengagement and opposing nuclear arms for the Bundeswehr, directly countered German government policy. Heuss' speech was welcomed by the Protestant press, and the general sentiments he expressed continued to gain its support until the Berlin crisis of 1958 brought to an end all hopes for an improvement in East-West relations.

While disengagement, detente, and denuclearization enjoyed a relatively wide support among Protestants, the government decision to equip the Bundeswehr for tactical nuclear operations confronted many Protestants with another difficult political issue. At the same time, however, German church leaders, in common with church leaders elsewhere, were beginning to face the tough moral and theological problem posed by nuclear weaponry. The issue completely dominated the annual session of the EKD synod, which met in East Berlin in April 1958. The synod was opened by Bishop Dibelius, who up to that time had taken essentially the same view as the federal government, to the effect that the Bundeswehr had to be equipped with the most modern (that is, nuclear) weapons. Now he revealed a complete change of mind; the *Frankfurter Allgemeine* quoted him on April 28, 1958, as having said:

> If I were fifty years younger and were ordered to take up a weapon of mass destruction, I would go to my military chaplain, and I would say to him: Help me out of this assignment. I cannot do it!

He explained that he had come to the conclusion that the whole nature of war had changed so radically, involving the possibility of death to persons not

---

31. This confessional distinction should not be overemphasized. Gerstenmaier was to a large extent motivated by a consuming ambition to be foreign minister. Furthermore, a few Catholics, such as von Brentano and Strauss, were somewhat uneasy over Adenauer's policies, while Schröder, the party's leading Protestant, stood firmly behind the Chancellor. It was largely because of this loyalty that Adenauer made Schröder foreign minister in 1961.

remotely involved, that the concept of a "just war" had dissolved. While a majority inclined to Dibelius' view, other members of the synod insisted that the employment of nuclear weapons under certain circumstances was not theologically or morally unjustified. The synod would not therefore go so far as to denounce the employment of nuclear weapons in self-defense as un-Christian, but its final declaration called upon the East and West German governments "to avoid arming German military forces with nuclear weapons." In short the Evangelical church once again opposed Adenauer's policy. [32]

Since the government was unswayed by this appeal, the council asked Chancellor Adenauer and Defense Minister Strauss to extend the provisions for conscientious objectors to those "who on the basis of their Protestant religious convictions believe they must decline training with nuclear weapons." The government refused to support the proposal, and in fact made it more difficult, on the basis of a law of 1935, for Protestant pastors to appear as counsels with conscientious objectors before the examining boards that determined a person's suitability for exemption from service. A Social Democratic proposal introduced in the Bundestag in 1960 to give the churches the right to aid conscientious objectors was voted down by the Christian Democrats, joined by some Free Democrats. Not until 1962 did the Bundestag finally bow to pressure from Protestants and others to enact legislation recognizing the right of religious officials to represent conscripts during their examination. Largely as a consequence of the Evangelical church's efforts, the Federal Republic today has the most lenient regulations of any state for acceptance as a conscientious objector to military service. [33]

---

32. *Frankfurter Allgemeine*, April 31, 1958. This issue nearly caused another open ecclesiastical split in the Evangelical church, since Niemöller and the "church brotherhoods" had insisted that the Evangelical church make it an article of faith that a Protestant might not serve in a nuclear-armed Bundeswehr. Unity was preserved by an agreement to have the question examined by a committee on nuclear questions. This body, under the chairmanship of Professor Carl-Friedrich von Weizsäcker, pondered the matter for several years and finally determined that the two sides would have to agree to disagree.

33. The council's statement quoted in *Kirchliches Jahrbuch*, 1960 p. 118-119. The Evangelical church has continued to take the lead in defending the interests of conscientious objectors and Joachim Beckmann (President of the Rhineland Provincial Church) has been delegated the responsibility of negotiating with the government on the membership of the examining boards, the procedures for recognition of conscientious objectors, and the sort of duties to be performed instead of military service. Up to 1962 there were 6,519 recognized conscientious objectors; 51 percent were members of the Evangelical Church, 14 percent were Jehovah's Witnesses, 12 percent were Catholics, 9 percent had no confession, and on the remaining 3 percent no information was available. A Defense Ministry source cited in Neyer, *Wie hast Du's mit der Bundeswehr?*

The reaction of the vast majority of Catholic politicians and of Catholic lay groups to the changed international climate in 1957 was to man the defenses and snipe at every new proposal that appeared. Their attitude was typified by a manifesto sent to the Bundestag by a large group of prominent Catholics who—as it was put in *The Observer* of January 5, 1958—"in view of the alarming signs of German policy taking the wrong turn," emotionally warned against any reliance on agreements with the Russians. (Shortly thereafter Cardinal Ottaviani became the first curial cardinal in twenty-four years to make a political comment in the press, when he attacked an Italian government minister for supporting disengagement and advocating consideration of the Rapacki plan.) In February 1958 the Catholic weekly, *Echo der Zeit,* called for the explusion from the CDU of Peter Nellen, a Catholic Bundestag member, because he had praised disengagement as a step toward reunification. At about the same time Rainer Barzel organized a movement called "Save Freedom Today" to combat proposed new foreign policy ventures and to defame their main Social Democratic advocates. These themes were all picked up and repeated in the Catholic lay movement and press.

On the nuclear arms issue, the Catholic hierarchy itself gave the government its full support. As in the case of rearmament, the church's position was announced earlier than that of the government and, as in 1950, it was probably intended to prepare Catholic opinion. The cue was again given by Cardinal Frings. In a speech, reported in *Der Tagesspiegel* on May 12, 1957, and given, inappropriately enough in Japan, where Frings was visiting, he declared simply, "The Catholic Church does not advocate the outlawing of atomic and hydrogen bombs at the present time." He referred to a recent papal affirmation of the right of national self-defense and stated that Germany might claim access to weapons her neighbors had refused to give up. The statement was clearly support for government policy as his Bonn speech on rearmament had been, and it was recognized as such.

But brushing aside the hard moral issue in this way was little help to Catholic politicians. When, during one of the tempestuous Bundestag debates on nuclear arms in March 1958, Heinemann ridiculed the members of "the Christian party" for ignoring the moral aspects of the nuclear issue, Catholic parliamentarians consequently were ill-prepared to respond. The Social Democrats could not overturn the CDU majority in the Bundestag but, hoping to capitalize on an unpopular policy to deal Adenauer a sensational defeat, they decided to make what they labeled "nuclear death" the main issue of the 1958 election campaign in North Rhine-Westphalia, where elections always had a great impact on federal politics. It appeared in the spring that the SPD had the CDU on the run, and Catholics in the CDU asked their church for a theological statement on the nuclear issue.

The church responded handsomely with a declaration, drafted by seven of its most prominent theologians, that went out of its way to defend every point of Adenauer's policies and that attacked all the main themes of the SPD's campaign. On the central question of the right of self-defense with nuclear weapons, the statement declared:

> When it is a matter of the propagation by force of an ideology and a way of life that denies any "ideological coexistence" and that ruthlessly combats all contrary types of belief and life and tries systematically to root them out . . . , the statement of our Holy Father is applicable: "There are objects of such importance for human social life that their defense against aggression is fully justified."

Then, one by one, it picked up the arguments Adenauer had been using to defend his policies. After endorsing the membership of weak states in an alliance system, the theologians went on:

> If, then, a state belongs to such a defense alliance and carries out all the implicit obligations for defense, including acquisition of the appropriate weapons, it is only fulfilling the obligation to its own citizens and to the international community.

While controlled disarmament remained an overriding objective,

> The aim of such disarmament must be to improve the chances for peace in the world without endangering maximum security for all nations. To this end neither the mere renunciation of experiments with nuclear weapons nor the establishment of demilitarized zones suffices: rather, all the measures together and in conjunction with a general control of armaments are necessary.

The theologians warned that the Christian must be realistic and keep in mind that, as long as the communists justify any means to their ends,

> confidence in negotiations and agreements rests on a weak basis. Their aggressiveness toward the rest of the world makes it impossible to trust or be trusted by them.

In conclusion, Christians must reject false alternatives and their vulgar conclusion of "better red than dead." [34] The declaration was so obviously for a political purpose that it offended even some theologians, priests, and laymen who were well within the bounds of orthodox political Catholicism. It expressed none of the doubts that tortured many Catholic theologians and

---

34. Auer et al., *Christliche Friedenspolitik und atomare Aufrüstung.*

intellectuals and made no apparent attempt to reconcile conflicting Catholic views—as the EKD synod had tried to do—but simply swept all uncertainties out of sight. The operative sections of the statement, which could just as well have been drafted in the foreign office or the ministry of defense, mixed theology and politics so indistinguishably as to leave ambiguous where Catholic moral philosophy ended and where the right of individual judgment in international affairs began. Walter Dirks put it mildly when he commented,

> The declaration amounts in effect to a Catholic moral *and* political justification of the policies of Adenauer. It is an excellent and impressive moral-political contribution to the subject, written by moral theologians who approve of those policies.
> The seven Catholic theologians have attempted to ensure, through ecclesiastical unity, the unity of the political front. [35]

The theological declaration was issued in May. The following month the five bishops of North Rhine-Westphalia issued their election pastoral message which, echoing the twin themes of the CDU campaign, stressed that use of nuclear weapons in self-defense was the right, and in certain circumstances the duty, of a nation and that the danger of communism was as great as ever. The campaign against nuclear arms was in this way politically and (for Catholics) morally defused. The July election was a tremendous victory for the CDU, which won an unprecedented absolute majority in the Land parliament. In due course the moral aspect of the nuclear problem faded from public attention, and the passion with which the issue had been debated somehow vanished, presumably finding a place in the overcrowded museum of lost causes.

These issues—reunification, rearmament, conscription, and nuclear arms—were the most contentious and important in postwar Germany. For the Social Democrats, however, they were essentially tactical political issues. Within two years of the "nuclear death" controversy the Social Democrats had formally accepted Adenauer's foreign and defense policies in their totality. For the Evangelical church, however, the issues ran much deeper, for both ecclesiastical and moral reasons. Even though its leaders often had difficulty articulating the moral issue with clarity, the church gave the debate on these problems a genuineness and depth that they would otherwise have lacked. It is significant that the Bundestag debate on nuclear weapons reached

---

35. *Frankfurter Hefte,* June 1958. Professor Hirschmann denied that the declaration was concocted for a political purpose but admitted that it had been made to shield the CDU "from charges made on the basis of a distortion of the church standpoint"; *Stimmen der Zeit,* July 19, 1958.

its height with a speech by the SPD's leading Protestant layman, Gustav Heinemann. It is also perhaps symptomatic that the SPD's acceptance of Adenauer's western policy has never been echoed by Heinemann.

What ultimately lay behind the Evangelical church's approach to Deutschlandpolitik was a sense of repentence for the war and a longing for reconciliation with the East. Rather than diminishing with time, these emotions perceptibly increased. In 1965 the church issued an "Eastern memorandum," which avowed that a settlement with the East could not be without German sacrifice—that is, unqualified acceptance of the loss of the territories east of the Oder-Neisse border. This view was reiterated by the church three years later in a declaration on "The Responsibility of the German People for Peace." Both statements were released at a time when it was still impossible for the political parties to advocate recognition of the German-Polish border and when (the later) Ostpolitik was nothing more than a dream of Brandt's advisor, Egon Bahr. Although their impact on German public opinion cannot be known, they clearly broke the public taboo on the subject and, as with the guilt question in 1945, forced the German people to face bitter facts—in this case that the loss of territory to Poland and the Soviet Union was not only final but morally just. The last point was especially important, and the church admonished Germans to forgive the expulsion of millions of their countrymen from their homes and in turn to seek forgiveness for German crimes in the East.

While the Ostpolitik that Brandt pursued after this election victory in 1969 was for dispassionate reasons, there was at the core of his policy—which amounted to de facto peace settlements with Poland and the Soviet Union— an identical sense of repentence. This was emotionally symbolized by Brandt's spontaneous gesture of kneeling before the memorial to the victims of the Warsaw ghetto during his 1971 visit to Poland. Finally, after the troubled relationship between the Evangelical church and the government during the foreign and defense policy disputes of the 1950s, the church and the government were now perfectly attuned on a major issue of East-West relations. There developed throughout the Evangelical church strong support for the eastern treaties, typified by a church renunciation of any legal claim to its extensive properties, including six thousand churches, in the former German territory.

Then came the anticlimax. As the public and parliamentary controversy was reaching its peak—the most impassioned political dispute since the rearmament controversy—the Evangelical church council announced that it would not advocate either acceptance or rejection of the treaties. It maintained that the church had no better information or political judgment on the issue than the German parliament. While intended solely to keep the church out of a partisan political dispute, the council's position made nonsense of the church's advocacy up to then of a course of action essentially identical to the Ostpolitik, as a group of twenty-five eminent church leaders lost no time in pointing out in a counterstatement. It was a feeble denouement to an otherwise lustrous chapter in the Evangelical church's postwar history.

During the entire discussion of Ostpolitik, the Catholic hierarchy was silent.

10 | *Social Policy*

ARCHITECTURALLY a Gothic cathedral has been described as "a balance of two equally vehement drives towards two opposite directions." Christian Democracy has also been a delicate balance of opposing forces: German Catholicism, with its intense stress upon social welfare, and the Protestant business community, with its equally strong pressure for economic and fiscal liberalism. Failure to achieve and maintain an equilibrium would have been as disastrous for the Christian Democrats as it proved for many a medieval builder. Adenauer's solution—like Bismarck's—was to support an economic policy favorable to the business community, a social policy in the interest of the workers, and a foreign policy binding both groups together. Through this formula—and under church pressure—working-class Catholics for nearly twenty-five years gave their full backing to the CDU, even though Protestant control of economic policy along with the party's selection in 1949 of the Free Democrats rather than the Social Democrats as its main coalition partner meant that economic liberalism would have priority over social welfare. Erhard's economic miracle and Adenauer's brilliant success in foreign affairs carried the CDU to a series of election victories and kept social dissatisfaction within safe bounds. But neglect of low-income groups—pensioners, refugees, farmers, and unskilled laborers—was the price. The price would have been greater still had not both the churches, though largely at Catholic initiative, together exerted strong pressure on behalf of a broad range of social measures. Because of their influence in the CDU, they were able to play a central role in the conception, drafting, and enactment of social legislation in the twenty years between 1949 and 1969.

This involvement is particularly remarkable on the Protestant side. Before 1933 social issues were simply beyond the ken of the Evangelical church. The idea of social *reform* was so unthinkable that, as the Göttingen theologian, Ernst Wolf, has commented, "One of the main arguments against Karl Barth until late in the 1930s and beyond was that he was a 'Social Demo-

269

crat.' "[1] It was a consequence of this belief that religion and social ethics were separable that German Protestants at the end of the war had no tradition of social activity, no guidelines to follow, and neither a laity nor a pastorate with any experience in social, industrial, or labor problems. Yet in keeping with their resolution in 1945 that the church must never again ignore its responsibility for the condition of German society, Protestant leaders gradually felt their way to a fresh approach to social problems. In October 1946 the Westphalian church synod, for instance, declared that economic security and a decent standard of living were rights everyone could claim. Employers, it insisted, should be more concerned to maintain full employment at adequate wages than to make large profits. Nationalization of industry and the break-up of large agricultural estates were justifiable if the lot of the people were improved as a result and if due process of law prevailed. Similarly, even such a conservative as Bishop Dibelius could criticize his church for having in the past merely preached to the poor while ignoring the economic system which was responsible for their poverty. Capitalism, he said, did not fulfill the demands of the Christian creed; Christian socialism was needed. Wages should be as high as possible and ideally related to employers' profits.

These statements are indicative of both the strength and weakness of the Protestant position. The positive side was the church's openness to social reform and its desire for an understanding with the trade union movement, the Social Democratic party, and the workers generally. To help this process along, a variety of institutions were established, such as a committee on the social structure (created in 1949 to advise the EKD council on social problems), a committee for labor problems (founded in 1951 to foster contacts with workers and trade unionists) and a committee for family problems (formed in 1953 to study problems of marriage, divorce, and financial assistance to families). Many provincial churches organized similar bodies, and both the academies and the church assemblies devoted a fair portion of their meetings to social issues. The entire session of the 1955 EKD synod was devoted to "The Evangelical Church and the World of Labor."

The effect was enormous. In a remarkable short time the barriers between the church and the trade union movement fell. By 1956 a Protestant specialist in labor relations could write:

> No worker who today wants to attend a social seminar of the Evangelical Church finds any resistance from the DGB [Deutscher Gewerkschaftsbund—German Trade Union Federation]. One is tempted to say,

---

1. *Barmen*, p. 16.

"What a change!" At every course for workers either the main speaker or one of the two main speakers is a DGB official. Previously it used to be extremely difficult to find participants for one of the church's week-long courses; nowadays 30 requests to attend the next course have to be turned down. In reciprocity for the participation of leading trade union officials in church courses, churchmen as well as young theologians have for years been attending the DGB academy in Hamburg.[2]

By such methods the Evangelical church gradually found a place somewhat to the left of center and gained a reputation as a progressive force in German society. Distressing as this was to some middle-class churchgoers, there has always, no matter how deep differences ran over political issues, been virtual unanimity among church leaders in the realm of social problems.

On the other hand, for all its good will, the church has been limited by its lack of pragmatic concepts or practical proposals for social reform. This circumstance is due not only to its lack of practical experience but, as in politics, to a doctrinal inability to develop a specific Protestant program. "Such an official action program," one lay expert has written, "could not be reconciled with the substance of Protestant belief. Protestant freedom does not permit such constraint. . . . It is in any case not the task of the Evangelical Church to proclaim a uniquely holy way to reform social relations."[3] Although the church has been more willing in recent years to risk definite policy suggestions through its semiofficial memoranda, this theological inhibition remains. Where goodwill has been useful to the problem at hand, the Evangelical church has been a force for an enlightened policy. Where this was not enough, the church has had either little to contribute or has tended to follow the lead of the Catholic church, which had no reluctance even in helping parliamentarians to draft legislation.

This contrasting Catholic involvement in social affairs was similarly the result of the interaction of creed and experience. Catholicism vigorously combats the notion that a dichotomy can exist between church and society. In practice Catholic teachings therefore have a direct and specific application to the social situation and legitimize direct ecclesiastical participation in such matters. In substance this doctrine, as summed up by Troeltsch, "simply means a return to the Law of Nature, and that means to the unpolitical class society guided by the Church, in which the State has only utilitarian tasks, while the Church hopes to lead society back to peace through the ideas of

---

2. Gerhard Schlosser, in *Die Mitarbeit,* June 1956.

3. Gerhard Heilfurth, "Gibt es ein evangelisches Sozialprogramm?" in *Die Mitarbeit*, June 1957.

self-restraint and of group-solidarity which are involved in the 'class idea.' "[4] This Thomistic approach—equally critical of liberal, individualistic capitalism and of materialistic, atheistic socialism—had tremendous meaning for mid-nineteenth century Germany suffering from the effects of rapid industrialization, particularly since most German Catholics were workers and peasants. Out of this milieu emerged such men as Bishop von Ketteler and Father Adolf Kopling, who not only championed the cause of the poor at home but also led the entire Catholic church in the social field. From 1871 until 1933 Catholic political leaders drew upon this heritage and, having little other outlet in public life for their energies (the grand affairs of state being almost exclusively in the hands of Protestants), devoted themselves with energy and devotion to social legislation.

At the end of the war the Catholic church and Catholic politicians consequently had not only a well-developed social ethic but also a great fund of experience in dealing with social problems. Their approach, as Troeltsch implied, was not a matter simply of alleviating social ills but of creating a Christian society. "Social policy" to the Catholic church therefore encompassed not just welfare legislation but an almost unlimited range of issues, extending from family and youth affairs through property ownership to labor relations. In almost every sphere the church had definite programs, a body of proposals that became increasingly explicit as Pius XII in the period between 1945 and 1958 made one pronouncement after another—often with his eye on Germany—regarding outstanding social issues. No bishop was as absorbed in the social question as was Cardinal Frings, and since his influence was commanding, the hierarchy usually followed his lead. But if his involvement was great, his approach tended on the whole to be conservative as a result of his fear of the political left, socialization, and the threat to bourgeois values in the aftermath of the war.

Catholic political leaders, particularly those from the industrial areas of the Rhineland and Westphalia, were persons whose chief political aim was to put Catholic social ideals into practice. These men all came from the Center party or the Christian trade union movement, and their long interest in social problems was intensified by the immediate postwar situation. Their tacit price for helping to form the CDU with conservative Protestants was a party program with a strong social policy. This was clearly reflected in the British Zone CDU's first program—the Ahlen program of 1947—which they largely drafted. This advocated the transfer of large industries to the control of

---

4. *The Social Teachings of the Christian Churches,* vol. 1, p. 310.

public, somewhat corporative, bodies. It called for a mixed economy with limited government powers and state planning. As such, the Ahlen program was an elegant delineation of the narrow Catholic path between capitalism and socialism.

Significantly, the "social committees of the CDU" were founded in the same year. These were quite frankly designed as straightforward pressure groups within the CDU on behalf of the Catholic social viewpoint and policies favoring the workers. Probably at no other point was the Catholic lay movement and the CDU so perfectly aligned as here. The members of the social committees were all members or leaders of Catholic workers organizations, and thanks to the CDU's policy of reserving a block of election constituencies or places on the Land election lists for them, a large number of representatives of these organizations sat in the Bundestag and of course in the social committees. Many of the leading officials of the social committees and the workers organizations were at the same time members of the central committee of German Catholics or of the special committees of the Catholic Office. In the first half-dozen years of the Federal Republic, Johannes Albers, for example, was chairman of the social committees, deputy CDU floor leader, chairman of the committee on social housing, and a member of the national executive committee of the CDU. Josef Gockeln, who succeeded him as chairman of the social committees in 1957, was at the same time chairman of the federation of Catholic employees organizations, chairman of the Catholic workers movement, vice president of the central committee of German Catholics, a member of the Bundestag, and president of the North Rhine-Westphalian Landtag. Johannes Even succeeded Gockeln in 1959 as vice president of the central committee of German Catholics, as chairman of the social committees, and as chairman of the Catholic workers movement; at the same time he was president of the Christian Trade Union Movement.

These institutional relationships were of fundamental importance. Their effect was to give the Catholic workers' organizations a vested interest in the CDU and the Catholic workingman a sense of identity with Christian Democracy. They became all the more vital to the CDU in the course of time. For the Ahlen program marked, not the take-off point of Catholic influence over the party's social policy, but its high-water mark. The party's economic committee under Franz Etzel, a corporation lawyer, soon eclipsed the social committees, which were reduced to a pressure group within the party and in time shifted their own emphasis from social reform to social amelioration. By 1948 Erhard became the architect of the party's economic policy, and this quickly gained priority over social policy. The liberal Düsseldorf program of 1949 replaced the Ahlen program, and following the first national election, the CDU looked to the right rather than the left for its coalition partners. But by this time the bonds of the Catholic church and its lay movement to the CDU were so firm that there was no undoing them. Catholic social doctrine was from then on at the mercy of the party's economic policy. The Catholic "labor wing" would always be a force in the party, and one or another of its leaders–Kaiser, Storch, Katzer, Lücke–could always claim a place in the cabinet. But by the time the Federal Republic was founded, the scope for the social committees, and with them the Catholic church, was already severely limited. It fell to the relatively independent religious orders–notably the Walberberg Dominicans, such as Welty, Nawroth, and Fridolin Utz as well as the Frankfurt Jesuits, such as von Nell-Breuning, Hirschmann, and Wallraff– to make real contributions to Catholic social thinking. Given the relations between the CDU and the Catholic church, these theologians were virtually the only Catholics who enjoyed influence in trade union circles and in the SPD.

The contrast in the attitude of the two churches–the relatively passive, progressive, and tolerant Protestant approach as against the relatively active, conservative, and dogmatic Catholic approach–became increasingly evident in the course of the postwar period as the churches grappled with one after another of the social issues that arose. This can be illustrated most concisely by means of examples rather than by a general survey of the entire field. The cases are unrelated, extending from industrial relations and trade unionism to family assistance and captial-savings incentives. But each of them shows an aspect of the churches' position on social questions as well as the interaction of their viewpoints and those of the political parties.

After the war leaders of the three pre-1933 trade union groups favored the establishment of a single trade union. This attitude was strongly endorsed by British and American military governments, and a request by Cardinal Frings along with several other British Zone bishops for permission to establish a Catholic trade union was rejected. The Catholic church had to bow to the decision, though the Pope had warned Cardinal Faulhaber shortly after the war that a unified trade union "is fraught with dangers which you will have to guard against–to see that Catholic workers do not stray from the church's social policy."[5]

Within days of the establishment of the Federal Republic, the DGB was founded. In response to the Catholic church's warnings that Catholics could remain in the federation only so long as it did not pursue policies repugnant to the church, the union leadership promised both to maintain political and

---

5. Quoted in *Herder Korrespondenz*, September 1946.

"ideological" neutrality and to give members of Catholic and Protestant workers' groups a share in that body's administration and policy direction. In practice the president has always leaned in the direction of the SPD, while the vice president has been a Catholic lay group official. In the view of almost everyone outside the Catholic church and the Catholic lay movement, the union maintained its neutrality—at times to a fault, succumbing to a passivity incompatible with the workers' interests. However, in the 1950s, when the bishops regarded anyone who was not for them to be against them, this was not enough. The KAB—the Catholic workers' movement—repeatedly claimed that the DGB favored policies similar to those of the SPD and opposed confessional schools. In the fall of 1952 a spokesman for the KAB warned trade union leaders that their criticism of the government's social policy played into the hands of the communists. The West German bishops, meeting a short time later, concurred in this warning and called upon the entire clergy to support the KAB on this issue. Cardinal Frings was the central figure behind the attacks on the DGB. To him they were the continuation of war against the SPD by other means. In December 1952 he came out into the open with "A Serious Word to the DGB," as his article in the KAB paper, *Ketteler Wacht,* was entitled:

> We bishops understand and share the concern of the KAB over the evolution of the unified trade union. We are grateful to those who, out of deep Christian responsibility, draw the trade union members' attention to increasingly dangerous trends and who have appealed in the interests of the union itself for the maintenance of ideological neutrality and genuine tolerance.

The DGB's slogan for the 1953 election campaign, "Elect a Better Bundestag," noncommittal as it was, amounted to either the last straw or the excuse Frings was looking for. Claiming that the union had broken its political neutrality, he moved toward a showdown. In September 1953 a number of Catholic trade unionists who were in agreement with Frings sent letters on behalf of the KAB and the CDU social committees to the DGB, insisting that Christian groups be formed and representatives from Christian workers movements be appointed in all branch unions and at all levels of the DGB itself. The union viewed these demands as inconsistent with its charter but was willing to discuss the issue. Even before it could dispatch a reply in this sense, however, Frings remarked in a speech to the KAB that he had never been convinced that a unified trade union could properly represent the interests of all the workers. At the same meeting Johannes Even, the secretary of the KAB, was even more menacing. The *Neuer Vorwärts* of September 25, 1953, quotes him as stating, "If the DGB does not change, Catholics will have to leave the unified trade union; it is religion that is at stake." Behind the scenes the decision had apparently already been taken to found a Christian trade union. Plans went forward largely under the direction at first of Monsignor Hermann Schmidt, director of the KAB and later three Bundestag members— Johannes Even and Bernhard Winkelheide, who were both Catholics, and Erwin Voss, a Protestant taken in tow by the others.

As the battle lines formed in the summer and fall of 1955, it became obvious how drastically Cardinal Frings had overreached himself. Almost no one outside his direct range of influence—specifically the Catholic workers movement 'and the Catholic working youth—wanted a Christian secession from the DGB. The social committees of the CDU, the Christian Social workers movement (the Catholic workers' movement in Bavaria), the CDU as a whole, Chancellor Adenauer, Ruhr industrial circles, leading trade union Catholics, and prominent DGB Catholics led by Matthias Föcher (DGB vice president), were all opposed. Some Catholics felt that representatives of the Catholic workers' groups had too little and socialist extremists too much influence within the DGB.[6] But they did not doubt that these difficulties could be overcome, and in any case they did not want to break up the unified trade union movement over this issue. Even inside Frings' Trojan horse—the Catholic Workers Movement—fewer than one in five was willing to leave the DGB. Undaunted, the so-called committee for the foundation of a Christian Trade Union (Christliche Gewerkschaftsbewegung Deutschlands–CGD) on October 15 presented an ultimatum to the DGB demanding the creation of "Christian groups" and specific "Christian representation" at all levels of the trade union movement. If this was not permitted forthwith, it threatened to "liberate itself from the existing hold of socialism upon the DGB and establish an independent Christian trade union movement." Nothing could more blatantly have exposed the pitiful narrowness of the group's support than a DGB-sponsored rally a few days later, on the tenth anniversary of the reestablishment of a free German trade-union movement. Kaiser, Arnold, and Anton Storch—Catholics, Christian Democrats, and trade unionists—all attended the meeting, and Adenauer sent a telegram expressing his wish for a flourishing development of the organization. When a "Christian Trade Union Movement

---

6. The "Agartz Affair" was symptomatic. Viktor Agartz was head of the DGB's Economic Research Institute, a center of extreme and dogmatic left-wing ideology. Advocating a much more leftist course for the DGB, the group was strongly anticlerical and attacked such pro-DGB theologians as von Nell-Breuning. In mid-1955, as Catholic criticism of the DGB reached a critical point, the trade union dismissed Agartz and his associates.

of Germany" was nonetheless founded on October 30, the DGB executive committee could without much, if any, tendentiousness deplore this action of "a small group of narrow-minded fanatics." [7]

Frings had had his way. But few of the bishops were pleased at the outcome, and Frings failed to persuade them to give the new union more than the coolest support:

> We bishops have been extremely reserved toward the establishment of Christian trade unions. . . . If Christian employees, out of genuine inner compulsion and after long, independent reflection, have now decided in favor of this, we respect this objectively justified decision and expect others, especially in church circles, to do so as well. [8]

As in the rearmament controversy, a number of bishops and a few lay leaders had imposed their will upon the mass of Catholics. In this case, however, the hierarchy was divided, and the "loyal" laity was a tiny minority. Frings fought a lonely battle. He supported the CGD publicly and privately—according to a persistent rumor, financially as well—and coaxed his clergy into doing the same. As at election time, they together summoned up the hoary specter of a "socialist and communist threat." But this time the workers could not be frightened. While the church had conditioned them into believing that they could not be Catholics and Social Democrats at the same time, it failed to show them that there was an inconsistency between their religion and their membership in the DGB.

By contrast, the Evangelical church, the Protestant press, and Protestant lay groups gave their full support to the DGB. Their instinctive bias was completely against a confrontation between "Christian" and "non-Christian." They were generally satisfied with the administration and the policies of the DGB, and when Catholic attacks upon the union grew serious in the fall of 1953, the Protestant committee for labor matters declared that it stood fully behind the federation. A short time later the EKD council subscribed to this statement. As Catholic agitation continued, the committee for labor matters formed a special committee in the fall of 1954 to work against any Christian secession from the DGB and to prevent opponents of the DBG from claiming they spoke for "the Christians." This was followed by a forthright statement by a group of bishops, theologians, and laymen, warning that moves to break up the DGB would endanger confidence, not only between

---

7. Numbers based on a poll conducted by Winkelheide in *Frankfurter Allgemeine,* July 5, 1955; committee statement in *Kölnische Rundschau,* October 24, 1955; DGB executive quoted in *Die Welt,* November 2, 1955.

8. Quoted in *Herder Korrespondenz,* December 1955.

the churches and the trade union movement, but also between Catholics and Protestants. To this chorus were added the voices of several leading Ruhr Protestants. including the heads of the churches of Rhineland and Westphalia, and such prominent laymen as Gustav Heinemann and Friedrich Karrenberg:

> We consider this antithesis of "Christian" and "socialist" to be no longer possible since a Protestant Christian at least can be a member of socialist groups and parties and still be loyal to his faith.[9]

The establishment of the CGD in 1955 was as a consequence deplored by Protestant churchmen. When the handful of Protestants who had gone over to the new union asked for the official view of the Evangelical church, the council responded that the Protestant was free to be guided by his own conscience in public affairs. But, the church leaders declared, the founding of a Christian trade union and the use of 'Christian" in its title were regrettable. The social effects would be deeply unfortunate:

> Cooperation in existing unions is an important means of overcoming the alienation that previously existed between church and labor. The exchange of views that had begun will be more difficult with the establishment of an organization that is to segregate Christian employees.[10]

The stand of the Evangelical church and Protestant laymen forestalled any possiblity of a genuine religious split of the DGB and from the start isolated the few Catholic enemies of the organization. A Christian secession from the DGB could have endangered not only the interests of the workers through competing and hostile trade union movements but even the political and social stability of the country. Here was a clear case where the Evangelical church had, in no direct self-interest, intervened on behalf of the liberal democratic order in Germany. In the end very few workers, Catholic or Protestant, ever left the DGB. Most of the CGD's modest number of early recruits were workers who had previously not belonged to a trade union. Even after the integration of the Saar with Germany and the consequent fusion of the already existing Christian unions there with the CGD, membership in the Christian union movement probably never exceeded 300,000 at most and is now thought to be about half that number.[11]

---

9. Quoted in *Kirchliches Jahrbuch,* 1955, p. 79.

10. Quoted in *Die Mitarbeit,* January 1956.

11. The CGD does not issue membership statistics; the figures cited are widely-held estimates.

A second important industrial issue in which the churches followed different courses was that of worker participation in industrial management. In the immediate postwar period leaders of both churches—like the German people generally—were critical of big industry on the ground that the concentration of economic power had been unhealthy for German democracy. As a step toward limiting and dispersing such power, British Military Government in 1947 introduced into the Ruhr coal and steel industry a scheme known as codetermination. This gave workers' representatives a place on the management bodies and in this way a voice in the decisions of the industry. Both churches welcomed this move. However, the 1949 Catholic lay assembly at Bochum went much further and, in a display of spontaneity not repeated until the 1968 meeting in Essen, adopted a resolution enthusiastically calling for codetermination in all German industry. It characterized the scheme as a "natural right of the God-given order." This, in the view of some bishops, was going far too far. In a book on the subject, *Verantwortung und Mitverantwortung in der Wirtschaft*, which appeared at about the same time, Cardinal Frings expressed strong reservations toward applying the scheme throughout industry. Better results, he maintained, could be achieved if employers were guided by Christian charity. Angered by the Bochum pronouncement, he gave a speech within days of the assembly's action and sought to strip the resolution of all meaning. "When the resolution speaks of a 'natural right of the God-given order,' it means only a compatibility with natural rights," he argued; "when it speaks of codetermination in personnel, social, and economic matters, it does not mean all three to the same extent or to an unlimited degree in any of the three." [12]

From this point on, the Catholic church fell into disarray over the issue. While broad application of the scheme was defended by some theologians and lay leaders as well as by Bishop Keller of Münster, it was attacked by others. In June 1950 the Pope sought to end the dissension by publicly announcing his disapproval of codetermination, insisting that it endangered private property rights, especially when the influence of outside organizations (that is, the trade unions) was involved. It was not, Pius insisted, a "just claim" of the workers. Elaborating upon the Pope's remarks in an article entitled "The End of the Wrong Road," the *Rheinischer Merkur* commented on June 10, 1950:

> That Germany and her problems take up so much space in a papal address to representatives of the entire earth is a cause both for concern

---

12. Bochum statement and Frings' reply in *Herder Korrespondenz*, October-November 1949.

and for consolation. Consolation because it shows how—increasingly eager to help—Rome watches developments in Germany, this experimentation field of Europe, upon whose strength or weakness the defeat of bolshevism depends; concern because it proves that the overheated discussion of social policy, which broke out after Bochum (obscuring the central point of the rally), began to alarm the universal church at a decisive moment of history and that the differences among German Catholics could not be settled by themselves and forced the Pope to the extreme and rare step of a personal statement.

Progressive Catholics in many countries have often tended to ignore any papal pronouncements that they regarded as not only fallible but also fallacious. Progressive German Catholics, on the other hand, have usually tried to square the circle. Walter Dirks, for instance, declared that the Pope's words should be taken seriously but not considered binding. After all, he contended, Catholics live in a world with non-Catholics and must be willing to compromise on such practical matters. Writing in *Frankfurter Hefte* in July 1950, he pointed out that codetermination was a way of preventing a possible recurrence of what had happened in Germany in the 1930s. "For that very reason," he concluded, "the papal message can be neither the only nor the last word. . . . It would be a sin against the Pope himself to impose upon him the responsibility for a political decision." The Jesuit theologian Johannes Hirschmann argued on a still different tack at the following year's lay assembly, by maintaining that the Pope's statement was not really inconsistent with the Bochum resolution. At the same session Johannes Even insisted that Catholics must in any case carry on with codetermination because it was beneficial to both workers and society.

By this time—the summer and fall of 1950—codetermination had become one of the major issues facing the recently established government, since some sort of legislation had to be enacted to replace the 1947 Allied regulations. The result was one of the greatest muddles imaginable. The prevailing view of German industry and the CDU was one of Protestant-influenced economic liberalism, which opposed codetermination. However, the Evangelical church and the Protestant press strongly favored it. The Protestant lay assembly resolved at its 1950 session:

> Employer and worker! In the efforts for codetermination, strive for a real partnership. Free the industrial worker from being a mere cipher.

And a short time later the council of the EKD repeated the same theme in its own declaration:

The intent of codetermination is to end the mere wage-work relationship and to have the worker regarded as a human being and a colleague. Its implementation would be a salutary influence on our social relationships not only for the employee but for the employer and the community. [13]

In view of the Pope's declared position, the Catholic bishops did not feel free to make any comments on the impending legislation. The social committees of the CDU and Catholic trade unionists, however, strongly backed it. Under pressure from the Trade Union Federation as well as from Catholic trade unionists in the CDU, Adenauer finally decided early in 1951 in favor of maintaining codetermination in the coal and steel industries. The necessary legislation was passed with the support of the SPD and against the votes of the CDU's right-wing coalition partners. A year later a similar coalition of forces—again with the support of the Evangelical church and Catholic workers' organizations, but with the silence of the Catholic church—passed "the industrial relations law," giving employees in medium-sized and large firms certain consultative rights in personnel and related matters. There the matter has stood, and codetermination remains one of the controversial issues of the present coalition of Social Democrats and Free Democrats. With the former officially committed to a rapid introduction of broader codetermination and the latter just as officially opposed, it is widely believed that codetermination could be the most troublesome issue of the second Brandt administration.

Even though social policy took second place to economic and fiscal policy, it laid the basis for a creditable advance in social welfare. Both in the terms of initiative and substance, social legislation has been greatly, perhaps decisively, influenced by the two churches. The Catholic church in particular had a comprehensive catalogue of social programs relating not only to family and youth affairs, housing, and property ownership, but also to such broad social-welfare matters as pensions and social insurance. The hierarchy, often under the prodding of Cardinal Frings, exerted steady pressure after 1949 for the enactment of legislation in these fields. These programs were fully supported by leading Catholics in the CDU, such as Kaiser, Arnold, Albers, Storch, and more recently, Hans Katzer and Paul Lücke. The social committees of the CDU acted not only as the social conscience of the CDU, but working closely with the Catholic Office, the central committee of German Catholics, and the hierarchy (often in the person of Frings), they also operated as initiators of all CDU-sponsored social legislation.

---

13. Both resolutious in *Kirchliches Jahrbuch,* 1950, pp. 17, 26–27.

The principal emphasis in social legislation lay in two areas. One was social security. After the establishment of the Federal Republic, social security legislation was largely a matter of amending or expanding the Bismarckian legislation of the 1880s. Early in the 1950s the CDU, with the support of the Social Democrats, enacted reforms which liberalized old-age, survivor, accident, unemployment, and sickness benefits. Church officials—Böhler for the Catholic church along with Kunst and Hansjürg Ranke for the Evangelical church—were deeply involved at every stage of this legislation. This collaboration was mostly for the purpose of encouraging as generous coverage as possible but also out of a sense of competition between the two church representatives. The Protestants would normally have been willing to state their view and let matters take their course, but they did not want to appear less interested or active than their Catholic counterparts.

The second principal sphere of social policy was family affairs. One of the notable characteristics of the German social scene since the war and one which bears the clearest marks of Catholic influence is the quasipolitical status which has been given to the family. In Catholicism "the family" has deep theological significance. The sociological effects of the Third Reich and the war reinforced this doctrinal viewpoint and spurred the German bishops to make family affairs the centerpiece of their social aims. With their unprecedented political power after the war, they were able to influence events in a decisive way. The Parliamentary Council was persuaded to endow the family with a constitutional status. Once the Federal Republic was founded, members of the hierarchy and Catholic lay organizations repeatedly exhorted the government to pursue a "positive" family policy—by which they meant one which would confer upon the family unit certain legal and financial advantages designed to strengthen family ties and aid large families.

Primarily they wanted the enactment of specific legislation. But Bishop Keller of Münster, supported by Cardinal Frings and several lay organizations, also favored the establishment of a ministry which would promote "family policy" on a continuing basis. Monsignor Böhler opposed the idea out of fear that such a body might develop into a federal "Kultus ministry" which would encroach upon the autonomy of the Länder in educational and ecclesiastical affairs. In 1953, however, when Adenauer's plan to appoint a militant Catholic, Franz-Josef Wuermeling, as minister of interior ran into stiff Protestant opposition, on the ground that the ministry of interior had always been headed by a Protestant, Adenauer found a way out of his dilemma by creating a family ministry for Wuermeling.

With the press and, apparently, the public uncertain about the functions of the new ministry, Wuermeling spent much of his first months in office outlining its objectives. From his remarks it became clear that he wanted not only legal and financial advantages for families but also a stiffening of the divorce laws. "Even if our view of the indissolubility of marriage can no longer find legal recognition," he told a Catholic lay group, "we should nonetheless try to limit the dissolution of the vital cell of the state—marriage and the family." He also indicated that the ministry intended to administer a strong dose of Catholic puritanism to the public media, especially to films and popular magazines. These were to be subject to what he labeled "people's censorship," a phrase that many persons found uncomfortably reminiscent of the Third Reich. [14] Wuermeling further recommended a popular boycott of films starring actors and actresses who were divorced. Although the minister's proposals were generally applauded by Catholic lay groups and the Catholic press, most of the German public found them laughable. The sober *Neue Zürcher Zeitung* on January 24, 1954, saw in them "a new offensive by the clerical forces in the CDU." Wuermeling's incautious imputations—such as the assertion that a higher number of divorces were being granted by judges who had taken a purely civil oath of office than by those who had taken a religious oath—eventually caused the CDU such humiliation that both party leaders and Chancellor Adenauer formally disavowed him on occasion. The Social Democrats and most of the Free Democrats were so incensed by his clericalism and his wild allegations that in 1954 they refused to support a budget authorization for the family ministry.

Once the family ministry had been established, however, Catholic circles worked for the transfer of the youth affairs section of the ministry of interior to the family ministry. Although the Evangelical church opposed this move, Adenauer bent to Catholic pressure and, following the 1957 election, a ministry for family and youth affairs was established, headed by Würmeling.

Over the years the ministry's work concentrated on assisting families with large numbers of children and, after 1957, on the coordination and financing of youth activities. The child-allowance law of 1955, for instance, gave families an allotment for two or more children, the sum increasing with each additional child. A housing-allowance scheme enacted in 1963 provided payments to families in accordance with the number of children. This was followed by the so-called Lücke plan, which promoted the construction of houses for large families. Other legislation encouraged home ownership by providing for low-cost mortgages. Apart from this, however, the ministry has achieved very little over the years, inasmuch as primary responsibility for

---

14. Federal Press Office *Bulletin,* November 21, 1953; February 4, 1954.

drawing up legislation for family and youth matters has remained in the hands of other ministries. When asked in an interview whether the agency had any continuing purpose other than as a channel of funds to church groups, one official of the ministry laughed and said, "We sometimes ask ourselves that question." When pressed, the official acknowledged that the main support for the ministry came from Catholic circles and that their principal interest was in its dispensing of funds to church groups. The ministry, all of whose heads up to 1969 had been Catholics, was regarded in Bonn as the "blackest" agency of the government. After every election the question arose whether the ministry should be dissolved and its sections returned to the ministries of justice and interior. The SPD-FDP government formed in 1969 merged the ministry with the ministry of health, though the staff remains intact.

Another Catholic interest in the social sphere—in addition to certain legislation and the establishment of a family ministry—was to channel funds for social purposes through church organizations. Again Catholics were successful. For instance, the Social Assistance Act permitted ecclesiastical bodies, such as Caritas, to operate as carrier organizations for implementing public-assistance programs. A youth-welfare law made similar provision for ecclesiastical youth organizations. The Social Democrats always opposed such arrangements, regarding them as clericalist in nature and fiscally illegitimate in practice. To Catholic officials this was a central difference in outlook and an insurmountable barrier between the church and the SPD. "The ultimate basis for the church's legal status vis-a-vis the state," the deputy director of the Catholic Office, Johannes Niemeyer, once summed up the Catholic position in a speech in 1969, "rests on the fact that the pluralistic state has to turn to social groups that establish and preserve values, and this the churches are better able to do than other social groups." The Social Democrats' attitude was consequently regarded as symptomatic of their desire to shut the churches out of public life and to secularize society. For this reason the hierarchy regarded the issue, along with the school question, as the acid test of the SPD's sincerity of desire for understanding and cooperation with the Catholic church. This was one of the main points mentioned in Cardinal Frings' sermon on the SPD's 1959 party program, which sought to reconcile the party and the churches. "It is typical of the parties growing out of liberalism and rationalism," he stated, "that they do not want to give the church a real chance for public influence in the state." [15]

---

15. *Katholische Nachrichten-Agentur,* dispatch 80, April 4, 1960.

The question of the church's place in social affairs has also been much disputed from a different quarter in the long controversy over capital-savings incentives for workers. The specific idea of giving workers a share of the national economy's capital formation was raised as early as 1950 on the ecclesiatical side when the Jesuit economist, Oswald von Nell-Breuning, suggested it at a meeting of an advisory council of the ministry of economics. Though the idea was not then taken up, Karl Arnold kept it alive. As German economic recovery neared completion at the end of the 1950s, the churches, along with the trade unions, the Social Democrats, and the left wing of the CDU, became increasingly critical of the unfair distribution of income. For the period 1950 to 1964, according to trade union estimates, workers and pensioners (together 80 percent of the population) received only 17 percent of the total capital growth of 600 billion marks. In 1961, as an election-year sweetener, the CDU enacted a law which permitted voluntary employer-employee agreements by which 312 marks per employee might be annually invested in specific ways, with tax benefits to both parties. The scheme failed to catch on. Workers found the amount of money too small. Trade unionists feared that the savings incentives would be at the expense of wage increases. Employers insisted that the sum was a cost factor that must affect prices. However, the churches—or at least church specialists in social affairs—were determined to keep the concept from languishing. In the Evangelical church there was a strong feeling that a capital savings program would only achieve its goal of spreading capital holdings if it were based on compulsory, industry-wide agreements rather than on individual, voluntary arrangements. Reflecting this point of view, the council of the EKD in April 1962 issued a memorandum, a crucial passage of which declared: "It can be no contradiction of a free social structure if forced savings are put to the advantage of those who up to now have had no part in capital formation." [16] The point was that if voluntary schemes did not contribute to some redistribution of income, then compulsory arrangements should be adopted. The memorandum was universally applauded—then ignored.

To give the idea a further impetus, a group of Catholic and Protestant social experts in January 1964 issued an "appeal on capital formation," calling for collective bargaining on the matter. This challenge, interestingly enough, was taken up, not by the Christian Democrats (despite the efforts of Katzer, Arnold's successor as head of the CDU labor wing), but by Georg Leber, head of the construction workers' union and later SPD minister of

---

16. Müller (editor), *Eigentumsbildung in sozialer Verantwortung,* p. 89.

transport. The "Leber plan," announced in June 1964, envisaged the creation of a central investment fund which would administer the workers' savings. With this things began to move. The government drafted a bill to revise the "312-mark law," and as this work progressed, Chancellor Erhard turned—sometimes privately, sometimes publicly—to church representatives, especially Kunst and Wissing, to lay out the Protestant and Catholic views. The final legislation, the "second law on furthering capital savings by employees," was passed in July 1965 and permitted collective bargaining over the issue in a way that met the point raised by the churches.

It was against this background that the two churches were openly criticized for the role they had been playing in social affairs. One of the boldest attacks came from Hanns-Martin Schleyer, a director of the Daimler-Benz company and a prominent industrialist. In the *Frankfurter Allgemeine* of May 21, 1965, Schleyer accused the churches of having let themselves be beguiled by "bogus social romanticism" and warned that if they thought of making themselves the "third social partner"—between labor and management—management "would have to use against them the same weapons" it employed against labor.

The postwar history of the Federal Republic indicates that when the two churches worked together on social issues, they were able to exert a decisive influence on social policy and social legislation. During this period nothing in this field was—or probably could have been—enacted into law or have even reached the floor of the Bundestag against the clear opposition of the two churches. All too often, however, and especially during the republic's early years, the motor of this ecclesiastical activity, especially on the Catholic side, was less one of helping the unfortunate at the bottom of the social scale than of working for a doctrinal concept of what is good for society. The end result may be the same, and probably most of the theologians and laity devoting themselves to social problems were motivated by a desire to relieve social distress as such. However, this approach undermined the Catholic church's social tradition. The bishops' overriding objective was to "save" the workers from the Social Democrats. Only the Jesuits and Dominicans, intellectually and ecclesiastically relatively independent, took the view that social justice could be best fostered by encouraging the party that was historically and doctrinally dedicated to social justice. Significantly enough, it was the school issue and not the removal of social injustice that was chosen by the Catholic bishops as a matter of conscience for their faithful. As late as 1960 Cardinal Frings could still bring himself to have a pastoral letter read in all of the churches of his diocese on May Day which admonished Catholics "to have an examination of conscience as to whether they could possibly justify, before God and Catholic children, any form of support for a trade union that disapproved of Catholic school objectives." [17] Nothing could more clearly have demonstrated the hierarchy's order of priorities. It was significant also—and perhaps ominous for the churches—that the theologians and laymen who fought for social programs did so without using theological arguments. In recent years church leaders themselves have begun to follow a similar course. In dealing with social issues, they have been acting less as churches, which by their status could command authority, and more like impartial bodies anxious to cooperate in improving society. This situation illustrates both the change the churches themselves have undergone since 1945 and their altered position in German society.

---

17. *Die Welt,* May 2, 1960.

THE CHURCHES AND PARTY POLITICS

11 | *The Churches and Christian Democracy*

CHRISTIAN Democracy has determined the domestic and foreign policies of the Federal Republic to such an extent that it is impossible to imagine how Germany, or Europe as a whole, would look today without this political movement. For this very reason, perhaps, one is far too prone to read the present into the past and to take for granted a political phenomenon that was virtually a product of chance. Christian Democracy was created by a few men—many of whom, being under death sentence for anti-Nazi activities, had no right to be alive in 1945—who confounded some of the elementary rules of society and politics. This small group of persons, who happened to be in politically strategic places at the war's end, succeeded in establishing an inter-confessional political party in Berlin within a month of the collapse of the Third Reich and in most other parts of Germany within six months after that. This they did despite the fact that

• Germany was the homeland of the Reformation, where confessional differences divided society more deeply than anywhere else in the world.

• Unlike Social Democracy, communism and liberalism, an interconfessional party had no tradition or organization to rely upon, no political infrastructure to build upon.

• The German people at the war's end craved reliable, trusted traditions, rather than political experiments.

• Political meetings in the Western zones were forbidden for months after the war, and contacts among Germans through travel or post were nearly impossible. Symptomatically, when Adenauer was approached in April 1945 by some former Center party colleagues about a possible interconfessional party, he explicitly used some of these arguments in rejecting the overture. He remarked that the idea was "premature" and "too idealistic" and commented that it was not the moment for novel political ventures.[1]

---

1. Schwering Diary (entry of April 9, 1945), *Fasz I/Sch,* Schwering Papers, Cologne.

Later on, when a Christian Democratic group was started in Cologne anyway, Adenauer refused to participate on the ground that attendance would violate the British ban on meetings of more than eight persons.

How did this novel political phenomenon come about at a time of material and spiritual chaos? Politically, 1945 was the "year zero" of modern German history. The entire political and governmental apparatus of the Third Reich was buried in the ruins of the final collapse, and the German state passed into the hands of four occupying powers. For politicians the end of the war created a tabula rasa. Although the Social Democrats and communists quickly refounded their old parties, many Germans were seized with a desire to set their country's political life on an entirely new course. These persons were conservatives and socialists, pastors and priests, industrialists and trade unionists, bankers and left-wing intellectuals. Their political outlook was as mixed as were their backgrounds. A belief in the applicability of general Christian principles to political problems and the desire to establish a new German state based on Christian ideals were all that united them on a religious basis. A determination to correct the mistakes of the Weimar era, to heal somehow the moral wounds inflicted by the Third Reich, and to erect a barrier against Marxism was all that united them on a political basis.

The idea of a joint Catholic-Protestant party was not new in German politics. As early as 1906 a Catholic journalist-historian, Julius Bachem, had argued that, since the Catholic church was no longer politically threatened in Germany, the Zentrum should come out of its "tower" of "confessional isolation" and join Protestants in a broader Christian party.[2] Sentiment in favor of this ideal gradually increased, and in 1920 Adam Stegerwald, a Catholic labor leader and politician, called for an interconfessional "Christian National People's party." But these and similar proposals came to nothing, since they attracted few Catholics and almost no Protestants. A tiny Protestant group merged with the Zentrum late in the Weimar era, but it did not alter the party's Catholic character. In fact, the Center party's clerical nature

---

2. "Wir müssen aus dem Turm heraus!" in *Historisch-politische Blätter,* March 1, 1906. Bachem was still alive in 1945 and on November 15 wrote to Lambert Lensing, chairman of the Westphalian CDU: "I welcomed the founding of the Christian Democratic Party with great joy. . . . I deeply regret that in my 88th year my strength is no longer sufficient for me to participate in the practical work of the new party in our beloved fatherland. . . . Nothing is more necessary today for our fatherland than the close collaboration of all Christian-minded groups. . . . The new times demand new forms, and the Christian Democratic Party is the only practical form. . . . So go confidently forward with the Christian Democratic Party! To it alone belongs the future." File *Stellungnahmen,* Archives of the Westphalian-Lippe CDU, Dortmund.

was starkly emphasized in 1928 when Monsignor Ludwig Kaas, professor at the Trier Theological Seminary, became its chairman.

It was toward the end of the Third Reich that a sufficient degree of harmony among Catholics and Protestants developed to make genuine interconfessional cooperation possible. National Socialist pressure against the two churches brought together the clergy and laity of both in a common concern for humanity that made separate ecclesiastical interests appear unimportant. There developed in Germany at that time an ecumenical spirit that was not to be seen in the world again until the time of the Vatican Council of 1962. Even as uncompromising a theologian as Bonhoeffer, for instance, found himself in 1940 wondering how the two churches might someday come together and, during the very last days of his life, his thoughts returned again and again to the relationship between Protestants and Catholics after the Third Reich. Several times during the war he held discussions with a number of the German Jesuits close to Pius XII, and they were apparently of one mind that, following the Nazi collapse, the Center party and other confessional parties should not be refounded, that Protestants and Catholics would have to stand together, and that the two churches would have to assume a joint political responsibility. Pius himself, as already noted, at least for a time shared this "ecumenical" sentiment.

As the barriers between Protestants and Catholics were coming down, non-Marxist, anti-Nazi groups such as the Kreisau circle and the Freiburg circle were turning increasingly to basic Christian values—the absolute worth of the individual, the existence of inalienable rights, and so on—in their planning for the future. These persons had no intention of taking up where things had left off in 1933; instead, they envisaged a state explicitly based on Christian ideals. Carl Goerdeler, not a particularly religious man, well summed up the general view when he wrote in 1943:

> The religious consciousness in Germany has been enormously deepened and broadened by the oppression of the last decade. The Christian religion and its teachings will constitute for us the basis and guiding principle in all domestic and foreign affairs. We consider it necessary that even the fundamentals of foreign policy should be brought into conformity with Christian moral principles.[3]

While there is no evidence that the members of the various opposition and resistance groups ever explicitly discussed the establishment of an inter-

---

3. Quoted in Ritter, *Carl Goerdeler und die deutsche Widerstandsbewegung,* p. *333.*

confessional political party, the desire for cooperation among Catholics and Protestants, coupled with the conviction that the future German state would need the impetus of Christian ideals, proved enduring. In this sense German Christian Democracy is the most important and tangible outgrowth of the intense ecumenical spirit that developed in the Nazi era. It was one thing for this spirit to exist and another for it to be put into definite form, however, and here chance played a role.

German Christian Democracy was founded in Berlin in June 1945 by a small group of former politicans, trade union leaders, and a variety of others. The remnants of the July plot, they had been brought together by Andreas Hermes, then deputy Mayor of Berlin.[4] Although the Russians pressed for the reestablishment of the Center party, the members of the group, which was interconfessional from the start, unanimously agreed at the outset of their meetings in early May that a revival of the Zentrum was out of the question. Instead they wanted a party of an entirely new sort, one which would spread out from the center of the political spectrum, uniting non-Marxist socialists with conservatives, and which would put an end to the confessional antipathy that had poisoned German political life since unification in 1871.

Although it was taken for granted that the party would rest on general Christian values, the founders' approach was otherwise completely secularist. The two clergymen in the group, Provost Grüber and Father Peter Buchholz, did not play an important role in the deliberations, and although Bishop von Preysing and Bishop Dibelius were kept informed of events, they exerted no appreciable influence on them. Most of the Catholic members of the group felt that Catholic politicians had been abandoned by the Catholic church in 1933 with the conclusion of the Reichskonkordat and the dissolution of the Center party. As a result, they had little respect for the political views of their church and no intention of drawing it into their deliberations. If Catholic interests needed to be protected, they themselves could effectively accomplish this end. Such feelings were particularly strong with Hermes, whose contact with church leaders during the Third Reich left him dismayed with their political naiveté. Even the less skeptical Catholics were careful to pre-

---

4. Andreas Hermes (1878–1964) was one of the leading agricultural authorities and governmental administrators of the Weimar Republic, twice a minister and Zentrum member of the Prussian Landtag and the Reichstag. Sentenced to death in 1944 for his connection with the July plot, he was freed from prison upon arrival of the Russian forces. The only non-Marxist to serve in a top position in the Berlin civil government in 1945, he was banned from political activity by the Russians for refusing to support their land-reform program. Hermes moved to the Rhineland, but after Adenauer thwarted his attempts to play a role in the British Zone CDU, he dropped out of politics.

serve a distance from the church to avoid any seeming compromise of the party's interconfessional, secular nature.

Nonetheless, the only important differences within the Berlin group were of a confessional sort. Hermes had proposed that the new party be called "Democratic Union"—"democratic" to emphasize its antithesis to Nazism, and "union" to advertise its breadth of appeal. Several Catholics in the group, led by Heinrich Vockel, the former secretary general of the Zentrum, insisted that the term "Christian" be added, both as a further definition of the party's character and as "a signal to Catholics, showing them politically the way to go."[5] Most of the Protestants agreed with Father Buchholz, who objected that this decision would associate the party too closely with the churches. Dibelius, when informed of the dispute, agreed. But in the end the Protestants considered interconfessional political cooperation too vital to come to grief over the party's name, and they gave way. Grüber, however, withdrew from the group as a result; he was followed by several others, who later founded the Liberal Democratic party. The quarrel was the most serious point at issue among the Berliners, affecting as it did the very identity of the party. It was a dispute that was reenacted throughout Germany in the following months in most other nascent Christian Democratic groups, when Protestants would object again and again to this arrogation by one party of the name and characteristic "Christian." The other difficult question among the Berliners was the school question, and here, in the ecumenical spirit of the time, the Catholics agreed to a party program advocating nonconfessional schools.

Only in one other way did religious notions enter the picture, and this was in the party's advocacy of "socialism based on a sense of Christian responsibility." This proposal was the contribution of trade union leaders, notably Jakob Kaiser, who only relinquished their long-cherished idea of founding a non-Marxist "labor party" after several rebuffs from the Social Democrats.[6] More clearly developed in Berlin than anywhere else in Germany, Christian socialism became the principal motor of the planning sessions and shifted the new party's balance to the left without compromising its liberal, bourgeois values. By spanning the political spectrum, by incorporating general Christian ideals in a nonclerical party, and by attracting prominent laymen of both churches, the Berlin CDU was at its birth the only genuinely broadly based, interconfessional party of the sort intended, but not for many

---

5. Frau Elfriede Kaiser (wife of Jakob Kaiser), in an interview.
6. Discussed in Chapter 12, pp. 295–296.

years achieved, by Christian Democrats in other parts of Germany. By attracting those who wanted a fresh start in German political life no less than those
who saw in it primarily a refuge from Marxism, the Berlin group devised the
magic formula that would eventually make Christian Democracy a dominant
force in German political life.

Both Bishop Dibelius and Bishop von Preysing welcomed the new party,
though for different reasons. Von Preysing, thanks largely to his contact with
the Kreisau circle, was one of the few Catholic bishops who considered interconfessional political cooperation desirable for its own sake. The presence of
the Red Army and the danger of communist dominance in Germany were
additional arguments for a large non-Marxist party. He consequently fell in
easily with the decision against reviving the Zentrum and even with the party's school program. Dibelius, on the other hand, was at first unable to shake
himself free of a very old-fashioned brand of Lutheran skepticism of democracy and political affairs. Nor was he worried by communism, telling an
American military officer in July, "Because of recent German experience
with USSR occupation, Communism will not command the support of more
than a small percentage of Germans and therefore will not take root in
Germany." [7] Dibelius would have kept completely aloof from party politics
had he not found the Berlin Social Democrats at that time so strongly anticlerical as to constitute a threat to the church. As a personal gesture he
therefore joined the party just after it was founded and later explained his
decision to a pastor of his provincial church:

> A pastor should normally not appear publicly in party meetings, and he
> must in any event act in such a manner that his political behavior is not
> detrimental to his pastoral relationship to the members of the parish. It
> should also be understood that the Church does not in principle associ-
> ate itself with a single party but instead prefers that there be devout
> Protestant Christians in all camps. But it should not be forgotten that
> the Evangelical Church today finds understanding and support practi-
> cally only from the Christian Democratic Union of Germany.
> ... This makes it clear how much depends on the number of party
> members being as large as possible. ... Consequently I have myself be-
> come a member, even though I should have preferred, in view of my
> office, to have remained outside.[8]

Christian Democracy had a greater and more immediate appeal in the
Russian Zone than anywhere else; with 250,000 members by the end of

---

7. "Report on Conference with Dr. Dibelius" July 28, 1945, by Marshall Knappen, in *Evangelical Church, Lutheran,* Modern Military Records.

8. Copy of letter of December 22, 1945, to Pastor Schian, in Hermes Papers,
Königswinter.

1945, it enjoyed a larger membership than the CDU in West Germany has ever had. Its amazing growth frightened the Russians into taking steps to prevent its further spread. Determined to keep nonsocialist forces divided, Russian authorities refused to license CDU local organizations in a third of the communities of their zone in time for the elections of 1946 and virtually dictated that a Liberal Democratic party be established. The Russian tactic succeeded in draining away some Protestant support from the CDU. Almost all Catholics but only a relatively modest number of Protestants joined the party; as a result, Catholics, who constituted roughly 10 percent of the population, represented 50 percent of the party membership. In addition, Catholic priests and church leaders were far more active than the Protestant clergy in helping to organize the party, and some local organizations in the early days tended to be dominated by Catholics. All these circumstances occasionally aroused Protestant suspicion. Though the imbalance was gradually corrected, by that time the Russians and Adenauer had both seen it in their interest to isolate the Berlin-East German organization, which soon lost all influence in the West.

The Berlin CDU had always consciously sought to be the center of an all-German party. Although this preeminence was never acknowledged in the Western zones, the Berlin development was nevertheless decisive for the rest of Germany by acting as a powerful catalyst. There was a great revival of German particularism in 1945, and regional political leaders feared that if they did not move quickly, they might find themselves as local officials of a "Prussian" party. If the Berliners could launch a novel political idea, therefore, it was for the West Germans to decide how far it would go. The three Western zones were not only more than twice as populous as the Russian Zone, they were also the locus of political and ecclesiastical power after 1945 and therefore the site of the vital decisions.

Christian Democracy in western Germany took root first and most deeply in the Rhineland. Events there were set in their course in the Cologne area by four prominent Catholic political and lay leaders shortly after the arrival of American forces in March. As one of the four explained their outlook at the time:

> In our view, the immediate postwar years would be most difficult. The danger of secularist and communist influences would be acute. A fusion of communists and socialists or a popular front of the two threatened to dominate German political life. The only way of resisting the menace from the left and establishing a Christian State would be to establish a political movement uniting everyone with a Christian out-

look. A joint Catholic and Protestant party would constitute a power base that Catholics alone could not have.[9]

These arguments, vehemently debated among local Catholic political leaders, finally prevailed over the intense devotion which the Center party still inspired in the Rhineland. On June 17 a small group of Catholic politicians agreed to try to organize an interconfessional party rather than revive the Zentrum. In the Rhineland, fear of the left was the most compelling consideration. "Bear in mind at all times," as Adenauer later admonished his deeply divided political colleagues in Bavaria, "that only the planned merger of all forces standing on a Christian and democratic basis can protect us from the impending danger from the East."[10] At its inception, therefore, the Cologne brand of Christian Democracy was characterized less by the enthusiastic, fresh approach of the Berliners than by a cautious, defensive attitude of "defending old positions from new dangers" as it was put in an interview by Otto Schmidt, one of the Rhineland Protestant founders.

Two dramatic departures from old positions were originally intended, but attempts to insert them in the party's program had to be dropped because of the Catholic church's opposition. With the program's general provisions, which reflected a distinctly Catholic outlook, there were no difficulties. These attributed the downfall of the Weimar Republic to the "widespread, acquisitive materialism" of the interwar period and to the failure of the German people to maintain Christian moral standards. They went on to advocate a "new union of the population" in "social justice and social love" and—reviving a traditional archprinciple of German Catholicism—called for a strongly federalist system in the new German state. The difficulties arose over economic policy and education.

Neo-Thomist economic and social philosophy was the speciality of two Dominican theologians in the Cologne group, Eberhard Welty and Laurentius Siemer, and their intellectual influence, which generally dominated the program committee's discussions, was especially strong on these questions. Welty and Siemer, whose ecumenism embraced not only Protestants but socialists as well, believed that the prewar capitalistic, bourgeois order was finished in 1945. In a monograph, *Was Nun?*, written during the war and published on the eve of the program committee's first meeting, Welty argued that there

9. Wilhelm Warsch, in an interview. Warsch was pre-Nazi mayor of Krefeld-Uerdingen and a leading member of the Center party in the Weimar Republic.

10. Letter of August 21, 1945, to Karl Scharnagl, Mayor of Munich, in File 117: *Gründung der CDU Rheinland*, Archives of the Rhineland CDU, Cologne.

would have to be a fundamental reorientation of the system of property ownership. Sweeping nationalization of industry was inescapable; the only question was whether it would be done by Marxist brute force or in accord with Christian natural law. Welty and Siemer accordingly recommended that the program provide for broad-scale nationalization and that the party call itself the "Christian Socialist Association" to reflect its generally socialist aims. These proposals were an anathema to Frings, however, and did not go over well with the conservatives in the committee; they were either rejected altogether or watered down to such an extent that Siemer walked out of the drafting sessions.

The major clash with the church was over education. Although the original Cologne group was comprised of Catholics alone, in the best ecumenical spirit they had advocated nonconfessional schools with religious instruction as part of the curriculum. This radical break with traditional Catholic policy was simply the logical extension of their political premise that confessional differences were essentially unimportant and should be deemphasized as much as possible. But Frings would have none of this, and the program committee retreated to the position that, while confessional schools were preferable, nonconfessional schools would be acceptable. This position, in the archbishop's view, was still unsatisfactory, and the founding ceremony of the Rhineland party had to be postponed for several weeks while a settlement was negotiated. In the end, party leaders conceded, and the program advocated confessional schools wherever requested by parents.

Once the program was amended, Frings agreed to support the party, though initially he had been opposed to the new political course. One of the four originators of Christian Democracy in Cologne, Dr. Leo Schwering, recorded in his diary, "He considers us 'crazy' people." Above all Frings was afraid that joining Catholics and Protestants in one organization would endanger Catholic unity and compromise Catholic political aims. By mid-July, however, he recognized that a Catholic party was not possible, and when asked by a representative of Field Marshal Montgomery whether the Zentrum would be refounded, he said flatly, "No." He made it clear that the communist political threat was uppermost in his mind. In the Rhineland, the archbishop of Cologne's word was as good as law, and though, in the light of the church's desire to minimize its political activity, Frings was discreet in his involvement, his decision was crucial, as the party's organizers fully appreciated. Tradition-

---

11. Entry of June 16, 1945, from Schwering's diary, *Fasz I/Sch,* Schwering Papers, Cologne; memorandum of conversation between Frings and an unidentified British officer on July 19, 1945, File *CR 25/18,* Diocesan Archives, Cologne.

ally Cologne was the heart of German Catholicism and before 1933 the "capital" of the Catholic political and lay movement. The decision of Catholic laymen and ecclesiastical officials there in favor of an interconfessional party was consequently a key step in the development of the CDU.

Even so, it was a gamble since the whole concept depended upon recruiting a sufficient number of Protestants to make the party reasonably interconfessional. While this was impossible in Catholic Cologne, in the predominantly Protestant area of Wuppertal an interconfessional party had begun to develop under Protestant leadership and independently of events in Cologne. The contrast in approach was striking. If the first question facing the Cologne group was over the kind of Christian party to have—interconfessional or Catholic—the initial problem for the Ruhr Protestants was whether a "Christian" party as such was possible. With less difficulty than most of their coreligionists in other areas, these Protestants decided affirmatively. The state could never be Christian, and it would not be their aim to make it so; but the Christian citizen must be politically active out of a sense of responsibility toward others. The political and religious lessons of the Third Reich and the new understanding between Protestants and Catholics made a Christian party possible and necessary, they concluded.

A Wuppertal Christian Democratic party was formed in August, though not on the basis of a specific political and social program—even these Protestants would not go so far as to claim the existence of an identifiable body of Christian policies—but simply as the manifestation of "politics stemming from belief," as they often put it. This vague expression is to be understood in a Barthian sense—that the Christian, though recognizing that the state can never achieve absolute morality, has an obligation to work for the relative social justice that the state alone can secure. In other words, this brand of Christian Democracy was a mode of action, not a body of policy. The Wuppertal group as a result took strong exception to the Cologne program when they learned of it, condemning its narrowly Catholic tone and substance as well as most of its concrete economic and political proposals. This in turn frightened many local Catholics, and the dean of the Catholic Church in Wuppertal took steps to revive the Center party as a means of protecting Catholic interests. "Whenever Catholics were in a minority," Otto Schmidt later remarked in an interview, "they normally wanted to go their own way. They were interested in cooperation only when they were in control." This difference of political approach and the Protestant suspicion of Catholic motives were typical throughout Germany, and neither situation has entirely disappeared with the passage of years.

Despite these differences the two groups felt they had an adequate basis for cooperation and, along with a Christian Democratic group in Düsseldorf, founded a Rhineland party on September 2, 1945. A weak sister party in Westphalia was formed at the same time, despite the lack of interest of most Protestants and the hostility of many of the Catholic clergy and laity in the area. The Catholic bishops north of the Main met in mid-August and decided to support the new political movement. Concerned over the Catholic minority which remained opposed to an interconfessional party, the bishops pleaded against the revival of the Zentrum. As Frings later explained the bishops' decision to a recalcitrant Zentrum supporter:

> Rest assured that none of the gentlemen [the bishops] decided in favor of the CDU because he considered its program fundamentally better or more correct; rather, this was done for tactical reasons, to deprive the world of the spectacle of political division and of mutual animosity within German Catholicism. Your party had the disadvantage of being too late on the scene. [12]

These decisions in the Rhineland and in Westphalia meant that the most influential Catholic political and ecclesiastical leaders in Germany had decided in favor of an interconfessional movement. With this, the decisive step had been taken toward the establishment of a national Christian Democratic party.

The Berlin Christian Democratic Union, secularist in origin, outlook and aim, and the Rhineland Christian Democratic party, tinged with Catholic clericalism and Protestant theology, represented the two poles between which, broadly speaking, Christian Democracy developed in other parts of Germany. In Frankfurt the impetus came less from former Zentrum politicians than from left-wing Catholic intellectuals who had initially hoped to forestall the reestablishment of both the Center party and the SPD in order to construct a socialist people's party from the two. Unable to evoke SPD interest, the group came to regard a party based on general Christian principles as the best way of achieving the ultimate objective of a socialistically inclined, strongly federalist German state. Although a number of Catholic and Protestant clergymen participated in the meetings, the general approach was as

---

12. Quoted in Wieck, *Die Entstehung der CDU und die Wiedergründung des Zentrums im Jahre 1945*, p. 66.

secularist as that in Berlin. The Frankfurt group advocated a strict separation of church and state, including nonconfessional schools, as well as a program of Christian socialism envisaging the nationalization of basic industries and large industrial firms. Though not pleased with the program, Bishop Albert Stohr of Mainz went along with the party quite easily. Niemöller was skeptical about founding political parties before Germans had political responsibility. He was not, however, opposed to the CDU in principle at that point, though he did not like its calling itself "Christian" and remained aloof. He became increasingly critical as—conversely to Cardinal Frings—he thought he saw Protestants in the party being ideologically corrupted through their affiliation with Catholics; by 1955 he was openly calling them a "Catholic-infected Protestant group." [13]

In southwestern Germany, Catholic church officials had the controlling hand in the party's development. In Baden immediately at the end of the war Monsignor Föhr began carrying out his long-established plan to refound the Center party, broadened to include—as he put it in an interview—sympathetic Protestants, as "a genuinely ideological Christian party . . . not an interconfessional party based on general Christian ideals, since these amount to little or nothing and would give the party no real foundation or clear aims." But Archbishop Gröber had no intention of permitting Föhr to be the political power in the area and was quite radical in his desire for interconfessional cooperation, even opposing the establishment of confessional schools and forbidding the publication of a Catholic newspaper in his diocese. He therefore launched an interconfessional group, locally known as the "archbishop's party," which competed throughout the summer with Föhr's "monsignor's party." By autumn, Gröber had obtained French support and finally brought sufficient pressure on Föhr's group to disband. An interconfessional party was duly founded in December, and Gröber himself largely wrote its program.

In Württemberg Catholic church officials of the diocese of Rottenburg were directly involved in the earliest political discussions; but like Catholic politicians in the area, they toyed at first with the idea of refounding the Zentrum. According to Auxiliary Bishop Wilhelm Sedlmeier in an interview diocesan officials did not seriously think this move was feasible, recognizing that "we would only secure power if Protestants and Catholics joined forces." In any event, they were encouraged in this direction by Gröber and Augustin Rösch, the Jesuit provincial of Bavaria who visited Rottenburg in the summer of 1945 and in discussions with church officials stressed the importance of

---

13. Quoted in *Kirchliches Jahrbuch,* 1955, p. 22.

interconfessional cooperation. Once Catholic politicians had decided in favor of an interconfessional party, diocesan officials did all they could to help it along. In addition to their general encouragement of the clergy and laity to support the party, they permitted parish priests to help organize local party groups, recommended the names of sympathetic laymen to party organizers, and authorized a diocesan official, Gebhard Müller (later minister president of the Land and head of the federal constitutional court), to become manager of the CDU in south Württemberg.

Finding Protestant partners was not difficult, since Württemberg had been the center of the Christian Social People's Service (Christlich-sozialer Volksdienst–CSVP), a small Protestant party founded during the last years of the Weimar Republic. Its former leaders decided soon after the war that their party should not be refounded, and that an interconfessional party was vital both as a Christian influence in the reconstruction of Germany and as an expression of a Christian obligation to society. The Protestants, however, had no contact with provincial church officials. "We knew that Wurm had no objection to an interconfessional party," Wilhelm Simpfendörfer, the CSVP's chairman, stated in an interview. "But even if he had, we would have done what we felt the circumstances demanded." The Württemberg church itself was careful to avoid any association with the new party, both as a matter of principle and because some of its officials suspected the Catholics of intending to use the party for their own purposes. Roughly half the Protestant clergy in Württemberg had similar reservations and skeptically regarded Protestant Christian Democrats as so much "vote fodder" for the Catholics. These views were not, however, shared by Wurm himself, whose long-standing antipathy toward the "free-thinking liberals" (the later Free Democrats) led him to welcome a party of confessing Christians.

An interconfessional party developed relatively slowly in Bavaria as a result of the incompatibility of the political aims and the personal ambitions of local politicians. The Catholic church could give no lead, since here more than anywhere else in Germany, it was itself politically adrift. The Bavarian bishops, all old men who were exhausted by the tribulations of the Third Reich, were overwhelmed by the aftermath of the war and the problems of the occupation. Moreover, Cardinal Faulhaber and several other bishops were more interested in a restoration of the Wittelsbach monarchy than in the revival of political parties. As a result, the hierarchy at first committed itself to no definite political course or political figure and soon saw its clergy associated with a wide variety of political movements. Fritz Schäffer, the last chairman of the Bavarian People's party, the Bavarian branch of the Zentrum, favored the revival of his old party and a restoration of the monarchy, ideally with himself as prime minister of an autonomous Bavaria. In Würzburg, Adam Stegerwald saw his long-awaited chance to unite Catholics and Protestants, along with workers and farmers, in a mass party occupying the ground between the left and right extremes. Only in northeastern Bavaria, which is predominantly Protestant, were Catholic church officials really active, and there, with the approval of the ecumenically minded archbishop of Bamberg, helped to organize an interconfessional party with a Catholic and corporativist program that had little appeal to Protestants.

All of this activity came to nothing. Schäffer found no popular support for a Catholic party, the Americans would not permit Crown Prince Rupprecht to return to Germany, Stegerwald died in the fall, and Bamberg was without wide influence. Munich was in any case the vital center of Bavaria, and there an interconfessional party had begun to develop late in the summer under the leadership of Josef Müller. Müller—who had played a central role in the efforts of Pope Pius XII to reach an understanding in 1940 between German resistance circles and the British government, designed to lead to the removal of the Nazi regime and an end to the war—had had close contact with Bonhoeffer and Ivo Zeiger during the war. The three agreed that confessional divisions must never again be carried into the political sphere. The Pope himself received Müller in June 1945, and according to the latter in an interview, Pius remarked that just as Protestants and Catholics had stood shoulder to shoulder against Hitler, now they would have to stand together against the communist threat. Neither the Pope nor Müller had drawn any specific political conclusions from this, but following a meeting with Stegerwald in July, Müller immediately embraced the idea of a party joining Protestants and Catholics. It was to be conceptually an expression of the ecumenical feeling of the time and pragmatically a counterpoise to Marxist collectivism. The name eventually chosen for the party, Christian Social Union, was to reflect the general idea of Chrisitian solidarity against political extremism and not the economic notions of the Berlin or Frankfurt groups or the Rhineland Dominicans.

The new party found considerable favor with Bishop Meiser and a fair proportion of the Protestant clergy in Bavaria. However, none of the Catholic bishops, except Simon Kolb of Bamberg gave Müller any support, while Bishop Simon Landersdorfer of Passau actively opposed him. Cardinal Faulhaber, perhaps the most conservative member of a deeply conservative group of bishops, shared Landersdorfer's apprehension that an interconfessional party would deprive Catholics of the influence they could exert through a party of their own. For their part, the Catholic clergy in southern Bavaria was completely caught up in the nostalgia of Bavarian monarchism, which in turn became involved with the romantic notion of Bavarian separatism and a Danube confederation. But the shock caused by the American replacement of Schäffer by the Social Democrat Hoegner in September 1945, the hopelessness of the monarchist cause, and the spread of Christian Democracy elsewhere in Germany finally persuaded most of the Bavarian hierarchy in January 1946 to espouse the CSU, though more in an effort to consolidate Catholic political forces than in the conviction that an interconfessional party was a wise idea. Even so, much of the Catholic clergy refused to support the CSU even for tactical reasons, backing instead the clericalist and autonomist Bavarian party.

In northern Germany the idea of a Christian party took root even more slowly. In most areas there were no Catholics to take the lead, and in the others, they wanted to revive the Zentrum. Protestant church leaders let it be known that they had serious reservations about a party calling itself Christian, fearing that such a party would be an encumbrance on the church. Eventually, however, a modest start was made. In Schleswig-Holstein a conservative Protestant group was organized by Hans Schlange-Schöningen, a leading representative of agrarian interests in the Weimar Republic. In Hamburg former Center party leaders organized a party based on the Cologne program. In Lower Saxony, where the Catholic bishops of Hildesheim and Osnabrück supported the Zentrum, Bishop Marahrens actively encouraged the establishment of an interconfessional party, and two of his clerical officials became founding members of the Hanover CDU. Despite the coolness of most Protestant bishops, clergy, and laity, the development of Christian Democracy in northern Germany was highly important in giving the party both geographical balance and, after the isolation of the East German CDU, its largest bloc of Protestant supporters.

Christian Democracy clearly began without either organizational or philosophic coherence. Its very origins nonetheless gave rise to certain traits that have influenced the subsequent course of the party. Catholic predominance is the most obvious. That, with a few notable exceptions, the major regional party groups were organized at the initiative of Catholics was an entirely natural development. The long tradition of Catholic political involvement and lay activity in social affairs had produced a large body of Catholic laity with great experience in organized politics. Despite the dissolution of the Zentrum and the Catholic lay movement in 1933, Catholic political leaders had maintained contact with one another during the Third Reich, and in 1945 they quickly resumed their political collaboration. Moreover, the Catholic body of natural rights and the broad social program adumbrated in papal encyclicals gave them an organizational coherence, a set of aims, and a clear relationship to their religion and their church. Thanks to a common political origin—the Center party—they had a fundamentally similar political outlook, which was essentially pragmatic and power-directed. As a result Catholic political leaders had been able relatively quickly and easily to agree at the end of the war that the Center party, largely because it had discredited itself, had no future and would have to be replaced by a party promising a fresh political start and able to raise an effective challenge to the Social Democrats and communists. Catholics differed only over the tactical question of what sort of party could best achieve this objective. While several years were required to settle this issue, Catholics were able from the beginning to march together, assisted by their church and confident of the support of a high proportion of the laity. With this degree of inner cohesion and strength, most of the party's Catholic founders took for granted that leadership would lie in Catholic hands.

Protestants almost totally lacked this unity and self-confidence. They had no substantial tradition of organized political and social cooperation on which they could draw. In the summer of 1945 they had, with few exceptions, no contact with one another and differed substantially in their approach to political, social, and economic matters. Their religion not only provided them no social philosophy on which they could draw, but also ruled out both the concept of identifiable "Christian" policies and a "Christian" party as such. Far from constituting a source of strength, the Protestant laity and clergy were a completely incalculable political factor. Even the motivations of the Protestant founders varied greatly, ranging from simple conservative agrarianism to a vague semireligious sense of responsibility to society, which Catholics tended to find naive and at times exasperating. All these circumstances left Protestants both psychologically and numerically much the weaker partner.

This disparity was further emphasized by the vividly contrasting attitudes of the two churches to the party. Despite the desire of church officials and politicians on the Catholic side to maintain some distance, the Catholic bishops had become entangled from the outset in the party's development. At the end of the war many of the bishops tended to take for granted, with varying degrees of enthusiasm, the fact that the Center party would be reestablished. While Gröber, Kolb, von Preysing, and von Galen supported an interconfessional party almost at once and with conviction, the other bishops accepted this view only gradually. The factors involved in their decision are so interrelated that it is difficult to distinguish cause from effect. In some cases the CDU was already on the scene; in other cases the party had evolved with the bishop's consent or even his encouragement; in still other cases the arguments of Catholic politicians favoring an interconfessional party were seen as compelling. The distinguished group of German Jesuits—August Bea, Robert Leiber, Zeiger, Rösch, Hirschmann, Nell-Breuning, and Gundlach—were all convinced of the wisdom—at least on tactical grounds—of an interconfessional party and were influential both in arguing the case for it and in spreading the word that the Vatican was inclined to look with favor on such a party. In their efforts the Jesuits had the enthusiastic support of Professor Paul Simon, the ecumenically minded Provost of Paderborn and in 1945 the Fulda Bishops' Conference's adviser on political questions.

In all these deliberations one argument proved decisive: Catholics alone would not be able to assure a Catholic or Christian or conservative influence in the new German state. Protestants were the only possible ally. Even acknowledging this situation, some of the bishops, such as Frings, would have preferred separate Catholic and Protestant parties, each fighting the left in its own way. But a Protestant party was not in the cards and Protestants, the Jesuits argued, if left to themselves would fall into the hands of the liberals and the Social Democrats. The bishops were therefore swept along, occasionally master but usually victim of events. With little enthusiasm for interconfessional partnership and some apprehension that Catholic aims might be watered down by a fuzzy sort of Protestantism, the bishops eventually concluded that the danger from the left was greater than were the risks of a Catholic-Protestant party. Some bishops, such as Frings and Jäger, grasped the logic of the situation quickly; others, such as Faulhaber, only slowly; still others, such as the bishops of Hildesheim, Speyer, and Passau, never lost their personal preference for a Catholic party but had to fall in line anyhow.

The support of the Catholic church was important in getting the party established. Bishops and priests often helped organize local party groups, provided meeting places (usually halls belonging to Catholic lay organizations), and suggested the names of potential party workers. In the months following the war, when clergymen could travel much more freely than ordinary civilians, church officials were sometimes the main link among the various nascent Christian Democratic groups. In this way the Catholic church compensated for the Christian Democrats' lack of an organizational infrastructure and helped to cement the various party units into a cohesive whole. The church's price for its support was that it receive satisfaction in the various party programs on church-state matters and especially on the school question. In this way the bishops were able to take a political movement about which they had some reservations and nudge it in a direction more to their own liking. There was a lesson in this for both sides. While Catholic politicians and church leaders wanted to maintain their political independence, each recognized that neither could do without the other. But this very fact meant that the relationship between the two was pragmatic rather than organic; it would therefore be subject to political circumstances and would change with these.

The Protestant church was generally a passive element in the development of Christian Democracy. Though some Protestant bishops were informed of the efforts to establish an interconfessional party, they were never consulted as such and, with the partial exception of Meiser and Marahrens, neither played a role in organizing the party nor exerted influence on its program. Apparently none of the Protestant church leaders cared for the party's calling itself "Christian" but, after fifteen years of National Socialism and at a time of profound national uncertainty and insecurity, they could not but welcome the establishment of a party explicitly dedicated to Christian values and implicitly interested in good relations with the churches. In addition, many churchmen were sympathetic to the CDU as an influence for humane and conservative values and as a counterforce to the anticlericalism of the Social Democrats and the Free Democrats. However, it was agreed on all sides that the church should cultivate good relations with all democratic parties and must remain neutral among them. This was made clear in the church's first postwar statement on political affairs, the Treysa conference's Declaration Regarding the Responsibility of the Church for Public Life, which stated with reference to the CDU:

> The attempts already under way in many areas to remove political differences between Protestantism and Catholicism, to make joint cause against secularism—and in that way to prepare a common spiritual and political reconciliation of the two confessions—deserve our support just as do the efforts of the Catholic clergy and laity to prevent a reestablishment of the Center party and make possible instead political cooperation between the two confessions on the basis of a Christian union. Needless to say, care must be taken that the cooperation of the two parties should be based on complete equality. [14]

At the same time, however, the declaration was careful to emphasize that the "utmost care will have to be taken . . . to avoid falling under any suspicion of partisanship toward the Christian personalities of other parties or to contribute to the isolation of one group of society from the others." This made plain the Evangelical church's view that no politician could make exclusive claim to the Christian label and that Protestants should not permit a political confrontation to develop between Christians and non-Christians.

---

14. Merzyn (editor), *Worte und Erklärungen*, p. 4.

The Christian Democratic Union, in short, took its place on the political scene without its progenitors' having reached agreement either on the practical meaning of any of the three words in the party's title or regarding the relationship of this "Christian" party to the churches. Reduced to its lowest common denominator, Christian Democracy at the time of its establishment stood simply for a restoration of the rule of law after a period of despotism and for social justice tempered by political caution rather than revolutionary social change. From the beginning the party's basic appeal was not so much to religious feeling as to political moderation, in contrast to socialism, communism, and the sort of developments taking place in East Germany. It was in this sense that Adenauer's slogan in the national elections from 1949 until 1961–"The coming Bundestag election will above all determine whether Germany will remain Christian or not" [15] –was popularly understood, and it was for this reason that it was so successful. But such slogans could not conceal the party's ideological barrenness. What the CDU stood for at its birth was something essentially novel in German political history: an *approach* to social and political problems rather than a specific social and political philosophy. While this pragmatic attitude had an appeal to a population sated with political doctrine, it might easily have led to electoral disaster. What made the CDU a major force in German politics from a very early stage was its ability to build on the Zentrum tradition and to count on the Catholic church's support. Indispensable though they were, they were not, however, an unqualified advantage.

In the first two or three years of the CDU's development the party was scarcely more than nominally interconfessional. In Catholic areas it was strong but, in terms of leadership and electoral support, almost a purely Catholic party. This was the simple consequence of the fact that, thanks largely to the Catholic hierarchy's direction, after 1945 as before 1933, a large proportion of Catholics acted politically as a bloc and now merely shifted their support from the Zentrum to the CDU. In Protestant areas (with the exception of East Germany), on the other hand, the CDU experienced great difficulty in gaining even a foothold. The Evangelical church was politically neutral, and the Protestants, in any case skeptical toward a Christian party, divided their support among a variety of parties, as they, too, had before 1933. Catholic domination of the CDU was further emphasized by the rapid ascendancy of the Rhineland-Westphalian group over all the other CDU organizations. Between 1945 and 1948 four regional groups vied for suprema-

---

15. *Süddeutsche Zeitung*, June 28, 1957.

cy—the agrarian North German Protestants, led by Hans Schlange-Schöningen; the interconfessional Christian socialist group in Berlin, under Jakob Kaiser; the Bavarians, under Josef Müller; and the conservative Catholic Rhineland-Westphalian group, led by Adenauer. Adenauer's purposeful climb to the top of the CDU fundamentally affected the character of the party, representing as it did a victory at once for the right wing, the Catholics, and the Rhineland. During this period the party's growth was primarily fostered by Catholic clerical, theological, and lay figures. As one acute observer noted in 1948, "One may pass from Church to Catholic Action to Christian party and still be under the same roof and surrounded by the same faces." [16] The relatively few Catholics who were opposed to this conservative and clericalist trend found themselves powerless to stem the tide. Since they could not bring themselves to join the Social Democrats, they had nowhere to go. While most remained in the party, a few, such as Walter Dirks and some of the other founders of the Frankfurt party, dropped out of active politics.

For Protestants, however, this trend was far more provocative. In the earliest postwar years, as already noted, Christian Democracy was widely regarded among the Protestant clergy and laymen as a salutary, almost healing force in German politics. While accepting the numerical superiority of Catholics, they regarded this dominance as temporary and believed that the party would in any case be interconfessional in tone and operation. When the CDU instead fell more deeply into the control of Catholics, Protestant suspicions were aroused and a significant backlash developed. In Schleswig-Holstein, for instance, the CDU vote declined from 44 percent in the 1947 Land election to 31 percent in the 1949 federal election, and to a disastrous 20 percent in the 1950 Land election. This trend was reflected in most other Protestant areas as well between 1948 and 1952.

Expunging its image as a Catholic party became the CDU's major task, which Adenauer was the first to recognize. Indeed, one of the reasons given for his refusal to commit himself to Christian Democracy in the summer and fall of 1945 was his skepticism of the party's chance of recruiting Protestants. Once the party was established, he realized that its survival as well as the extent of its success would depend upon the achievement of an acceptable psychological balance between the confessions. After securing control of the CDU in the British zone early in 1946, Adenauer actively cultivated Protestant support through influential Protestant laymen, such as Gustav Heine-

---

16. Almond, "The Christian Parties of Western Europe." "Catholic Action", which did not exist as such in Germany, here refers to the organized Catholic lay movement in general.

mann, Friedrich Holzapfel, Robert Pferdmenges, and Otto Schmidt. As an institutional means to this end, for instance, he encouraged Schmidt to organize a Protestant group within the Rhineland and Westphalian parties to help compensate for Protestant numerical inferiority and to attract further support from Protestants in the area. Out of this effort came the so-called Evangelische Tagung der CDU in late 1946. Although this group had only limited success, a strong core of Protestant Christian Democratic politicans gradually developed in North Rhine-Westphalia, from which emerged such prominent party figures as Heinemann and Gerhard Schröder. In Protestant areas of the southwest as well as in Hesse and northern Germany, the CDU's growth was also slow, largely as a result of the party's Catholic image. However, here, too, it was gradually developing strong Protestant leadership.

It had been one of the assumptions of the party founders everywhere that Catholics as a whole could be counted on to support the CDU and that the extent of Protestant support would determine whether and by what margin the party would prevail in elections. This evaluation set strict limits on the extent to which the party could be controlled by Catholics. The problem was one of recruiting Protestants while allowing Catholics to have enough of an edge to remain thoroughly tied to the party. It was a mark of Adenauer's skill that he turned this dilemma into a recipe for electoral success. Organizationally the party was kept in Catholic hands while ideologically it moved in a direction attractive to Protestants.

This change in party philosophy was most clearly reflected in the evolution of the party's programs. The key element of most early CDU programs was their economic and social provisions, and these were more often than not based on Catholic social doctrine and expressed in Catholic terminology. The main emphasis was on "Christian socialism," and this was entirely of Catholic origin, developed by Dominicans and Jesuits such as Welty, Siemer, and von Nell-Breuning; by Catholic intellectuals such as Walter Dirks and Eugen Kogon; and by Catholic trade unionists such as Kaiser and Arnold. The Ahlen Program of 1947, calling for a new noncapitalist economic and social order, was in this vein. The Düsseldorf program of July 1949, on the other hand, rejected all economic planning and limited state activity to taxation and import policy. This shift marked the decisive triumph of liberal economics over Catholic social philosophy, a victory of Erhard (and Adam Smith) over the Catholic scholastics (and Thomas Aquinas).

By the time the Federal Republic was established, the CDU had shed most of the doctrinal elements that were objectionable and even incomprehensible to non-Catholics. In this way a practical modus vivendi evolved, with Catholics occupying the leading positions in the national party while Protestants called the tune in the economic sphere. This division amounted in effect to emptying party "ideology" of anything more specific than the vague notions of political freedom and material prosperity. Such an approach was sufficient to check the CDU's loss of its "soft" Protestant support and to anchor a solid portion of the Protestant bourgeoisie in the party. This degree of Protestant backing—which was probably in the neighborhood of 20 percent of Protestant voters—in combination with the votes of the great majority of Catholics, enabled the Christian Democrats, against general expectation, to edge out the SPD in the 1949 federal election.

It was when Germany became self-governing with a CDU-dominated government in 1949 that interconfessional political cooperation was put to the real test. Since the emotional enthusiasm in which the political partnership between Catholics and Protestants had developed after the war had already largely dissipated, confessional differences over the CDU's character were increasingly exposed. During the half-dozen years after 1949 the main course of the Federal Republic's domestic and foreign policies were charted. In foreign affairs it was the period when Adenauer tied Germany to the West through interrelated economic, political, and defense arrangements, against the vehement opposition of the Social Democrats and the Niemöller-Heinemann wing of the Evangelical church. Adenauer's success depended not only upon the CDU's ability to withstand the political attacks of the SPD but equally in preventing the party's policies from taking on a confessional character, with Protestants on one side of the argument and Catholics on the other. The problem was complicated by the fact that during the same period the entire federal government machinery had to be reconstructed, and this led to the bitter confessional dispute over Personalpolitik that has already been described. There was dynamite in this situation, not only for the CDU but also for the West German state. That it was successfully defused was due to two men—Adenauer and Ehlers.

It was obvious to all Germans that Adenauer's absorbing interest was in grand foreign policy strategy. In essence this strategy was thoroughly Western-oriented and anticommunist. While both characteristics may have had their deepest roots in Adenauer's Rhenish Catholicism, they unquestionably reflected the strongest political emotions of the majority of Germans, whether Protestant or Catholic. Whatever residual suspicion some Protestants may have had of Adenauer's ultimate motivation, the policies themselves were so widely accepted as being what the times called for—and what the Western Allies wanted—that any possible ulterior aim on Adenauer's part was considered even by most skeptics to be essentially irrelevant. As a result, neither Niemöller and Barth on the one hand nor Schumacher on the other were able to convince an appreciable number of Protestants that the country's foreign policy was in reality a design to weaken German Protestantism and perpetuate the division of the country. Even when the majority of Evangelical church leaders differed in substance or tactics from Adenauer, they never regarded these differences as confessional ones.

To the extent that confessional issues were involved in domestic policy matters, Adenauer demonstrated both as chairman of the Parliamentary Council and over the years as chancellor that he was ecclesiastically nonpartisan and fully capable of rejecting Catholic church demands. Through masterful legerdemain he succeeded in letting the churches feel appeased while in fact he more and more ignored them. His clear distance from the Catholic hierarchy and his good relations with key Protestant bishops, particularly with Dibelius, further satisfied the broad mass of Protestants that he maintained a careful balance between the two institutions. Such fear of (Catholic) clericalism and "counter-Reformation" tendencies in the federal government as did exist concerned precisely two areas of government—social policy and Personalpolitik—which Adenauer left essentially to others. In these cases suspicion generally fastened on the conservative Catholics in Adenauer's cabinet, and above all on State Secretary Glokbe, because of his own activities as well as his dealings with Monsignor Böhler. From these intrigues Adenauer was believed to have remained aloof. Moreover, Catholic advantage in these spheres was effectively offset by Adenauer's making economic policy virtually the exclusive preserve of the Protestant business community. In sum, although there was always a small minority of Protestants who withheld their support from the CDU because it was led by a Catholic, they were acting upon simple confessional prejudice and not upon any plausible evidence that Adenauer was motivated in his policies by confessional considerations.

Adenauer did not frighten Protestants away from the CDU. The man who enticed decisive numbers into the party was Hermann Ehlers. When Ehlers, an eminent Protestant layman and a man with a political tenacity and strength of character equal to Adenauer's, took his seat as a member of the first Bundestag in 1949, he found that Protestants in the CDU were a small, completely disorganized minority and that Catholics dominated the party's affairs largely because no one was looking after Protestant interests. Ehlers, a Berliner and accustomed to the Protestant-dominated governments of the pre-Nazi period, was shocked by his initial encounter with the militant Catholicism of some of his CDU colleagues. He at once launched a virtual crusade both to defend the party from its enemies in the Evangelical church and to force Catholics to give Protestants equality in the CDU. To Protestant laymen he argued that Protestant weight in the CDU would increase only if more of them were active in the party. To his Catholic colleagues he insisted that he could secure Protestant support only if Protestants held an equal share of the top jobs in the party and in the government. Suggestions, occasionally put to him by Protestant laymen and clergy, that Protestants should break away from the CDU and organize their own party, were rejected by Ehlers out of hand on the ground that such a move would lead directly back into darkest clericalism and confessional strife. But he warned Adenauer and other party officials that, despite Catholic numerical predominance, confessional parity both in the party and in the government must be achieved if the party was not to break apart.

Ehlers' main weapon was the Protestant committee of the CDU/CSU (Evangelischer Arbeitskreis der CDU/CSU) which he organized in 1952 over Adenauer's strong objection. The Chancellor was at first intensely mistrustful of Ehlers, and their relationship improved only slowly and to a limited extent. Although Adenauer had in earlier days favored the formation of a Protestant faction in the Rhineland and Westphalian parties, he now feared that the existence of a larger national body would interfere with his absolute control of the party and would give Ehlers more power than Adenauer wanted anyone else in the CDU to have. This outcome is in a way what Ehlers intended and what in fact happened. The committee gave Protestants a measure of the cohesiveness which Catholics had had from the start. It became a watchdog of government operations, particularly in the sphere of Personalpolitik and forced Catholics to accept compromise all along the line. Ehlers himself, who was elected president of the Bundestag in 1950, rose swiftly to become the second most influential person in the CDU and the heir-apparent to the chancellorship. But just after his fiftieth birthday in 1954, he died suddenly. It was long rumored in anti-CDU Protestant circles that Ehlers was embittered at the end because he felt that his best efforts had not prevented the CDU from following "Catholic policies." The truth, according to those who knew him best, is that though Ehlers was not fully content with the confessional balance in the party, he held Protestants themselves responsible, because so few of them were willing to devote their careers to politics. He was far more deeply hurt that the Evangelical church was not friendlier to the CDU and that many Protestant churchmen spoke of the CDU only to condemn it.

Ehlers was succeeded as Bundestag president by Eugen Gerstenmaier. Though a prominent Protestant layman, Gerstenmaier had always refused to have any dealings with the Protestant committee of the CDU, the contretemps over Personalpolitik, or Bishop Kunst's office. Gerhard Schröder succeeded Ehlers as chairman of the Protestant committee, but he used the committee less as an instrument for Protestant interests than to further his personal career. Robert Tillmanns, a minister in the second Adenauer cabinet, replaced Ehlers as the prime defender of Protestant interests; but Tillmanns, like Ehlers and a number of other important Protestants in the CDU, suffered an untimely death. Thereafter the protection of specific Protestant interests in the government passed largely out of the party and into the hands of Bishop Kunst. But Ehlers did succeed in establishing in the party a rough confessional equality—both psychological and in terms of political influence—which has endured. As a result, the party was spared either a confessional split or what Protestants at large might have viewed as a surrender to Catholic clericalism.

Thanks to Ehlers, the CDU was poised for its decisive breakthrough into Protestant ranks. Between 1949 and 1953 it gained a momentum of success in Landtag elections that took it further into Protestant strongholds and the territory of the various minor parties on its periphery. With each victory its character as a politically moderate, nonideological coalition of forces was more firmly established. And as it grew, it increasingly took on the confessional coloration of the area itself. In northern Germany it became a preeminently Protestant party with an exclusively Protestant leadership. While the process of "Protestantization" of the CDU in Protestant areas never reached this extent in Berlin, Württemberg, and Hesse, even in these sectors the CDU became more and more acceptable to the Protestant bourgeoisie, which felt it could vote for the CDU without supporting a Catholic party. Its Catholic base assured and Protestants now swinging over to its support, in 1953 the CDU became the first party in German history to win an absolute parliamentary majority—a victory for which Ehlers (who had spoken at over 100 campaign rallies in Protestant areas) was given much of the credit. The trend continued, and in the 1957 election the party's success was even greater.

Now the Catholics were frightened. The CDU's successes and its secularization had become mutually reinforcing developments, and the Catholic bishops realized that the potential danger—which some had foreseen in 1945—of Catholics and Protestants together in one party was actually at hand. The Catholic salt had, politically speaking, lost its savor. In broadening its base, Catholic church and lay circles felt, the CDU had surrendered its Christian character. It had evolved, as the conservative Catholic monthly *Wort und Wahrheit* complained in February 1957, from a party oriented toward Christianity to a party oriented toward liberalism, where policies were merely a "political act" without religious significance. The politically active religious orders, particularly the Frankfurt Jesuits and the Walberberg Dominicans, shared this pessimism; they found the situation all the more galling in view of their original encouragement of an interconfessional party. Their first shock had come in 1949 when the CDU formed a coalition with the FDP, a party they judged as having most of the worst characteristics of the Social Democrats and none of the SPD's social conscience. The increasingly stark liberalism of the CDU's economic policies deepened their woe. By 1958 Professor Gundlach, for instance, made no attempt to conceal his profound disillusionment with the liberal tendencies resulting from interconfessional cooperation. These, he commented in an interview, had reduced Christian Democracy to such an "ideological mish-mash" that it differed little if at all from the other parties.

Gundlach was right. And the Catholic church was consequently on the spot. The major premise of the church's political tactic had always been that the CDU was literally a "Christian" party and as such was inherently superior to any other party on the political scene. The reason Catholic theologians, laymen, and politicians had over the years devoted tens of thousands of words to discussions of the CDU as an ideological party was in reality an effort to determine in what sense the CDU was Christian. Some argued that its policies, ultimately reflecting Christian values, were innately Christian. This view not only failed to convince even the most credulous but also left the party vulnerable to the arguments of pro-SPD Protestants, who insisted that opposite policies were in fact Christian. Others maintained that the CDU, as a party of Christians, had a unique grasp of Christian social values and the sanctity of personal and property rights and was therefore uniquely qualified to institute social reform while protecting the freedom of the individual. Yet most Catholic and Protestant theologians had long believed that the CDU's record of social reform was inadequate at best and that CDU-controlled governments had instead instilled such a materialist approach into German life that the very mission of the churches was endangered as a result. Still others argued that the CDU was guided by such Christian virtues as tolerance, honesty, and moderation; but no one outside the party and few inside it ever took this claim seriously.

In fact, the interminable discussion of the topic has always had the pointlessness of a medieval disputation. The relationship between the Catholic church and the CDU was pragmatic, not platonic. It ultimately rested less on the party's policies as such, about which the bishops and theologians had mixed views, than on the close historic and institutional links between the two, which the hierarchy believed to be its guarantee of influence in the party. It was the change in *this* relationship that was causing Catholic church circles such anxiety. Whether through contact with Protestants or as a result of broad trends in European political life, by the mid-1950s most Catholic politicians and laymen had no interest in papal encyclicals, had lost touch with the church's political views, and were generally unwilling to fight for the church's aims in the public sphere. As early as December 1954 *Wort and Wahrheit* had observed among Catholic lay groups "partly a flabby indifference, partly a resigned acquiescence, partly overexaggerated confidence—'Let the parties do as they will, we have other concerns; our representatives must decide things for themselves; they will do the right thing; if they do not, well, we are not married to one another; the Church has no business in party politics.' " This attitude had increasingly infected Catholics in the Bundestag, who tended to see the Catholic church as just one, and not the most important, of the interest groups with which they had to deal.

Catholic church officials planned to counteract this development in two ways. Monsignor Böhler, in concert with the Catholic lay groups led by the central committee of German Catholics and some of the Jesuits and Dominicans, made elaborate plans to reestablish ideological and organizational links between Catholic parliamentarians in the CDU and the church. These proposals ranged from simple encouragement of the Catholic parliamentarian "to keep himself continuously informed of the concerns and wishes of the Church" and "to ask for and accept the word and advice of the Church in questions of religious of ethical significance" to such practices as the screening of potential candidates for the Bundestag so that "candidates who do not exhibit the necessary prerequisites are eliminated." [17] In short, Catholics were to remain a separate, self-conscious, church-directed group. This was an openly acknowledged Kulturkampf state of mind, aimed at creating a sort of neo-Zentrum within the CDU. The 1958 plenary session of the central committee of German Catholics actually mapped out the precise ways of making the CDU an ideological party, with Catholics permanently in control.

The second part of the strategy was to resist the growth of the CDU, since, as Father Hirschmann argued to the Catholic Institute for Social Work in Paderborn in 1958, this growth had proved incompatible with the party's Christian character. A reform of the election law was under consideration by the government at that time; if enacted, it would have favored the two major parties, the CDU and SPD, thus broadening the CDU even further. Hirschmann recommended dropping the proposed law. In the judgment of these Catholic circles, the liberal influence of the FDP would be easier to control if

---

17. *Wort und Wahrheit,* February 1957; Zentralkomitee der deutschen Katholiken, *Arbeitstagung Saarbrücken,* p. 249.

it were an independent coalition partner than if it were directly absorbed into the CDU. Although Catholic pressure was probably of only marginal influence, the proposal was eventually abandoned.

The concern among Catholic ecclesiastical and lay group leaders over the control and character of the CDU came to a head over the question of Adenauer's succession. It was increasingly obvious by the end of the 1950s that Ludwig Erhard's popularity in the party and with the voters made him the obvious sucessor. But Erhard, the paramount symbol of Protestant liberalism, economic materalism, and political secularism, was the outstanding bête noir of the Catholic church. Adenauer, moreover, was utterly convinced that Erhard was politically incompetent and would align the Federal Republic with Britain rather than France, thereby destroying Adenauer's long dream of Franco-German reconciliation. The chancellor's intimates, Globke and Krone, further saw the party and the government faced with a Protestant takeover, since they anticipated that Erhard would surround himself with the party's leading Protestants—Gerstenmaier, Schröder, and von Hassel. The question of party doctrine, party aims, and party control now became caught up in the leadership question, and in 1959 the CDU was squarely confronted with its inherent Catholic-Protestant problem in a particularly acute form. The idea of solving the problem by shifting Erhard into the presidency was unacceptable both to Erhard and to the CDU parliamentarians, who wanted Erhard to lead the party in future elections.

Early in 1959 a solution seemed to present itself to Adenauer's inner circle. Adenauer himself would become president. Finance minister Franz Etzel, a Protestant, would be made chancellor but would in fact be Adenauer's puppet. A Catholic would in turn succeed Adenauer as party chairman. To this end Globke put together a legal commentary on the Basic Law which was designed to appeal to Adenauer by stressing the potential influence of the president over the entire government—authority which Heuss had putatively neglected to use. At the same time Krone and other friends reported to Adenauer that confessional relations in the party were becoming frayed and that Protestants considered that their hour had come; they could only be deterred from seizing control of the party if Adenauer fell in with their scheme. They observed that Gerstenmaier, whose dearest wish was to be foreign minister, was encouraging Erhard while organizing Protestant support for him behind the scenes. They noted that the majority of Catholics in the CDU Bundestag delegation, although insisting on a Catholic's being party chairman, was willing to accept a Protestant as chancellor. Armed with Globke's legal commentary and these arguments, the group pointed out to Adenauer that he could retain political power, keep the chancellorship from

Erhard, and prevent the Protestants from capturing the party's leading positions only by becoming president himself.

Adenauer finally agreed to this stratagem on the conditions that the parliamentary party accept Etzel as his successor, that Globke remain state secretary at the chancellery for at least a year, that a Catholic be foreign minister, and that he himself be succeeded as party chairman also by a Catholic. Accordingly, on April 7, 1959 he announced his decision to stand as CDU candidate for president. When the parliamentary CDU could not be persuaded to accept Etzel, however, the key element of the plan collapsed, and Adenauer withdrew his candidacy. [18]

Part of the cost of this decision was the sharpest decline in Protestant support for the Christian Democrats since the 1948-1952 period. Protestant mistrust of the CDU had again been so inflamed that the 1961 national election saw a significant Protestant defection to the Free Democrats and, to a lesser extent, the Social Democrats. "In communities with a population over 50% Protestant," the Statistisches Bundesamt found, "the CDU/CSU suffered electoral losses . . . so great in the 1961 election that it lost the leading position there that it had up to then held." [19] Moreover, when Adenauer finally had to give up the chancellorship in 1963, there was, as his friends had predicted, no way of preventing Erhard and his Protestant colleagues—chief of whom were Schröder, Gerstenmaier and von Hassel—from dominating the government. But now Protestants could for the first time consider the CDU to be *their* party, with the result that the Christian Democrats received an appreciable increase in Protestant support. The 1965 election marked in fact the greatest victory for Protestant Christian Democrats since the party was founded. Significantly, it was in Protestant Länder and in communities throughout Germany with a population 50 percent or more Protestant that the CDU made its greatest gains, more than counterbalancing Catholic losses. [20] What had happened was that most of the remaining uncom-

---

18. While Globke in an interview confirmed the view that Etzel's unacceptability to the party was the sole reason for Adenauer's decision, rather than the foreign policy considerations which the Chancellor cited at the time, this account of the presidential crisis did not otherwise find favor with him and with several other of the principals with whom it was discussed. It was, however, derived from officials who were in an unquestionable position to know the facts and had no reason to feel embarrassed by them.

19. Statistisches Bundesamt, *Fachserie A, Bevölkerung und Kultur, Reihe 8, Wahl zum 4. Deutschen Bundestag am 17. September 1961, Heft 4, Textliche Auswertung der Wahlergebnisse* (1965), p. 45.

20. Ibid., *Fachserie A, Bevölkerung und Kultur, Reihe 8, Wahl zum 5. Deutschen Bundestag am 19. September 1965, 9. Textliche Auswertung der Wahlergebnisse (1967),* passim.

mitted Protestant conservatives (including the residue of those who had here-tofore shied from the CDU as a Catholic party) abandoned the Free Demo-crats for the CDU.

When this trend—of increasing Protestant and declining Catholic sup-port—was reinforced in the North Rhine-Westphalian Landtag election the following year, some scholars drew the over-hasty conclusion that the CDU was, as one of them put it, "running the danger of becoming a party of the Protestant conservative middle class". [21] It was true that a threshold had been passed in the mid-1960s and the CDU had become interconfessional to an extent and in a way that it had never been before. But Protestants would never have either the intimate links or the commitment to the CDU that Catholics had had during the previous two decades. Misapprehension of this point was in any case dispelled with the fall of the Erhard government at the end of 1966. When the CDU Bundestag delegation passed over Schröder as Chancellor, a number of the party's foremost Protestants became convinced that their Catholic colleagues comprised a Fronde that intended to keep power in their own hands whenever possible. Kurt Georg Kiesinger was in fact elected Erhard's successor by an avowedly Catholic coalition of south Ger-mans and Rhinelanders. The resolution of the 1966 crisis—in toppling the party's three leading Protestants and depriving Schröder and von Hassel of influence in the government—evoked bitterness among some of the party's Protestant leaders. This was intensified when it became clear that the grand coalition's policy-making body, the so-called Kressbronn circle, was limited (apart from Social Democratic representatives) to CDU Catholics. For a time there was serious fear among the party's Protestant leadership that this marked an attempt to revive in contemporary form the old Weimar partner-ship between the Center party and the SPD. Fortunately for the CDU this internal tension never broke out into the open and dissipated as soon as the CDU went into opposition in 1969. In the following years the leadership crisis and the stress between left and right in the party were without confes-sional undertones. By 1970 it could be said that the Christian Democrats had mastered their confessional problem.

While the CDU was consolidating its hold on Protestant conservatives and drawing in the last of the politically homeless Protestants, it was for the first time beginning to lose Catholic support. The general tone of Vatican II, the changing attitude of Catholics toward their church, the hierarchy's dimin-ishing political partisanship, the growing role of Protestants in the CDU along with developments in the SPD together had the effect of cracking the politi-

---

21. Rudolf Wildenmann in *Die Welt*, July 19, 1966.

cal unity of Catholics and opening the way for significant numbers of them to defect to the SPD. In the 1965 federal election, when this first became visible, the Christian Democrats barely held their own in Catholic Länder as a whole and in communities more than 50 percent Catholic they suffered a uniform decline. [22] North of the Main the Christian Democrats lost Catholic votes not only in industrial areas but in rural areas as well. The contrasting Protestant-Catholic trends were particularly stark in Baden-Württemberg, where constituencies predominantly of one confession are in many cases situated side by side with those strongly of the other. In Protestant districts the CDU vote rose generally by about 10 percent while in Catholic constituencies it often declined and was at best stagnant. This trend continued in other Land elections until the 1969 national election witnessed still further Catholic defections, this time by the middle class generally and white collar workers specifically. What had occurred from 1965 on was a change of deep significance—for the Catholic church no less than for the CDU. An increasing proportion of Catholics were now tending to vote in accordance with their professional, social and class interests rather than in response to confessional considerations and ecclesiastical guidance (which was in any case muted). The sum result, as *Der Spiegel* (August 28, 1972) indicated, was that the Christian Democrats lost roughly 2½ percent of their Catholic voters throughout the country between 1965 and 1969. It was this that led to the CDU's ejection from power in North Rhine-Westphalia in 1966 and from the federal government three years later.

"For every Catholic we lose to the SPD, we gain one Protestant", the CDU's general secretary, Bruno Heck, observed in an interview in 1969 of this situation. To some extent this development was self-reinforcing; the more genuinely interconfessional the CDU became the more it attracted Protestant conservatives and the less some Catholics felt committed to support it. The second half of the 1960s consequently saw a mutation not only in the CDU's confessional make-up but also in its political tone. As it absorbed Protestants from the right and lost Catholic workers on the left, the CDU became more unambiguously conservative, a tendency that was reinforced when the Social Democrats and Free Democrats maneuvered it into the opposition in 1969. Symptomatically, the social committees of the CDU, a powerful voice in the part during the 1950s, all but vanished as an influence and in fact came to be regarded by the leadership more as a political nuisance than as the party's social conscience.

---

22. Statisches Bundesamt, *Fachserie A, Bevölkerung und Kultur, Reihe 8, Wahl zum 5. Deutschen Bundestag am 19. September 1965, 9. Textliche Auswertung der Wahlergebnisse*, passim.

These developments, combined with the continued breakdown in Catholic cohesiveness and the Catholic bishops' further loss of control over their laity, largely accounted for the Christian Democrats' election disaster in 1972. Although heavily Catholic constituencies remained safely in CDU hands, more Catholic voters than ever slipped over to the Social Democrats. According to *Der Spiegel* (December 11, 1972), the SPD's election gains in Catholic constituencies were 4½ per cent above its national average. Proving Adenauer's point in reverse—that the CDU's success depended upon Catholic women—the marked shift to the SPD of female Catholic voters was a strong contributory element to the CDU's 1972 defeat. In sum, by the beginning of the 1970s the Protestant vote had become relatively stable and calculable, with roughly two-thirds of it falling to the SPD and FDP together and the remainder to the CDU. It was the Catholic vote that had become the open question, the crucial political variable.

The CDU's ouster from the federal government at the hands of an SPD-FDP coalition caused the Catholic bishops to check their tentative steps on the road toward nonpartisanship. As a result of the close links between the CDU and the Catholic lay movement, the CDU's departure from office had the effect of simultaneously removing almost all Catholic political figures from government positions. This pragmatic coincidence of fortune quickly brought Catholic back into the arms of the Christian Democrats on the basis of the syllogism that if Catholics control the CDU and the CDU controls the government then Catholics and Catholic influence could be restored to the government once the CDU was back in office. Ecclesiastical election pronouncements again began, if cautiously, to favor the CDU. In the quarter-century after the war the Catholic church had not altered its dominant political tactic.

The disparity of this clericalist approach with the pragmatic secularism of Christian Democracy is even more obvious now than it had been in the party's earlier days. In philosophy and practice the CDU is, for all the changes it has undergone, essentially what Hermes and Stegerwald intended it to be: a flexible, non-ideological party occupying essentially the middle ground of the German political spectrum. For all its hortatory dedication to Christian values, the CDU was always the least doctrinaire of German parties and for all its closeness to Catholic lay groups, it was on the whole consistently secularist. Symbolically, as Catholics have abandoned attempts to give meaning to "Christian" in the party's title, Protestants have stopped trying to have the word deleted. In fact, the fig leaf is necessary precisely because it hides nothing. The best the party's 1968 program could manage was only the most backhanded reference to Christianity. "The Christian Democratic Union," it avowed, "does not deny its origin; it holds to its objective as a Christian people's party." It did not bother to spell out what a "Christian people's party" might be. In any case, in the future as in the past, the vital question regarding the party's character is whether it will maintain its comprehensiveness—its unprecedented but now no longer unique coalition of classes, professions and interests. Its relationship to the Catholic Church will help to determine the answer to this question.

12 | *The Churches and Social Democracy*

GERMAN political history since 1945 marks an evolution from the ideological to the pragmatic. This holds especially true for the relationship between the Social Democratic party and the churches. German Social Democracy traditionally regarded religion and the churches in a Marxist light. Party philosophy was an all-embracing, millenial doctrine that had no place for Christianity. The churches were considered central pillars of an oppressive class structure. The churches in turn regarded Social Democracy as an atheistic, materialistic ideology completely incompatible with the Christian revelation. Prior to World War I neither the progressive social aims of the Catholic church nor the tiny Christian Social movement inside the Evangelical church altered the mutual antipathy between the churches and the party. During the Weimar Republic the Center party and the SPD were often in coalition but never reached any real understanding. Social policies proposed by the Zentrum were automatically rejected as "clericalist" by the Social Democrats, while SPD proposals were regarded with equal skepticism by the Zentrum. On the Protestant side the collapse of the throne-altar relationship and the support for Social Democracy by such theologians as Karl Barth and Paul Tillich (along with the establishment of the Federation of Religious Socialists) tended to reduce the tension between the SPD and German Protestantism. For its part the SPD went along with the "church articles" of the Weimar constitution, which left church privileges intact. Doctrinally, however, the party had not changed at all. Early party programs confined themselves to declaring religion a "private matter" and to calling for a separation of church and state. Before World War I this attitude was an understatement of socialist doctrine, which really looked forward to the time when religion would disappear from socialist society. After World War I it overstated the party's attitude, which was, at least tactically, to accept the status quo. But fundamentally the two institutions remained completely at odds over the place of religion in society and the church's role in the state.

During the Third Reich this antagonism was somewhat reduced. Many

324

Catholic and Protestant laymen came to the view that in refusing to vote for the Enabling Act and the dissolution of the SPD in 1933, the "atheistic" Social Democrats had done more for German democracy and humane values than either of the churches by their actions at the time. Some Social Democrats recognized that, apart from the political left, the main opposition force in the Third Reich came from Christian groups, and they gradually developed a basis of cooperation with them. Consequently, just as Catholics and Protestants tended to draw together after 1933, so some Christians and Social Democrats developed a mutual respect and a determination to work together in a post-Nazi state. Most of the leaders of this coterie, however, were executed by the Nazis late in the war. Immediately after the war the strong predilection of most Social Democrats throughout Germany was to make common political cause with the communists. Moreover, many emigré Social Democrats returned to Germany with the anticlerical sentiments of the pre-1933 period. The sum result was that, while a residue of sympathy among some Christian laymen and theologians and a few Social Democrats remained, the SPD in effect closed the door on Christian laity and adopted a strongly anticlerical tone.

Probably no major European political party committed as many tactical errors in the postwar period as did the SPD, and its failure—or inability—in 1945 formally and explicitly to renounce its Marxist doctrine must count as its supreme mistake. This is not because, as has sometimes been maintained, a Labor party of Protestants, Catholics, and non-Marxist Social Democrats would have been formed instead of the CDU. Although this idea enjoyed some popularity, particularly among Catholic trade union circles in Berlin and the Ruhr, it never had a real chance of success. Social Democrats, such as Wilhelm Leuschner and Julius Leber, who might have supported a party of this sort were executed in connection with the July 1944 plot. After the war the surviving leaders were completely unreceptive to the approaches of Jakob Kaiser, the chief proponent of the idea.

Yet even had their reaction been entirely favorable, it is highly doubtful that Kaiser would have been able to carry many nonsocialists with him. The notion of a worker's party did not figure in Hermes' scheme of things, and the majority of the Berlin group inclined to Hermes rather than to Kaiser. Kaiser might nevertheless have attempted to establish such a party in the British zone, where his influence in Catholic workers' circles was enormous. But a record exists of a conference of Catholic church and lay leaders held in the Ruhr on June 18, 1945 and this shows the unlikelihood of his success:

> The views of the group were deeply divided. The vast majority favored a Christian People's Party. . . . Only such a party grouping could constitute a strong enough dam against communism. In a party with

socialists, the Christian workers would be condemned to an insignificant minority. All influential positions would be held by socialists. The example of the English Labour Party is not relevant to the decision. . . . How would such a unified party treat educational and ecclesiastical matters— as, for instance, the question of confessional schools? In addition, there is the question of the condition our country will find itself in after the withdrawal of occupation forces. East of the Elbe, it would probably not be a Christian state. But that would be precisely the great opportunity for a Christian party. So far it has not been possible to find enthusiasm for a unified party among Catholic workers. [1]

But though a Christian Democratic party would have been founded even had the SPD been less doctrinaire, Social Democratic ideology did have an important quasireligious impact. While the party's philosophy was no stumbling block to most Protestants inclined to socialism, it was an insurmountable barrier to Catholics, including Catholic trade unionists, such as Karl Arnold. Even Catholics who considered the CDU too conservative went their own political way by forming the Zentrum. For Protestants the door to the SPD, unlocked in the 1920s by Barth and Tillich, was ajar and would open completely in the course of a decade after the war. Their decisions were individual ones, based on political preference. But as long as Catholics formed a self-conscious and disciplined group and the hierarchy was radically opposed to the SPD, the existing gulf was too wide for the faithful to cross, whatever their political views. The competition for the loyalty of left-wing Catholics and Catholic workers was therefore not between the SPD and the CDU (which had increasingly little to offer them), but between the SPD and the Catholic church. The church won this contest because the party made no attempt to narrow the psychological and doctrinal gap. As a consequence, and in defiance of normal political rules, Catholic worker support went to the CDU and became what Jakob Kaiser in 1950 could legitimately acclaim as "the most loyal bloc of voters in the Union". [2] In this way the CDU avoided becoming a class party while the SPD could not secure even the support of all the workers, trade unionists, and leftist intellectuals.

The further consequence of the SPD's inability to part with Marxist

---

1. "Protokoll der Konferenz vom 18.6.45," in *Sitzungsprotokolle 1945,* Archives of the Westphalia-Lippe CDU, Dortmund. The meeting, probably held in the town of Wattenscheid, was convened and chaired by Monsignor Caspar Schulte, the head of Catholic workers' groups in the diocese of Paderborn. By July 2 the group decided in principle against cooperation with socialists and in favor of an interconfessional party, on the ground that a Christian party would best meet the demands of the time and that agreement with socialists on educational and ecclesiastical issues would not be possible.

2. "Sozialausschüsse der christlich-demokratischen Arbeitnehmerschaft," *Essener Kongress 1950 der christlich-demokratischen Arbeitnehmerschaft* (undated).

dogma was that it prejudiced the party's attitude toward the churches in a way that antagonized church leaders and long prevented any real understanding between the two sides. Although the SPD's complexion varied from area to area—in predominantly Catholic areas it was relatively conservative—there was everywhere an antichurch bias. In Berlin, Hesse, and areas of northern Germany this attitude was quite pronounced in the early postwar period. It was this that pushed some Protestant bishops—such as Dibelius—who wanted to be politically neutral into the arms of the CDU. And it was this that strengthened the resolve of the Catholic bishops to fight the SPD with all the means at their disposal.

The SPD's ranks included party workers who neither believed nor practiced the socialist dictum of the private nature of religion. To them, Social Democracy and Christianity were mutually exclusive, and a believing Christian was unacceptable for party position or for nomination to elective office. While the national party leadership was immune from such intolerance, it had no appreciation either for the churches' point of view or for their social and political importance in postwar Germany. Schumacher never tired of assuring the churches that they were in no political danger. In his view this should have extinguished all their anxieties. But for churchmen it was cold comfort to be told that the Kirchenkampf begun by the Nazis would not be continued by the Social Democrats. Schumacher also thought he was being quite conciliatory when he wrote in 1945 and later often repeated:

> It makes no difference whether someone becomes a Social Democrat through the methods of Marxist economic analysis, for philosophical or ethical reasons, or through the spirit of the Sermon on the Mount. Everyone has . . . the same right in the party. Because of this respect for the individual and in the interest of the common good, it is necessary for the Social Democratic Party to be neutral and independent toward every church and ideology.[3]

For the SPD in 1945 this may have been going very far, but it also missed the point. The key issue was whether the SPD was prepared to grant the churches the role in German social and political life which church leaders had every intention of playing after their experiences in the Third Reich. This Schumacher and his party had no thought of doing; they could not even comprehend the churches' point of view. To them, the churches were simply part of the old order, with an instinctive tendency toward reaction. Indicative was Schumacher's warning to the churches, contained in his "Appeal" to the

---

3. "Aufruf," quoted in Scholz and Oschilewski (editors), *Turmwächter der Demokratie*, pp. 44–45.

German people in the summer of 1945, not to become associated with the CDU. "It is precisely the Nazis and reactionaries who for better or worse want to keep what they have in hand and who would as gladly camouflage this under the term 'Christian' as they previously did under the term 'national,' " he noted.[4] The prevailing party view was even more skeptical; it was expressed in a typical way by Willi Eichler, the party's "ideologue," at the first postwar party congress in May 1946:

> A word about Christianity. We must also be clear what we mean when we say—quite correctly—that it is possible to become a socialist through the spirit of the Sermon on the Mount. But we must also be clear that no less a person than Karl Marx described "religion as opiate of the people" and no less a person than August Bebel said: Christianity and Socialism have the same relationship as fire and water. These two socialists, however, certainly wrote no gospel. We only need to be clear what we think about this today. This is also necessary from a propaganda point of view.
>
> For the clarification of Military Government, something else is necessary in this connection. There is a widespread superstition in Military Government that the church is merely a religious institution, having nothing to do with politics. There can be no more false view than this. If there is any tightly organized, stable body which survived the war and National Socialism and which supports reaction and even to some extent nationalist reaction, that, in Germany at any rate, is the church.[5]

Schumacher was blinded from seeing—much less coming to terms with—the ecclesiastical factor in the postwar political equation. It would never have crossed his mind to try to reach a compromise with the Catholic church on, for instance, the school issue, even for tactical political advantage. This attitude delineates a major difference between him and Adenauer. The latter was no more prepared than Schumacher to take political advice from the churches, but he recognized that it would be better to have them behind him than against him. Adenauer was no proponent of confessional schools; but he was willing to handle this and other Catholic interests pragmatically, unimpeded one way or the other by party dogma. It was just this difference that assured Adenauer the support of the Catholic church and the Catholic voter. When this trend became apparent in 1949, Schumacher was enraged. Noting the sizable role played by the Catholic church in the first Bundestag election, he rounded on the hierarchy and accused it of being "the fifth occupation

---

4. Scholz and Oschilewski, pp. 34–35.

5. *Protokoll der Verhandlungen des Parteitages der SPD vom 9. bis 11. Mai 1946 in Hannover* (1947) p. 107.

power." As reported in *The New York Times* on August 1, 1949, his statement included the revealing comment: "We have absolute understanding for all doctrines rooted in Christian ethics and morality. But we have no understanding for outspoken power politics exercised by ecclesiastical authorities."

"No understanding" of the churches' importance in public affairs was precisely the SPD's problem. This was still the case in 1954, when at the party conference Willi Eichler declared that churchmen had no right to give binding political advice, since they could be as politically mistaken as anyone else. He cited as an example the "sympathy which fascism enjoyed among many clergymen and in part still enjoys today." Clergymen, he stated, had the right to express their political opinions, but if they did so, they risked "making the pulpit an instrument of politics"[6]–a view shared by the National Socialists and doubtless as repugnant to a Niemöller as to a Frings. Eichler, who was later one of the main proponents of better relations with the churches, admitted candidly in an interview that until 1959 the SPD did not know how to come to grips with its problem with the churches and was not even able to be a serious interlocutor with them.

The two churches had almost diametrically opposed attitudes toward Social Democracy after 1945. Decisive for German Protestantism was the policy inaugurated at Treysa. This not only established the neutrality of the Evangelical church toward the political parties but also promised its cooperation with all political and social institutions in establishing a strong democratic state. No church leader, whatever his personal political leanings, regarded the SPD's philosophy or program as unacceptable in principle. Indeed, the Evangelical church was anxious to have laymen in all the major parties, on the ground that this was salutary for the parties and for the church. For these reasons and in order to try to establish some contact with Protestant workers, most Protestant bishops made a conscious effort at the end of the war to establish a friendly working relationship with Social Democratic leaders. Even as conservative a church leader as Bishop Meiser, for instance, was convinced that the church had neglected its responsibility to the workers and believed that only as it broke with its bourgeois outlook would it have any chance of reaching them. Meiser personally inclined to the CSU, where he found greater sympathy for church interests than in the SPD, but he established and maintained good relations with Wilhelm Hoegner, the Bavarian SPD leader and minister president (1945–1946 and 1954–1957). In short, with the Evangeli-

---

6. *Protokoll der Verhandlungen des Parteitages der SPD vom 20. bis 24. Juli 1954 in Berlin* (1954), p. 159.

cal church's official neutrality, the practical relationship between the SPD and Protestants was largely a matter between each provincial church and the local SPD. In due course and for the first time in German history some church leaders (such as Wilm, Held, Scharf, and occasionally Niemöller) became open SPD sympathizers, though none of them ever joined the party. Only a few churchmen (such as Dibelius) remained consistently cool to the SPD—both out of personal conservative leanings and in reaction to the party's anticlericalism in their areas. Even in these cases, however, the provincial church administration and the synod included many strong SPD sympathizers.

In the light of this situation, the SPD's relationship to the Evangelical church was of little interest to party leaders on the national level. It was the prosocialists in the church who were determined to bring the two sides closer together. These persons were for the most part disciples of Karl Barth—theologians such as Helmut Gollwitzer, Hans-Joachim Iwand, Ernst Wolf, Heinrich Vogel, and Karl Kupisch. Behind them was a sprinkling of pastors who were drawn to the SPD because of its concern for the workers and the poor. Together they wanted a "socially conscious" church and were not offended by the Social Democrats' philosophy or materialist approach. They rejected, and deeply resented, the CDU's appropriation of the term "Christian" for itself and its policies. In time they bitterly opposed the domestic and especially the foreign policy course of the Adenauer government. As early as July 1947 Niemöller and Iwand arranged for Protestant leaders (including all the members of the council of the Evangelical church) to meet with a number of prominent Social Democrats. At this session the churchmen made it clear that the Evangelical church recognized its past failures, was determined to follow a progressive social course, and wanted to "undertake a fundamental revision in its relationship to Social Democracy." Schumacher, significantly not going beyond the position he enunciated in 1945, was reported to have responded that the SPD and the church were no longer enemies and that "Ratio and religio are no longer polar opposites." Although Schumacher described the meeting as one of the finest experiences of his life and Niemöller as his "greatest day since leaving the concentration camp," neither side met again until Niemöller and his anti-Adenauer friends discussed the rearmament controversy with Schumacher in October 1950.[7] On neither occasion did Schumacher pursue the matter and try to cultivate Protestant support. So long as the Evangelical church would not fight the SPD, he was content to ignore it.

---

7. Schumacher in *Rhein-Neckar Zeitung,* July 26, 1947, quoted in Scholz and Oschilewski, p. 133. Niemöller quoted by Iwand in an interview.

The important consideration from the political point of view was that no impediment existed, as far as the Evangelical church was concerned, to support the SPD—almost the contrary. Since Protestants had never been politically allied to any party, the church's position probably had only marginal influence on Protestant political behavior. The novelty of the situation lay in the fact that prominent laymen and some clergymen began to join the SPD. Since two-thirds of the SPD's voters were Protestant, these men could draw on significant support. On the Land level they soon achieved important positions in SPD governments. In the Bundestag a small Protestant SPD wing began to develop around such persons as Adolf Arndt, Ludwig Metzger, Wilhelm Mellies and Hans Merten (a pastor who took a leave of absence to stand for the Bundestag). This trend was strongly reinforced by the entry of Heinemann and his friends from the All-German People's party, some of whose younger members rose quickly in the party—such as Erhard Eppler, who became minister for development aid in 1969, and Johannes Rau, who became SPD floor leader in the North Rhine-Westphalia parliament in 1966. This was capped, in a way, in the mid-1950s, when Herbert Wehner reentered the Evangelical church and even became an occasional lay preacher in St. Michael's Church in Hamburg.

The same period saw the emergence of a remarkable coincidence of views over important domestic and defense issues between the SPD and the Evangelical church (these are observed in other chapters). Where the SPD and the CDU were at odds, the Evangelical church found itself more often than not on the side of the Social Democrats. Where the two churches differed, the SPD was usually on the same side as the Protestants. In these ways relations between the Evangelical church and the SPD steadily improved through the 1950s, and a dramatic reconciliation never became necessary. It had often been said that the Protestant Social Democrats were no more representative of the SPD than the socialist Protestants were of the Evangelical church. But by the end of the 1950s not only was a strong friend of the SPD, Bishop Scharf, chairman of the council of the EKD, but Protestants such as Arndt, Heinemann, Metzger, Mellies, Helmut Schmidt, Fritz Erler, and Wehner were all members of the SPD federal executive board. With Erler as the party's foreign policy expert, Schmidt as defense policy expert, and Wehner as the strongest influence in the party, the SPD had slipped into the hands of active Protestant laymen.

For nearly two decades after the war the Catholic church expressed profound suspicion and hostility toward the SPD. Indeed, fear of Social Democracy was the dominant political sentiment of the Catholic bishops after 1945. They anticipated that the SPD would show no understanding for the Catholic position on the school issue. It would not want to give the churches a broad role in social and political affairs. And it would neither heed social encyclicals nor recognize the sanctity of private property.

The bishops' initial suspicions proved largely justified. The SPD was dogmatic in its opposition to confessional schools, considering them a divisive force in society and a source of intentional and unintentional indoctrination that was ideologically stultifying and politically anti-SPD. The Social Democrats were also of the view that the state should be neutral toward all social institutions and therefore saw no reason to give the churches a privileged position. In Länder where the SPD was in power in the early postwar period, the constitutions provided—either in word (as in Bremen) or in spirit—for a separation of church and state. Church taxes and in most cases state subsidies to the churches were maintained, but in decisions on the Land and local level—on whether, for instance, to build a "secular" hospital or enlarge Catholic and Protestant ones, whether to dispense certain monies through governmental offices or church lay organizations, and whether to support a community public library or Catholic and Protestant parish libraries—the SPD usually decided in favor of the state. Finally, after the war the SPD enacted nationalization legislation in North Rhine-Westphalia which only failed of implementation because of an Allied veto.

For these reasons the Catholic church and the SPD were completely at odds over an important range of issues from the outset of the postwar period. These differences were not new. It was Germany's situation in 1945 that made the bishops obsessively frightened of the party. The SPD was the only political party apart from the communists to survive the Third Reich. It appeared to stand a good chance of dominating German politics for a long time. The hierarchy, moreover, still looked at the country as a whole, and with Germany as far as the Elbe in the control of Russians bearing communism, it was braced for a wave of radical socialism throughout the country. The bishops' fears were still further inflamed by British favoritism toward the SPD and the American underestimate of the danger of the political left. The bishops were deeply concerned by the assessments of their political counsellors, who foresaw the possibility of economic and social chaos which might lead to political extremism of the most dangerous sort.

These considerations caused the hierarchy in 1945 to mount a full-scale campaign against the Social Democrats and to support a political union of Protestants and Catholics. The church's resultant total commitment to the CDU and its largely successful efforts to bind the Catholic faithful to the party turned the Catholic church into the purely political foe of the SPD. Inevitably Social Democrats viewed the CDU and the Catholic church as almost a single target. Schumacher became as suspicious as Niemöller of the

Catholic church, and for essentially the same reasons. In an election speech in 1949 he cited Cardinal Frings by name and warned against continued ecclesiastical interference in party politics. "Christianity is not in danger in Germany," he insisted: "Never in the past 100 years has the Church been so strong as it is today." Embittered by the election outcome, he accused the bishops of having seduced voters away from the SPD and over to the CDU, adding, "We have the impression they would like to make a second Spain in Germany." Later he opposed the inclusion of the Federal Republic in a Western European federation because it would establish a "conservative, clerical, capitalist and cartellist" Europe.[8] This line of thought was echoed by his successor as SPD chairman, Erich Ollenhauer, who argued that Germany should only join a European defense community if it included Protestant countries such as Denmark, Norway, and Britain. Even when it was unnecessary to his point, Schumacher could not resist taking a swipe at the Catholic church. Socialism is no dogma, he once said, for instance; it requires neither a Politburo nor a Holy Office.

The antipathy between the SPD and the Catholic church was thus a cumulative and self-reinforcing process. In the course of time relations between them became, if anything, worse. Even though the SPD had dropped its demand for broad nationalization by 1952; though it financed Catholic schools liberally on a private basis in some Länder (such as Hamburg); and though it did not harm the confessional school systems when it came to power in Bavaria and North Rhine-Westphalia in the 1950s; foreign and defense issues then took the party and the church even further apart. Pope Pius' fervent anticommunism and his view of Germany as the fulcrum of the East-West conflict were fully shared by the German hierarchy and, as already noted, dominated the political outlook of the bishops during the fifteen years after the war. Consequently the SPD's policy on rearmament, conscription, and nuclear arms was in the bishops' view not only politically wrong and militarily dangerous, but also theologically mistaken. The hierarchy's attitude was well expressed by a priest who said, "If Adenauer followed the foreign policy of Ollenhauer and Ollenhauer the foreign policy of Adenauer, I would consider myself bound in conscience to vote for Ollenhauer—despite the school policy of the SPD"[9]

The hierarchy therefore did not merely support the CDU, it actively

---

8. *The New York Times,* July 25, 1949; *Manchester Guardian*, August 31, 1949; Klaus Schütz, "Die Sozialdemokratie im Nachkriegsdeutschland," in Lange, Schulz, and Schütz, *Parteien in der Bundesrepublik*, p. 255.

9. Quoted in Kafka (editor), *Die Katholiken vor der Politik,* p. 141.

fought the SPD. At election time the bishops' pastoral letters coupled advice to vote for the CDU with the admonition that the SPD was not a party that a Catholic could in conscience support. Although the election appeals became increasingly explicit, the bishops themselves normally shunned actually using the party's title. Twice, however, Catholics were warned away from the SPD by name. While Bishop of Würzburg, Döpfner stated in a New Year's Eve sermon in 1952 that friends of Christ could not vote for the KPD, the SPD, or the FDP. In June 1957 Bishop Keller of Münster declared in a speech to the KAB (the Catholic worker's movement) that he had often been asked whether a believing Catholic could vote for the SPD and whether a member of the KAB could belong to the party. He said he considered this a "genuine matter of conscience and by no means a question of purely political judgment." Despite the good intentions of many Social Democrats, he went on, the SPD both lacked a natural-rights basis and had followed policies (on schools, civil marriage, and family matters) contrary to those favored by the Catholic church. He continued, as reported in *Deutsche Tagespost* on June 18-19, 1957:

> The question that has been raised—"May a Catholic worker—indeed, any believing Catholic—reconcile it with his conscience to vote Social Democratic? Or, is it consistent to be active in the Social Democratic Party and at the same time remain a member of the KAB?"—must be answered with an unequivocal "no." For the present and for our area, the assertion of *Quadragesimo anno*—"It is impossible to be at the same time a good Catholic and a true Socialist"—still remains valid.

In the campaign atmosphere of that summer, this statement caused a minor sensation, particularly in conjunction with a statement by Archbishop Jäger of Paderborn made a few days earlier which criticized Catholics for indolence, fatigue, and cowardice for their talk about coexistence and tolerance of non-Catholic groups. The two pronouncements together created the impression of a reactionary hierarchy spoiling for an ideological crusade. In reality, however, the churchmen's motives were somewhat more defensive than offensive. In the preceding February the FDP and SPD had united to bring down North Rhine-Westphalia's CDU government headed by the prominent Catholic layman, Karl Arnold, and this deeply angered the bishops of the Land. To add insult to injury, the new socialist-liberal government became fairly popular; it confounded the Catholic church's dire predictions that an ecclesiastical calamity would result from such a regime when it signed an agreement with the Papal Nuncio establishing a new diocese of Essen (the main purpose of which, according to CDU sources, was to fight socialism in the RUHR). In the preceding summer's local elections, moreover, there had been a serious defection of Catholic workers to the Social Democrats. Now, with the approaching elections to the Bundestag, the CDU persuaded Bishop Keller to fire a broadside that would teach the SPD a lesson and keep Catholic workers in the CDU camp. The result was, as *The Times* of June 5, 1957, gravely remarked, to give the election campaign "religious undertones, reminiscent in some degree of the old Kulturkampf."

Not every member of the hierarchy approved either of the matter or of the manner of Bishop Keller's intervention. Far from settling the issue for good, the 1957 pronouncement confronted Catholics squarely with the ambiguity of their church's position on postwar European social democracy. That the church did not like the SPD for practical, political reasons was obvious. But whether this was a dogmatic position, binding upon a Catholic, remained uncertain. Father Gundlach, along with Oswald von Nell-Breuning, the principal author of *Quadragesimo anno,* firmly insisted after the war that the 1931 encyclical remained fully applicable to the SPD and that any Catholic who supported the party did so either in ignorance or in violation of the church's teachings. With his usual intellectual vigor, he rejected the counterargument that the SPD had evolved into a party like the British Labour party and was therefore open to Catholics. "For no papal document exists specifically recognizing the socialism of the English Labour party," he observed in 1958 before SPD leaders. "In fact, no papal document exists removing the socialism of the English Labour Party from the judgment of Pius XI"–i.e., *Quadragesimo anno.* [10] The central error of socialism was its liberalism, particularly its rejection of natural rights, and in this respect the SPD had not changed, he concluded. That the CDU was no less liberal than the SPD, Gundlach was the last to deny. In short, the church's position did in fact boil down to a tactical preference for the CDU over the SPD. Such an attitude was perfectly legitimate but, even in the church's own terms, not a matter of conscience. The ideological fiction had therefore to be maintained, though some bishops would have preferred doing so less ostentatiously than Keller.

A small group of Catholic outsiders–known collectively as "left Catholics"–had consistently resisted the hierarchy's position. The members of this group were, roughly speaking, the editors and "adherents" of two monthly publications, *Frankfurter Hefte* and *Werkhefte katholischer Laien,* along with a few theologians, such as von Nell-Breuning. Their general line of argument was that the popes had condemned the atheism and arch-materialism of socialism and that, as the SPD had in practice altered its stand in these respects

---

10. "Katholizismus und Sozialismus," in *Christentum und demokratischer Sozialismus,* p. 23.

after the war, it was immune from papal condemnation. They believed that the SPD after 1950 favored economic and social objectives more consistent with the outlook of the Catholic church than any other party. Some of them even maintained that the SPD had an arguable case with respect to the school question. Most of all they insisted that the best way of creating understanding between the SPD and the Catholic church was for the bishops to stop bludgeoning the party and to establish contact with it.

However, the hierarchy (with the CDU's encouragement) followed a policy of total ostracism of the SPD. Bishops themselves shunned meetings with Social Democrats, and their occasional conferences with Catholic Bundestag and Landtag delegates in their diocese always excluded the few Catholic SPD members. For many years the hierarchy forbade the appearance of any priest or theologian at Social Democratic functions. As late as 1957, for instance, the committee of Social Democratic academicians held a meeting on the topic "Christianity and Politics"; while the participants included Gerhard Jacobi, the Protestant bishop of Oldenburg, not a single Catholic clergyman would attend.

Secretly, however, meetings between a small number of Social Democrats and Catholic theologians began to take place shortly after the war. These were held with the knowledge of the leaders of the party and the church. Secrecy was a precondition from the Catholic side, but the SPD was no less anxious to keep its left-wing anticlericalists in the dark. The theologians were the Walberberg Dominicans, such as Welty and Siemer, and—later on—the Frankfurt Jesuits, including von Nell-Breuning and Hirschmann. These churchmen did not want to see the SPD in power, and they had helped to establish the CDU in 1945; but they were critical of the capitalist, liberal bourgeois order and were in sympathy with the social aims of the SPD. They felt that, by keeping a channel open between the party and the church, some measure of practical understanding might be reached, differences might be kept from exploding into corrosive public attacks, and a gradual reform in Social Democracy might be set in train.

The first meeting took place in January 1946 at Walberberg between Schumacher, Eichler, Welty, and Siemer. The session, at which Schumacher made it clear that he rejected Marxist ideology, went well, and a second one was planned for a discussion of the school problem and nationalization. However, both sides felt they had already gone further than their "rank and file" would like, and therefore the second meeting was cancelled. Early in the 1950s the meetings were resumed and became increasingly frequent. The regular participants included Welty, Hanssler, and Böhler from the Catholic side and Eichler, Heinz Kühn (later minister president of North Rhine-Westphalia), and Walter Seuffert (later vice-president of the federal constitutional court) from the SPD. The attendance of Böhler, who was adamantly against any rapprochement with the SPD, guaranteed that the talks would have limited practical consequences as far as the church was concerned. But the Walberberg talks are considered, especially by SPD leaders, to have been an indispensable step toward a modus vivendi. Through them misunderstanding and mistrust were removed, and the two institutions started down the road that eventually led to the concept of a partnership between the parties and the church in dealing with social problems. Since the death of Welty in 1961, the talks have been held primarily with Nell-Breuning, Hirschmann, and Wallraff.

"The Church will never change; the SPD will have to come into conformity with her doctrines"—Gundlach's statement in an interview summed up the general feeling of the hierarchy. The Social Democratic attitude was almost as unbending. Up to the late 1950s each wanted a solution essentially on its own terms. The first direct efforts to break out of this vicious circle were made by Karl Forster and Herbert Wehner. Monsignor Forster (then head of the Catholic Academy in Bavaria), like many another churchman, took a cold, hard look at the church's relationship to the CDU following the 1957 election and what appeared to be the dawn of an Erhard era. In connection with the Reichskonkordat litigation, this period also saw the beginning of a reassessment of the Catholic church's position in 1933, and this underscored the risks to the church of close involvement with a political party—a view endorsed by the bishops in 1945 and then quickly forgotten. Forster also considered the chairman of the CSU, Franz Josef Strauss, to be a travesty of a Christian politician. Moreover, he felt that Strauss wanted the church's support but would give nothing in return. Forster looked forward to the time when the Catholic church could be politically neutral, and he intended to do his best to hasten that moment. He established contact with Waldemar von Knoeringen (chairman of the Bavarian SPD and a deputy chairman of the national SPD) and a number of other Social Democrats. In 1958 the taboo on public meetings between Catholics and Social Democrats was broken when Forster (with the support of Cardinal Josef Wendel of Munich and against the strong opposition of Böhler and the CDU) arranged a meeting for fifty Social Democrats and fifty Catholic priests, theologians, and laymen. Although the event aroused a good deal of sharp criticism in church circles, it marked the first crack in the frozen relationship between the church and the party.

It was the SPD that made the next and more significant move toward peaceful coexistence. The party's successive failures at the polls demonstrated that the SPD was not offering the mass of the German electorate what was desired. It was doctrinaire in a pragmatic era; it appealed to the working class when this was disappearing; it was cut off from the middle class and, above all, from the Catholics. Until it could break into these ranks, it appeared destined never to get much more than one-third of the national vote. After each election defeat party workers gathered to press a new batch of sour grapes: the Christian Democrats had numbed the people with prosperity; they had fooled the people with a slick, American-type campaign; the Catholic church had enticed at least a million voters away from the SPD; and so on. Herbert Wehner finally decided that the CDU's and the church's actions were less important than what the SPD did for itself. He was determined to enter territory the party had left to the CDU—the middle class as a whole, and Catholics specifically. He recognized more clearly than most others in the party that this approach would involve not so much a change of party ideology as a "deideologization" of the party. He also saw that the central problem in the relationship between the SPD and the churches was not philosophical—if the Catholic church could swallow Professor Erhard's "Marktwirtschaft," it could swallow the pallid socialism of the SPD; rather it was the role the party intended to allow the churches in social and political affairs. Significantly enough, it was only when command of the party was in the hands of active Protestants that a campaign could be launched to reach a genuine understanding with the Catholic church.

Against the resistance of a small but stubbornly anticlerical group in the ranks, Wehner pressed ahead for a new party program. This was presented for adoption at a party conference in Bad Godesberg in 1959. The Godesberg program accomplished essentially two ends. It formally cut the party's ties with Marxism (neither "Marx" nor "Marxism" was even mentioned in the document), and it adopted a new attitude toward religion and the churches. The section on "Fundamental Values of Socialism" made it clear that Social Democracy was not in competition with Christianity as a philosophy of life:

> Democratic Socialism, which in Europe is rooted in Christian ethics, humanism and classical philosophy, does not proclaim ultimate truths— not because of any lack of understanding for or indifference to philosophical or religious truths, but out of respect for the individual's choice in these matters of conscience in which neither the state nor any political party should be allowed to interfere.

The section on "Religion and Church" then proclaimed:

> Socialism is no substitute for religion. The Social Democratic Party respects churches and religious societies. It affirms their public and legal status, their special mission and their autonomy.

It is always ready to co-operate with the churches on the basis of a free partnership. It welcomes the fact that men are moved by their religious faith to acknowledge their social obligation and their responsibilities towards society.

Freedom of thought, of religion and of conscience, and freedom to preach the gospel must be protected. Any abuse of this freedom for partisan or anti-democratic ends cannot be tolerated. [11]

Old-line socialists considered it bad enough to declare that Social Democracy was not an all-encompassing ideology; to advocate cooperation with the churches was going much too far. No other section of the program received so many objections. One outraged delegate remarked that oppressed Spanish workers knew what cooperation between church and state could mean in terms of social injustice. Referring to Ollenhauer's introductory comments on the SPD's new relationship to the churches, he added,

> When it is . . . stated that this is not a tactical formulation, I would just like to say: this is precisely the fear of many of us, that it is not just a tactical formulation but that it is to be put into practice. (Laughter) . . . What is in the final analysis at issue here . . . is that every step forward till now required a hard and often bloody fight against all religious power institutions. Knowing this, many members of our party are afraid that these things will be disregarded for the sake of transitory success.
>
> If I may express my own opinion, I fear that we will achieve nothing with concessions of this sort if we do not give practical proof that we are not prepared to give in to the hegemonic claims of various religious institutions. [12]

It was only thanks to Wehner's autocratic control of the conference and the able defense of the church provisions by their authors (Eichler, Heinemann, Arndt, and Metzger) that the section remained virtually intact and was approved—though against the largest number of opposition votes of any portion of the program.

While Protestant circles welcomed the program, the reaction of the Catholic church (to which it was principally addressed) varied, from cool to hostile. The hierarchy still felt psychologically bound to the CDU and remained

---

11. Social Democratic Party of Germany, *Basic Programme of the Social Democratic Party of Germany* (1959).

12. *Protokoll der Verhandlungen des ausserordentlichen Parteitages der Sozialdemokratischen Partei Deutschlands vom 13.–15. November 1959 in Bad Godesberg* (1959), p. 74.

in terror of standing alone in German society unprotected by a political praetorian guard. An SPD proclaiming its friendship for the churches threatened to undermine the basis of the Catholic opposition to the party. An SPD able to cut into the Catholic vote endangered not only the dominance of the CDU in German politics but also the dominance of Catholics in the CDU. With that, the church's whole postwar political tactic would come tumbling down. The main Catholic rebuttal, logically enough, was that the program was fraudulent. Gustav Kafka of the central committee of German Catholics wrote a vicious book, *Der freiheitliche Sozialismus in Deutschland*, to demonstrate this point and to warn Catholics against being taken in. "Marx without a Beard," was the way *Mann in der Zeit* (the organ of the Central Committee for Men's Religious Affairs) headlined a report on the draft program. The *Rheinischer Merkur* commented on February 19, 1960, "Salvation through Christ has no place in this program of self-redemption." Father Gundlach, not surprisingly, found original political sin in the program: "All in all the new 'humanitarian' socialism is the descendant of the laicism of the liberal bourgeoisie." His conclusion could not have been more crisp: "The good Catholic who wants to be a good socialist is in an objectively contradictory situation." [13]

Wehner and the SPD leadership refused to be deterred from their general course. Step by step they succeeded in neutralizing their Catholic critics. In terms of practical policies the Catholic church's two main differences with the SPD were on the school problem and foreign policy. In 1960 Wehner settled the foreign policy issue with one stroke in a remarkable speech before the Bundestag, associating the SPD with the tenets of Adenauer's foreign policy. The following year the Social Democratic government of predominantly Protestant Lower Saxony entered into negotiations with Bishop Keller of Münster, and following his death in the same year with the Papal Nuncio, regarding the school question. The outcome of these discussions was not simply an agreement, but a full-fledged concordat between the Land and the Vatican, the first such treaty since the Reichskonkordat. The concordat itself was suggested by the Land government and was pressed upon the Nuncio; its terms were so generous as to create some misgivings on the part of Protestant church officials and to set off riots by some non-Catholics in the Land. The concordat began:

> His Holiness Pope Paul VI and the Lower Saxony Minister President, who are united in the wish to strengthen and promote the relationship

---

13. "SPD-Kirche, Katholisch gesehen," *Politisch-Soziale Korrespondenz*, December 1959.

between the Catholic Church and Lower Saxony in a friendly spirit, have arrived at a solemn agreement through which the legal status of the Catholic Church in Lower Saxony ... will be strengthened and maintained.

According to the text in the *Frankfurter Allgemeine* on May 7, 1965, the treaty went on to guarantee Catholic religious holidays, undertook to establish a Catholic theological faculty at Göttingen University, promised to maintain the Land Catholic pedagogical college, guaranteed the maintenance of existing and the opening of new Catholic confessional schools, promised to employ Catholic teachers in proportion to Catholic students in nonconfessional schools, guaranteed Catholic religious instruction as a normal part of the curriculum in all public schools, promised generous financial support for Catholic private schools and adult education centers, undertook that radio programs would "not offend the religious feelings of the Catholic population," promised to collect church taxes and guaranteed a minimum annual financial subsidy of 3.25 million marks to the dioceses of the Land. The form of agreement, the wording of the opening paragraph, and the terms would have been unthinkable a mere half-dozen years earlier.

Another dramatic step was taken in 1964, when an SPD delegation was received by the Pope. The idea of such a meeting grew out of informal discussions and correspondence between Ludovico Montini, a member of the Italian Senate and brother of Pope Paul VI, and Ernst Paul, an SPD Bundestag member. Both were representatives at the Council of Europe, and at these Strassburg sessions they became friends. Montini was enthusiastic about the Godesberg program, which expressed much of his own point of view, and he strongly favored an improvement in relations between the SPD and the Catholic church. In November 1963 Paul secured Wehner's approval to pursue the subject with Montini, and early in December Montini said he thought it would be a good idea for the SPD to seek an audience with the Pope. The SPD executive committee approved the idea and in January dispatched Alexander Kohn-Brandenburg, a party official whose liaison activities with Italian Socialists and Social Democrats had given him the opportunity of cultivating contacts in the Vatican, to take soundings in Rome. Finding the reaction of the curia favorable, Kohn-Brandenburg returned to Bonn, and armed with an official letter signed by Wehner and addressed to the Papal State Secretary, he called upon the Papal Nuncio and requested him formally to recommend that the Pope receive an SPD delegation. The Nuncio refused, stating (according to Kohn-Brandenburg's report in an interview at the time) that he "could not recommend such a meeting in good conscience, since an audience would signify approval of what the SPD seeks and does." As grounds for his decision, Bafile cited the party's policy on schools, the Reichskonkordat, and the birth-control issue, as well as SPD press approval of Hochhuth's play *The Deputy* and criticism of the Godesberg program in the party ranks. With this veto, the formal SPD proposal had to be dropped.

Knowing, however, that the Vatican itself was willing to receive an SPD delegation, Kohn-Brandenburg took up the matter on a personal basis with his contacts in the curia. These officials indicated that the approach to the conservative Nuncio had been a blunder, but that they were prepared to try to revive the idea of a meeting with the Pope. By the end of February the Pope's assent to an audience had been secured. It was strictly understood that the party delegation would be small, that the Pope's remarks to the group would not be publicized, and that the meeting would be treated with extreme discretion and not played up for political purposes.

On March 4, 1964 an SPD delegation for the first time in history entered the Vatican. In a private audience with the Pope the delegation head, Fritz Erler, presented Paul VI with a copy of the Godesberg program and emphasized the party's desire for good relations with the Catholic church. The two also reportedly discussed European questions and the Berlin problem. Then, receiving the remainder of the delegation (Waldemar von Knoeringen, Kohn-Brandenburg, Peter Nellen, and Paul), the Pope read a brief address in German expressing his interest in the evolution of the SPD, praising its contribution to German economic and social life, and implying that the differences between the church and the SPD were in the past.

The delegation was extremely pleased with the Pope's statement, which, they felt, formally signified the party's acceptability to the Catholic church. Pope Paul doubtless realized that the meeting would make it impossible for the German hierarchy or the CDU any longer to claim that the Social Democrats were an atheist brotherhood, for whom Catholics could not in conscience vote. It is therefore logical to assume that the Pope deliberately sought to weaken the church's intimate association with the CDU and to foster some basis of understanding with the SPD. The Pope is believed to have been well aware of how the German church (and, indeed, the Vatican) had, because of its connections with the Center party, become involved in political developments in 1933, and he evidently wanted to avoid having ecclesiastical interests so tightly bound up with the destinies of a single party.

The general reaction of German Catholic circles and the CDU was much less dispassionate. The CDU press spokesman commented, "The CDU cannot tell the Holy Father whom he should receive"—a delicious remark, in view of the party's efforts to do exactly that through frantic appeals to the Vatican to cancel the meeting. For its part, the hierarchy took the unusual step of announcing through the Catholic news agency that "Church authorities in Germany were a party neither to the preparations for the audience nor to the attempts to prevent it at the last minute." The latter part of the remark was presumably intended to quash reports (which nevertheless have persisted) that representatives of Archbishop Schäufele of Freiburg and Bishop Leiprecht of Rottenburg flew to Rome to try to have the meeting cancelled. In any event, the matter had been handled by the Vatican and the SPD with such discretion that the German government, the German hierarchy, and the CDU did not learn of the meeting until the arrangements were absolutely firm. By then it was too late to alter the Pope's decision. [14]

The Vatican's liberality contrasted starkly with the German hierarchy's intransigence. If SPD leaders thought they would get the best robe and fatted calf due the prodigal son, they soon learned otherwise. Upon his return to Bonn, Erler was interviewed on television by a Catholic priest whose questions became so offensive that Erler felt compelled to break off the interview. The hierarchy's boundless skepticism came out in Cardinal Döpfner's May Day sermon of 1964 to Munich workers, as reported in dispatch 86 of the Catholic news agency on the same day:

> In the Godesberg program the party of democratic socialism has undoubtedly begun to build a bridge over the gulf that has always divided the church and socialism. . . . But, after thorough reflection, I think I must still say—without going into details—that the bridge is not usable, the gap is not at the moment closed.
>
> Much of the program is still unclear and definitely unsatisfactory. The view of many Catholics that the Godesberg program is already completely consistent with Catholic social teaching is scarcely convincing.
>
> It might also be mentioned that considerable doubt remains about a party that is so clearly based upon liberalism.

A short time later Brandt, as SPD chairman, wrote to both Bishop Scharf and Cardinal Frings (as de facto heads of the two churches) to propose a meeting for an exchange of views. While Scharf promptly accepted, Frings rejected the request on the ground that such an encounter would not be useful. He complained that the SPD had voted in the Bundestag against certain legislation of interest to the Catholic church, that the party's position on the school issue was still unsatisfactory, and that the (SPD-controlled) Berlin city government had given an award to Hochhuth.

---

14. The CDU's remark and the hierarchy response in *Katholische Nachrichten-Agentur,* dispatch 46, March 6, 1964.

To some extent the problem was that the Catholic church had—could have—no single leader like Herbert Wehner in its ranks single-handedly to cut through such churlish recalcitrance and cajole the hierarchy to accept the view that the church's long-range interest no less than the stability of German democracy required a substantial measure of conciliation between the two institutions and that the church would have to make its contribution to this. With their poorly developed sense of compromise the bishops saw no reason to settle for less than unconditional surrender. A polarization of political forces did not worry them. Indeed, political Catholicism in Germany owed its existence to a sense of external menace. It was therefore difficult for Catholic churchmen and lay leaders to part with their last great secular enemy. It was all the harder as a result of the emotional and institutional links of the church and its lay movement to the Christian Democrats. This consideration was in fact the unarticulated premise of an appeal by the 1966 plenary session of the central committee of German Catholics when secretary-general Friedrich Kronenberg called for a return to the time when the church, the lay movement and the CDU were fully allied. "It seems urgently necessary," he maintained, "for the hierarchy, the central committee and Catholic politicians together to find the ways and means." [15] The central committee's attempt to perpetuate the division between the German Catholics and the Social Democrats ignored all of the changes in the party—its clear acceptance of the CDU's foreign, defense and economic policies—along with the evidence—such as the Lower Saxon concordat and Erler's visit to the Vatican—that the party leadership meant what it said in the Godesberg program about cooperating with the churches. This was also to act as though the social encyclicals of Pope John XXIII and the general approach of the Vatican Council, to say nothing of the changes in German Catholicism and the CDU, had never occurred. More than a year before, Monsignor Forster had felt it necessary publicly to warn that Catholics were standing helpless before the changes in Social Democracy and that once the SPD translated these changes into policies "the traditional disapproval would then be insupportable". [16]

A warning of another sort undoubtedly meant even more to the bishops. One of the most remarkable and remarked upon results of the 1965 federal election was the SPD's breakthrough in Catholic areas. The party's greatest successes were precisely in strongly Catholic constituencies. In communities 50 percent or more Catholic, the SPD enjoyed an increase in its vote that was uniformly higher than its national average. In contrast to the significant Prot-

15. *Parlamentarisch-Politischer Pressedienst,* December 21, 1966.
16. *Katholische Nachrichten-Agentur,* October 16, 1965.

estant shift in that year to the Christian Democrats, unprecedented numbers of Catholics in industrial areas, large cities and, most surprisingly, in rural areas went over to the SPD. For the first time the Social Democrats received the votes of almost as many Catholics as Protestant workers. In the North Rhine-Westphalian election the following year, the SPD again achieved its greatest gains in strongly Catholic areas, averaging an almost 10 percent increase in industrial constituencies and as much as 7 percent in conservative rural Catholic communities. Since it was largely at the expense of the CDU, this represented a swing of almost 20 and 14 percent between the two large parties. Although no mass Catholic exodus from the CDU, this marked a watershed in the postwar development of the SPD. For Catholics of all classes the Social Democrats had now become *wählbar*—a party one could legitimately support (even if at this point one did not make the full step and vote for it). The shift was in fact sufficient to bring down the Christian Democratic Land government and ultimately the Erhard government in Bonn.

The advent of the grand coalition at the end of 1966, which to some extent presupposed a taming of the animosities between the Catholic church and the SPD, inaugurated a period of detente between the two. Catholic critics were unable convincingly to attack policies of SPD ministers without reputiating the conservative Catholic Chancellor. Even the school controversy which raged between 1966 and 1969 could not be turned against the Social Democrats. On the one hand Wehner effectively moderated Social Democratic reform proposals in North Rhine-Westphalia, Rhineland-Palatinate and Bavaria. On the other hand the CDU eventually jumped on the school reform bandwagon and in some cases even took it over. The hierarchy was as a result unable to condemn the benighted reds for a policy supported by *Christian* Democrats.

During this period formal contacts were established between ecclesiastical and party leaders. Beginning in 1965 regular meetings were held under the auspices of the Catholic Office between such figures as Bishop Tenhumberg, Monsignor Forster and Monsignor Hanssler on the one side and Wehner, Schmid, Leber and Eichler on the other. The meetings were privately described by both sides as a useful means of exchanging views and of grappling with outstanding practical differences, such as the school issue. Although the meetings were to some extent self-seeking—with the Social Democrats interested in partisan advantage and Tenhumberg in personal political influence—the talks destroyed the Christian Democrats' almost exclusive contact with the Catholic hierarchy and signaled the church's willingness to take a cautious step toward non-partisanship. One important agreement that is said to have emerged from these sessions—perhaps the only positive achievement—was an undertaking by the Social Democrats not to press for a reform of the church tax system in response to a promise that the Bishops' Conference would be neutral in the 1969 federal election.

As a cumulative result of ecclesiastical and political developments, there was by 1969 a new spirit in the Catholic church. Symptomatically, in June of that year, *Konradsblatt,* the weekly newspaper of the Archdiocese of Freiburg, commented that Catholics would vote in the forthcoming election for the Social Democrats if they believed their policies were better than those of the Christian Democrats. The paper added that the church would violate its apostolic mission if, for political reasons, it appealed to the faithful not to vote for a specific party. This was going too far for many bishops and in some dioceses priests were threatened with punishment if they joined or supported the SPD. For the first time, however, the hierarchy was formally neutral and issued no electoral guidance. As in 1965, and subsequent Land elections, the Social Democrats made further significant inroads into Catholic constituencies, this time gaining the votes of unprecedented numbers of the urban middle class. This breakthrough enabled the SPD for the first time in its history to get more than 40 percent of the vote in a German national election and for the first time since 1930 to form a government.

With the Catholic church now formally non-partisan, the Social Democrats began their term of office in 1969 with high hope of reaching a durable accommodation. The hierarchy appeared to be moving toward political neutrality, Catholic voters were shifting to the SPD, the central committee of German Catholics elected Georg Leber as its first Social Democratic member, and calls upon the Pope by SPD leaders were becoming almost routine. To prevent friction with the churches, government ministers were instructed to discuss any matter touching upon ecclesiastical interests with the Bonn representatives of the two churches. As a further measure Georg Leber, transport minister and lone Catholic of the Social Democratic ministers, established a small staff in his ministerial office to monitor the government's relations with the Catholic church. He himself devoted considerable time to speeches and meetings with Catholic groups to hammer home the theme that a good Catholic could be a Social Democrat and vice versa.

But as it turned out the period of the grand coalition was not a prelude to reconciliation but an interlude between periods of mutual misunderstanding, mistrust and occasional open clashes. It rapidly became clear that the psychological and organizational bonds between the CDU and the Catholic church and its lay movement were too firm to permit a disengagement of the two. Now as before Social Democrats were systematically excluded from the work of the central committee of German Catholics, the Catholic Office and many of the lay organizations. With the CDU still the steppingstone to political success, most Catholic lay leaders retained their vested professional and intellectual interest in maintaining and even widening the gulf between the church and the SPD. No longer shielded by coalition with the CDU, the SPD could now be attacked unreservedly for the first time since 1966. From the moment the new government was formed the Furies of the right-wing Catholic press lavished their invective upon what they regarded an illegitimate coalition. According to the *Deutsche Tagespost*, the formation of the new government was the first stage of the downfall of the West, while the *Rheinischer Merkur*, with more restraint if more ambiguity, predicted (in the headline with which it greeted the new government) "The Sell-Out Begins". Moreover, in forcing the CDU from office, the SPD-FDP coalition inevitably removed Catholics from positions of power. The normal bureaucratic reorganization, in fact extraordinarily mild by any standard, was described by some Catholic journals as an "anti-Christian blood-bath", while the Katholische Nachrichten-Agentur claimed that Christians in government were being " 'slaughtered' as in Nero's time". In view of the drastically different confessional composition of the two parties, a reduction of Catholics at high levels of government was as unintentional as it was inevitable. This did not make the new government any more palatable in Catholic circles.

Paradoxically the effect of the Social Democratic ascent to power was therefore to weaken rather than intensify the relationship between the SPD and the church. An unravelling process was soon underway. The SPD, as the self-proclaimed party of social justice, felt politically and philosophically obliged to make it a first order of business to correct the blatant incongruity between the antiquated German penal code and the contemporary attitude toward such matters as marriage and sexual conduct. In Europe as a whole, Protestant churches have generally favored liberal reform in this sphere while the Catholic church has fought any change. Legislation that was consequently unproblematic in Protestant northern Europe and rarely even attempted in Catholic southern Europe was bound to blow up into a first-class controversy in confessionally divided Germany. Partisan politics made it even more explosive. Social legislation that might have had a chance if introduced under the leadership of the Christian Democrats, thanks to the church's confidence in them, evoked infinite suspicion when proposed by the SPD. Thus in 1969 the grand coalition without much ado abolished penalties for adultery, blasphemy and homosexual offenses. Only a year later the Catholic bishops were up in arms at the new social-liberal coalition's plans to liberalize laws regarding divorce, abortion and "pornography". It was in fact a Catholic theme throughout Europe at this time, once well articulated by *L'Osservatore Ro-*

mano, that Social Democrats had unleashed upon Europe a wave of sexual libertinism. [17] The proposed divorce law, which followed years of study by a commission of jurists and which was fully supported not only by secular experts but by the Evangelical church's commission on marriage law, ran into immediate opposition. As it turned out the hierarchy had little trouble demolishing it. In a spirit of exuberant ecumenism and personal conservatism, Bishop Dietzfelbinger—to the consternation of the Protestant laity and many church officials—brought the council of the Evangelical church to support the general Catholic position. About the same time Herbert Wehner, appalled at the sight of the imminent collapse of the detente for which he had worked so long, launched a public attack on the draft law for its failure to give adequate weight to the views of the Catholic bishops. With both churches and his own party's parliamentary floor leader against him, justice minister Gerhard Jahn had no choice but to delete the key elements of his reform.

The growing tension between the government and the Catholic church exploded with an attack by the Vatican upon the German government of a violence unparalleled in the postwar period. On February 12, 1972 *L'Osservatore Romano* condemned the government's plan to permit abortion during the initial three months of pregnancy and likened the further proposal to permit voluntary sterilization for birth control purposes to Nazi schemes for sterilization and euthanasia. No sooner had the outraged German government's protest to the Nuncio brought some verbal softening of the Vatican's denunciation than Cardinal Höffner pronounced his own curse: any parliamentarian who should vote for the implementing legislation could not receive the vote of Catholics at election time. With this the cold war between the SPD and the Catholic Church was revived. Jahn, who had discussed his reform proposals with the hierarchy's representative, Monsignor Wöste, at least a dozen times, publicly complained that he had been victimized by slander and misrepresentation. The Association of Social Democratic Jurists accused the bishop of totalitarianism. The Catholic side countered by claiming that basic social values had been at stake and that the dispute between the two was an ideological and moral one.

By this time the Social Democratic detente policy was in ruins and the relationship between the two institutions was back to where it had been before 1965 if not before the adoption of the Godesberg program. What had gone wrong? The SPD had confronted an invidious choice: whether to follow

---

17. "Sexwelle, SPD und Vatikan; Zu einer Ausserung des Osservatore Romano," in *Frankfurter Allgemeine*, March 11, 1970.

Wehner's course and give priority to good relations with the Catholic church or to reform harsh and repressive laws at the risk of a clash with the Catholic church. Perhaps the cabinet never faced up to this issue in such stark form; perhaps it thought compromises could be reached and the dilemma evaded. But ultimately the Catholic church's social principles are incompatible with a liberal, secularized society and Catholic officials were to that extent right in maintaining that the dispute was not simply over certain legislation but rather who—church or parliament—should determine society's values. For the church it was therefore a critical battle, probably its last chance to prevent the final secularization of society. In the end the Social Democrats were bitter that, as they saw it, their efforts for a more humane, tolerant and progressive society had been frustrated by an inflexibly doctrinaire group which, allied to the political opposition, had used the reform for partisan political purposes. To church leaders the SPD's reform proposals amounted to a catalog of violations of Christian principles which made confidence in the government's intentions impossible and betrayed the party's Marxist origin.

In retrospect at appears probable that the confrontation could only have been avoided, reform achieved and detente between the SPD and the Catholic church maintained if (as Wehner had recommended) the grand coalition had been continued in 1969. From the CDU or the CDU and SPD together the Catholic bishops would have had no choice but to swallow the bitter medicine of social reform. A social-liberal coalition with a majority of twelve was in no position to have a show-down with the Catholic church. The relationship between the two was not nearly strong enough to stand a test of strength and as a consequence the armistice collapsed. The 1972 national election once again found the Catholic church openly allied with the Christian Democrats and if this alliance was now discreet it was only because greater frankness would have been counter-productive by splitting the Catholic ranks and provoking a minority to open partisanship on behalf of the SPD.

In sharp contrast to the Evangelical church which did its best after 1945 to promote the closest possible contact and understanding between Protestants and Social Democrat, the Catholic hierarchy, far from feeling any compulsion toward social reconciliation, continued to demand full acceptance of Catholic social principles as the price of good relations. This was yet another sign that the bishops were not too politically involved but too politically indifferent. They cared only for the narrow interests of the church rather than the broad interests of society—indeed they were congenitally unable to see that the two might clearly diverge. In this situation it is natural that as long as there is a party with which the church has organizational links and thereby at least the feeling of influence, the hierarchy is bound to favor that party over any other. Although the Catholic bishops have undoubtedly lost influence over the laity, they can, directly and by means of the Catholic lay movement, continue to exert political influence both through general conditioning and outright electoral guidance. With the Protestant vote now fairly stable and the difference in the strength of the SPD and CDU marginal, the Catholic middle class vote has become a critical element in any electoral situation. Given the church's generally assumed ability still to sway some Catholic voters, the hierarchy and its lay organizations may well be able to tip the electoral balance in the CDU's favor. However, while putting the SPD out of power may be to the church's short term advantage, this risks not only polarizing society but also radicalizing the SPD by supporting their extremist's claim that the approach of the Godesberg program is neither expedient nor authentic. The question is not whose social principles are right but whether the church may legitimately play a partisan role to achieve them. The answer will be of importance for the future of German democracy.

Conclusion

Jesus came to establish a spiritual kingdom on earth, one which in separating the theological system from the political system destroyed the unity of the state and produced those internal divisions which ever since have troubled Christian peoples.

... Since there have always been a prince and civil laws, the result of this division of power has been an unending conflict of jurisdiction which has made good government in Christian states thoroughly impossible; and no one has ever been able really to determine whether it is the ruler or the priest who must be obeyed.

The Social Contract

THROUGHOUT most of the postwar era—and, indeed, the course of modern history—the dilemma stated by Rousseau had a central relevance to German political life. At the present time it has almost none. During much of the quarter-century after the war the churches played a major role in political affairs. By 1970 they were merely one of a number of actors on the stage, little more than a pressure group. In 1945 the churches, as the only institutions to survive the Third Reich, stood at one of the pinnacles of their prestige and influence. Yet by the mid-1950s many Protestant theologians were already troubled by the prospect that the churches, having just withstood National Socialism, would succumb to the more subtle menace of a materialistic society. Today some German Jesuits publicly assert that, since believing Christians have become a tiny minority, Germany has already ceased to be a Christian nation.

Between 1945 and the present one of the most important changes in German history occurred. Traditional social attitudes and political patterns disintegrated. The positive ideological nature of German political life dissolved, and the parliamentary system took on the image of Anglo-American liberal democracy, with all its strengths and weaknesses. The party system came to be completely dominated by two great groupings, practical coalitions in themselves, less and less divided from one another. Pragmatism and stability increasingly characterized the entire political scene. The individual, with new emotions and a new attitude toward the world, felt more concern for national prosperity than for national power. While these changes were part of a phenomenon occurring throughout Western Europe after 1945, in Germany they were especially marked because the psychological distance covered was greater. Political concepts that entered English political philosophy with Hobbes and French thinking with Montesquieu replaced the Hegelian outlook of the Germans only after the collapse of the Third Reich.

In the process, German society became secularized, and the confessional element in German political and social life steadily diminished. Popular ideals were no longer, consciously or unconsciously, otherworldly but were concentrated on immediate human satisfaction. When ecclesiastical views differed from those of the government, the church could no longer successfully raise a prior claim to allegiance, since politicians were increasingly disinclined to treat church interests or their own religious views as relevant to their political decisions. The concept of religion and politics, church and state, as two spheres competing for the loyalty of the citizen and the politician practically disappeared. Although stronger than ever in formal legal terms, the church lost a controlling influence over popular attitudes and with that its commanding position in society. The end of the post-Reformation era thus strangely coincided with the end of the post-World War II era.

This radical reorientation of German political and social life was both cause and consequence of a gradual but revolutionary change in the way the Germans thought and acted about their society. Prior to 1933 popular political and social conceptions, even though in many important respects liberal and thoroughly democratic, were basically inclined toward the utopian, the authoritarian, and the ideological. In party terms this was as true of the communists and Social Democrats on the left and the conservatives and fascists on the right as of the Center party in the middle. After the war the view spread that political life should be a matter not of millenial, ideological principles or of a struggle for a perfect society, but of compromise, cooperation, and the acceptance of politics as, in Aristotles's apothegm, a practice of the second-best. At the same time it was recognized that the political integration rather than the exclusion of important social groups and a broad agreement on a minimum rather than a maximum catalog of the ends of society was what were required for a workable democracy. This change of outlook—which boiled down simply to an acceptance of the essential tenets of liberal democracy—was the key that opened the door to the only successful period of self-government in German history. Without this development, it is impossible to calculate how German political life would look today. Now Germany, in its free part, has at last joined the mainstream of Western democracy, and it is difficult to believe that it will ever again break away. The great flaw in German political behavior—the inability satisfactorily to manage power—appears to have been corrected.

To some extent this development grew quite naturally out of the general postwar mood: the widespread determination to avoid the corrosive, divisive politics of the Weimar Republic, the popular revulsion from all-encompassing social philosophies, the aversion to nationalism, and the general attraction to pragmatic politics of the Anglo-American sort. But the central element was the radical change of approach by those institutions professing a broad social philosophy—the political parties and the churches—and the manner in which each, acting and reacting upon one another, to some extent fostered and directed this evolution even while to some extent resisting and only reluctantly adjusting to it. That this process involved a greater change and a greater sacrifice on the part of the Catholic church and the Social Democratic party than of other bodies—and that these two would be the major adversaries in the evolution of events—was inevitable. They were the two institutions most ideologically committed to a specific social creed and least inclined to compromise with those who did not share it.

Echoing Rousseau, Leonard Woolf, in *After the Deluge,* maintained that democracy and Christianity are in practice incompatible, since the one is concerned with human happiness in this world while the other is devoted to salvation in eternity and consequently indifferent to just government. Though some branches of Protestantism were the handmaiden of democracy in England and the United States, the record of Christian churches as a whole tends to support Woolf's contention. In the case of Germany the two churches—however impressive their intellectual and cultural contribution to the life of the nation—have in the course of history on balance been more of an obstacle than an encouragement to democratic developments. At any given point they gave precedence to social stability, property and personal rights over political liberalism and liberal constitutionalism. How has the balance looked since 1945?

Liberal democracy requires the general acceptance of certain political premises and procedures: tolerance, pluralism, compromise, and cooperation. For all its internal bickering over political issues, the Evangelical church generally did all that any church could have done to contribute to the development of these characteristics in German public life. At the war's end conservative Lutherans no less than liberal Calvinists faced up to the church's reactionary, Erastian, and authoritarian past and reversed course. Together they actively worked for good relations with all democratic parties and, directly and through the various bodies they established, cultivated ties with the trade unions and other important social groups which they had previously ignored. They urged their laity to participate in politics and encouraged such activity in all the parties dedicated to the democratic order. The church itself took a stand on every issue of domestic and foreign significance without ever compromising its basic political neutrality. It exercised independent judgment of the government's policies, did not shrink from disagreeing with them, and in fact at times advocated a course that differed from Adenauer's policies toward the East and in defense affairs. Through its synodal meetings, academies, church assemblies, and countless informal meetings at all levels, the church sought to awaken lay interest in public affairs. Protestant lay activities became virtual training institutes for self-government. Everything the church did was directed toward social conciliation, understanding, and cooperation. This was the opening wedge that eventually cracked the barrier between Christians and non-Christians in German society generally and between the churches and Social Democracy specifically. This approach also harbored the seeds of an attitude that eventually blossomed into broad support for the Ostpolitik. The Evangelical church was a major contributor to the conditions and practices that have made liberal democracy a success in Germany.

Where the Evangelical church fell short was in determining what role it would itself play in the political process. Given the nature of Protestantism and the structure of the Evangelical church, there was never any real chance that the church would speak with a single, strong voice—much less be a decisive power—in German political life. In any case, torn between those Lutherans, like Meiser, who thought the church should not become involved in specific issues, and the disciples of Barth who wanted it to be an active, partisan force, the church could never go beyond the vague consensus that it had to play a role, without ever being able to decide how or how much of one. As a result, the church more and more abdicated the direct and substantive role which it might have played even within Protestant bounds.

A further consequence was to leave a good deal of confusion in the minds of many Protestants over how a Christian should relate his religion to day-to-day political problems. The old-fashioned Lutherans, as politically passive as ever, could contribute nothing to a clarification of the question. The Niemöller-Heinemann group may have done as much harm as good. Although they occasionally forced their church as a whole to face up to and take a position on some issues it might have preferred to ignore, essentially they worked against the very political conciliation to which the church as a whole was dedicated. Whatever strength there may have been to the point that their views acted as a useful corrective to the general complacency of German public opinion in the 1950s, opposition for opposition's sake is otiose. And so it proved in this case.

For the Catholic church the problem was how to find its way, not into, but out of active politics. Since it was plain to most bishops—as to virtually all Catholic politicians—that political Catholicism had failed in 1932 and 1933, the majority of the hierarchy was determined that the church should not again become directly involved in politics. But whether through the force of tradition, an exaggerated fear of communism and socialism, or the prompting of Pope Pius XII, the bishops were no less intent than ever to be a decisive force in the state. This basic contradiction between their doctrinal claim to a role in political affairs and their own practical inhibition from playing one was a principal mark of postwar German Catholicism. In practice it amounted to trying to exercise political influence while pretending not to. The church tried to evade the contradiction by riding two horses at the same time, though in the end it fell between them. On the one hand it decided against reviving the Center party, enjoined priests from open political activity, and refrained from specifically endorsing the Christian Democrats. On the other hand it tried to mobilize the laity into a political army, aligned itself unqualifiedly with the CDU, and tried to transform practical politics into a struggle over ultimate, ideological values. In the end its tactics undermined its strategy.

The church's fateful act, its most important in the postwar period, was the decision not to reestablish the Center party but instead to support an interconfessional party independent of the church. In giving up the institutional link between church and party, the bishops crossed a great practical and psychological divide. The ultimate, if unintentional, effect was to emancipate German Catholics politically. The CDU, though at first clearly dominated by Catholics but even then not under clerical control, necessarily pursued its own course and inevitably followed an inner dynamic that led it further and further from the church. Moreover, since the party was not explicitly Catholic, it was sooner or later destined to have difficulty in justifying a unique claim to Catholic support. The party quickly went its own way, therefore, and the laity eventually went theirs. As a consequence, the church found itself politically on its own. Far from making the CDU the Center party by other means, the bishops became the CDU's hostages, and to their mortification saw their miscalculation sealed first in 1963 with the rise of Protestants to dominance in the party (and government) and three years later with the invitation to the Social Democrats, whom they wanted to keep out of power forever, to join in a coalition government.

The Catholic church's great problem in the postwar period was how, in the face of this shrinking political influence, to achieve its unchanged and sweeping objectives. In the hierarchy's eyes the measure of public policy was its consistency with "Christian social values" and the security of the church. Probably no characteristic of the Catholic church has raised a deeper challenge to democratic government and pluralist society than its insistence on having its moral and social concepts enacted into law or otherwise recognized by the state and imposed upon non-Catholics and Catholics alike, irrespective of whether either accepts them. Since the bishops regarded their claims as rights—even as divine rights—their approach tended in practice to rule out any possibility of compromise. Moreover, remote from the public mood and absorbed in traditional, often archaic demands upon the state, they worked toward goals more and more irrelevant to comtemporary society's needs and less and less in correspondence with the outlook of their own laity.

What these developments demonstrated was that political Catholicism in Germany was a negative rather than a positive phenomenon, in the sense that it was aimed at protecting Catholic rights rather than at making Germany a Catholic state. But precisely because Catholics for the first time since 1871 enjoyed a secure place in the state, their confessional impulse in politics steadily waned. It was this situation that the bishops made every effort to control and reverse. Their politics were the politics of the cynic. They had near-contempt for the laity and no apparent qualms about depriving them of their independent judgment. From the CDU they expected policy concessions in return for Catholic votes. The SPD and other parties which refused to endorse ecclesiastical claims were denigrated as politically and morally unfit to govern. The hierarchy's clericalist tactics, relics of a Protestant and Prussian-dominated Germany, were often used to circumvent and frustrate legitimate democratic procedures. Its political subterfuge was often so blatant, its lobbying activities were until recently so close to the conspiratorial as to debase the church's standing in the eyes of everyone but Catholics and eventually a good many of them as well. If the bishops ultimately helped to destroy popular respect for authority, this was by presenting a conspicuous example of its misuse. In sum, the hierarchy had singular difficulty in understanding, much less contributing to, democratic processes and in practice operated as a hindrance to them. The irony of the situation is that the single institution that had most to do with the changed nature of German politics to which the church found itself unable to adjust was the CDU.

No postwar political event did more to foster a workable liberal democracy in Germany than the establishment of Christian Democracy. Despite the confessional adjective in its title, the CDU was from its inception the prototype of mass Anglo-American party, a unique phenomenon in German politics. Although religious concepts and a deep streak of idealism were among the motivations of many of the party's founders, these soon diminished. As events proved, the CDU's success derived chiefly from its lack of doctrine. Its very reason for being was comprehensiveness rather than exclusiveness, tolerance and pragmatism rather than dogmatism and fixed social creed. By creating an alliance of Protestants and Catholics, workers and farmers, trade unionists and industrialists, the CDU substantially attenuated ideological divisions and contributed to a degree of social unity that the country had previously lacked. It both responded to and accentuated a popular longing for flexibility and pragmatism with just a touch of idealism. In these ways Christian Democracy altered the foundations of German political life and went a long way toward establishing the political terms on which all parties had to compete.

Had a Catholic party been founded instead by Catholic political leaders with church support, it would undoubtedly have enjoyed the backing of a high proportion of Catholics. Since they were half the Federal Republic's population, this situation would have left the political spectrum sharply fragmented, with Protestants scattered in a variety of parties and the Social Democrats no doubt fixated in their early twentieth-century brand of Marxism. With parties of this sort, each representative of narrow ideological and social interests, the political process would once again have been ideologically overcharged. The probable result would have been a society deeply riven by religious and social differences, an unstable political balance and weak governments of shifting coalitions. Bonn would after all have been Weimar. By contrast, the CDU promoted the social and political circumstances which have given the Federal Republic the most stable, pragmatic political system on the continent.

It was clearly a reflection of its whole approach that the CDU, far from stressing religion, should have tried to remove it from parliamentary politics. In fact, given the broad political divergence between the two churches on the one hand and the party's need to placate both the churches and its own confessional wings on the other, the CDU had little choice but to minimize religious considerations. Attitude counted as much as anything; a general emollience toward ecclesiastical views and an occasional concession in social matters broadly sufficed to appease the churches and permit party leaders otherwise to ignore them. But if only a Rhineland Catholic could have had the necessary cynicism toward the Catholic church to curb it and force it to accept compromise, only north and east German Social Democrats could have attributed to the churches, above all to the Catholic church, great and sinister significance. Not until the Social Democrats solved the problem of their own identity did they learn how to take the churches in stride.

The long march of German socialism from Gotha to Bad Godesberg ended with an "about face." By 1959 the party leadership had concluded that the way to power was to play the CDU's game and play it better. The SPD would give the people what they wanted rather than what it thought they should want, in that way ridding the party of the ideological shibboleths of a preconsumer economy. Unlike the British Labour party, which has never been able to solve its doctrinal problem, or the Italian Socialists, who split in the attempt to do so, the SPD in 1959 faced down its past, put Marx aside, and stopped treating politics as a matter of ultimate social values.

A central point of the Godesberg program was to allow the party to come to terms with the churches. On the Protestant side this was not difficult; its practical and philosophic differences with the SPD were marginal, and the church had been anxious for an understanding since 1945. Its achievement depended solely upon the party and was already largely realized by 1959. But with the Catholic church, the party's chief ideological foe, the long antagonism could not be easily overcome. Although both sides had about equal reason to feel aggrieved, the church was unwilling to accept the Godesberg program as adequate payment for the past. For this reason the Social Democratic leaders had to outflank the hierarchy by going directly—and literally—to the Vatican, which, removed from the fray, was able to take a cooler and more sagacious view of German developments. Once Pope Paul VI in clear effect acknowledged the party's good intentions, and after the party had generally translated its words into deeds, the hierarchy's recalcitrance become unconvincing. So in the general mood of change in the 1960s, the church cautiously set out in the direction of detente with the Social Democrats.

The mid-1960s therefore saw a new political-ecclesiastical environment in Germany. With the two dominant parties equally committed to broad partisanship with the churches and accepting their role in the state, the churches gained complete bipartisan recognition of the status they had sought since 1945. At the same time, however, they committed themselves in effect openly to work with the government in power and to refrain from political combat with it. Paradoxically the highpoint of the churches' political success was in this way linked with their political neutralization. While the Catholic church was not able fully to accept this fact, the essential nature of the churches' relationship to politics had nevertheless changed fundamentally by the eve of the grand coalition, which itself further emphasized the end of the confrontation between Christian and non-Christian in Germany.

The churches' new position both reflected and reinforced radical changes in German society resulting from the aftermath of the war and the reconstruction of the country. In destroying the confessional-geographic pattern of local society, the mass migration of Germans from the East put an end at once to the dominance of a single church in the community and to the de facto "apartheid" of Catholics and Protestants. It also broke the hold of the church, not only in terms of direct influence, but also through the compulsion of social conformity. As a result the way was opened to full social reconciliation between the confessions. At the same time the laity became freer to follow, ignore, or reject ecclesiastical guidance. This development was especially significant in Catholic areas, and most of the hierarchy's activities in the social and political sphere during the past twenty years should be seen ultimately as a vain attempt to maintain its authority over the individual and the community. Not surprisingly, when the first postwar generation of Catholics reached maturity in the mid-1960s, it had an outlook perceptibly different from that of its predecessors and was markedly skeptical of the church's views on any topic—moral, political, or social. Its mood was evident, for instance, at election time, at the Essen Catholic assembly, in the referenda on the school issue and in the reaction to *Humani vitae.* In just such ways, a mode of life—of intense ecclesiastical influence in the community—which in important respects grew out of the treaties of Augsburg and Westphalia came to an end. Parallel with these confessional developments occurred the rapid ascendancy of liberal politics and economics, bringing with it the new values of a progressively industrialized, technocratic, prosperous consumer society. This was a phenomenon that occurred throughout Western Europe and everywhere swept away interest in ideology, demoted the preeminence of politics, removed passion from social differences, and resolved disputes into disagreements over means rather than ends.

The position religion and the churches had for centuries occupied in Germany was consequently buried beneath layer upon layer of social change. By the end of the 1960s the age-old concept of the spiritual and secular as two overlapping realms—which had given rise to the centuries of tension between religion and politics and of the conflict between church and state to which Rousseau had referred—largely disappeared from the public consciousness. As postwar developments had altered the values, perceptions, and mode of life of the individual, the general attitude toward religion had necessarily changed at the same time. With peace between the confessions, an assertion of religious identity became less important. With the triumph of secular values and ideals, some fell away from religion while others reinterpreted their old concepts of it. But to almost all, religion—and to some, confessional allegiance—appeared to lose its relevance to practical affairs. The small decline in church attendance and the relatively few resignations (until quite recently) tended to disguise the fact that religion was no longer a motivational factor in the average individual's life and that, even for the person to whom it remained important, it no longer played an essential role in his political and social behavior. What all this change amounted to was in part a displacement, in part a reinterpretation of religious impulses and ideals in favor of the values and mode of life of a society that had become materialistic, pluralistic, relativistic, and pragmatic.

It is not surprising that a drastic decline in the authority and prestige of the church accompanied this evolution. If the church's place in the state was now politically uncontested, this position was increasingly subject to public tolerance. Popular attitude rather than tradition have already begun to determine what status and privileges the churches may enjoy in practice. Moreover, when political and social issues of interest to the church now arise, organizational loyalty to one church or the other has become marginal at most. On all sides there has been increasing skepticism that there can be an identifiable "Christian" policy on practical issues. Instead, it has been increasingly felt that there are merely ecclesiastic interests over which judgments can honorably differ and compromises be creditably reached. This was the political manifestation of the secularization of society.

This fundamental reorientation of German society has not been difficult for the Evangelical church to accept. Because of its concept of the church, Protestantism everywhere has found it fairly easy—sometimes, as in Germany in the 1930's, too easy—to draw a line between religion and politics, between church and state. Historically the profound influence of Protestantism on the Germans was not expressed in the form of direct political influence or organized political activity, but through the subtle and indirect shaping of the nation's Weltanschauung. Since it was the essence of Protestantism that the individual should assert his own judgment on all practical and moral questions, the Evangelical church had neither the will nor the means of exercising open political power. Its theological position not only ruled out the concept of a "Christian party" and of "Christian policies," but also required the church to be neutral in elections and to refrain from justifying its own interests in terms of divine will. Traditionally Protestantism also adjusted fairly smoothly to new ideas and social trends. Religious values among Protestants were on the whole mutable and marginal when it came to practical considerations. In sum, the Evangelical church lost relatively little from secularization because it had relatively little to lose.

To the Catholic church secularization has been a grave blow. The older bishops have found it intolerable that the church should be merely one co-equal institution in a pluralistic society. Although the Vatican Council responded to postwar European trends by altering somewhat the traditional Catholic position regarding church-state relations, Catholicism continues to reject a strict separation of the two and maintains all its established social aims. That these, however, tend to differ sharply from the ideals of a secularized society further limits the church's social authority. The church still appeals, but even the laity listen less. In the great test of strength over school reform, for instance, Catholics abandoned the church so demonstratively that the bishops have been unwilling so far to risk another showdown over any issue. Although they have made a few minor concessions to the new society, the bishops find it more natural to fight change of any sort. Since they are bound to lose in this struggle, the danger is that they may be tempted as a result to repeat the mistake of a century ago by taking the church into social isolation.

Under the circumstances, what role remains to the churches? Although secularization has gravely weakened their authority, it has by no means limited their activity in the social and political sphere. While the churches now have to stand more on their own, they are for that reason freer, at least in principle, to act independently. At the same time they retain great institutional strength and some unique social advantages. They continue to enjoy broad acceptability to all important social groups. Unlike the American churches, for example, which are so subservient to—indeed, such a symbiotic emanation of—the bourgeoisie and its narrow class ethos as to be beyond all promise as a progressive social force, the German churches have an essentially classless character. They are, in fact, the sole institution other than the government itself which spans the breadth of society. Consequently they have a potential for action which every other social institution lacks.

The resources on which they can draw are enormous. Their vast and impressive organizational infrastructure—comprising newspapers, journals, lay groups, official representation to the government, synods, church assemblies, and special advisory councils—offers the churches an ideal platform from which to launch social and political proposals. Their various ecclesiastical groups together constitute a professional staff capable of providing church leaders with well-researched briefs on any problem facing the country. Both churches, but especially the Evangelical church through its synods and advisory councils, have succeeded in engaging professionally eminent laymen in church activities in the political and social sphere. As a result, and because of the continuing high standard of the Catholic monastic orders and the Protestant pastorate, the German churches have been able to maintain their long tradition of intellectual vigor which has probably been without parallel in any other country in the postwar period.

With ample opportunities and resources, the decisive variables in the churches' role in public affairs lie in the political and legal sphere. Since both the Christian Democrats and Social Democrats have demonstrated their desire for practical partnership, there is for the first time in German history genuine basis for peace between the churches and the country's dominant political forces. In the case of the Evangelical church, the amity is firm and has developed into a productive relationship, with a genuine exchange of views between church and the parties and a determination on both sides to reach mutually satisfactory solutions to problems of joint interest. As a consequence, the Evangelical church will be able to work with any government elected to power and to enjoy roughly equal goodwill and influence.

On the Catholic side, however, the church's psychological and organizational ties continue to be entirely with the CDU. Indeed, in the mind of the bishops and the broad mass of Catholics, "CDU" still more or less equals "Catholic" and this equation remains one of the central elements of German politics. Consequently, the division between the Catholic church and the SPD is less a gulf—to which Cardinal Döpfner likened it in 1964—than a barrier, and the barrier is the CDU. By the mid-1960s this barrier was beginning to weaken and had the Social Democrats not come to power as soon as they did, a modus vivendi between the party and the church might gradually have been reached. But by 1969 the relationship had not gone beyond talks and meetings and it was too weak to withstand the social-liberal coalition's ejection of the Christian Democrats from power. The new government's steps toward social reform plunged the party into an area where the Catholic bishops are intensely sensitive and notoriously conservative. The resultant disagreement largely negated the modest rapprochement that had been achieved.

Ultimately the clash between German Catholicism and Social Democracy demonstrated that there remains a significant distance not simply between the Catholic church and the SPD but between the Catholic church and German democracy. The hierarchy still has a concept of the state and its own worldly mission that is incompatible with the democratic requirement of tolerance and compromise. The bishops not only refuse to acknowledge that the interests of secular society (as decided by a parliamentary majority) may legitimately differ from the morality of the church but are willing to frustrate these interests by threatening electoral vengeance (through the political manipulation of the laity) upon those who support them. Acutely sensitive to the moral state of society, they remain indifferent to the long-term political health of that society.

In the legal sphere the churches also face a test. Their privileges are so extraordinary, in many respects unique in the world, that these are bound to be increasingly questioned. While the German churches have not as a result of legal advantage sunk into the languor of, for instance, the Church of England, they enjoy privileges—especially financial ones—that will have to be scaled down if they are to maintain their credibility with the public as institutions interested in the general national welfare. Ultimately the churches' position in society will rest less on their formal status than on their standing with the public. Should they hold on to antiquated privileges, they will take on the character of relics of an outmoded social system and will not be in a position to convince a secularized society that in acting and speaking on public affairs they are dedicated to social justice and political impartiality rather than ecclesiastical advantage and doctrinal selfishness.

In the end the role the churches play will depend upon their concept of themselves. The Catholic church is right in maintaining that there is nothing that affects humanity that does not touch the church; the Evangelical church is right in insisting that the church should not treat its views on public affairs as either innately Christian or immutable and must emphatically avoid trying to coerce its adherents into accepting them. But these principles are scarcely enough. Protestant and Catholic leaders will have to formulate a clearer notion, free of any nostalgia, of their role in a secularized society. If the Evangelical church should join the Catholic church in seeking to purvey outmoded moral and social concepts rather than fearlessly challenging all forms of social repression and injustice, including those arising from accepted convention, both will well deserve the strictures Marx pronounced upon all moralists who fail to relate their ideals to social conditions.

Since 1945 the German churches, whatever their mistakes, have had a vigor and strength that few, if any, other churches in the world can claim. Today they are alive and responsive to the problems of their country in a way that perhaps no other churches are. What continues to make the two institutions exciting is that the challenge to them and their opportunity for response are so evenly balanced. But unless the Evangelical church resumes its progressive course and a fortiori the Catholic church reverses the pull of reaction, they will both run the grave danger of being reduced to the role of constitutional monarch—a relic of a past age, of ceremonial importance, the object of devotion by the old and conservative, symbolically (if vaguely) representing the best of the nation, but politically impotent and of little practical relevance to contemporary life.

Appendix

The Structure of the Evangelical Church in Germany

	number of communicants*	head
Evangelical Church of the Union		
Church in Berlin-Brandenburg	3,550,000	Bishop Kurt Scharf
Church of the Province of Saxony	2,125,000	Bishop Werner Krusche
Pomeranian Evangelical Church (Greifswald)	415,000	Bishop Friedrich-Wilhelm Krummacher
Church of Silesia (Görlitz)	210,000	Bishop Hans Joachim Fränkel
Church of Westphalia	3,510,000	President Hans Thimme
Church of the Rhineland	3,915,000	President Joachim Beckmann
Other Union Churches:		
Church in Hesse and Nassau	2,310,000	Church President Helmut Hild
Church of Kurhessen-Waldeck	1,145,000	Bishop Erich Vellmer
Church of Baden	1,390,000	Bishop Hans-Wolfgang Heidland
Church of the Palatinate	750,000	Church President Theodor Schaller
Church of Anhalt	275,000	Church President Martin Müller
Church of Bremen	520,000	President Arnold Rutenberg
United Evangelical Lutheran Church of Germany:		
Church of Saxony	2,910,000	Bishop Gottfried Noth

*Figures for West German churches as of January 1, 1967; figures for East German churches as of 1964.

364

Church of Hanover	3,915,000	Bishop Hanns Lilje
Church of Schleswig-Holstein	2,370,000	Bishop Friedrich Hübner
Church of Bavaria	2,540,000	Bishop Hermann Dietzfelbinger
Church of Thuringia	1,210,000	Bishop Moritz Mitzenheim
Church of Mecklenburg	850,000	Bishop Niklot Beste
Church in Hamburg	685,000	Bishop Hans-Otto Wölber
Church of Brunswick	690,000	Bishop Gerhard Heintze
Church in Lübeck	210,000	Bishop Heinrich Meyer
Church of Schaumburg-Lippe	70,000	Bishop Johann-Gottfried Maltusch

Other Lutheran Churches:

Church in Württemburg	2,520,000	Bishop Erich Eichele
Church in Oldenburg	540,000	Bishop Heinrich Harms
Church of Eutin	85,000	Bishop Wilhelm Kieckbusch

Reformed Churches:

| Church in Northwestern Germany | 215,000 | Church President Gerhard Nordholt |
| Church of Lippe | 245,000 | Superintendent Udo Smidt |

Source: Evangelical Church Chancellery.

The Structure of the Catholic Church in Germany

Church Province of Cologne	number of communicants*	head
Archdiocese of Cologne	2,712,071	Cardinal Joseph Höffner
Diocese of Trier	1,908,838	Bishop Bernhard Stein
Diocese of Osnabrück	812,401 (West) 118,745 (East)	Bishop Helmut Hermann Wittler
Diocese of Münster	2,113,219	Bishop Heinrich Tenhumberg
Diocese of Aachen	1,469,721	Bishop Johannes Pohlschneider
Diocese of Limburg	903,404	Bishop Wilhelm Kempf
Diocese of Essen	1,417,048	Bishop Franz Hengsbach

Church Province of Munich and Freising

*Figures for all provinces except Meissen for 1967.

Archdiocese of Munich and Freising	2,206,388	Cardinal Julius Döpfner
Diocese of Augsburg	1,500,598	Bishop Joseph Stimpfle
Diocese of Passau	508,454	Bishop Anton Hofmann
Diocese of Regensburg	1,312,242	Bishop Rudolf Graber
Church Province of Bamberg		
Archdiocese of Bamberg	833,840	Archbishop Josef Schneider
Diocese of Speyer	700,223	Bishop Friedrich Wetter
Diocese of Würzburg	932,655 (West) 26,324 (East)	Bishop Josef Stangl
Diocese of Eichstätt	388,190	Bishop Alois Brems
Church Province of Freiburg		
Archdiocese of Freiburg	2,243,818	Archbishop Hermann Schäufele
Diocese of Mainz	858,894	Bishop Hermannn Volk
Diocese of Rottenburg	1,909,069	Bishop Carl Josef Leiprecht
Church Province of Paderborn		
Archdiocese of Paderborn	1,942,787 (West) 337,954 (East)	Cardinal Lorenz Jaeger
Diocese of Hildesheim	727,357 (West) 6,510 (East)	Bishop Heinrich Maria Janssen
Diocese of Fulda	435,057 (West) 262,305 (East)	Bishop Adolf Bolte
Church Province of Breslau		
Archdiocese of Breslau	71,997	Vicar Capitular Gerhard Schaffran
Diocese of Ermland	–	Vicar Capitular Paul Hoppe
Diocese of Berlin	256,957 (West) 239,737 (East)	Cardinal Alfred Bengsch
Free Prelature of Schneidemühl	–	Vicar Capitular Wilhelm Volkmann
Diocese of Meissen	354,199	Bishop Otto Spülbeck
Archdiocese of Olmütz (German part)	–	Canonical Visitator Eduard Beigel
Archdiocese of Prague (German part)	–	Canonical Visitator Leo Christoph

Sources: *Annuario Pontificio* (1969) and Franz Groner (editor), *Kirchliches Handbuch, Amtliches statistisches Jahrbuch der Katholischen Kirche Deutschlands,* Band XXCI, 1962-1968 (1969)

Sources

THIS study relies heavily on unpublished documents and interviews. Both, however, are generally used for background purposes and are not usually referred to in the text. Such is especially the case with interviews where the statements of several persons are frequently synthesized into broad conclusions. In identifying these persons below, only the position of relevance to this study is given; where the name is marked with an asterisk, the interview was conducted by correspondence. Most of the interviews took place between 1968 and 1970. Published material was also indispensible. The bibliography does not cite every book and article available but lists rather the important ones as well as titles offering a cross-section of contrasting and contentious points of view. Strictly theological works are excluded and, since the religious journals mentioned below are such excellent sources of information and comment on every aspect of the ecclesiastical situation, only articles of special pertinance are cited.

PART I: UNPUBLISHED MATERIAL AND INTERVIEWS

The Churches, their Political Approach and their Position on Political and Economic Issues (Chapters 1, 2, 5, 6, 9 and 10)

Documents

The best unpublished material on the critical period of the Evangelical church's history from May 1945 to 1949 are Bishop Theophil Wurm's extensive papers in the Württemberg Church archives in Stuttgart. These are usefully supplemented by some of the archives' other records. For this and the later period, the EKD's central archives in Hanover and the Rhineland Church in Düsseldorf provided, upon request, copies of such requested documents as were available. The latter's holdings, including Church-President Heinrich Held's papers, were not adequately ordered in 1969 and 1970 to permit examination. Bishop Otto Dibelius is said to have left no collection of papers, although some of his letters are among the papers of Robert Tillmanns in Bonn. The Bavarian Church rejected several requests for permission to read the diary and papers of Bishop Hans Meiser.

On the Catholic side, Cardinal Frings made available eighteen dossiers of papers covering the 1945-1950 period (*CR 25/18,* Diocesan Archives, Cologne). While this material primarily concerns the military occupation, it includes a number of important documents on ecclesiastical developments as well. Requests to see the records of several other dioceses were rejected. The papers of Cardinal Muench were presented in November 1972 to the Catholic University of America, Washington, and opened to research. The collection, 162 boxes of material, includes diaries, memoranda, and correspondence though very few official reports to the Vatican. Despite the latter limitation, the papers are an excellent body of information on ecclesiastical-political affairs in Germany from 1946 through 1959, even if they contain no new points of high significance. Since this manuscript was already in print when these documents became available, it was not possible to make more than the most limited use of them.

Fragmentary but often valuable material is also available from non-ecclesiastical sources. American government records, both those of the military government and the Department of State (discussed below), contain reports on ecclesiastical affairs as well as records of interviews with church leaders both by military officials and by Ambassador Robert Murphy. The archives of the Rhineland CDU in Cologne and the Westphalian CDU in Dortmund, along with the papers of a number of CDU leaders (mentioned below), contain much useful material on the political views and activities of church leaders and lay groups, particularly on the Catholic side, from the end of the war to the present.

The role of confession in electoral behavior and party preference has been amply investigated over the years in public opinion polls. Since the mid-1950s these polls have been conducted by one or another of the well-known German polling institutes; for the early postwar period the results of the polls conducted by the American Military Government and the U.S. High Commission for Germany are held in the archives of the United States Information Agency, Washington. A set of the military government polls are also held by the Roper Public Opinion Research Center at Williams College, Williamstown, Massachusetts. The results of the former are summarized in the book by Anna and Richard Merritt listed in the bibliography; a companion volume on the latter by the same authors is forthcoming. The general topic has also been studied in two doctoral theses: Heinz Striebich, *Konfession und Partei; Ein Beitrag zur Entwicklung der politischen Willensbildung im alten Lande Baden*; Heidelberg, 1955; and Karl-Heinz Diekershoff, *Das Wahlverhalten von Mitgliedern organisierter Interessengruppen; Dargestellt am Beispiel der Bundestagswahlen 1961,* Cologne University, 1964.

Interviews

Becher, Paul. Social affairs expert, Central Committee of German Catholics.
Blank, Theodor. Catholic trade unionist; CDU Bundestag member; commissioner for defense matters; Defense Minister.
Dirks, Walter. Cofounder of CDU, Frankfurt; copublisher of *Frankfurter Hefte.*

Fischer, Professor Martin. Professor of theology, Kirchliche Hochschule, Berlin.

Forster, Monsignor Karl. Director, Catholic Academy in Bavaria; secretary general, German Bishops' Conference.

Grüber, Heinrich. Protestant Dean of Berlin; representative of EKD to East German government.

Gundlach, Professor Gustav, S.J. Professor of social philosophy, Gregorian University, Rome.

Hamm, Justin. Special assistant to Konrad Adenauer.

Hanssler, Monsignor Bernhard. Religious adviser, Central Committee of German Catholics.

Heinemann, Gustav. Member of EDK council; president of EKD synod; Interior Minister; cofounder of All-German People's party; Justice Minister; President of Federal Republic.

von Heyl, Church Counselor Cornelius-Adalbert. Social affairs expert, EKD Chancellery, Bonn.

Hirschmann, Professor Johannes, S.J. Professor of moral theology, Hochschule St. Georgen, Offenbach.

Hochhuth, Rolf.* Author of *The Deputy*.

Iwand, Professor Hans-Joachim. Professor of theology, Bonn University.

Kafka, Gustav. Political expert of Central Committee of German Catholics.

Kalinna, Church Counsellor Hermann. Adviser to representative of EKD to federal government.

Köppler, Heinrich. Chairman of Federation of German Catholic Youth; secretary general, Central Committee of German Catholics; parliamentary state secretary of interior ministry.

Koppe, Karlheinz. Secretary, Bensberg circle.

Kronenberg, Friedrich. Secretary general, Central Committee of German Catholics.

Kruska, Professor Harald. Professor of theology, Kirchliche Hochschule, Berlin.

Kunst, Bishop Hermann. Representative of EKD to federal government.

Kupisch, Professor Karl. Professor of church history, Kirchliche Hochschule, Berlin.

von Mutius, Albrecht. Protestant Deacon General, German armed forces.

Nawroth, Edgar, O.P. Director, Albertus Magnus Academy, Walberberg.

von Nell-Breuning, Professor Oswald, S.J. Professor of Economic and Social Studies, Hochschule St. Georgen, Offenbach.

Niemeyer, Johannes. Deputy director, Catholic Office.

Niemöller, Church President Martin. President of Church of Hesse and Nassau; Member, EKD council.

Niemöller, Pastor Wilhelm. Expert on Evangelical church in Third Reich and on relations between provincial churches and British Military Government.

Prausz, Herbert. Eastern expert, Central Committee of German Catholics.

Ranke, Church Counselor Hansjürg. Representative, EKD Chancellery in Bonn.

Rittberg, Church Counselor Else, Countess von. Adviser to representative of
EKD to federal government.
Rommerskirchen, Josef. Chairman, Federation of German Catholic Youth;
CDU member of Bundestag.
Schmidt, Church Counselor Hans. Bavarian provincial church.

The Occupation and Denazification (Chapters 3 and 4)

Documents

Of the four occupation powers, only the American government grants
access to its military occupation records, the bulk of which are comprised of
the files of military government and the War (Army) Department. These are
part of the Modern Military Records of the National Archives. While this
material is subject to screening by the Army Adjutant General, authorization
for use was in my case withheld only for a few documents relating to denazification proceedings and several mail intercepts (letters from Bishop Wurm to
the Archbishop of Canterbury, copies of which are in any case among the
Wurm papers). Material on American policy toward the churches and on
general ecclesiastical affairs are primarily contained in the files of the Religious Affairs Administration Branch (Boxes 337–344, shipment 5) as well as,
though to a much lesser extent, the Political Affairs Branch (Boxes 147–148,
shipment 15). These files are usefully supplemented by the typescript and
mimeographed cumulative reports of the Land military governments, which
were issued periodically from 1945 to 1949. The reports are unclassified and
are accessible both in Washington and at USAREUR headquarters in Heidelberg.

The records of the Department of States are an additional but compara-
tively meager source on church matters. For the period 1945 to 1949 the
major part of these documents is filed in two boxes (862.404—Religion and
Churches), which contain Foreign Service telegrams, despatches, letters, and
interoffice State Department memoranda. There is some further interesting
material in the file containing correspondence between departmental officials
and the Apostolic Delegate (762.66A) as well as in Ambassador Murphy's
voluminous files (740.00119 Control (Germany)), which hold his letters and
reports from Germany on ecclesiastical affairs. While none of the State Department documents dated after December 31, 1945, may currently be used
for publication, those for the later period in fact contain no novel points and
only emphasize the themes presented in the text of this study. In general,
State Department officials had greater understanding than the military of the
German churches' point of view, but they rarely raised an aggressive challenge
to military policy.

Although not open to research, the French Archives de l'Occupation in
Colmar provided, upon request, copies of several documents on French policy. Helmut Kohl's doctoral thesis, *Die politische Entwicklung in der Pfalz
und das Wiedererstehen der Parteien nach 1945* (Heidelberg University,
1958), contains original and useful material on the Palatinate under the occupation. In response to inquiry, the Imperial War Museum in London stated
that British Military Government records remained subject to the thirty-year

rule and that no exceptions could be considered. The minutes of the meetings of the Allied Control Council for Germany also remain inaccessible.

Fortunately, the papers of Cardinal Frings and Bishop Wurm go some way in compensating for the unavailability of French and British records, containing as they do the exchange of correspondence between occupation officials and the church leaders. Wurm's records are also an excellent complement to American documents while Cardinal Muench's papers constitute an unrivalled source on the Catholic side. In addition, the diocesan archives in Cologne and the Württemberg Church archives hold useful material on denazification and in the latter case especially on the church's own denazification proceedings. The best studies on denazification in the American Zone are two unpublished works: William Griffith, *Denazification Program in the United States Zone of Germany* (Harvard University doctoral thesis, 1950) and John Kormann, *U.S. Denazification Policy in Germany, 1944–1950* (Office of the High Commissioner for Germany, 1952).

Interviews

Arndt, Karl.* Religious Affairs officer, American Military Government, Württemberg-Baden.

Beckmann, Joachim. President, Rhineland provincial church.

Bodensieck, Professor Julius.* Liaison representative, Federal Council of Churches, to American Military Government.

Bogner, Pastor. Son of Church Counselor Wilhelm Bogner.

Cavert, Samuel McCrea.* General secretary, Federal Council of Churches.

Clay, General Lucius.* Military Governor, American Zone of Germany.

Cube, Walter von. Domestic-affairs editor, *Die Neue Zeitung* (Munich).

Eagan, James.* Religious Affairs officer, American Military Government, Bavaria.

Griffith, Professor William. Official, American Military Government; Expert on denazification in American Occupation Zone.

Haug, Bishop Martin. Bishop, Württemberg provincial church.

Hermans, Hubert. Governing President, Rhineland-Hesse-Nassau.

Holborn, Professor Hajo.* Expert on American occupation policy.

Longford, 7th Earl of (Francis Aungier Pakenham). Chancellor, Duchy of Lancaster (Minister of State for German Affairs).

Olsen, Arild.* Religious Affairs officer, American Military Government in Germany.

Robertson of Oakridge, 1st Baron. Military Governor, British Zone of Germany; British High Commissioner in Germany.

Sedlmeier, Wilhelm. Auxiliary Bishop, Rottenberg.

Teusch, Joseph. Vicar general, Cologne.

The Legal Relationship between Church and State

(Chapters 6 and 7)
Documents

On the role of the churches in the work of the Parliamentary Council an unpublished source of some help is "Materialien zum Grundgesetz" in the Bundestag archives. It is an article by article compilation—though fragmentary—of working papers used in the deliberations of the Council's committees. In it can be found a copy of Bishop Wurm's letter, dated November 9, 1948, to Adenauer and related documents.

Interviews

Flatten, Professor Heinrich. Professor of Catholic church law, Bonn University.

Flor, Peter. Official, family ministry.

Globke, Hans. State secretary, federal chancellor's office (1949–1963).

Klein, Manfried. Director of studies, Federal Center for Political Education.

von Merkatz, Hans-Joachim. Advisor to German party delegation in Parliamentary Council; deputy chairman, German party.

Osner, Karl. Official, ministry of development aid.

Schmid, Professor Carlo. Chairman, main committee, Parliamentary Council (1948–1949); SPD member, Bundestag.

Schraaf, Monsignor Karl. Director, directorate for schools and education, Diocese of Cologne.

Wosnitza, Monsignor Franz. Expert on diocesan structure east of Oder-Neisse.

Wuermeling, Franz-Josef. CDU member, Bundestag; family minister; family and youth minister.

Zieger, Church Counselor Paul. Director, church statistics office, EKD.

The Churches and the Parties

(Chapters 11 and 12)

Documents

Anyone writing on the origins of the CDU will be much indebted to Hans Wieck for his two indispensable studies on the subject. But since the focus of this study differed from his, the research had to cover some of the same as well as some different ground in order to answer such questions as whether and to what extent the concept of an interconfessional party had been discussed before the end of the war either by Catholic and Protestant churchmen or by secular opposition groups; whether any suggestions of Catholic-Protestant political cooperation came from Rome or were completely spontaneous and indigenous to Germany; whether and to what extent churchmen encouraged and participated in the establishment of an interconfessional party and to what extent the party's founders were motivated by ecclesiastical considerations. Fortunately the key founders of the CDU/CSU maintained fairly extensive records, and it was possible to examine most of these. They included the papers of Andreas Hermes in Königswinter, Leo Schwering in Cologne, Otto Lenz in Bad Godesberg, Joseph Müller in Munich, and Adam Stegerwald in Cologne. These were most usefully supplemented by the files of the headquarters of the Rhineland and the Westphalian CDU. The files of these two party organizations, along with the papers of Richard Muckermann in Kettwig, were an excellent source of information on the revived Center party and the Catholic church's efforts on behalf of its fusion with the CDU. For the later period of the CDU's development, the records of the Rhineland and Westphalian CDU were once again of much help, while the files of the

Protestant Committee of the CDU and the papers of Robert Tillmanns in Bonn were useful in documenting the political differences in the CDU. For the background of the visit of Social Democratic leaders to the Vatican, Alexander Kohn-Brandenburg's records were indispensable.

Interviews

Bausch, Paul.* Cofounder, CDU in Württemberg.

Bethge, Eberhard. Biographer of Dietrich Bonhoeffer.

Brockmann, Johannes.* Cofounder, Center party.

Buchheim, Karl.* Cofounder, CDU in Leipzig.

Dörpinghaus, Bruno. Cofounder, CDU in Hesse.

Dovifat, Professor Emil. Cofounder, Berlin CDU.

Eichler, Willi. Member, SPD executive committee.

Encke, Pastor Hans. Cofounder, Rhineland CDU.

Eurel, Alfred. Cofounder, CSU in Nuremberg.

Föhr, Ernst. Vicar general, Freiburg.

Gronwald, Karl. Cofounder, CSU in northern Bavaria.

Heck, Bruno. Secretary general, CDU.

Heine, Friedrich. Member, SPD executive committee, and SPD press spokesman.

Hermes, Peter. Son of Andreas Hermes, Cofounder of CDU in Berlin.

Kaiser, Elfriede. Cofounder, CDU in Berlin.

Kohn-Brandenburg, Alexander, Member, SPD executive committee.

Krause, Alfred. Manager, CDU Eastern bureau, Berlin.

Krone, Heinrich. Cofounder, CDU in Berlin.

Lemmer, Ernst. Cofounder, CDU in Berlin.

Muckermann, Richard. Cofounder, Center party.

Müller, Gebhard. Cofounder, CDU in Württemberg.

Müller, Josef. Cofounder, CSU.

Nellen, Peter. SPD member, Bundestag.

Paul, Ernst. SPD member, Bundestag.

Ritter, Professor Gerhard.* Biographer of Carl Goerdeler.

Röhring, Pastor. Cofounder, CSU in northern Bavaria.

Rösing, Josef. Cofounder, Center party.

Schäffer, Fritz. Minister president, Bavaria.

Schmidt, Otto. Cofounder, Rhineland CDU.

Schneider, Josef. Cofounder, CDU in Rottenberg.

Schorr, Helmut. Biographer of Adam Stegerwald.

Schreiber, Hans. Manager, Rhineland CDU.

Schwering, Leo. Cofounder, Rhineland CDU.

Senfft von Pilsach, Baron von. Cofounder, Rhineland CDU.

Simpfendörfer, Wilhelm. Cofounder, CDU in Württemberg.

Steltzer, Theodor. Cofounder, CDU in Berlin and northern Germany.

Vockel, Heinrich. Cofounder, CDU in Berlin.

Warsch, Wilhelm. Cofounder, Rhineland CDU.

Weinzierl, Georg. Cofounder, CSU in Eichstätt.

Wessel, Helene. Cofounder, Center party.

Zürcher, Paul. Cofounder, CDU in Baden.

Source References of Muench Papers

page	initial words of quotation	source
30	"impervious to criticism" et seq.	diary, January 1, 1947
83	"Jews in control"	diary, August 9, 1946
86	"a Jew . . . morally corrupt . . ."	diary, June 19, 1955
86	"N.Y. Jew"	diary, November 9, 1948
173	"quite excited" et seq.	diary, December 17, 1954
175	"Excellent Catholic . . ."	diary, May 7, 1954
175	"Blackmailer's methods again"	letter, October 31, 1950, Zeiger to Muench, Box 85
176	"decorations from other governments" et seq.	diary, June 29, 1955
176	"Boehler seems to have pushed . . ."	diary, December 3, 1966
211	"past is enshrined . . ."	diary, November 6, 1949
211	"I was in the Nunciatur . . ."	letter, March 28, 1949, Lehnert to Muench, Box 85
211	"He thinks he is . . ."	diary, July 12, 1946
211	"Holy Father [is] more interested . . ."	diary, November 7, 1949
211	"Holy Father's principal concern . . ."	diary, July 12, 1946
211	"The juridically very ambiguous . . ."	report, spring 1947, Zeiger to Muench, Box 119
212	"we are at sea . . ."	diary, June 7, 1953
212	"some appropriate way . . ."	diary, April 30, 1949
215	"expect [the] Church to honor . . ."	diary, July 25, 1956
218	"Holy Father does not trust . . ."	diary, March 21, 1953

PART II: PUBLISHED MATERIAL

General

Ecclesiastical Encyclopaedias, Yearbooks, Handbooks, and Reports

Catholic
Adressbuch für das katholische Deutschland, 1965.
Annuario Pontificio, published annually.
Der grosse Herder: Nachschlagwerk für Wissen und Leben, 1956.
Herders Sozialkathechismus, Eberhard Welty, editor, 1953 et seq.
Katholisches Jahrbuch, 1948–1949 et seq.
Kirchliches Handbuch: Amtliches statistisches Jahrbuch der katholischen Kirche Deutschlands, volume 23: 1944–1957; volume 24: 1952–1956; volume 25: 1957–1961; volume 26: 1962–1968.
Lexikon für Theologie und Kirche Josef Höfner and Karl Rahner, editors, 2nd edition, 1958 et seq.

Reports of the Catholic Assemblies.

Staatslexikon, published by the Görresgesellschaft, 6th edition, 1957 et seq.

Wörterbuch der Politik, Oswald von Nell-Breuning and Hermann Sacher, editors, 1947 et seq.

Protestant

Evangelisches Kirchenlexikon, 1956 et seq.

Heidtmann, Günter, editor. *Kirche in Kampf der Zeit: Die Botschaften, Worte und Erklärungen der evangelischen Kirche in Deutschland und ihren östlichen Gliedkrichen,* 1954.

Karrenberg, Friedrich, editor. *Evangelisches Soziallexikon,* 1954.

Kirchliches Jahrbuch für die Evangelische Kirche in Deutschland, Joachim Beckmann, editor, 1948 et seq.

Merzyn, Friedrich, editor. *Kundgebungen, Worte and Erklärungen der Evangelischen Kirche in Deutschland 1945–1959,* 1959.

Taschenbuch der Evangelischen Kirche: Zusammengefasste Ausgabè, 1966.

Reports of the EKD synod. *Protokolbände der Synoden der EKD,* 1949 et seq.

Ecclesiastical and Lay Publications

Catholic

Diocesan gazettes. Official organ of each diocese.

Diocesan newspapers. Periodical journals of general diocesan news.

Catholic newspapers. Newspapers published under Catholic auspices.

Lay organization publications. Each lay organization issues a newspaper or periodical; two leading ones are *Mann in der Zeit* and *Ketteler Wacht.*

Dispatches of the Katholische Nachrichten-Agentur (KNA).

Frankfurter Hefte.

Herder-Korrespondenz.

Hochland.

Informationsdienst.

Die neue Ordnung

Rheinischer Merkur.

Stimmen der Zeit.

Werkhefte.

Wort und Wahrheit.

Studien und Berichte der katholischen Akademie in Bayern, edited by Karl Forster.

Protestant

Provincial church gazettes. Official organ of each provincial church.

Provincial church newspapers. Periodical journals of general comment and church news.

Christ und Welt.

Evangelische Kommentare.

Evangelisch-lutherische Kirchenzeitung.

Evangelische Verantwortung: Politische Briefe des evangelischen Arbeitskreises der CDU/CSU.

Junge Kirche.

Kirche im Volk.

Kirche in der Zeit.

Die Mitarbeit; Evangelische Monatshefte zur Gesellschaftspolitik.

Politisch-soziale Korrespondenz.

Politische Verantwortung; Evangelische Stimmen.

Die Stimme der Gemeinde.

General Newspapers and Periodicals

German

Coverage of church affairs is enormous by American standards. *Süddeutsche Zeitung, Frankfurter Allgemeine, Die Welt, Die Zeit,* and *Der Spiegel* are especially useful. *Die Neue Zeitung* and *Die Neue Rhein Zeitung* are helpful for coverage of the immediate postwar period in the American and British zones respectively.

Foreign

Neue Zürcher Zeitung has carried outstanding analytical reports on German Protestantism since 1945. *The Times* of London and *The New York Times* are useful for general coverage of the German scene.

Press Clipping Collections: Federal Press and Information Agency, Bonn; Bundestag press library, Bonn; Katholische Nachrichten-Agentur, Bonn; Royal Institute of International Affairs, London.

General Sociological and Political Analyses

Blankenburg, Erhard. *Kirchliche Bindung und Wahlverhalten: Die sozialen Faktoren bei der Wahlentscheidung Nordrhein-Westfalen 1961 bis 1966,* 1967.

Breitling, Rupert. *Die Verbände in der Bundesrepublik,* 1955.

Buchner, Rudolf. "Die konfessionelle Spaltung als deutsches Schicksal," *Archiv für Kulturgeschichte,* volume 47, 1965.

Burger, Annemarie. *Religionszugehörigkeit und soziales Verhalten,* 1953.

Freytag, Justus. *Die Kirchengemeinde in soziologischer Sicht,* 1959.

Goldschmidt, Dietrich, Franz Greiner and Helmut Schelsky, editors. *Soziologie der Kirchengemeinde,* 1960.

Greiffenhagen, Martin. *Christengemeinde und moderne Gesellschaft,* 1968.

Harenberg, Werner, editor. *Was glauben die Deutschen? Die EMNID-Umfrage, Ergebnisse, Kommentare,* 1968.

von der Heydte, F.A. and Karl Sacherl. *Soziologie der deutschen Parteien,* 1955.

Hirsch-Weber, Wolfgang and Klaus Schütz. *Wähler und Gewählte: Eine Untersuchung der Bundestagswahlen 1953,* 1957.

Kahn, K.G. *Les églises en Allemagne,* 1949.

Kitzinger, U.W. *German Electoral Politics: A Study of the 1957 Campaign,* 1960.

Köster, Reinhard. *Die Kirchentreuen: Erfahrungen und Ergebnisse einer soziologischen Untersuchung in einer grossstädtischen evangelischen Kirchengemeinde,* 1959.

Lohse, Jens Marten. *Kirchen ohne Kontakte?*, 1967.

Luckmann, Thomas. *Das Problem der Religion in der modernen Gesellschaft*, 1963.

Mahrenholz, E.G. *Die Kirchen in der Gesellschaft der Bundesrepublik*, 1969.

Matthes, Joachim, editor. *International Yearbook for the Sociology of Religion*, 1965 et seq.

Menges, Walter. *Die Zugehörigkeit zur Kirche*, 1964.

Reigrotzki, Erich. *Soziale Verflechtungen in der Bundesrepublik: Elemente der sozialen Teilnahme in Kirche, Politik, Organisationen und Freizeit*, 1956.

Rendtorff, Trutz. *Die soziale Struktur der Gemeinde*, 1958.

Scheuch, Erwin and Rudolf Wildenmann. *Zur Soziologie der Wahl*, 1965.

Statistisches Bundesamt. *Statistik der Bundesrepublik*: volume 100, number 2, *Die Wahl zum 2. Deutschen Bundestag am 6.9. 1953*, 1955; volume 200, number 3, *Die Wahl zum 3. Deutschen Bundestag am 15. September 1957*, 1959; series A, number 4, *Wahl zum 4. Deutschen Bundestag am 17. September 1961*, 1965; and series A, number 9, *Wahl zum 5. Deutschen Bundestag am 19. September 1965*, 1967.

Vogel, Reinhard and Peter Haungs. *Wahlkampf und Wählertradition*, 1965.

Chapter 1. German Protestantism—Character and Organization

Background (selected bibliography)

Bonhoeffer, Dietrich. *Gesammelte Schriften*, edited by Eberhard Bethge, four volumes, 1958–1961.

Brunotte, Heinz, editor. *Zur Geschichte des Kirchenkampfes: Gesammelte Aufsätze*, 1965.

Conway, John. *The Nazi Persecution of the Churches 1933–1945*, *1968*.

Diehn, Otto. *Bibliographie zur Geschichte des Kirchenkampfes 1933–1945*, 1958.

Fischer, Fritz. "Der deutsche Protestantismus und die Politik im 19. Jahrhundert," *Historische Zeitschrift*, 171 (1951)

Hermelink, Heinrich, editor. *Kirche im Kampf: Dokumente des Widerstands und des Aufbaus in der evangelischen Kirche Deutschlands von 1933–1945*, 1950.

Kupisch, Karl. *Zwischen Idealismus und Massendemokratie: Eine Geschichte der evangelischen Kirche in Deutschland von 1815–1945*, 1955.

Niemöller, Wilhelm. *Kampf und Zeugnis der Bekennenden Kirche*, 1948.

——— . *Die Evangelische Kirche im Dritten Reich: Handbuch des Kirchenkampfes*, 1956.

Schmidt, Kurt Dietrich. *Die Bekenntnisse und grundsätzlichen Äusserungen zur Kirchenfrage*, volume 1, *1933*, 1934; volume 2, *1934*, 1935; volume 3, *1935*, 1936.

———. *Dokumente des Kirchenkampfes II; Die Zeit des Reichskirchenausschusses 1935–1937*, 1964.

——— , editor. *Arbeiten zur Geschichte des Kirchenkampfes*, volume 1, 1958; volume 2, 1963.

Troeltsch, Ernst. *The Social Teachings of the Christian Churches*, two volumes, 1931: translation of *Die Soziallehren der christlichen Kirchen und Gruppen*, 1911.

Wolf, Ernst. *Barmen; Kirche zwischen Versuchung und Glaube*, 1957.

_____ , editor. *Karl Barth zum Kirchenkampf*, 1956.

Zimmermann, Wolf-Dieter, editor. *Begegnungen mit Dietrich Bonhoeffer: Ein Almanach*, 1964.

Since the War

Barth, Karl. *Zur Genesung des deutschen Wesens: Ein Freundeswort von Draussen*, 1945.

_____. *Die Evangelische Kirche in Deutschland nach dem Zusammenbruch des Dritten Reiches*, 1946.

_____. "Die christlichen Kirchen und die heutige Wirklichkeit," in *Evangelische Theologie*, new series, 1946–1947, pp. 212 ff.

_____. *The Germans and Ourselves*, 1945.

_____. *Ein Wort an die Deutschen*, 1946.

Beckmann, Joachim, and Gerhard Weisser, editors. *Christliche Gemeinde und Gesellschaftswandel*, 1964.

Boyens, Armin. "Treysa 1945 – Die Evangelische Kirche nach dem Zusammenbruch des Dritten Reiches," *Zeitschrift für Kirchengeschichte*, volume 82, number 1 (1971).

Brunner, Peter. *Das lutherische Bekenntnis in der Union*, 1952.

Brunotte, Heinz. *Das Zusammenleben der Konfessionen in der Evangelischen Kirche in Deutschland*, 1953.

_____ . *Die Grundordnung der Evangelischen Kirche in Deutschland: Ihre Entstehung und ihre Probleme*, 1954.

_____ . *Die Evangelische Kirche in Deutschland: Geschichte, Organisation und Gestalt der EKD*, 1964.

Casalis, Georges. "Les relations internationales du protestantisme allemand," in Alfred Grosser, editor. *Les relations internationales de l'Allemagne occidentale*, 1956.

Diem, Hermann. *Restauration oder Neuanfang in der evangelischen Kirche, 1946.*

_____. *Haben wir Deutsche etwas gelernt?*, 1948.

Ehlers, Hermann. "Struktur und Aufgabe der Evangelischen Kirche in Deutschland heute," *Europa-Archiv*, April 5, 1951.

Eisenach 1958; Protokollband, 1951.

Giesen, Heinrich, Heinz-Horst Schrey, and Hans Jürgen Schultz. *Der mündige Christ*, 1957.

Giesen, Heinrich, editor. *"Fröhlich in Hoffnung;" Der Deutsche Evangelische Kirchentag 1954 in Leipzig*, 1954.

_____. *Erlebter Kirchentag; Frankfurt 1956*, 1956.

_____. *Erlebter Kirchentag; München 1959*, 1959.

_____. *Erlebter Kirchentag; Berlin 1961*, 1961.

Heckel, Theodor. *Die Evangelische Kirche in der modernen Gesellschaft*, 1956.

Herman, Stewart. *The Rebirth of the German Church*, 1946.

Iwand, Hans-Joachim. *Um den rechten Glauben; Gesammelte Aufsätze,* 1959.

Jacob, Günter, Hermann Kunst, and Wilhelm Stählin. *Die evangelische Christenheit in Deutschland; Gestalt und Auftrag,* 1958.

Littell, Franklin Hamlin. *The German Phoenix,* 1960.

Mehl, Roger. "Le protestantisme allemand d'aujourd'hui," *Revue d'Allemagne,* April-June 1970.

Merzyn, Friedrich. *Das Verfassungsrecht der evangelischen Kirche in Deutschland und ihrer Gliedkirchen,* three volumes, 1957–1964.

Müller, Eberhard. *Die Welt ist anders geworden,* 1953.

Niemöller, Martin. *Zur gegenwärtigen Lage der evangelischen Christenheit,* 1946.

_____ . *Reden 1945–1954,* 1958.

_____ . *Reden 1955–1957,* 1957.

_____ . *Reden 1958–1961,* 1961.

_____ . *Eine Welt oder keine Welt: Reden 1961–1963,* 1964.

Ryssel, Fritz Heinrich, editor. *Protestantismus heute,* 1959.

Schempp, Paul, editor. *Evangelische Selbstprüfung,* 1947.

Schreiner, Helmut. *Vom Recht der Kirche: Grundsätzliches und Praktisches zur Neuordnung des evangelischen Kirchentums,* 1947.

Söhlmann, Fritz, editor. *Treysa 1945,* 1946.

Stammler, Eberhard. *Protestanten ohne Kirche,* 1960.

Vogel, Heinrich. *Von der Verantwortung der Kirche für die Welt,* 1948.

Waltz, Hans Hermann. *Das protestantische Wagnis,* 1958.

Weisser, Elisabeth. *Freiheit und Bindung: Beiträge zur Situation der evangelischen Jugendarbeit in Deutschland,* 1963.

Wendland, Heinz-Dietrich. *Die Kirche in der modernen Gesellschaft: Entscheidungsfragen für das kirchliche Handeln im Zeitalter der Massenwelt,* 1956.

Biographies, Autobiographies, and Festschriften

Bachmann, Jürgen, editor. *Zum Dienst berufen: Lebensbilder leitender Männer der evangelischen Kirche in Deutschland,* 1963.

Bartsch, Friedrich, and others. *Die Stunde der Kirche: Dem evangelischen Bischof von Berlin Otto Dibelius zum 15. Mai 1950,* 1950.

Beckmann, Joachim, and Herbert Mochalski, editors. *Bekennende Kirche: Martin Niemöller zum 60. Geburtstag,* 1952.

Beckmann, Joachim, and Gerhard Weisser, editors. *Christliche Gemeinde und Gesellschaftswandel: Friedrich Karrenberg zur Vollendung des 60. Lebensjahres,* 1964.

Bethge, Eberhard. *Dietrich Bonhoeffer,* 1967.

Dibelius, Otto. *Ein Christ ist immer in Dienst,* 1961.

Grüber, Heinrich. *Erinnerungen aus sieben Jahrzehnten,* 1968.

Hühne, Werner. *Thadden-Trieglaff: Ein Leben unter uns,* 1959.

Jacobi, Gerhard, editor. *Otto Dibelius, Leben und Wirken: Mit Grussworten zum 80. Geburtstag von Theodor Heuss, Eugen Gerstenmaier, Hanns Lilje, Willem A. Visser't Hooft,* 1960.

Karrenberg, Friedrich, and Joachim Beckmann. *Verantwortung für den*

Menschen; Beiträge für die gesellschaftliche Programatik der Gegenwart: Festschrift für Präses Dr. Held, 1957.

Metzger, Wolfgang, editor. *Karl Hartenstein: Ein Leben für Kirche und Mission,* 1954.

Niemöller, Wilhelm. *Aus dem Leben eines Bekenntnispfarrers,* 1961.

Schmidt, Dietmar. *Martin Niemöller,* 1959.

Vogelsanger, Peter. *Der Auftrag der Kirche in der modernen Welt: Festgabe zum 70. Geburtstag von Emil Brunner,* 1959.

Wolf, Ernst, editor. *Zwischenstation: Festschrift für Karl Kupisch zum 60. Geburtstag,* 1963.

Wolf, Uvo Andreas. *Hermann Diem, sine vi–sed verbo, Aufsätze–Vorträge–Voten: Aus Anlass der Vollendung seines 65. Lebensjahres am 2. Februar 1965,* Theologische Bücherei, volume 25, 1965.

Wurm, Theophil. *Erinnerungen aus meinem Leben,* 1953.

Chapter 2. German Catholicism—Character and Organization

General Background (selected bibliography)

Adolf, Walter. *Hirtenamt und Hitler-Diktatur,* 1965.

Bauer, Clemens. *Deutscher Katholizismus; Entwicklungslinien und Profile,* 1964.

Böckenförde, Ernst-Wolfgang. "Der deutsche Katholizismus im Jahre 1933; Eine kritische Betrachtung," *Hochland,* February 1961.

Buchheim, Hans. "Der deutsche Katholizismus in Jahre 1933: Eine Auseinandersetzung mit Ernst-Wolfgang Böckenförde," *Hochland,* August 1961.

Conrad, Walter. *Der Kampf um die Kanzeln: Erinnerungen und Dokumente aus der Hitlerzeit,* 1957.

Deuerlein, Ernst. *Der deutsche Katholizismus 1933,* 1963.

Friedländer, Saul. *Pius XII. und das Dritte Reich; Eine Dokumentation,* 1965.

Gurian, Waldemar. *Der Kampf um die Kirche·im Dritten Reich,* 1936.

Kinkel, Walter. *Kirche und Nationalsozialismus, Ihre Auseinandersetzung zwischen 1925 und 1945 in Dokumenten dargestellt,* 1960.

Leiber, Robert, S. J. "Pius XII." *Stimmen der Zeit,* November 1958.

Lewy, Guenter. *The Catholic Church and Nazi Germany,* 1964.

von Löwenich, Walter. *Der moderne Katholizismus,* 1955.

Müller, Hans. "Zur Behandlung des Kirchenkampfes in der Nachkriegsliteratur," *Politische Studien,* 12, 1961.

———, editor. *Katholische Kirche und Nationalsozialismus; Dokumente 1930–1935,* 1963.

Natterer, Alois. *Der bayerische Klerus in der Zeit dreier Revolutionen 1918–1933–1945,* 1946.

Neuhäusler, Johann. *Kreuz und Hakenkreuz,* 1946.

Volk, Ludwig. *Der bayerische Episkopat und der Nationalsozialismus 1930–1934,* 2nd edition, 1966.

Zahn, Gordon. *German Catholics and Hitler's Wars,* 1962.

Since the War

Amery, Carl. *Die Kapitulation, oder Deutscher Katholizismus heute,* 1963.

_____. *Fragen an Welt und Kirche*, 1967.

Arnold, F. X., and others. *Catholicisme Allemand*, 1956.

Böll, Heinrich. *Aufsätze, Kritiken, Reden*, 1967.

Forster, Karl, editor. *Katholizismus und Kirche, Zum Weg des deutschen Katholizismus nach 1945*, Studien und Berichte der Katholischen Akademie in Bayern, number 28, 1965.

_____. *Das Zweite Vatikanische Konzil*, Studien und Berichte der Katholischen Akademie in Bayern, number 24, 1963.

Greinacher, Norbert, and Heinz Theo Risse, editors. *Bilanz des deutschen Katholizismus*, 1966.

Grosche, Robert, Friedrich Heer, Werner Becker, and Karlheinz Schmidthüs, *Der Weg aus dem Ghetto*, 1955.

Heldt, Joachim. *Gott in Deutschland*, 1963.

Hirschauer, Gerd. *Der Katholizismus vor dem Risiko der Freiheit*, 1969.

Hoffmann, Joseph. "Situation et problèmes du catholicisme allemand aujourd'hui," *Revue d'Allemagne*, April-June 1970.

Lenz-Medoc, Paulus. "Les catholiques d'Allemagne dans les relations internationales," in Alfred Grosser, editor. *Les relations internationales de l'Allemagne occidentale*, 1956.

Maier, Hans. *Deutscher Katholizismus nach 1945: Kirche, Gesellschaft, Geschichte*, 1964.

van Onna, Ben, and Martin Stankowski, editors. *Kritischer Katholizismus: Argumente gegen die Kirchen-Gesellschaft*, 1969.

Rahner, Karl, and Herbert Vorgrimler. *Kleines Konzilskompendium: Alle Konstitutionen, Dekrete und Erklärungen des Zweiten Vaticanums in der bishöflich genehmigten Übersetzungen*, sixth edition, 1969.

Ratzinger, Joseph and Hans Maier. *Demokratie in der Kirche: Moglichkeiten, Grenzen, Gefahren*, 1970.

Roegele, Otto. *Krise oder Wachstum? Zu Gegenwartsfragen des deutschen Katholizismus*, 1970.

Ruta, J.C., and J. Straubinger. *Die katholische Kirche in Deutschland und ihre Probleme*, 1954.

Schäufele, Hermann, editor. *Zur Neuordnung im Staats- und Völkerleben. Ansprachen Papst Pius XII*, 1946.

Schultz, Hans Jürgen. *Kritik an der Kirche*, 1958.

Seeber, David Andreas. *Katholikentag im Widerspruch: Ein Bericht über den 82. Katholikentag in Essen*, 1968.

Sucker, Wolfgang. *Der deutsche Katholizismus 1945–1950: Eine Chronik*, 1951.

Zaborowski, Jan. *Die Kirche an der Oder und Neisse*, 1969.

Zeiger, Ivo, S. J. "Um die Zukunft der Katholischen Kirche in Deutschland" *Stimmen der Zeit*, January 1948.

Biographies and Autobiographies

Bierbaum, Max. *Nicht Lob, Nicht Furcht*, 1963.

Erb, Alfons. *Bernhard Lichtenberg, Domprobst von St. Hedwig zu Berlin*, 1949.

Portmann, Heinrich. *Kardinal von Galen,* 1953.

Rauch, Wendelin, Archbishop of Freiburg. *Testificatio Veritas: Ansprachen, Kriegsbriefe, Hirtenschreiben,* 1955.

Siemer, Laurentius, O. P. *Aufzeichnungen und Briefe,* 1957.

Zöller, Josef Othmar. "Julius Kardinal Döpfner," *Die politische Meinung,* October 1964.

Chapter 3. The Occupation Era

Almond, Gabriel, editor. *The Struggle for Democracy in Germany,* 1949.

Balfour, Michael, and John Mair. *Four Power Control in Germany and Austria,* 1956.

Bodensiek, Julius. *Ein brüderliches Wort,* 1949.

British Military Government. *Ordinances,* 1945 et seq.

Clay, Lucius. *Decision in Germany,* 1950.

Coles, Harry, and Albert Weinberg. *Civil Affairs: Soldiers Become Governors,* 1964.

Davidson, Eugene. *The Death and Life of Germany,* 1959.

Dollinger, Hans, editor. *Deutschland unter den Besatzungsmächten,* 1967.

Donnison, F. S. V. *Civil Affairs and Military Government Organization and Planning,* 1966.

Ebsworth, Raymond. *Restoring Democracy in Germany: The British Contribution,* 1960.

Friedmann, Wolfgang. *The Allied Military Government of Germany,* 1947.

French Military Government. *Ordonnances,* 1945 et seq.

Friedrich, Carl, and others. *American Experience in Military Government in World War II,* 1948.

Gimbel, John. *The American Occupation of Germany,* 1968.

Gross, Werner. *Die ersten Schritte,* 1961.

Holborn, Hajo. *American Military Government: Its Organization and Policies,* 1947.

Jasper, Ronald. *George Bell, Bishop of Chichester,* 1967.

Kaufmann, Erich. *Deutschlands Rechtslage unter der Besatzung,* 1948.

Kirkpatrick, Ivone. *The Inner Circle,* 1959.

Knappen, Marshall. *And Call It Peace,* 1947.

Köhler, Wolfram. *Das Land aus dem Schmelztiegel: Die Entstehungsgeschichte Nordrhein-Westfalens,* 1961.

Lemberg, Eugen, and Friedrich Edding, editors. *Die Vertriebenen in Westdeutschland,* 1959.

Litchfield, Edward, and associates. *Governing Post-War Germany,* 1953.

McClaskey, Beryl. *The History of U.S. Policy and Program in the Field of Religious Affairs under the Office of the U.S. High Commissioner for Germany,* Office of the U.S. High Commissioner for Germany, 1951.

Merritt, Anna, and Richard Merritt. *Public Opinion in Occupied Germany. The OMGUS Surveys, 1945–1949,* 1970.

Montgomery, John. *Forced to be Free,* 1957.

Murphy, Robert. *Diplomat among Warriors,* 1964.

Niethammer, Lutz. "Die amerikanische Besatzungsmacht zwischen Verwaltungstradition und politischen Parteien in Bayern 1945," *Vierteljahrshefte für Zeitgeschichte*, number 2, 1967.

Padover, Saul. *Experiment in Germany*, 1946.

Pakenham, Francis, Lord. *Born to Believe: An Autobiography*, 1953.

Poll, Bernhard. "Franz Oppenhoff (1902–1945)," *Rheinische Lebensbilder*, 1, 1961.

Pollock, James, and Edward Mason. *American Policy toward Germany*, 1947.

Pollock, James, James Meisel, and Henry Bretton. *Germany under Occupation: Illustrative Materials and Documents*, 1947.

Price, Hoyt, and Carl Schorske. *The Problem of Germany*, 1947.

Schwarz, Hans-Peter. *Vom Reich zur Bundesrepublik*, 1966.

Supreme Headquarters Allied Expeditionary Force, *Handbook for Military Government in Germany Prior to Defect or Surrender*, 1944.

United States Department of State. *Occupation of Germany, Policy and Progress*, 1947.

––––––. *Germany, 1947–1949: The Story in Documents*, 1950.

United States Forces, Headquarters, European Theater, Office of Military Government, U.S. Zone. *Military Government Regulations*, 1945 et seq.

Willis, F. Roy. *France, Germany, and the New Europe 1945–1963*, 1965.

Zink, Harold. *American Military Government in Germany*, 1947.

Chapter 4: Collective Guilt and Denazification

Bizer, Ernst. *Ein Kampf um die Kirche: Der "Fall Schempp" nach den Akten erzählt*, 1965.

Diem, Hermann. *Kirche und Entnazifizierung*, 1946.

Dorn, Walter. "The Debate over American Occupation Policy in Germany in 1944–1945," *Political Science Quarterly*, December 1957.

FitzGibbon, Constantine. *Denazification*, 1969.

Griffith, William. "Denazification in the U.S. Zone of Germany" in *The Annals of the American Academy of Political and Social Science*, January 1950.

Herz, John. "The Fiasco of Denazification in Germany," *Political Science Quarterly*, December 1948.

Jaspers, Karl. *The Question of German Guilt*, 1947.

Knappstein, Karl Heinrich. "Die versaumte Revolution," *Die Wandlung*, August 1947.

Napoli, Joseph. "Denazification from an American's Point of View," *The Annals of the American Academy of Political and Social Science*, July 1949.

Niebuhr, Reinhold. "Germany: Vengeance or Justice," *The Nation*, July 23, 1949.

Plischke, Elmer. "Denazification Law and Procedure," *American Journal of International Law*, October 1947.

––––––. "Denazifying the Reich," *Review of Politics*, April 1947.

Pribilla, Max. *Deutsche Schicksalsfragen*, 1950.

Raddatz, Fritz. *Summa iniuria oder durfte der Papst schweigen?*, 1963.

Roth, Guenther, and Kurt Wolff. *The American Denazification of Germany: A Historical Survey and an Appraisal,* mimeographed manuscript, 1954.

Schuster, Johann B. "Kollektivschuld," *Stimmen der Zeit,* November 1946.

Thielicke, Helmut. *Die Schuld der Anderen: Ein Briefwechsel zwischen Helmut Thielicke und Hermann Diem,* 1948.

Wilkens, Erwin. *NS-Verbrechen; Strafjustiz; deutsche Selbstbesinnung,* 1964.

Zink, Harold. "American Denazification Program in Germany," *Journal of Central European Affairs,* October 1946.

Chapter 5: The Political Ethic of German Protestantism

Aland, Kurt, and Wilhelm Schneemelcher, editors. *Kirche und Staat: Festschrift für Bischof D. Hermann Kunst zum 60. Geburtstag am 21. Januar 1967,* 1967.

Althaus, Paul. "Die Christenheit und die politische Welt," in *Jahrbuch des Martin Luther Bundes,* 1948.

Asmussen, Hans. *Rom, Wittenberg, Moskau: Zur grossen Kirchenpolitik,* 1956.

_____. *Der Christ in der politischen Verantwortung,* 1961.

Bahr, Hans-Eckehard, editor. *Weltfrieden und Revolution: Neun politisch-theologische Analysen,* 1968.

Barth, Karl. *Christengemeinde und Bürgergemeinde,* 1946.

_____. *Christliche Gemeinde im Wechsel der Staatsordnungen: Dokumente einer Ungarnreise 1948,* 1948.

_____. *Politische Entscheidung in der Einheit des Glaubens,* 1952.

_____. *Against the Stream; Shorter Post-War Writings, 1946–1952,* edited by Ronald Smith, 1954.

_____. *Der Götze wackelt: Zeitkritische Aufsätze, Reden und Briefe von 1930 bis 1960,* edited by Karl Kupisch, 1961.

Beyer, Franz. *Menschen Warten: Aus dem politischen Wirken Martin Niemöllers seit 1945,* 1952.

Brunner, Emil. *Die Kirche zwischen Ost und West,* 1949.

Calliess, Rolf-Peter. *Kirche und Demokratie,* 1966.

Dehn, Günther. *Unsere Predigt heute,* 1946.

Delekat, Friedrich. *Die politische Predigt,* 1947.

_____. *Kirche über den Zeiten und in der Zeit, Aber wie?,* 1953.

Dibelius, Otto. *Grenzen des Staates,* 1949.

_____. *Obrigkeit,* 1963.

Diem, Hermann. *Luthers Predigt in den zwei Reichen,* 1947.

_____. *Die Kirche zwischen Russland und Amerika,* 1948.

_____. *Die politische Verantwortung des Christen heute,* 1952.

Dombois, Hans, and Erwin Wilkens, editors. *Macht und Recht: Beiträge zur lutherischen Staatslehre der Gegenwart,* 1956.

Fischer, Hans Gerhard. *Evangelische Kirche und Demokratie nach 1945: Ein Beitrag zum Problem der politischen Theologie,* 1970.

Fischer, Martin. *Die öffentliche Verantwortung des Christen heute,* 1952.

_____. *Obrigkeit,* 1959.

Friedrich Naumann Stiftung. *Politischer Liberalismus und evangelische Kirche,* 1967.

Gerstenmaier, Eugen, and others. *Die Kirche in der Öffentlichkeit,* 1948.

Gogarten, Freidrich. *Die Kirche in der Welt,* 1948.

Gollwitzer, Helmut. *Christ und Bürger in der Bundesrepublik: Eine Disputation mit Dr. Eugen Gerstenmaier,* no date.

———. *Forderungen der Freiheit: Aufsätze und Reden zur politischen Ethik,* 1962.

———. *Die christliche Gemeinde in der politischen Welt,* 1955.

———. "Einige Leitsätze zur politischen Beteiligung am politischen Leben," *Junge Kirche,* 1964, pp. 620-623.

Hahn, Friedrich. *Evangelische Unterweisung zwischen Theologie und Politik,* 1958.

Hahn, Wilhelm. "Die Bewältigung unserer Vergangenheit als politisches und theologisches Problem," *Evangelische Verantwortung,* number 7/8, 1964.

Hammelsbeck, Otto. *Um Heil oder Unheil im öffentlichen Leben,* 1947.

Heinemann, Gustav. "Zur theologischen Bemühung um Politik aus christlicher Verantwortung," *Die Stimme der Gemeinde,* May 1951.

———. "Politisierung der Kirche?" *Die Stimme der Gemeinde,* July 1957.

———. "Gedanken zur politischen Ethik," *Junge Kirche,* July 1957.

———. "Kirchen und Parteien in der Bundesrepublik Deutschland," *Die neue Gesellschaft,* June 1966.

Kraus, Hans-Joachim. *Prophetie und Politik,* 1952.

von Krause, Wolfram. *Die politische Verantwortung der Kirche nach der Lehre der lutherischen Bekenntnisschriften,* 1952.

Künneth, Walter. *Politik zwischen Dämon und Gott; Eine christliche Ethik des Politischen,* 1954.

Kunst, Hermann. *Die politische Aufgabe der Kirche,* 1954.

Kupisch, Karl. *Vom Pietismus zum Kommunismus; Historische Gestalten, Szenen und Probleme,* 1953.

Lilje, Hanns. *Kirche und Welt,* 1956.

Chapter 6: The Political Ethic of German Catholicism

von Aretin, Karl Otmar Freiherr. "Kardinal Faulhaber—Kämpfer oder Mitläufer?," *Frankfurter Hefte,* May 1966.

Barzel, Rainer. "Die persönliche religiöse Verpflichtung der Christen zur Politik," in *Ihr sollt mir Zeugen sein: 76. Deutscher Katholikentag, 1954, Fulda,* 1954.

———. *Mater et Magistra und praktische Politik,* 1962.

Baukloh, Friedhelm. "Deutsche Katholiken vor der Wahl," *Der Monat,* March 1965.

Beckel, Albrecht. *Christliche Staatslehre: Grundlagen und Zeitfragen,* 1961.

———. *Mensch, Gesellschaft, Kirche bei Heinrich Böll,* 1966.

———. *Demokratie—Idee und Praxis,* 1966.

Bergmann, Bernhard, and Josef Steinberg, editors. *In Memoriam Wilhelm Böhler: Erinnerungen und Begegnungen,* 1965.

Böckenförde, Ernst-Wolfgang. "Das Ethos der modernen Demokratie und die Kirche," *Hochland,* January-February 1959.

Böhm, Anton. "Voraussetzunglose Politik," *Wort und Wahrheit,* July 1957.

Buchheim, Karl, and Johannes Binkowski. *Die Pflicht zur Politik,* 1957.

Dirks, Walter. "Die Kirchen und die CDU," *Frankfurter Hefte,* June 1957.

_____. *Das schmutzige Geschäft? Die Politik und die Verantwortung der Christen,* 1964.

_____. "Ein 'anderer' Katholizismus?; Minderheiten im deutschen Corpus catholicorum," *Frankfurter Hefte,* April 1966.

Forster, Karl, editor. *Das religiöse Geheimnis der Stadt,* Studien und Berichte der katholischen Akademie in Bayern, number 6, 1958.

_____, editor. *Staat und Gewissen,* Studien und Berichte der Katholischen Akademie in Bayern, number 8, 1959.

_____, editor. *Christentum und Liberalismus,* Studien und Berichte der Katholischen Akademie in Bayern, number 13, 1960.

_____, editor. *Frankreich und Deutschland,* Studien und Berichte der Katholischen Akademie in Bayern, number 23, 1963.

_____, editor. *Katholik und christliche Partei,* Studien und Berichte der Katholischen Akademie in Bayern, number 31, 1965.

Garaudy, Roger, Johannes Metz, and Karl Rahner. *Der Dialog, oder ändert sich das Verhältnis zwischen Katholizismus und Marxismus,* 1966.

Gundlach, Gustav, S. J. "Die Katholiken und die Bundesrepublik," *Stimmen der Zeit,* August 1957.

Hanssler, Bernard. *Das Gottesvolk der Kirche,* 1960.

_____, editor. *Die Kirche in der Gesellschaft,* 1961.

Höffner, Joseph. "Der deutsche Katholizismus in der pluralistischen Gesellschaft der Gegenwart," in Joseph Höffner, editor. *Jahrbuch des Instituts für christliche Sozialwissenschaften der Westfälischen Wilhelms-Universität Müster,* 1960.

Horné, Alfred, editor. *Christ und Bürger heute und morgen,* 1958.

Kafka, Gustav, editor. *Die Katholiken vor der Politik,* 1958.

_____. "Christliche Parteien und katholische Kräfte," *Die neue Ordnung,* March-April 1958.

Le Bras, Gabriel, and others. "Catholicisme et politique en France et en Allemagne," *Allemagne,* February-March and April-May, 1957.

Lenz, Hubert. *Die Kirche und das weltliche Recht,* 1956.

Maier, Hans. "Politischer Katholizismus, sozialer Katholizismus, christliche Demokratie," *Civitas,* volume 1, 1962.

Mikat, Paul. "Kirche, Gesellschaft, Staat: Wandlungen seit dem II. Vatikanischen Konzil," *Die politische Meinung,* June 1966.

Müller, Eberhard, and Bernard Hanssler. *Klerikalisierung des öffentlichen Lebens?,* 1963.

von Nell-Breuning, Oswald, and Hermann Sacher. *Zur christlichen Staatslehre: Beiträge zu einem Wörterbuch der Politik,* 1948.

_____, editors. *Wörterbuch der Politik,* 1947.

Pfeil, Hans. "Individualismus und Liberalismus, Ihr Einbruch in die Frömmigkeit," *Die neue Ordnung,* September-October and November-December, 1955.

Rahner, Karl. *Der Christ in der modernen Welt. Sendung und Gnade,* 1959.

Roegele, Otto. "Der deutsche Katholizismus im sozialen Chaos; Eine nüchterne Bestandsaufnahme," *Hochland,* February 1949.

_____. *Kirche und öffentliche Meinung,* 1953.

_____. *Kirche und Politik,* 1956.

_____. *Was geht uns Christen Europa an?,* 1964.

Rovan, Joseph. *Le catholicisme politique en Allemagne,* 1956.

Spital, H. J., and E. W. Böckenförde. "Noch einmal: Das Ethos der modernen Demokratie und die Kirche," *Hochland,* June 1958.

Steinkämpfer, Manfred, editor. *Kirche und Politik,* 1966.

Vogt, Wolfgang. *Der Staat in der Soziallehre der Kirche,* 1965.

Zeiger, Ivo, S. J. "Die religiös-sittliche Lage und die Aufgabe der deutschen Katholiken," in *Der Christ in der Not der Zeit: Der 72. Deutsche Katholikentag vom 1. bis 5. September 1948 in Mainz,* 1949.

Zentralkomitee der deutschen Katholiken. *Arbeitstagung Saarbrücken, 16.- 19. April 1958,* 1958.

Chapter 7: The Legal Relationship between Church and State

Arndt, Adolf. "Die Konfessionalisierung der Bundesrepublik," *Geist und Tat,* May 1954.

Böhler, Wilhelm. "Katholische Kirche und Staat in Deutschland," *Politische Bildung,* number 44, 1953.

Conrad, Wolfgang. *Der Öffentlichkeitsauftrag der Kirche; Eine Untersuchung über den Rechtscharakter der Einigungsformel der deutschen Staatskirchenverträge seit 1945,* 1964.

Eschenburg, Theodor. *Herrschaft der Verbäde?,* 1956.

_____. *Ämterpatronage,* 1961.

Fischer, Erwin. *Trennung von Staat und Kirche; Die Gefährdung der Religionsfreiheit in der Bundesrepublik,* 1964.

_____. *Das Bundesverfassungsgericht über Staat und Kirche,* 1965.

_____. *Kirchenaustritt und Kirchensteuer,* 1966.

Flatten, Heinrich. *Fort mit der Kirchensteuer?,* 1964.

Forster, Karl, editor. *Das Verhältnis von Kirche und Staat,* Studien und Berichte der Katholischen Akademie in Bayern, number 30, 1965.

_____, editor. *Klerikalismus heute?,* Studien und Berichte der Katholischen Akademie in Bayern, number 26, 1964.

Giese, Friedrich. *Deutsches Kirchensteuerrecht,* 1965.

_____ and Albert Königer. *Grundzüge des katholischen Kirchenrechtes und des Staatskirchenrechts,* 3rd edition, 1949.

Golay, John. *The Founding of the Federal Republic of Germany,* 1958.

Grundmann, Siegfried. *Die Ordnung des Verhältnisses von Kirche und Staat auf der Grundlage des Vertragskirchenrechts,* 1960.

Hamann, Andreas, editor. *Das Grundgesetz für die Bundesrepublik Deutschland vom 23. Mai 1949,* 3rd revised edition, 1970.

Hering, C. J., and H. Lentz. *Entscheidungen in Kirchensachen seit 1946.* Volume 1: *1946 bis 1952;* Volume 2: *1953 bis 1954;* Volume 3: *1957-1958,* 1963-1968.

Hanssler, Bernard. "Klerikalismus ein Kinderschreck," *Politische Studien,* January 1957.

_____. "Die Entwicklung des Staatskirchenrechts seit 1945," in *Jahrbuch des öffentlichen Rechts,* new series, volume 10, 1961.

Hesse, Konrad, Siegfried Riecke, and Ulrich Scheuner. *Staatsverfassung und Kirchenordnung: Festgabe für Rudolf Smend zum 80. Geburtstag am 15. Januar 1962,* 1962.

Hollerbach, Alexander. *Verträge zwischen Staat und Kirche in der Bundesrepublik Deutschland,* 1965.

Kern, Eduard. *Staat und Kirche in der Gegenwart,* 1951.

Leibholz, Gerhard and Hermann von Mangoldt. *Jahrbuch des öffentlichen Rechts der Gegenwart,* new series, volume 1: *Entstehungsgeschichte der Artikel des Grundgesetzes,* 1951.

Liermann, Hans. *Kirchen und Staat,* volume 1, 1954; volume 2, 1955.

von Mangoldt, Hermann. *Das Bonner Grundgesetz; Kommentar,* 1950–1953.

Martens, Klaus. *Wie reich ist die Kirche?; Versuch einer Bestandsaufnahme in Deutschland,* 1969.

Merkl, Peter. *The Origin of the West German Republic,* 1963.

Mikat, Paul. *Das Verhältnis von Kirche und Staat in der Bundesrepublik,* 1964.

Model, Otto, and Klaus Müller. *Grundgesetz für die Bundesrepublik Deutschland,* 4th edition, 1965.

Osner, Karl. *Kirchen und Entwicklungshilfe,* 1965.

Quaritsch, Helmut and Hermann Weber, editors. *Staat und Kirchen in der Bundesrepublik: Staatskirchenrechtliche Aufsätze 1950–1967,* 1967.

Rahner, Karl, and others. *Religionsfreiheit: Ein Problem für Staat und Kirche,* 1966.

Ranke, Hansjürg. "Evangelische Kirche und Staat," *Politische Bildung,* number 43, 1953.

Schelz, Sepp. *Die fromme Schröpfung; Zum Streit um das Geld der Kirche,* 1969.

Scheuner, Ulrich. *Rechtsgrundlagen der Beziehungen von Kirche und Staat,* Veröffentlichungen der Evangelischen Akademie in Hessen und Nassau, number 47, 1962.

Smend, Rudolf. *Staatsrechtliche Abhandlungen und andere Aufsätze,* 2nd edition, 1968.

_____ . "Staat und Kirche nach dem Bonner Grundgesetz," *Zeitschrift für Evangelisches Kirchenrecht,* volume 1 (1951).

Steck, Karl Gerhard. "Klerikalismus und Antiklerikalismus in evangelischer Sicht," *Politische Studien,* March 1957.

Veröffentlichung der Vereinigung der Deutschen Staatsrechtslehrer. Number 11, *Die Gegenwartslage des Staatskirchenrechts,* 1952; number 26, *Die Kirchen unter dem Grundgesetz,* 1968.

Weber, Hermann. *Die Religionsgemeinschaften als Körperschaften des öffentlichen Rechts im System des Grundgesetzes,* 1966.

_____ . *Staatskirchenverträge: Textsammlung,* 1967.

Weber, Werner. *Die Ablösung der Staatsleitungen an die Religionsgesellschaften,* 1948.

_____ . *Spannungen und Kräfte im westdeutschen Verfassungssystem,* 1951.

_____ . *Die deutschen Konkordate und Kirchenverträge der Gegenwart,* 1962.

Wilken, Waldemar. *Unser Geld und die Kirche,* 2nd edition, 1964.

Zeiger, Ivo, S. J. "Das Bonner Verfassungswerk," *Stimmen der Zeit,* volume 145 (1949–1950).

Ziegler, Paul. "Die Kirchensteurer in Deutschland," *Lutherische Monatshefte,* February, 1965.

Chapter 8: The Schools and other Problems of the Reichskonkordat

Abelein, Manfred. *Die Kulturpolitik des deutschen Reiches und der Bundesrepublik Deutschland: Ihre verfassungsgeschichtliche Entwicklung und ihre verfassungsrechtlichen Probleme,* 1968.

Albrecht, Alfred. *Koordination von Staat und Kirche in der Demokratie: Eine juristische Untersuchung über die allgemeinen Rechtsprobleme der Konkordate zwischen der katholischen Kirche und einem freiheitlich-demokratischen Staat,* 1965.

Bauer, Clemens. "Das Reichskonkordat," *Hochland,* December 1956.

Becker, Hans-Joachim. *Zur Rechtsproblematik des Reichskonkordats,* 2nd edition, 1956.

Böhler, Wilhelm. "Elternrecht, Schulfragen und Reichskonkordat im Parlamentarischen Rat und in der Politik der Deutschen Bundesrepublik und ihrer Länder," Hans Seidel, editor. *Festschrift zum 70. Geburtstag von Dr. Hans Ehard,* 1958.

Bracher, Karl-Dietrich. *Die Auflösung der Weimarer Republik: Eine Studie zum Problem des Machtverfalls in der Demokratie,* 1955.

von Carnap, Roderich, and Friedrich Edding. *Der relative Schulbesuch in der Bundesrepublik, 1952–1960,* 1962.

Deuerlein, Ernst. *Das Reichskonkordat: Beiträge zur Vorgeschichte, zum Abschluss und Vollendung des Konkordates zwischen dem Heiligen Stuhl und dem Deutschen Reich vom 20. 7. 1933,* 1956.

Ellwein, Thomas. *Klerikalismus in der deutschen Politik,* 1955.

Erlinghagen, Karl. *Vom Bildungsideal zur Lebensordnung: Das Erziehungsziel in der katholischen Pädagogik,* 1960.

――――. *Die Schule in der pluralistischen Gesellschaft,* 1964.

――――. *Katholisches Bildungsdefizit in Deutschland,* 1965.

――――. and others. *Konfessionalität und Erziehungswissenschaft: Eine Diskussion,* 1965.

Esterhues, Josef. *Zur Geschichte der Bekenntnisschule: Grundsätze katholischer Schulpolitik,* 1958.

Fleig, Paul. *Das Elternrecht im Bonner Grundgesetz,* 1953.

Frings, Cardinal Joseph, and Bishop Franz Hengsbach. *Schulkampf '66,* 1966.

Giese, Friedrich, and Friedrich August von der Heydte, editors. *Der Konkordatsprozess,* 4 volumes, 1956–1959.

Groppe, Herbert. *Das Reichskonkordat vom 20. Juli 1933: Eine Studie zur staats- und völkerrechtlichen Bedeutung dieses Vertrages für die Bundesrepublik Deutschland,* 1956.

Hammelsbeck, Oskar. *Volksschule in evangelischer Verantwortung,* 1961.

Heuser, Adolf. *Die katholische Schule,* 1961.

von der Heydte, Friedrich August. "Die katholische Kirche in Deutschland und das Konkordatsurteil des Bundesverfassungsgerichts," *Zeitschrift für Politik,* number 3, 1957.

Kaiser, J. H. *Die politische Klausel der Konkordate,* 1949.

Kupper, Alfons. *Staatliche Akten über die Reichskonkordatsverhandlungen 1933,* 1969.

Leiber, Robert, S. J. "Reichskonkordat und Ende der Zentrumspartei," *Stimmen der Zeit,* December 1960.

Morsey, Rudolf. "Zur Problematik und Geschichte des Reichskonkordats," *Neue politische Literatur,* number 1, 1960.

_____, editor. "Tagebuch 7.–20. April 1933, Ludwig Kaas; Aus dem Nachlass von Prälat Ludwig Kaas," *Stimmen der Zeit,* September 1960.

Nellessen-Schumacher, Traute. *Sozialstruktur und Ausbildung der deutschen Katholiken: Statistische Untersuchung aufgrund der Ergebnisse der Volks- und Berufszählung 1961,* 1969.

Picht, Georg. *Die deutsche Bildungskatastrophe,* 1964.

Pöggeler, Franz, editor. *Das Wagnis der Schule,* 1962.

_____, editor. *Katholische Erziehung und Schulreform im 20. Jahrhundert: Das Wagnis der Schule,* 1962.

Reis, Hans. "Konkordat und Kirchenvertrag in der Staatsverfassung," in *Jahrbuch des öffentlichen Rechts der Gegenwart,* new series, volume 17, 1968.

Samuel, R. H., and R. Hinton Thomas. *Education and Society in Modern Germany,* 1949.

Stein, E., N. Joest, and Hans Dombois. *Elternrecht; Studien zu einer Rechtsphilosophie und evangelisch-theologischen Grundlegung,* 1958.

Volk, Ludwig, editor. *Kirchliche Akten über die Reichskonkordatsverhandlungen 1933,* Veröffentlichungen der Kommission für Zeitgeschichte bei der Katholischen Akademie in Bayern, Series A, 1969.

Wenner, Joseph. *Reichskonkordat und Länderkonkordate,* 7th edition, 1964.

Zentralkomitee der deutschen Katholiken. *Die deutschen Katholiken und die Bildungsaufgaben der Gegenwart,* 1965.

Chapter 9: Reunification, Conscription, and Nuclear Arms

Allemann, Fritz René. *Bonn ist nicht Weimar,* 1956.

Amelung, Eberhard. "Soldat-Bürger-Demokratie," *Evangelische Verantwortung,* July-August 1964.

Andersen, Wilhelm and others. *Lutherische Stimmen zur Frage der Atomwaffen,* 1958.

Auer, Alfons. "Atombombe und Naturrecht," *Die neue Ordnung,* July-August 1958.

_____, Richard Egenter, Heinz Fleckenstein, Johannes Hirschmann, Joseph Höffner, Nicolaus Monzel, and Eberhard Welty. *Christliche Friedenspolitik und atomare Aufrüstung,* 1958.

Baring, Arnulf. *Aussenpolitik in Adenauers Kanzlerdemokratie; Bonns Beitrag zur Europäischen Verteidigungsgemeinschaft,* 1969.

Barth, Karl. "Fürchtet euch nicht!" *Unterwegs,* November 1, 1950.

_____. *Die christliche Verkündigung im heutigen Europa,* 1946.

_____. *Die Kirche zwischen Ost und West,* 1949.

_____. *Zur Wiederaufrüstung in Deutschland,* 1950.

Bienert, Walther. *Krieg, Kriegsdienst und Kriegsdienstverweigerung; Nach der Botschaft des Neuen Testaments,* 1952.

Delekat, Friedrich and others. *Evangelische Stimmen zur Frage des Wehrdienstes,* 1956.

Deutsch, Karl and Lewis Edinger. *Germany Rejoins the Powers; Mass Opinion, Interest Groups and Elites in Contemporary German Foreign Policy,* 1959.

Evangelische Kirche in Deutschland. *Kirche und Kriegsdienstverweigerung,* 1956.

Evertz, Alexander. *Der Abfall der evangelischen Kirche vom Vaterland,* fourth edition 1966.

Forster, Karl, editor. *Kann der atomare Verteidigungskrieg ein gerechter Krieg sein?* Studien und Berichte der Katholischen Akademie in Bayern, 1960.

Gollwitzer, Helmut. *Die Christen und die Atomwaffen,* 1957.

_____. *Militär, Staat und Kirche,* 1965.

Gross, Erwin. *Das Geheimnis des Pazifismus: Theologie und Politik der Kirchlichen Bruderschaften,* 1959.

Heinemann, Gustav. *Deutsche Sicherheit,* 1950; reprinted in *Kirchliches Jahrbuch,* 1950.

_____. *Deutsche Friedenspolitik; Reden und Aufsätze,* 1952.

_____. "Neue Achsenpolitik," *Die Stimme der Gemeinde,* April 1952.

_____. "Was Dr. Adenauer vergisst; Notizen zu einer Biographie," *Frankfurter Hefte,* July 1956.

_____. *Im Schnittpunkt der Zeit: Reden und Aufsätze,* 1957.

_____. *Verfehlte Deutschlandpolitik: Irreführung und Selbsttäuschung; Artikel und Reden,* third edition 1971.

Henkys, Reinhard, editor. *Deutschland und die östlichen Nachbarn; Beiträge zu einer evangelischen Denkschrift,* 1966.

Hirschmann, Johannes, S.J. "Kann atomare Verteidigung sittlich gerechtfertigt sein?" *Stimmen der Zeit,* July 1958.

Howe, Günter, editor. *Atomzeitalter, Krieg und Frieden,* 1959.

Institut für europäische Politik und Wirtschaft. *Der deutsche Soldat in der Armee von morgen,* 1954.

Jahn, Hans Edgar. *Für und gegen den Wehrbeitrag: Argumente und Dokumente,* 1957.

Jentsch, Werner, editor. *Christliche Stimmen zur Wehrdienstfrage,* 1952.

Koch, Dieter. *Heinemann und die Deutschlandfrage,* 1972.

Kogon, Eugen. *Die unvollendete Erneuerung: Deutschland im Kräftefeld 1945–1963; Aufsätze aus zwei Jahrzehnten,* 1964.

Küchenhoff, Erich. "Atomkrieg zum Schutze der Menschenwürde?," *Blätter für deutsche und internationale Politik* (1958), pp. 507–513.

Künneth, Walter. "Das Problem der Kriegsdienstverweigerung und die Kirche der Reformation," *Deutsches Pfarrerblatt,* numbers 3 and 4, 1951.

Luchsinger, Fred. *Bericht über Bonn; Deutsche Politik 1955–1965,* 1966.

Neyer, Harry. *Wie hast Du's mit der Bundeswehr?,* 1963.

Niemöller, Martin. *Deutschland wohin? Krieg oder Frieden?,* 1952.

―――― and others. *Frieden: Der Christ im Kampf gegen die Angst und den Gewaltgeist der Zeit,* 1954.

―――― . *Zur atomaren Rüstung; Zwei Reden,* 1959.

Noack, Ulrich. *Die Sicherung des Friedens durch Neutralisierung Deutschlands und seine ausgleichende weltwirtschaftliche Aufgabe,* 1948.

Ökumenische Studiengemeinschaft Berlin/Brandenburg. *Die Kirche zwischen Ost und West: Beitrag der Ökumenischen Studiengemeinschaft Berlin/ Brandenburg zur Weltkirchenkonferenz in Amsterdam 1948,* Ökumenische Reihe, number 6, 1948.

Pribilla, Max, S.J. "Die Kirche zwischen Ost und West," *Stimmen der Zeit,* January 1951.

Rand Corporation. *The Attitude of the Christian Churches Toward a German Defense Contribution,* Rand Monograph 927, 1952.

Schardt, Alois. "Das Gewissen bleibt unruhig," *Rheinischer Merkur,* October 17, 1958.

Scheuner, Ulrich. "Zur Frage der Kriegsdienstverweigerung," *Evangelische Verantwortung,* volume 9, 1955.

Schmidthüs, Karlheinz. "Atomwaffen und Gewissen," *Wort und Wahrheit,* June-July 1958.

Schröter, Martin, editor. *Kriegsdienstverweigerung als christliche Entscheidung,* 1965.

Seidlmayer, Michael. "Der Atomkrieg als politisches und ethisches Problem," *Blätter für deutsche und internationale Politik,* August 20, 1958.

Stehle, Hansjakob. "Katholische Kirche und Koexistenz," *Aussenpolitik,* May 1956.

Thielicke, Helmut. "Der Christ und die Verhütung des Krieges im Atomzeitalter," *Zeitschrift für Evangelische Ethik,* number 2, 1957.

Varain, Heinz Josef. "Die Auseinandersetzung innerhalb der Evangelischen Kirche wegen der Wiederaufrüstung," *Geschichte in Wissenschaft und Unterricht,* July 1958.

Wilkens, Erwin. *Kirchlicher Beitrag zur deutschen Ostpolitik,* 1966.

―――― , editor. *Vertreibung und Versöhnung: Die Synode der EKD zur Denkschrift "Die Lage der Vertriebenen und das Verhältnis des deutschen Volkes zu seinen östlichen Nachbarn,"* 1966.

Chapter 10: Social Policy

Protestant

Beckmann, Joachim, and Gerhard Weisser, editors. *Christliche Gemeinde und Gesellschaftswandel: Friedrich Karrenberg zur Vollendung des 60. Lebensjahres,* 1964.

Bienert, Walther. *Die Arbeit nach der Lehre der Bibel: Ein Beitrag zur evangelischen Sozialethik,* 1956.

von Bismarck, Klaus. *Kirche und moderne Arbeitswelt,* 1955.

―――― . "Die Kirche in der industriellen Welt," *Der Mensch in der Wirtschaft,* number 1, 1960.

―――― . and others. *Aufgabe der gesellschaftlichen Diakonie; Kirche im Volk,* number 25, 1960.

Dibelius, Otto. *Volk, Staat und Wirtschaft aus christlichem Verantwortungs-bewusstsein,* 1947.

Gollwitzer, Helmut. *Die reichen Christen und der arme Lazarus: Die Konsequenzen von Uppsala,* 1968.

Heckel, Theodor, and others. *Die evangelische Kirche in der modernen Gesellschaft,* 1956.

Heilfurth, Gerhard. *Church and Labour in Western Germany,* 1954.

———. "Gibt es ein evangelisches Sozialprogramm?," *Die Mitarbeit,* June 1957.

Hillerdal, Gunnar. *Kirche und Sozialethik,* 1963.

Karrenberg, Friedrich. *Stand und Aufgaben christlicher Sozialethik;* Kirche im Volk, number 4, 1951.

———. *Gestalt und Kritik des Westens: Beiträge zur christlichen Sozialethik heute,* 1959.

Karrenberg, Friedrich, and Joachim Beckmann, editors. *Verantwortung für Menschen: Beiträge zur gesellschaftlichen Problematik der Gegenwart,* 1957.

Karrenberg, Friedrich, and Wolfgang Schweitzer, editors. *Spannungsfelder der evangelischen Soziallehre: Aufgaben und Fragen vom Dienst der Kirche an der heutigen Gesellschaft,* 1960.

Kunst, Hermann, and Gerhard Heilfurth, editors. *Wir sind gefordert: Fragen christlicher Verantwortung,* 1954.

Lutz, Hans. "Einheitsgewerkschaft in evangelischer Sicht," *Gewerkschaftliche Monatshefte,* (1953) pp. 714–719.

Matthes, Joachim. *Die Emigration der Kirche aus der Gesellschaft,* 1964.

Müller, Eberhard, editor. *Eigentumsbildung in sozialer Verantwortung: Der Text der Denkschrift der Evangelischen Kirche in Deutschland; Erläutert von Eberhard Müller,* 1962.

Müller-Schwefe, Hans-Rudolf. *Die Kirche und die Arbeiter,* 1950.

Rendtorff, Trutz, and Heinz Eduard Tödt. *Theologie der Revolution: Analysen und Materialien,* 1968.

Schrey, Heinz-Horst. "Soziale Verkündigung oder Social Gospel?," *Zeitschrift für Evangelische Ethik,* number 2, 1957.

Stork, Hans. *Die Kirche im Neuland der Industrie,* 1959.

Suhr, Georg, editor. *Evangelische Stimmen zum Sozialhilfegesetz und Jugendwohlfahrtsgesetz,* 1962.

Synode der Evangelischen Kirche in Deutschland. "Die Kirche und die Welt der Arbeit," in *Kirchliches Jahrbuch für die Evangelische Kirche in Deutschland,* 1955.

Wendland, Heinz-Dietrich. *Die Kirche in der modernen Gesellschaft: Entscheidungsfragen für das kirchliche Handeln im Zeitalter der Massenwelt,* 2nd edition, 1958.

———. *Botschaft an die soziale Welt: Beiträge zur christlichen Sozialethik der Gegenwart,* Studien zur evangelischen Sozialtheologie und Sozialethik, volume 5, 1959.

———. "Die Grundlagen unseres sozialen Handelns: Evangelische Sozialethik als Fundament christlicher Bewährung," *Die Mitarbeit: Evangelische Monatshefte zur Gesellschaftspolitik* (1959) pp. 454–461.

_____. *Eigentum für alle?: Eigentum und Gesellschaftsordnung im Lichte der evangelischen Soziallehre*, 1960.

_____. *Person und Gesellschaft in evangelischer Sicht*, 1965.

_____. *Die Kirche in der revolutionären Gesellschaft*, 1967.

Catholic

Achinger, Hans, Ludwig Preller, and Hermann Josef Wallraff, editors. *Normen der Gesellschaft: Festgabe für Oswald von Nell-Breuning zu seinem 75. Geburtstag*, 1965.

Arnold, Franz Xaver. *Zur christlichen Lösung der sozialen Frage*, 1949.

_____. *Das Mitbestimmungsrecht im Lichte christlicher Soziallehre*, 1951.

Auer, Alfons. *Weltoffener Christ; Grundsächliches und Geschichtliches zur Laienfrömmigkeit*, 1960.

Becher, Paul. "Zur sozialen Situation der Bundesrepublik," *Die neue Ordnung*, February 1965.

Beckel, Albrecht, and others: *Mensch sein im Betrieb*, 1960.

Braun, Siegfried. "Eine soziale Stellungnahme zur katholischen Soziallehre," *Werkhefte*, August-September 1964.

Dirks, Walter. "Das gesellschaftspolitische Engagement der deutschen Katholiken seit 1945," *Frankfurter Hefte*, November 1964.

Fellermeier, Jakob. *Abriss der katholischen Gesellschaftslehre*, 1957.

Frings, Cardinal Josef. *Grundsätze christlicher Sozialarbeit*, 1948.

_____. *Verantwortung und Mitverantwortung in der Wirtschaft*, 1949.

Gundlach, Gustav, S. J. *Die Ordnung der menschlichen Gesellschaft*, 1964.

Häring, Bernhard, C.SS.R. "Mitbestimmung und Mitbeteiligung als Wege zur Entproletarisierung," *Stimmen der Zeit*, May 1951.

Höffner, Joseph. *Christliche Gesellschaftslehre*, 1962.

Hirschmann, Hans. *Was sagt Bochum zum Mitbestimmungsrecht*, 1951.

Klüber, Franz. *Grundriss der katholischen Gesellschaftslehre*, 1971.

Külp, Bernard. *Kurzgefasste katholische Soziallehre*, 1962.

Jostock, Paul. *Das Sozialprodukt und seine Verteilung*, 1955.

_____. *Grundzüge der Soziallehre und der Sozialreform*, 1946.

Muhler, Emil. *Die Soziallehre der Päpste*, 1958.

Nawroth, Egon Edgar, O. P. *Die wirtschaftspolitischen Ordnungsvorstellungen des Neoliberalismus*, 1962.

_____. *Zur Sinnerfüllung der Marktwirtschaft*, 1965.

von Nell-Breuning, Oswald, S. J. *Wirtschaft und Gesellschaft heute*, 1956.

_____. *Die Gesellschaft, in der wir leben*, 1957.

_____. *Eigentumsbildung in Arbeitnehmerhand*, 1953.

_____. *Kapitalismus und gerechter Lohn*, 1960.

_____. "Die Christen im DGB," *Gesellschaftspolitische Kommentare*, September 15, 1957.

_____. *Christliche Soziallehre*, 1964.

_____. *Mitbestimmung*, 1968.

_____ and Hermann Sacher, editors. *Zur christlichen Gesellschaftslehre*, 2nd edition, 1954.

_____ and Hans Lutz. *Katholische und evangelische Soziallehre: Ein Vergleich*, 1967.

Prinz, Franz, S. J. "Werkgemeinschaften christlicher Arbeitnehmer," *Stimmen der Zeit,* January 1960.

Ratzinger, Joseph. *Naturrecht, Evangelium und Ideologie in der katholischen Soziallehre,* 1964.

Risse, Heinz Theo. "Die Situation der christlichen-sozialen Arbeitnehmerschaft in der Bundesrepublik," *Frankfurter Hefte,* May 1960.

Thalhammer, Dominik, S. J. *Bewältigte Gegenwart,* 1963.

Wallraff, Hermann Josef, S. J. *Kirche und Wirtschaft; Auftrag und Verantwortung,* 1959.

Welty, Eberhard, O. P. *Recht und Ordnung in Eigentum,* 1947.

Chapter 11: Christian Democracy

Albers, Johannes. *Die Aufgabe der Christlich-Demokratischen Union des deutschen Volkes,* no date.

Almond, Gabriel. "The Christian Parties of Western Europe," *World Politics,* October 1948.

Amelung, Eberhard. "Die Konfessionen in der Politik," *Civis,* May 1954.

Ansprenger, Franz. "Katholische Verbände im Vorfeld der CDU," *Die neue Gesellschaft,* May-June 1958.

Arnold, Karl. *Worum geht es?,* 1957.

Barzel, Rainer. *Die deutschen Parteien,* 1946.

———. *Die geistigen Grundlagen der politischen Parteien,* 1947.

———, editor. *Karl Arnold: Grundlegung christlich-demokratischer Politik in Deutschland; Eine Dokumentation,* 1960.

Berberich, Walter. "Die CSU als neue interkonfessionell-christliche und föderalistische Mehrheitspartei: Ein Beitrag zur Geschichte der Christlich-Sozialen Union in Bayern," in *Politisches Jahrbuch der CSU,* 1954.

Buchheim, Karl. *Geschichte der christlichen Parteien in Deutschland,* 1953.

Deuerlein, Ernst. *CDU/CSU 1945-1957: Beiträge zur Zeitgeschichte,* 1957.

Dirks, Walter. *Die zweite Republik,* 1947.

———. "Die christliche Demokratie in der Bundesrepublik," *Frankfurter Hefte,* September 1953.

———. "Die Kirchen und die CDU," *Frankfurter Hefte,* June 1957.

Ehlers, Hermann. *Drei Jahre Deutscher Bundestag,* 1952.

——— and others. *Deutschlands Aufgabe: Stimmen evangelischer Politiker,* 1953.

———. *Die geistige Struktur unserer Zeit,* 1954.

———. *Hat unsere Demokratie einen Sinn?,* no date.

——— and others. *Die politische Verantwortung der evangelischen Christen,* 1954.

———. *Um dem Vaterland zu dienen: Reden und Aufsätze,* edited by Friedrich Schramm, 1955.

——— and others. *Reden zur politischen Verantwortung,* 1956.

———. *Gedanken zur Zeit,* edited by Karl-Heinz Meyer, 1955.

Fogarty, Michael. *Christian Democracy in Western Europe, 1820-1953,* 1957.

Friedrich, Bruno. "CDU ohne katholische Laienverbände?" *Vorwärts*, July 24, 1963.

von der Gablenz, Otto Heinrich. *Uber Marx hinaus*, 1946.

Gerstenmaier, Eugen. *Reden und Aufsätze*, 1956.

_____. "Eine grundsätzliche Besinnung," *Civis*, March 1956.

_____. "Darf sich die CDU christlich nennen?," *Civis*, May 1957.

_____. "Der Kreisauer Kreis," *Vierteljahreshefte für Zeitgeschichte*, July 1967.

_____. *Deutschland in der weltpolitischen Situation der Gegenwart: Antwort an die Herren Dr. Dehler und Dr. Heinemann*, CDU Bundesgeschäftsstelle, 1958.

_____. *Verschleuderung des christlichen Namens? Eine Disputation mit Helmut Gollwitzer*, CDU Bundesgeschäftsstelle, 1960.

Gundlach, Gustav, S. J. "Christliche Demokratie," *Stimmen der Zeit*, January 1954.

Heidenheimer, Arnold. *Adenauer and the CDU: The Rise of the Leader and the Integration of the Party*, 1960.

Hermes, Peter. *Die Christlich-Demokratische Union und die Bodenreform in der Sowjetischen Besatzungszone Deutschlands im Jahre 1945*, 1963.

Hirschauer, Gerd. "Der westdeutsche Katholizismus und die christlichen Demokraten," *Die neue Gesellschaft*, May-June 1958.

Kafka, Gustav. "Christliche Parteien und katholische Kräfte," *Die neue Ordnung*, March-April 1958.

Klenk, Friedrich, S. J. "Die Kirche und die Macht," *Stimmen der Zeit*, November 1952.

Meyer, Karl-Heinz, editor. *Gedanken zur Zeit*, 1955.

Morsey, Rudolf. "Die deutsche Zentrumspartei," in Erich Matthias and Rudolf Morsey, *Das Ende der Parteien 1933*, 1960.

Müller, Josef. *Die geistige Erneuerung*, 1946.

Muhler, Emil. "Die ideologischen Grundlagen der CSU," in *Politisches Jahrbuch der CSU*, 1954.

Narr, Wolf-Dieter. *CDU-SPD: Programm und Praxis seit 1945*, 1966.

von Nell-Breuning. *Zur Programmatik politischer Parteien*, 1946.

_____. *Was hat die Kirche mit der Politik zu tun?* 1947.

Risse, Heinz Theo. "Der 'linke Flügel' der CDU," *Frankfurter Hefte*, May 1962.

Ritter, Gerhard. *Carl Goerdeler und die deutsche Widerstandsbewegung*, 1954.

Scharmitzel, Theodor. *Christliche Demokratie im neuen Deutschland*, 1946.

Schempp, Paul. *Die Stellung der Kirche zu den politischen Parteien und das Problem einer christlichen Partei*, 1946.

Schlange-Schöningen, Hans. *Am Tage danach*, 1946.

_____. *Die Politik des Möglichen*, 1949.

Schulz, Gerhard. "Die CDU—Merkmale ihres Aufbaus," in Max Gustav Lange, Gerhard Schulz and Klaus Schütz, *Parteien in der Bundesrepublik*, 1955.

Schwering, Leo. *Die Entstehung der CDU*, 1946.

_____. *Vorgeschichte und Entstehung der CDU*, 1952.

_____. *Frühgeschichte der Christlich-Demokratischen Union*, 1963.

Siemer, Laurentius. "Zum Problem des 'Christlichen Sozialismus,' " *Die neue Ordnung*, June 1948.

Stegerwald, Adam. *Wo stehen wir?*, 1945.

_____. *Wohin gehen wir?*, 1946.

Steltzer, Theodor. *Von deutscher Politik; Dokumente, Aufsätze und Vorträge*, 1949.

Welty, Eberhard. *Was nun?*, 1945.

_____. *Die Entscheidung in die Zukunft; Grundsätze und Hinweise zur Neuordnung im deutschen Lebensraum*, 1946.

_____. "Christlicher Sozialismus," *Die neue Ordnung*, October 1946.

_____. "Ein 'nicht' übersehen?," *Die neue Ordnung*, October 1948.

Wieck, Hans Georg. *Die Entstehung der CDU und die Wiedergründung des Zentrums im Jahre 1945*, 1953.

_____. *Christliche und Freie Demokraten in Hessen, Rheinland-Pfalz, Baden, und Württemberg 1945/46*, 1958.

Zimmermann, Karl. *Erste Reichstagung der Christliche-Demokratischen Union in Godesberg am 14., 15. und 16. Dezember 1945*, no date.

Biographies and Autobiographies

Adenauer, Konrad. *Erinnerungen.* Volume 1: *1945-1953;* Volume 2: *1953-1955;* Volume 3: *1955-1959;* Volume 4: *1959-1963, 1965-1968.*

Altenhöfer, Ludwig. *Stegerwald: Ein Leben für den kleinen Mann*, 1965.

Börner, Weert. *Hermann Ehlers und der Aufbau einer parlamentarischen Demokratie in Deutschland*, 1967.

Brügelmann, Hermann, and Klaus Simon, editors. *Robert Tillmanns; Eine Lebensleistung*, 1956.

Conze, Werner, Erich Kosthorst, and Elfriede Nebgen. *Jacob Kaiser.* Volume 1: *Der Arbeitsführer;* Volume 2: *Der Widerstandskämpfer*, 1967-1968.

Först, Walter. *Robert Lehr als Oberbürgermeister*, 1962.

Kaiser, Jakob. *Der soziale Staat: Reden und Gedanken*, 1946.

Kunst, Hermann, editor. *Für Freiheit und Recht: Eugen Gerstenmaier zum 60. Geburtstag*, 1966.

Konrad Adenauer Stiftung für politische Bildung. *Christliche Demokraten der ersten Stunde*, 1966.

McBride, Will, and Hans-Werner Finck von Finckenstein. *Adenauer: Ein Porträt*, 1965.

Reichard, Fritz. *Andreas Hermes*, 1953.

Rodens, Franz. *Konrad Adenauer: Der Mensch und der Politiker*, 1963.

Schorr, Helmut. *Adam Stegerwald*, 1966.

Schramm, Friedrich, and others. *Hermann Ehlers*, 1955.

Schröder, Georg. *Konrad Adenauer: Porträt eines Staatsmannes*, 1966.

Steltzer, Theodor. *Sechzig Jahre Zeitgenosse*, 1966.

Weymar, Paul. *Konrad Adenauer*, 1957.

Wighton, Charles. *Adenauer—Democratic Dictator*, 1963.

Chapter 12: Social Democracy

Abendroth, Wolfgang. *Aufstieg und Krise der deutschen Sozialdemokratie: Das Problem der Zweckentfremdung einer politischen Partei durch die Anpassungstendenz von Institutionen an vorgegebene Machtverhältnisse,* 1964.

Arndt, Adolf. *Die geistige Freiheit als politische Gegenwartsaufgabe,* Parteivorstand der SPD, 1956.

_____ . *Humanität–Kulturaufgaben des Politischen: Ein Beitrag zur Neubegründung des Humanismus und zur Auslegung des Godesberger Grundsatzprogrammes,* 1963.

_____ . *Geist der Politik: Reden,* 1965.

_____ and others. *Christlicher Glaube und politische Entscheidung,* 1957.

_____ and others. *Christentum und demokratischer Sozialismus,* 1958.

Beckel, Albrecht and Günther Triesch. *Wohin steuert die SPD?,* 1961.

Chalmers, Douglas. *The Social Democratic Party of Germany: From Working-Class Movement to Modern Political Party,* 1964.

Dirks, Walter. "Deutscher Katholizismus und Sozialdemokratie," *Geist und Tat,* May 1960.

_____ . "Ein Grundsatzprogramm–zum 'neuen Weg' der Sozialdemokratischen Partei Deutschlands," *Frankfurter Hefte,* January 1960.

Edinger, Lewis. *Kurt Schumacher: A Study in Personality and Political Behavior,* 1965.

Eichler, Willi. "Demokratische Sozialisten und Katholiken im Gespräch," *Geist und Tat,* February 1958.

_____ . "Weltanschauung und Politik," *Geist und Tat,* October 1959.

_____ . "Katholiken und demokratischer Sozialismus," *Geist und Tat,* April 1960.

_____ . "Gedanken zur Sozialenzyklika 'Mater et Magistra,' " *Die neue Gesellschaft,* July-August 1962.

_____ . *Weltanschauung und Politik; Reden und Aufsätze,* 1967.

Eppler, Erhard. *Spannungsfelder: Beiträge zur Politik,* 1968.

Erler, Fritz. *Politik für Deutschland,* 1968.

Forster, Karl, editor. *Christentum und demokratischer Sozialismus,* Studien und Berichte der Katholischen Akademie in Bayern, number 3, 1958.

Friedrich, Manfred. *Opposition ohne Alternative,* 1962.

Fuchs, Ernst. *Christentum und Sozialismus,* 1946.

Gaus, Günter. *Staatserhaltende Opposition, oder hat die SPD kapituliert?,* 1966.

Hildebrand, Wigbert. *Der Mensch im Godesberger Programm der SPD,* 1967.

Hoegner, Wilhelm. *Der Weg der deutschen Sozialdemokratie, 1863–1963,* 1965.

Kaden, Albrecht. *Einheit oder Freiheit: Die Wiedergründung der SPD 1945/1946,* 1964.

Kafka, Gustav. *Der freiheitliche Sozialismus in Deutschland: Das Godesberger Grundsatzprogramm der SPD in katholischer Sicht,* Zentralkomitee der deutschen Katholiken, 1960.

Kreiterling, Will. *Kirche-Katholizismus-Sozialdemokratie; Von Gegnerschaft zur Partnerschaft,* 1969.

Kübler, Franz. "Freiheitlicher Sozialismus und katholische Gesellschaftslehre in der Begegnung," *Die neue Gesellschaft,* January-February 1964.

Kupisch, Karl. *Das Jahrhundert des Sozialismus und die Kirche,* 1958.

Langner, Albrecht, editor. *Katholizismus und freiheitlicher Sozialismus in Europa,* 1965.

Lutz, Hans. *Protestantismus und Sozialismus heute,* 1949.

Matthias, Erich. *Sozialdemokratie und Nation,* 1952.

Mozer, Alfred. "Warum sind die sozialistischen Parteien gegen Europa?", *Frankfurter Hefte,* August 1953.

Ollenhauer, Erich. *Reden und Aufsätze,* edited by Fritz Sänder, 1964.

Ortlieb, Heinz Dietrich. *Wandlungen des Sozialismus,* 1947.

Osterroth, Franz, and Dieter Schuster. *Chronik der deutschen Sozialdemokratie,* 1963.

Pirker, Theo. *Die SPD nach Hitler,* 1965.

Ritter, Waldemar. *Kurt Schumacher: Eine Untersuchung seiner politischen Konzeption,* 1964.

Schempp, Paul. "Sozialdemokratie und Religion," *Sozialistische Monatshefte,* January 1947.

Schenkel, Gotthilf. *Kirche, Sozialismus, Demokratie,* 1946.

Schmid, Carlo. *Die verlorene Revolution,* 1948.

Scholz, Arno, and Walther Oschilewski, editors. *Turmwächter der Demokratie: Ein Lebensbild von Kurt Schumacher;* Volume 2: *Reden und Schriften,* 1953.

Schütz, Klaus. "Die Sozialdemokratie im Nachkriegsdeutschland," in Max Gustav Lange, Gerhard Schulz, and Klaus Schütz, *Parteien in der Bundesrepublik,* 1955.

Schulz, Klaus-Peter. *Sorge um die deutsche Linke,* 1954.

_____ . *Opposition als politisches Schicksal,* 1958.

Schumacher, Kurt. *Sozialismus und Demokratie,* 1945.

_____ . *Aufgaben und Ziele der deutschen Sozialdemokratie,* 1946.

_____ . *Nach dem Zusammenbruch: Gedanken über Demokratie und Sozialismus,* 1948.

_____ . *Reden und Schriften,* 1962.

Seuffert, Walter. "Neue Wege des Sozialismus," in *Geist und Tat,* February 1949.

Social Democratic Party of Germany. *Basic Programme of the Social Democratic Party of Germany,* 1959.

Strohm, Theodor. *Kirche und demokratischer Sozialismus,* 1968.

Vereinigung Katholischer Publizisten, Rheinische Gruppe. *SPD—das Fiasko einer Partei: eine kritische Analyse in fünf Kapiteln,* 1960.

Vorstand der SPD. *Der Katholik und die SPD,* 1959.

_____ . *Katholik und Godesberger Programm: Zur Situation nach den Enzykliken Johannes XXIII und Paul VI,* 1965.

Wesemann, Friedrich. *Kurt Schumacher: Ein Leben für Deutschland,* 1952.

Index

Academies, Catholic, 132

Academies, Protestant, 20, 132–134, 262

Acheson, Dean, 56, 59

Adenauer, Paul, 174–175

Adenauer, Konrad, sought organized Catholic support, 41, 150; dismissed as mayor of Cologne, 98; seeks Protestants in government, 131, 310–311; and Zentrum-CDU fusion, 153, 154; on Catholic women's voting behavior, 159, 322; gains mass Catholic support, 164; his relationship to Catholic church, 170, 171–175, 177, 313; his religious approach, 171–172, 244; on Russian intentions, 172; irked by clericalism, 173, 175; appeases Protestants, 173; his attitude to Reichskonkordat litigation, 173, 218; seeks papal award, 175; his relations with Böhler, 176, 177; wants to avoid church-state issues, 183; abandons confessional schools, 187; opposes school referendum, 188; proposes church programs in Third World, 202; his integration policy, 239, 312; clashes with Niemöller, 240, 245; not supported by EKD, 241; gains support of hierarchy, 241–242; attitude to reunification, 242 & n.; his rearmament policy, 243; clashes with Heinemann over, 243–245; not opposed by EKD, 246; policy supported by Catholic church, 246, 248, 249; and Schumacher, on rearmament, 251; irked by Niemöller's Moscow visit, 252; informed of Protestant disaffection, 253; Protestants differ from, 254–255; GVP's campaign against, 256; and 1953 election, 257–258; political decline begins, 261; and Schröder, 262n.; and conscientious objectors, 263; his nuclear policy attacked by SPD, 264; supported by theologians, 265–266; his foreign policy adopted by SPD, 266–267, 340; his recipe for political success, 269; supports unified trade union, 276; creates family ministry, 282; adds youth affairs, 283; sceptical about interconfessional party, 291–292; thwarts Hermes, 294n.; isolates eastern CDU, 297; animated by fear of Russians, 298; his election slogan, 309; rises to CDU leadership, 310; gains Protestant confidence, 312–313; and Ehlers, 314; and crisis over successor, 318–319 & n.; contrasted with Schumacher, 328; opposed by some Protestants, 330; contrasted with Ollenhauer, 333; mentioned, 176, 213, 216

After the Deluge, 353

Agartz, Viktor, 276n.

Ahlen program, 272–273, 311

Ahrweiler, constituency of, as index of Catholic voting behavior, 159–160

Albers, Johannes, 273, 281

Albertz, Heinrich, 251

All-German People's party (GVP), as "political sect," 139; confessional appeals of, 142, 256–257; no Catholic equivalent of, 157; its program, 164; its aims, 251, 257; and

1953 election, 256–258; accepts East German funds, 258; dissolves itself, 258; leaders shift to SPD, 331; mentioned, 157

Allemann, Fritz René, 64

Allied Control Council (ACC), annuls "German Evangelical Church" law, 10; leaves churches' legal status intact, 57; issues confessional school directive, 58n.; and policy on concordats, 58 & n., 210; receives Protestant protest on collective guilt, 94; establishes denazification guidelines, 95–96 & n.

American Military Government, consults churches on appointments, 53–54, 97–98; policy directive on churches, 54–55; policy in church-state sphere, 57–58, 194; differences with churches, 59–62; attitude to churches, 75–88; general denazification policy, 95–108; denazification of clergy, 108–110, 111–116; instructs Parliamentary Council, 185; represented at Eisenach conference, 237

Amery, Carl, 152

Annuario Pontificio, 216, 230

Aquinas, Thomas, 311

Aristotle, 352

Arndt, Adolf, 331, 339

Arnold, Karl, agrees to alliance with Zentrum, 155; supports unified trade union movement, 276; and social legislation, 281; encourages capital-savings incentives, 285; and Christian socialism, 311; repelled by SPD ideology, 326; ousted by SPD and FDP, 334

Asbury, William 66, 67

Asmussen, Hans, 10n., 93

Association of Catholic Men's Organizations of Germany, 248

Association of Catholic organizations, 179

Association of Dioceses of Germany, 35n.

Association of Social Democratic Jurists, 348

Augsburg, treaty of, 4, 12, 22, 359

Bachem, Julius, 292 & n.

Bafile, Corrado, 31, 33, 34, 214–215, 223, 224, 230, 340, 341, 348

Bahr, Egon, 133, 267

Balfour, Philip Maxwell, 67

Barmen, Reich synod at, 9n.; impact on postwar Protestantism, 12, 120

Barth, Karl, biography, 9n.; his influence at Barmen, 9; at Treysa, 10; his report to American army, 95; on interaction of church and politics, 122, 124–125, 126, 354; on East-West confrontation, 238–239; not supported by EKD, 241; antirearmament views, 250 & n.; stigma of being a Social Democrat, 269; fails to convince Protestants, 312; and support for Social Democracy, 324, 326; pro-SPD disciples of, 330; mentioned, 148

Bartsch, Hans Werner, 193

Barzel, Rainer, 264

Baudissin, Wolf, Count, 253

Bavarian party, 140, 305

Bavarian Patriots' party, 23

Bavarian People's party, 161, 303

Der Bayerische Klerus in der Zeit dreier Revolutionen—1918–1933–1945, 90

Bea, August, 307

Bebel, August, 328

Becher, Johannes, 256

Beckmann, Joachim, 263n.

Bell, George K. A., 65, 70; biography, 70n.; correspondence with Wurm, 71–72
Bender, Julius, 112
Bengsch, Alfred, 40 & n., 41, 233
Berger, Hans, 231
Bensberg circle, 157, 230
Berlin Ordinaries Conference, 40
Berning, Wilhelm, 27 & n.
Bertram, Adolf, 27 & n., 216
Beveridge, William Henry, 65
BHE (Block der Heimatvertriebenen und Entrechteten), *see* Bloc of those Driven from their Homes and Deprived of their Rights
Bidault, Georges, 74
Bishop, William H. A., 65
Bismarck, Klaus von, 133–134
Bismarck, Otto von, 7, 13, 24, 165, 173, 183, 269
Blank, Theodor, 248, 253
Bloc of those Driven from their Homes and Deprived of their Rights (BHE), 140–141
Bodensieck, Julius, 82, 88
Böckenförde, Ernst-Wolfgang, 91
Böhler, Wilhelm, works to eliminate Zentrum, 152–155; role in federal politics, 167–171, 175–177; decline and fall, 175–176; his legalistic approach, 184 & n.; his role in Parliamentary Council, 184–189; his role in Personalpolitik, 204–205, 313; lobbies for social legislation, 282; arouses Protestant suspicion, 313; and Catholic influence in CDU, 317; his contact with SPD, 336–337; and Catholic-SPD meeting, 337; mentioned, 175
Böhm, Anton, 161
Böll, Heinrich, 152, 198–199
Bonhoeffer, Dietrich, 7 & n.; attitude to Nazism, 9; and George Bell, 70n.; on German guilt, 93; metaphor on action in crisis, 119; on Catholic-Protestant relations, 293; contact with Josef Müller, 304
Bonner Rundschau, 227
Bornewasser, Franz Rudolf, 53, 73–75, 98, 153
Brandt, Willy, 223, 224, 226, 232, 267, 281
Braun, Herbert, 193
"Bremen clause," 213n.
Brentano, Heinrich von, 262n.
British Military Government, consults churches on appointments, 53–54, 97–98; policy directives on churches, 54–55; church-state policy, 57–58, 194; differences with churches, 59–62; relations with Catholic church, 62–70; with Protestant church, 70–72; general denazification policy, 95–100, 103, 107; denazification of clergy, 108–110; instructs Parliamentary Council, 185; vetoes nationalization bill, 332
Brockmann, Johannes, accepts electoral alliance with CDU, 155; warns Catholic church, 156; role in Parliamentary Council, 185
Brunner, Emil, 239
Buber, Martin, 249
Buchholz, Peter, 52, 294, 295
Bultmann, Rudolf, 193
"Bundeskonkordat," 224

Calvin, John, 4, 148
capital-savings incentives, 285–286
Caritas, 202, 284

Casaroli, Agostino, 229, 230, 231–232

Catholic Academy in Bavaria, 337

Catholic church (in Germany), before 1945, 22–28; at end of World War II, 28–31; attitude to Reichskonkordat, 30, 149, 190, 210, 213, 217, 230–231; its serenity broken, 31–32; organization of, 32, 34–35, 37–42; east of Oder-Neisse, 38, 215–217; in East Germany, 38–41; receives guidance from Pius XII, 56–57, 187–188, 211–212, 246–247, 272, 274, 279–281, 354; transmits letter to Eisenhower, 61; and British Military Government, 62–70; and French Military Government, 73–75; and American Military Government, 75–88; attitude to collective guilt, 89–93; attitude to denazification, 96–100, 103–105; and denazification of clergy, 109; political approach of, 149–157, 354–356; committed to CDU, chapter 6, passim; chapter 11, passim; 190, 332, 344, 346–347, 350, 361; strives for Catholic unity, 151–158; 161, 164; opposes Center party, 152–157, 354; exerts political pressure on laity, 156–158, 163–164, 166–167; opposes liberalism, 161–162, 343; parapolitical infrastructure and lobbying activities of, 167–171, 175–180; and Parliamentary Council, 183–190; attitude to confessional schools, 187, 212–213, 222–228; its privileged position in state, 190–203; criticizes Basic Law, 190; and Oder-Neisse issue, 233; and Ostpolitik, 232, 268; attitude to reunification, 241–242; supports rearmament, 246–250; opposes conscientious objection, 260; supports nuclear arms, 264–265; supports social legislation, 269, 271–272; opposes unified trade union, 274–278; attitude to codetermination, 279–281; and "family affairs," 282–284; and capital-savings program, 285–286; and origin of CDU, 294–305, 306–308; reacts to secularization of CDU, 315–318; and relations with SPD, 328–329, 331–337, 343–350; and Lower Saxony concordat, 340–341; neutral in 1969 election, 346; effect of secularization on, 355–357, 361–362

Catholic Club, 178

Catholic Farm Youth Movement, 176

CGD (Christliche Gewerkschaftsbewegung Deutschlands), *see* Christian Trade Union Movement of Germany

Catholic Institute for Social Work, 317

Catholic News Agency (KNA), 43, 168, 179, 343

Catholic Office, established, 167–168; its changing role, 176–179; open only to CDU, 178, 180; establishes contact with SPD, 180, 345; and programs in the Third World, 202–203; on school dispute, 224; and Oder-Neisse issue, 231; and Catholic workers groups, 273; fosters social legislation, 281, 284

Catholic Workers' Movement (KAB), ostracizes SPD, 179; supports rearmament, 248; harasses DGB, 275–276; supports codetermination, 281; mentioned, 43, 273, 334

Catholic Youth Movement, 43, 248, 249

Cavert, Samuel McCrae, 82

CDU/CSU (Christlich-Demokratische Union/Christlich-Soziale Union), *see* Christian Democratic Union/Christian Social Union

Center party, origin and nature, 24, 25–26; abandoned and dissolved, 28, 294; opposition to reestablishment of, 149, 293; reestablished, 152; efforts of hierarchy to destroy, 152–157; extraparliamentary substitute for, 179; in Parliamentary Council, 185; abstains on Basic Law, 189; Wessel leaves, 251; and Protestants, 292; revival of, intended by Russians, 294; opposed in Berlin, 294, 296; in Cologne, 297–299; by Catholic bishops, 301; in Frankfurt, 301; supported by Föhr, 302; opposed by Gröber, 302; decided against in Württemberg, 302; confusion over in north, 305; its heritage, 305–306; hierarchy's decision on, 306–307, 354; and SPD in Weimar, 324; as alternative to left-Catholics, 326; mentioned, 31, 91, 160, 161, 167, 175, 272, 291, 300, 320, 352, 355

Central committee of German Catholics, role of, 42, 168–170, 176, 178–179; and CDU,

179, 317, 344, 346–347; concern over Catholic education, 220; and Oder-Neisse issue, 231; and Catholic workers' groups, 273; and social legislation, 281; and SPD, 179, 346; mentioned, 151n., 161

Charlemagne, 257

Charles V, 3, 172

Christ und Welt, 21, 127

Christengemeinde und Bürgergemeinde, 124

Christian Democratic Union/Christian Social Union (CDU/CSU), passim but especially, and Protestants, 137–145, 310–311, 319–321; and Catholics, 157–161, 163–164, 178–180, 320–322; and Parliamentary Council, 185–190; origin and evolution of, chapter 11; historic significance of, 356–358

"Christian National People's party," 292

Christian People's party, 325

Christian Social People's Service (CSVP), 303

"Christian Socialist Association," 299

Christian Trade Union Movement of Germany (CGD), 273, 275–278

"Church articles," 188, 189n., 190–199, 207, 324

Church income, 55, 57, 193–199, 201–202, 332, 346

Church of England, 70, 363

Church of the Prussian Union (*see also* Church of the Union), 6

Church of Scotland, 70

Church of the Union (EKU), 16, 20

Church treaties, Protestant, 5n., 58n., 184, 185, 192, 200; with Baden, 188; Bavaria, 188, 192, 228; Hesse, 200; Lower Saxony (Loccum Treaty), 199–200; North Rhine-Westphalia, 200; Rhineland-Palatinate, 188, 200; Prussia, 188; Schleswig-Holstein, 200

Cicognani, Amleto, 51, 56, 59

Cillian, Adolf, 131

Clay, Lucius, attitude to churches, 76, 78; and Catholic petitions, 77; instructed to prevent Nazi revival in churches, 81; disengages from church affairs, 81; advises Bodensieck, 82; gives Apostolic Mission free contact with Vatican, 83; and expulsion of Muench, 87; doubts church influence, 88; declines to alter denazification law, 102; receives Catholic memorandum on denazification, 103; responds, 104–105; criticizes Niemöller, 105; clashes with Wurm on denazification of clergy, 113; alters denazification regulations, 114; represented at Eisenach conference, 237; mentioned, 84

Codetermination, 279–281

Colli, Carlo, 33, 83

Committee for education, training and instruction, 136

Commission for family legislation, 136

Commission for public affairs, 136

Commission for questions of sexual ethics, 136

Commission for social affairs, 136

Commission on marriage law, 348

Committee for family problems, 270

Committee for labor matters, 277

Committee for labor problems, 270

Committee for traffic and transportation matters, 136

Committee of Social Democratic academicians, 336

Committee on social structure, 270

Commonweal, 78

Concordats, Catholic (*see also* Reichskonkordat), 5n., 33, 51, 56, 59, 184, 185, 191, 200, 210, 211; with Baden, 58n., 188, 209; Bavaria, 58n., 188, 209, 228; Lower Saxony, 200, 340–341, 344; Prussia, 33, 38, 58n., 188, 209, 215, 225

"Confessing church," established, 9; and postwar church, 10n.; issues political statement, 120–121; adherents found academy movement, 132; members uncomfortable with institutions, 139

Confessional-geographic pattern of society, 4, 5, 12, 22, 48–50, 359

Confessional schools, their social foundation undermined, 50, 219–222; urged by Pius XII, 57, 212; occupation policies regarding, 57–59, 73, 75, 86, 213; ACC directive on, 58n.; as issue in revolt against hierarchy, 166–167, 220, 222, 225–226, 228; disputed in Parliamentary Council, 184, 186–188; before 1945, 208–209; and Reichskonkordat, 209–210, 212–214, 219; hierarchy's obsession with, 212; Protestant attitude to, 212, 222; changing view of Catholic laity, 220–222; and school reform in Baden-Württemberg, 222–224; North Rhine-Westphalia, 224–227, 345; Bavaria and Rhineland-Palatinate, 227–228, 345; and DGB, 275, 286–287; and establishment of CDU, in Berlin 295; Cologne, 299; Frankfurt, 302; Freiburg, 302; Wattenscheid, 326; and SPD, 331–332, 336, 340, 342, 343

Congress of Vienna, 13, 22

Conscientious objection, in Basic Law, 185–186; opposed by hierarchy, 260; supported by EKD, 260–261; and nuclear arms aspect, 263; religious affiliation of claimants, 263n.

Council of Europe, 341

CV (Cartellverband der Katholischen Deutschen Studentenverbindungen), 170 & n.

Czaja, Herbert, 231

Daily News (Chicago), 98

Davidson, Randall, 70n.

De rerum novarum, 25

Decision in Germany, 76

Defregger, Matthias, 31–32, 37

"Democratic Union," 295

The Deputy (Der Stellvertreter), 30, 31 & n., 91, 342

Deutsche Schicksalsfragen, 91

Deutsche Sicherheit, 250n.

Deutsche Tagespost, 334, 347

Diakonisches Werk, 202

Dibelius, Otto, 7 & n.; chairman of EKD council, 15; forbidden to travel in East Germany, 17; attitude to politics, 119–120; appeals for all-German elections, 255; conciliates Protestant political divisions, 127–128; debates rearmament, 129; opposes Catholic ambassador to Vatican, 204–205; on Heinemann's resignation, 244; appeals for reunification, 255; supports conscientious objection, 260; opposes nuclear arms for Bundeswehr, 262–263; criticizes capitalism, 270; and establishment of CDU, 294, 295; explains membership in CDU, 296; relations with Adenauer, 313; offended by SPD's anticlericalism, 327, 330; mentioned, 119, 123

Dieckmann, Johannes, 256

Dietze, Constantin von, 16n.

Dietzfelbinger, Hermann, chairman of EKD council, 15; considers church politically overextended, 123; political conservatism of, 148; supports hierarchy on marriage reform, 348

Dirks, Walter, ostracized by hierarchy for political nonconformity, 152, 249; denounces hierarchy's political pressure, 163–164, 266; on codetermination, 280; leaves politics, 310; and Christian socialism, 311

Döpfner, Julius, reads papal message, 31; biography, 36–37; attends Protestant academy, 133; his confessionalism angers Adenauer, 173; and school reform, 222, 223, 227; irks Vatican, 228; and diocesan reorganization, 232; forbids Catholic votes for SPD, 334; skeptical of SPD changes, 343, 362

Dorn, Walter, 104

Düsseldorf program 273, 311

DGB (Deutscher Gewerkschaftsbund), see German Trade Union Federation

East German government, policy of toward Evangelical church before 1955, 17; from 1955, 17–19; policy of toward Catholic church, 40–41; bans Erfurt lay assembly, 256; attitude of to Reichskonkordat, 215; presses for normalization of dioceses, 233

Ecclesiastical political group (kirchenpolitisches Gremium), 168, 178

Echo der Zeit, 248, 264

Economic Reconstruction League, 140

The Economist, 242n.

Ehlers, Hermann, enters politics, 131; cooperates with Kunst, 147; asked to defend government, 253; at Leipzig lay assembly, 256; leads CDU Protestants, 313–314; success of, 315

Eichler, Willi, 328, 329, 336, 339, 345

Eisenach conference, 12, 237

Eisenhower, Dwight, 61, 77

EKD (Evangelische Kirche in Deutschland), see Evangelical Church in Germany

EKU (Evangelische Kirche der Union), see Church of the Union

Eliot, T. S., 197, 198

Emergency League for the Peace of Europe, 251

Enabling Act, 28, 210, 218, 325

Encounter, 86

Eppler, Erhard, 331

Erhard, Ludwig, his economic approach prevails, 273, 311; contacts church representatives, 286; and Adenauer succession crisis, 318; becomes chancellor, 319; falls, 320, 345; mentioned, 216, 269, 338

Erler, Fritz, 331, 342, 343, 344

Ertl, Josef, 204

Eschwege, constituency of, as index of Protestant voting behavior, 141–142

Etzel, Franz, 273, 318, 319 & n.

European Defense Community, 248, 251, 259

Evangelical Church in Germany (EKD), provisionally established, 10; formally established, 12; structure of, 12–16, 20–21; Russian attitude to, 17; East German attitude to, 17–19; its organizational split, 19–20; lay activities of, 20–21; and British Military Government, 70–72; and French Military Government, 73; and American Military Government, 75–88; attitude to collective guilt, 93–95; attitude to general denazification, 96, 99, 100–102; attitude to denazification of clergy, 109–116; its political approach, 119–137, 145, 148, 353–354; its political neutrality, 121, 124, 137–138, 257, 308–309, 329, 330, 360; political divisions within, 124–130, 256, 263n.; encourages laity to be politically active, 130–136; and political figures' holding church office, 132; its pronouncements and memoranda, 134–136; lobbying activities of, 145–148; and Parliamentary Council, 183–187, 188; is silent on Basic Law, 189 & n.; its privileged position in state, 190–203; and school issue, 208, 212, 222; attitude to reunification, 240–241, 243, 254–256; attitude to rearmament,

243, 244, 245–246, 252 & n., 259; Heinemann and Niemöller decline to withdraw from, 250; favors reconciliation with East, 254–256, 267–268; opposes conscription, 259–260; supports conscientious objection, 260–261, 263 & n.; opposes nuclear arms, 262–263 & n.; declines to endorse eastern treaties, 267–268; and social policy, 269–271; and trade union movement, 270–271, 277–278; supports codetermination, 280–281; and family ministry, 283; and capital-savings program, 285; attitude to CDU, 308; to SPD, 329–331, 339; supports Catholic position on divorce, 348; a major contributor to liberal democracy, 354–355; effect of secularization upon, 360–361
Evangelische Tagung der CDU, 311
Even, Johannes, 273, 275, 276, 280

Fassbinder, Klara, 152, 249
Faulhaber, Michael von, 27 & n.; consulted by Americans on appointments, 53, 98; clashes with Americans over pastoral letter, 56; warned not to criticize American policy, 76; and Bavarian school reform, 86–87; praised by Pius XII, 90; and denazification, 98; attitude to Adenauer, 174; warned by Pius XII about trade union movement, 274; political uncertainty of, 303, 304, 307
FDP (Freie Demokratische Partei), *see* Free Democratic party
Federal Council of Churches, 81–82
Federation of Catholic employees organizations, 273
Federation of German Catholic youth, 248
Federation of German Industry, 180
Federation of Religious Socialists, 324
Filbinger, Hans, 223
Fink, Johannes, 74
Fischer, Geoffrey, 70–71, 78
Flor, Peter, 202
Föcher, Matthias, 276
Föhr, Ernst, 53, 73, 223, 302
Forster, Karl, 35, 337, 344, 345
Frankfurter Allgemeine, 37, 166, 217, 219, 222, 225, 226, 227, 262, 286, 341
Frankfurter Hefte, 43, 152, 280, 335
Frederick William III, 6
Free Democratic party (FDP), passim but especially, and Protestants, 140–145; and Catholics, 160; and Parliamentary Council, 185–189
Freiburg circle, 293
Der freiheitliche Sozialismus in Deutschland, 340
French Military Government, consults churches on appointments, 53–54; policy directives on churches, 54–55; policy in church-state sphere, 57–58; 75, 194; differences with churches, 59–62; relations with the Protestant church, 73; with the Catholic church, 73–75; denazification policy, 95; denazification of the clergy, 108, 110–111; instructs Parliamentary Council, 185
Friesenhahn, Ernst, 218n.
Frings, Joseph, receives report from Pius XII, 29; shocks Cologne Catholics, 30; problem of successor, 33; biography, 35–36; at 1945 Fulda conference, 56; warns British officers, 60–61; on mood of Germans, 61; and British Military Government, 64–70; complains about Clay, 77; denies Catholics were Nazis, 90; denounces collective guilt, 92; criticizes denazification procedures, 66, 96–97, 99–100, 103, 107; proposes priest for Bundestag, 150n.; wants monolithic Catholic unity, 151; opposes ·

Zentrum, 152–154, 301; joins CDU, 153; resigns at Pope's request, 212, 213; condemns liberalism, 162; relationship with Adenauer, 174; and Böhler, 176; role in Parliamentary Council, 187; attacks Dibelius, 205; on confessional schools, 212; resists school reform, 225 ff.; supports rearmament, 246–247; snubs Reinhold Schneider, 249; cited by GVP, 257; supports nuclear arms, 264–266; gives lead on social issues, 272; seeks permission for Catholic trade union, 274; attacks DGB, 275; fails to evoke support for CGD, 276; reserved toward codetermination, 279; presses for social legislation, 281; favors family ministry, 282; criticizes SPD social policy, 284; attacks DGB school policy, 286; attitude to CDU, 299, 302, 307; criticized by Schumacher, 333; declines to meet Brandt, 343; mentioned, 71, 167, 329

Füllenbach, Wilhelm, 98

Fuchs, Hans, 98

Fulda Bishops' Conference (see also German Bishops' Conference), lifts ban on Catholic membership in NSDAP, 28; role of, 34–35; origin, 35n.; headed by Frings, 35, 64; headed by Döpfner, 37; 1945 session, 56; appeals to Eisenhower, 61, 77; rejects collective guilt, 89; on Reichskonkordat, 210, mentioned, 27n., 64, 128, 167, 307

Gaitskell plan, 262

Galen, Clemens von, 27, biography, 27n.; asked to form provisional government, 53–54; attitude to occupation powers, 60; to denazification, 60; to British Military Government, 63–64; to collective guilt, 91–92, 93; supports CDU, 306

Gandhi, Mohandas, 260

Geiger, Willi, 218n.

George, Stefan, 25

German Bishops' Conference, established, 35; elects Döpfner chairman, 37; and Oder-Neisse dioceses, 38; its limited influence on East Germany, 40; neutral in 1969 election, 346

"German Christians," rise and decline, 7–9; Müller heads, 7n.; after 1945, 10, 109–110; as warning to East German clergy, 19; and denazification of clergy, 109–116; mentioned, 27

German Christian Faith Movement, 7

German Community, 140

"German Evangelical Church," origin, 7; its authority destroyed, 9; status at end of war, 10; legal basis annulled by ACC, 10, 58

German party, its appeal to Protestants, 140; in Parliamentary Council, 185; abstains on Basic Law, 189

German party of the Right, 140

German-Polish treaty, 38, 230, 232–233, 267

German Shakespeare Society, 249

German Trade Union Federation (DGB), supported by British, 67; and Evangelical church, 270–271, 277–278; established, 274–275; criticized by Frings and Catholic lay groups, 275–277; supported by some Catholics, 276; favors codetermination, 281; its school policy criticized, 286

Gerstenmaier, Eugen, as leading CDU Protestant, 131; defends liberalism, 162; reputed supporter of National Socialism, 253; attacks Niemöller, 257; his foreign policy views, 262 & n.; refuses to defend Protestant interests, 314; role in Adenauer succession crisis, 318–319; mentioned, 21.

Globke, Hans, as chancellery state secretary, 170–171 & n., 177; role in Personalpolitik, 204–206; enflames Protestant suspicions, 313; role in Adenauer succession crisis, 318–319 & n.

Gockeln, Josef, 273

Godesberg program, 284, 338–340, 341, 342, 343, 344, 348, 350, 358

Goebbels, Paul Josef, 225

Goerdeler, Carl, 293

Göring, Hermann, 238

Golay, John, 186

Gollwitzer, Helmut, 129, 193, 330

Gotha program, 358

Griffith, William, 102, 105, 107–108

Griffin, Bernard, 66

Gröber, Konrad, 26–27; biography, 27n.; 59, 73, 302, 306

Grosche, Robert, 152

Grotewohl, Otto, 255

Grüber, Heinrich, biography, 17n.; represents EKD in East Germany, 17; rejected, 18; appointed to Berlin city council, 52, 119; proposes Adenauer-Grotewohl meeting, 255; and origin of CDU, 294, 295

Gundlach, Gustav, condemns liberalism, 162; supports CDU, 307; disillusioned with CDU, 316; critical of SPD, 335, 337, 340

GVP (Gesamtdeutsche Volkspartei), *see* All-German People's party

Hack, Bernard, 218

Hanssler, Bernard, 176, 336, 345

Hartz, Franz, 216

Hassel, Kai-Uwe von, 318, 319

Haug, Martin, 108

"Haus Villigst," 133

Harnack, Adolf von, 193

Heck, Bruno, 321

Heinemann, Gustav, president of EKD synod, 16n.; opposes rearmament, 125, 127, 250 & n.; dropped as synod president, 128; debates rearmament, 129; enters federal politics, 131; political peregrination of, 139; establishes GVP, 139, 164, 251; tests Protestant solidarity, 142; nominated for federal presidency, 203; clashes with Adenauer over rearmament, 243–245; his impact on Protestants, 244–246, 258; remains loyal to EKD, 250; leaves CDU, 251; his impact on public opinion, 252–254; on 1953 federal election, 258; dissolves GVP, 258; ridicules CDU in nuclear debate, 264; never accepts western Alliance, 267; supports DGB, 278; and CDU's confessional balance, 311; strengthens Protestant influence in SPD, 331; his role in Godesberg program, 339; his overall influence, 354

Held, Heinrich, role in Parliamentary Council, 184 & n., 185; his attitude to Basic Law, 189n.; opposes rearmament, 251; sympathetic to SPD, 330

Hengsbach, Franz, 42, 226

Herder Korrespondenz, 43

Hermann, Franz, 150n.

Hermes, Andreas, appointed deputy mayor of Berlin, 52; biography, 294n.; takes lead in establishing CDU, 294–295, 325; and contemporary CDU, 322

Herrenchiemsee conference, 183

Hesse, Hermann, 249

Heuss, Theodor, despises Böhler, 175; his role in Parliamentary Council, 185–189; opposes Catholic ambassador to Vatican, 205; on Personalpolitik, 206; receives Muench's credentials, 214; rehabilitates Reinhold Schneider, 249; on rearmament referendum, 251; encourages East-West detente, 262

Hilfswerk, 20, 131

Hindenburg, Paul von, 210
Himmler, Heinrich, 225
Hirschmann, Johannes, contributes to Catholic social views, 274; on codetermination, 280; supports CDU, 307; on Catholic influence in CDU, 317; on theology of nuclear arms, 265–266 & n.; his contact with SPD, 336–337
Hitler, Adolf, 7, 28, 90, 120, 209, 210, 222, 225, 227, 238
Hlond, August, 215–216 & n.
Hobbes, Thomas, 352
Hochhuth, Rolf, 30, 31 & n., 91, 342, 343
Hochland, 43
Höffner, Joseph, 33, 348
Hoegner, Wilhelm, 98, 305, 329
Höpker-Aschoff, Thomas, 189, 218
Holy See, *see* Vatican
Holzapfel, Friedrich, 311
House of Commons, 72
House of Lords, 62, 71, 72
Humani vitae, 37, 359
Humboldt, Alexander von, 162
Hynd, John, 72

Innere Mission, 20
Institutes of Christian Religion, 4
Iwand, Hans-Joachim, 330

Jahn, Gerhard, 348
Jacobi, Gerhard, 336
Jäger, Lorenz, 92, 166, 225, 307, 334
JCS 1067, 81, 96n.
John XXIII, 150, 229, 344
Junge Gemeinde, 21
Junge Union, 225

Kaas, Ludwig, 28, 211, 293
KAB (Katholiche Arbeiterbewegung), *see* Catholic Workers' Movement
Käsemann, Ernst, 193
Kafka, Gustav, 152, 340
Kaiser, Elfriede, 295 & n.
Kaiser, Jakob, and rearmament memorandum, 251; and "labor wing" of CDU, 274; supports DGB, 276; and social legislation, 281; favors non-Marxist "labor party," 295, 325; leads Berlin CDU, 310; promotes Christian socialism, 311; cites Catholic worker support for CDU, 326
Kalinna, Hermann, 203
Kaller, Maximilian, 216
Karrenberg, Friedrich, 278
Kaspar, Walter, 193
Kassel, constituency of, as index of Protestant voting behavior, 141–142
Die Katholiken vor der Politik, 152
Katholikentag, *see* lay assemblies, Catholic
Katzer, Hans, 274, 281, 285
Keller, Michael, and Parliamentary Council, 187; supports codetermination, 279; advo-

cates family ministry, 282; bans Catholic votes for SPD, 334, 335; begins concordat negotiations, 340

Kennan, George, quoted, 79; his Reith lectures, 262

Ketteler, Emanuel von, 25, 272

Ketteler Wacht, 275

Khrushchev, Nikita, 242n.

Kiesinger, Kurt Georg, fosters educational reform, 222–223; discusses school reform with Pope, 227; elected chancellor, 320; mentioned, 216

King, Martin Luther, 36

Die Kirche, 244, 255

Kirche in der Welt, 21

Kirchentag, *see* lay assemblies, Protestant

Kirchenzeitung für das Erzbistum Köln, 224

Kirchlicher Anzeiger für die Erzdiözese Köln, 212

Kirchliches Jahrbuch, 8

Kirkpatrick, Sir Ivone, 55, 210n.

Klein, Manfried, 202

Knappen, Marshal, 79 & n.

Knoeringen, Waldemar von, 337, 342

Koblenz, constituency of, as index of Catholic voting behavior, 159–160

Kölnische Rundschau, 103

Koenig, Pierre, 74

Königgrätz, 24

Köppler, Heinrich, 164

Kogon, Eugen, 311

Kohn-Brandenburg, Alexander, 341–342

Kolb, Simon, 304, 306

Kolping, Adolf, 272

Kolping Family, 179

Konradsblatt, 346

Kottmann, Maximilian, 73

Kreisau circle, 27n., 293, 296

Kressbronn circle, 320

Kreuz und Hakenkreuz, 90, 91

Krone, Heinrich, 170n., 318

Kronenberg, Friedrich, 344

Krummacher, Friedrich-Wilhelm, 18, 261

Kühn, Heinz, 36, 226, 227, 336

Küng, Hans, 32, 193

Kulturkampf, 23, 24, 73, 151, 173, 180, 227, 335

Kunst, Hermann, as representative to government, 145–148; on Adenauer, 174; and Böhler, 176; role in Personalpolitik, 204–205; supports Adenauer's defense policy, 246; lobbies for social legislation, 282; lobbies for capital-savings legislation, 286; defends Protestant interests, 315

Kupisch, Karl, 330

KV (Kartellverband katholischer deutscher Studentenvereine), 170n.

La Follette, Charles, 105

Labour party (British), 67, 326, 335, 358

Landersdorfer, Simon, 304

Langenfass, Deacon, 130–131

Lateran treaty, 214

Law for Liberation from National Socialism and Militarism, 96n., 100–102, 103–106, 113–115

Lay assembly, Catholic (Katholikentag), unruliness at Essen, 31, 279, 359; hierarchy strengthens control over, 152; *Frankfurter Hefte* denounced at, 152; shuns Zentrum leaders, 156; its codetermination resolution irks hierarchy, 152, 279; 1922 Munich session, 174

Lay assembly, Protestant (Kirchentag), 20, political significance of, 134; as East-West link, 256; banned in East Germany, 256; mentioned, 203, 247

Leber, Georg, contact with Catholic Office, 177, 345; member of central committee of German Catholics, 179, 346; sole Catholic SPD cabinet member, 204; visit to Paul VI, 230; favors capital-savings incentives, 285

Leber, Julius, 325

"Leber plan," 286

Lehmann, Karl, 193

Lehnert, Sister Pasqualina, 34, 211

Lehr, Robert, 189n.

Leiber, Robert, 34, 175, 211, 307

Leiprecht, Carl, 223, 343

Lensing, Lambert, 184n., 253, 292n.

Lenz, Otto, 170

Leo XIII, 25

Leuschner, Wilhelm, 325

Liberal Democratic party, 295, 297

Lilje, Hanns, encourages Protestant unity, 13; passed over as EKD head, 15; on church's political role, 122; on Parliamentary Council, 185; on Basic Law, 189n.; angered by clericalism, 205; opposes rearmament, 243; and Heinemann's resignation, 244, 246

Lippmann, Walter, 242n.

Loccum Treaty, 199–200

Ludwig I, 23

Lübke, Heinrich, 148, 203

Lücke, Paul, 274, 281

Lücke plan, 283

Luther, Martin, 3, 120

McCarthy, Joseph, 84

McCloy, John J., 244

Manchester Guardian, 134, 242n.

Mann, Golo, 172

Mann in der Zeit, 340

Maritain, Jacques, 87

Marahrens, August, 8; at Treysa, 10, 119; nearly arrested by British, 110; encourages CDU, 131, 305, 308

Marx, Karl, 328, 338, 358, 363

Mater et Magistra, 150

Meiser, Hans, 8, biography, 8n.; opposes Nazi interference only in church matters, 9; at Treysa, 10, 119; threatens to withdraw Bavarian church from EKD, 10n.; reneges on guilt declaration, 11; and denazification, 110, 111; and Protestant political party, 130; reacts to Heinemann's resignation, 246; favorable to CDU, 304, 308; attitude to SPD, 329; view of church in politics, 354

Meixner, Georg, 87, 150n.

Mellies, Wilhelm, 331

Merten, Hans, 331
Metz, Johannes, 193
Metzger, Ludwig, 331, 339
Mit brennender Sorge, 27n., 29
Mitzenheim, Moritz, 19
Mochalski, Herbert, 251, 258–259
Der Monat, 86
Le Monde, 247
Montesquieu, Charles Louis de Secondat, 352
Montgomery, Bernard, 60, 61, 299
Montini, Giovanni, *see* Paul VI
Montini, Ludovico, 341
Morgenthau, Henry, 96
Morsey, Rudolf, 91
Muckermann, Richard, 154, 156
Müller, Eberhard, 132
Müller, Gebhard, 303
Müller, Josef, sought support of Catholic clergy, 150; and Pius XII, 304; adopts idea of interconfessional party, 304; leadership in Bavaria, 310
Müller, Ludwig, 7, biography, 7n.; 27 & n.
Muench, Alois, positions after 1945, 33–34, 83; reports to American hierarchy, 48; liaison role, 82–83; his anti-Semitism, 83–84, 86; his dispute over publications, 84–86; over schools, 86–87; clashes with French, 87; failed to alter policy, 88; forwards denazification memorandum, 103–104; calls on Adenauer about Reichskonkordat, 173; on Adenauer's attitude to hierarchy, 175; and Reichskonkordat, 211–212; Nuncio to "German people," 214; and Reichskonkordat litigation, 218 & n.; mentioned, 30
Muhler, Emil, 131
Murphy, Robert, 55, 76, 78, 79n., 84, 210

Napoleon, 5, 183
National Concentration, 140
National Democratic Party of Germany (NPD), 137
Natterer, Alois, 90
Naumann, Friedrich, 162
Nawroth, Edgar, 274
Nell-Breuning, Oswald von, criticized for SPD contacts, 152; as codrafter of *Quadragesimo anno*, 162; as influence on Catholic social views, 274; attacked by DGB institute, 276n.; proposes capital-savings incentives, 285; supports CDU, 307; and Christian socialism, 311; attitude to SPD, 335; contact with SPD, 336–337
Nellen, Peter, 264, 342
Die neue Gesellschaft, 152
Die neue Ordnung, 43
Neue Zürcher Zeitung, 51, 283
Neuer Vorwärts, 275
Neuhäusler, Johann, 90, 91
New York Herald Tribune, 240
The New York Times, interviews von Galen, 63; Walter Bedell Smith, 98; Wurm, 102; Clay, 105; La Follett, 105–106; quotes Schumacher, 329; cited, 77, 106, 150, 164, 213, 217
National Lutheran Council, 82
Niemeyer, Johannes, 284

Niemöller, Martin, 8, biography, 8n.; establishes Pastors' Emergency League, 8; at Treysa, 10; heads EKD foreign bureau, 10n.; claims role for church, 51; criticizes denazification procedures, 100–101, 105–106; criticized by Clay, 105; signals end of denazification, 115; denounces Erastianism, 119; his election advice, 125; meets with Social Democrats, 126, 127, 330; loses seat on EKD council, 128; debates rearmament, 129; and Basic Law, 189n.; advocates neutralism, 240; embarrasses Adenauer, 240 & n.; not supported by EKD, 240; and Heinemann's resignation, 244–245; denounced by Adenauer, 245; meets Schumacher, 245; loyal to EKD, 250; antirearmament views, 250, 251; proposes rearmament referendum, 251–252; visits Moscow, 252; dismissed from EKD foreign bureau, 252n.; impact on public opinion, 252–254; role in 1953 election, 257, 258; continues antirearmament campaign, 258–259; opposes nuclear arms, 263n.; attitude to CDU, 302; fails to convince Protestants, 312; attitude to SPD, 330; mentioned, 126, 247, 329, 332
Niesel, Wilhelm 189n.
Nietzsche, Friedrich Wilhelm, 3
Noth, Gottfried, 18
NPD (Nationaldemokratische Partei Deutschlands), see National Democratic party of Germany
Nuncio, role of, 33; status of in East Germany, 214–215
Nunciatur, history of, 33–34; hierarchy usurps functions of, 176
Nuremberg trials, 89
Nuschke, Otto, 256

The Observer, 262, 264
Occupation policy, see American, British, French, Soviet Military Government
Oder-Neisse issue, 38, 47, 61, 135, 136, 157, 193, 210, 214–217, 218, 223, 224, 229–233
Old Catholics, 23
Ollenhauer, Erich, 333, 339
Orsenigo, Cesare, 33, 83
Osborne, Sir Francis d'Arcy, 52
L'Osservatore Romano, 223, 347–348
Ott, Franz, 150 & n.
Ottaviani, Alfredo, 264

Pacelli, Eugenio, see Pius XII
Pakenham, Francis, Lord (Francis Aungier Pakenham; since 1961, Earl of Longford), 66, 67, 69, 72
Papan, Franz von, 209, 227
"Parents' rights," 186, 188, 208, 213, 219, 220, 222, 223, 225, 227; see also confessional schools
Parliamentary Council, 167, 173, 174, 183–189, 222, 224, 282, 313
Pastors' Emergency League, 8
Paul VI (Giovanni Montini), appoints successor to Frings, 33; relationship with Döpfner, 37; and British demarche on churches, 52 & n.; on Pius XII, 211; advised on Reichskonkordat, 211; and Kiesinger discuss schools, 227; and Oder-Neisse issue, 229–230; and Lower Saxony concordat, 340; receives SPD delegation, 341–343, 358
Paul, Ernst, 341, 342
"Persilscheine," 99
Personalpolitik, of interest to Kunst, 146; Catholic role in, 169, 170 & n., 176; its role in

government, 203–206; as problem for CDU, 312, 313–314; impact on of Brandt government, 347

Petrusblatt, 249

Pfeil, Hans, 162

Pferdmenges, Robert, 311

Pfleiderer, Kurt, 134

Pius XI, 27n., 162, 335

Pius XII (Eugenio Pacelli), attitude to Germany, 29, 211; first postwar statement of, 29, 89; "impervious to criticism," 30; Hochhuth's treatment of, 31; his German staff, 34; apprised of British demarche, 52; transmits directive on church-state relations, 56–57; appoints Muench Apostolic Visitator, 83; refuses to withdraw Muench, 87; told of school reform, 87; praises Catholics on Nazism, 90; denounces collective guilt, 92; relationship with Böhler, 171; and Adenauer, 173; concerned by hierarchy's political autonomy, 176; and Basic Law, 184, 187–188; attitude to Reichskonkordat, 209–212; to confessional schools, 212; to Oder-Neisse issue, 216 & n., 217; and Reichskonkordat litigation, 218; his Reichskonkordat intent confounded, 229; linked with Truman, 239; supports rearmament, 246–247 & n.; rules out conscientious objection, 260; cited in defense of nuclear arms, 265; provides guidance on social issues, 272, 355; warns about unified trade union, 274; rejects codetermination, 279–281; on Catholic-Protestant cooperation, 293; and Josef Müller, 304; fervent anticommunism of, 333; mentioned, 36, 84, 162

Pohlschneider, Johannes, 166

Political working group of Catholic organizations, 169–170, 179

Politische Entscheidung in der Einheit des Glaubens, 125, 126

Pollack, James, 134

Potsdam conference, 60, 95

Preysing, Konrad von, 27 & n.; submits petition to Truman, 77; and establishment of CDU, 294, 296, 306

Pribilla, Max, 91

Protestant committee of the CDU/CSU, 147, 205, 314–315

Publik, 43, 179–180

Puttfarken, Hans, 16n.

Quadragesimo anno, 162, 334, 335

Rahner, Karl, 37, 166, 193

Raiser, Ludwig, 16n., 136

Ranke, Hansjürg, 282

Rapacki plan, 262, 264

Rau, Johannes, 331

Reformed Federation of Germany (BRK), 16

Refugee party, 150

Reichsdeputationshauptschluss, 194

Reichskonkordat, concluded, 28, 209; defended by Pius XII, 29, 209, 210n.; German hierarchy embarrassed by, 30, 149, 210; applicability in East Germany, 41, 214–215; papal directive on, 56–57, 210–211; occupation policies regarding, 57–59, 75; intellectual impact of its litigation, 91, 337; and postwar politics, 149; Adenauer's attitude to, 173, 175, 218; in Parliamentary Council, 188–189; denounced by Heuss and Höpker-Aschoff, 189; buried in ambiguity, 189; its non-recognition disappoints hierarchy, 190; under Basic Law, 191ff.; guarantees church tax, 195; and school issue, 209–210, 212–214, 217–219, 222–224, 226–228;

Vatican's tactic regarding, 210–212, 214–218; and Oder-Neisse issue, 214–217, 218, 229–233; some of its provisions ignored, 216; appealed to constitutional court, 217–219 & n.; appealed to administrative court, 223; curia's changing attitude to, 229–232; invalidated in Oder-Neisse area, 233; undermined in East Germany, 233; attitude of Catholic politicians toward, 294; and SPD, 342; mentioned, 54, 184, 340

Reimann, Max, 67

Reith lectures, 262

Rheinischer Merkur, 43, 161, 248, 279, 340, 347

Riedel, Clemens, 231

Riedel, Heinrich, 8n.

Rilke, Rainer Maria, 25

Robertson, Brian (Baron Robertson of Oakridge), 69, 99, 187, 240n.

Rösch, Augustin, 302, 307

Rommerskirchen, Josef, 249

Roosevelt, Franklin D., 52

Rousseau, Jean-Jacques, 351, 353, 359

Der Ruf, 85

Rupprecht, Crown Prince, 304

Russian Orthodox church, 252

SA (Sturmabteilung), 111

Schäufele, Hermann, 223, 343

Schäffer, Fritz, dismissed as minister president, 98, 305; favors Catholic party, 303; finds no support, 304

Die Schar, 250

Scharf, Kurt, heads EKD council, 15; expelled from East Berlin, 18; on church's political responsibility, 123; attitude to SPD, 330, 331; agrees to meet Brandt, 343; mentioned, 331

Schian, Pastor, 296

Schiller, Friedrich von, 89

Schilling, Friedrich, 103

Schlange-Schöningen, 305, 310

Schleyer, Hanns-Martin, 286

Schmaus, Michael, 37

Schmid, Carlo, 122, 177, 345

Schmidt, Helmut, 331

Schmidt, Hermann, 276

Schmidt, Otto, 298, 300, 311

Schmidt-Vockenhausen, Hermann, 179

Schneider, Reinhold, 152, 249

School issue, *see* confessional schools

Schreiber, Monsignor, 150n.

Schröder, Gerhard, contact with Kunst, 147; loyalty to Adenauer, 262n.; rise to influence, 311, 318–319; becomes leading CDU Protestant, 314–315; loses influence, 320

Schulte, Caspar, 326n.

Schumacher, Kurt, wants to avoid church-state issues, 183; agrees to school referendum, 188; meets Niemöller, 245; impatience with Protestant antirearmers, 250–251; and Blank, 253; fails to convince Protestants, 312; attitude to churches, 327–329; contrasted to Adenauer, 328; angered by hierarchy's political role, 328–329, 332–333; meets with EKD leadership, 330; criticizes Frings, 333; meets with Dominicans, 336; mentioned, 69

Schuster, Johann, 92
Schweizer, Albert, 249
Schwering, Leo, 97, 299
Sedlmeier, Wilhelm, 302
Seigewasser, Hans, 233
Shell Oil Company, 195
Seufert, Walter, 337
Siemer, Laurentius, 298, 299, 311, 336
Simon, Paul, 307
Simpfendörfer, Wilhelm, 303
Simplicissimus, 85, 198
Smend, Rudolf, 199, 206
Smith, Adam, 311
Smith, Walter Bedell, 98
Social committees of CDU, 273, 275, 276, 281
Social Academy (Friedewald), 133
Social Contract, 351
Social Democratic party of Germany (SPD), passim but especially, and Protestants, 137–145, 245, 250–251, 258, 329–331; and Catholics, 158–160, 177, 179, 331–350; and Parliamentary Council, 185–189; evolution of, since 1945, chapter 12, 358
Socialist Reich party, 140
Sonntagsblatt, 21, 244, 255
South Schleswig Voters' League, 140
Soviet Military Government, attitude to churches, 17, 52–53 & n.; bans confessional schools, 57–58 & n.; wanted to abrogate Reichskonkordat, 58; attitude to political parties, 294, 297
SPD (Sozialdemokratische Partei Deutschlands), *see* Social Democratic party of Germany
Spellman, Francis, 83, 87
Spiecker, Karl, 154, 156
Der Spiegel, 31, 321, 322
Sproll, Johannes, 73
Stalin, Joseph, 238
Stegerwald, Adam, proposes interconfessional party, 292; favors party of the middle, 304; meets Josef Müller, 304; and contemporary CDU, 322
Stempel, Hans, 73
Stimme der Gemeinde, 21
Stimmen der Zeit, 43
Stohr, Albert, 302
Storch, Anton, 274, 276, 281
Strauss, Franz Josef, sought organized Catholic support, 150; supports school reform, 227; uneasy over Adenauer's policies, 262n.; and conscientious objectors, 263; considered a travesty of a Christian politician, 337
Strauss, Walter, 256
Stuttgart conference, acknowledges German guilt, 11, 93–95; contrasted with Catholic view, 30, 92; authorized by Americans, 55; declining influence of in EKD, 148
Süddeutsche Zeitung, 86, 136, 224
Süsterhenn, Adolf, 185, 189n.
Szczesny, Gerhard, 133

Der Tagesspiegel, 246, 264
Tardini, Domenico, 52 & n.; 211, 218

Die Tat, 64
Taylor, Myron, 52
Tenhumberg, Wilhelm, 177, 345
Thadden-Treiglaff, Reinhold von, 134, 247, 256
"Theology of revolution," 129
Thielicke, Helmut, 126–127, 132, 246
Tillich, Paul, 324, 326
Tillmanns, Robert, 131, 256, 315
The Times (London), 246, 256, 261, 335
Treysa conference, establishes provisional church government, 10; messages to congregations and clergy, 11; contrasted with Catholic view, 30; authorized by Americans, 55; approach to church-state relations, 57; misunderstood by Americans, 80; Niemöller's remarks at, 119; issues political declaration, 121 & n., 124, 130, 308, 329; its declining influence in EKD, 148
Troeltsch, Ernst, 6, 120, 271–272
Truman, Harry, 77, 84, 239
Tuesday circle, 168, 178; *see also* Wilhelm Böhler Club

Ulbricht, Walter, 53n., 225
Unfehlbar?, 32
United Evangelical Lutheran Church of Germany (VELKD), established, 12; and EKD, 16; splits, 19–20; Wölber as head, 148
Unsere Linie, 156
Utz, Fridolin, 274
UV (Verband der wissenschaftlichen katholischen Studentenvereine Unitas), 170n.

van der Velden, Johann Josef, 153
van Wagoner, Murray, 87
Vansittart, Sir Robert, 96
Vatican, and Reichskonkordat, 28, 29, 56, 209–212, 214–218; relations with German hierarchy, 34; and Döpfner, 37; and East Germany 40; and British demarche, 52; and Saar issue, 74, 75; and American Military Government, 83; initiates Reichskonkordat litigation, 173, 218; mistrusts Böhler, 176; and German Ambassador, 204–205; and Oder-Neisse issue, 215–217, 218, 223, 224, 229–233; and school reform, 222–224, 227–228; Niemöller on, 240; and CDU, 307; and SPD, 340–343, 344, 358; attacks abortion plan, 348; mentioned, 62, 87, 98, 175, 191, 203, 239
Vatican Council, 31, 35, 36, 37, 166, 175, 177, 193, 293, 320, 344, 360
VELKD (Vereinigte Evangelisch-Lutherische Kirche Deutschlands), *see* United Evangelical Lutheran Church of Germany
Verantwortung und Mitverantwortung in der Wirtschaft, 279
Viet Cong, 125
Vockel, Heinrich, 295
Vogel, Heinrich, 330
Volksverein für das katholische Deutschland, 41
Voss, Erwin, 276
Voting behavior, of Catholics, 157–161, 306, 309, 311, 320–322, 332, 344–345, 346, 350; of Protestants, 137–145, 257–258, 306, 309, 310, 311, 313, 315, 319–320, 321

Die Wacht, 250
Wallraff, Hermann, 274, 337
Warsaw treaty, *see* German-Polish treaty
Warsch, Wilhelm, 298n.

Wartburg, 257

Was Nun?, 298

Weber, Helene, 185

Wehner, Herbert, contact with Kunst, 147; contact with Catholic Office, 177, 345; visit to Paul VI, 230; reenters Evangelical church, 331; seeks to end Catholic-SPD animosity, 337, 349; presses for Godesberg program, 338, 339; associates SPD with Adenauer's foreign policy, 340; and SPD visit to Vatican, 341; moderates school reform proposals, 345; attacks marriage law reform, 348; mentioned, 344

Weizsäcker, Carl-Friedrich von, 263n.

Weizsäcker, Richard von, 203

Die Welt, 225

Welty, Eberhard, 274, 298, 311, 336, 337

Wendel, Josef, 150n., 173, 337

Werkhefte katholischer Laien, 335

Wessel, Helene, ostracised for political non-conformity, 152, 249; moves to SPD via GVP, 156, 251; codrafts GVP program, 164; role in Parliamentary Council, 185

Westphalia, treaty of, 22, 359

Weymar, Paul, 245

Wiesbadener Kurier, 240

Wilhelm Böhler club, 178

Wilm, Ernst, 251, 330

Winkelheide, Bernhard, 276

Wissing, Wilhelm, 176-177, 286

Wissmann, Erwin, 253

Wittenberg, 4, 257

Wölber, Hans-Otto, 148

Wöste, Wilhelm, 177, 232, 348

Wolf, Ernst, 124, 269, 330

Woolf, Leonard, 353

World Council of Churches, 7n., 8n., 18, 76, 82, 131, 252

Worms, Diet of, 3

Wort und Wahrheit, 315, 317

Wuermeling, Franz-Josef, 170, 282-283

Wurm, Theophil 8 & n.; begins reconstruction of church, 10; heads EKD, 10, 15; asked to form provisional government, 54; appeals for theological faculties, 55; corresponds with Bell and Fisher, 71-72; warned not to criticize American policies, 76, 78; meeting with Knappen, 79 & n.; acknowledges German guilt, 80, 94-95; comments on American occupation, 81; calls for changes in denazification law, 101-102; refuses to dismiss incriminated clergy, 112; clashes with Clay over clerical denazification, 113; and Heinemann's entry into government, 131; role in Parliamentary Council, 185-187; on conscientious objection, 259-260; welcomes CDU, 303; mentioned, 92, 119, 123

Wyszynski, Stefan, 217, 224

Yalta conference, 52

Zeiger, Ivo, reestablishes Vatican-hierarchy contact, 29, 210-211; on Pius XII, 30, 211; administers Apostolic Mission, 34; on Adenauer's "blackmailer's methods," 175; on Pius XII's attitude to Germany, 304; advised about Reichskonkordat, 211; contact with Josef Müller, 304; supports CDU, 307

Die Zeit, 227

Zentrum, *see* Center party

Zink, Harold, 70, 75